Secret Voices

Secret Voices

Edited by

Sarah Gristwood

BATSFORD

First published in the United Kingdom
in 2024 by
B. T. Batsford Ltd
43 Great Ormond Street
London
WC1N 3HZ

An imprint of B. T. Batsford Holdings Limited
Copyright © B. T. Batsford Ltd 2024
Introduction and text selection copyright © Sarah Gristwood 2024
For details of individual copyright permissions, please see pages 512–8.

ISBN 978 1 84994 815 9

A CIP catalogue record for this book is available from the British Library.

10 9 8 7 6 5 4 3 2 1

Reproduction by Mission Productions Ltd, Hong Kong
Printed and bound by Dream Colour, China

This book can be ordered direct from the publisher at
www.batsfordbooks.com, or try your local bookshop

Contents

Foreword

This was never going to be an exhaustive record of women's diaries. With so many individuals writing, under such different circumstances, a definitive record would be an impossibility. It is a personal take – but reflective, I trust, of the available evidence. Some women were writing in the deepest possible privacy; others had a reader in mind. But if I were to pick out the single strongest emotions voiced through all these diary entries I think it would be anger – frustration. And that is something that our cultural norms have allowed women to voice only secretly.

The diary has been the echo chamber for a woman's own voice, as opposed to what she was supposed to say. And, down the centuries, the need to utilize records in support of a male-oriented history has often kept those voices silent – until now. But thanks to new work, to a new foregrounding of women's history (and, in no small part to the internet's role in making such work internationally available), they can be heard with increasing clarity.

A number of these diarists did contemplate the possibility of their diary being read. Many pioneers and emigrants, indeed, kept daily journals to be sent to relatives back home. I have limited the use of these journal-letters, though not excluded them entirely. More invidiously, perhaps, Dorothy Wordsworth read her famous diaries to her brother (who made use of her observations in his poetry), and Virginia Woolf speculated as to what kind of a book her husband might eventually make of hers. Oscar Wilde had a wry word for it: 'it is simply a very young girl's record of her own thoughts and impressions,' says Cecily in *The Importance of Being Earnest*, 'and consequently meant for publication.'

Two of the most famous female diarists, Anne Frank and Fanny Burney, addressed their diaries respectively to an imaginary 'Kitty', and to 'a Certain Miss Nobody'. What that implies, of course, is that they could not find a live auditor to whom they could speak freely. A diary, wrote P. D. James, noting the prevalence of the 'Dear Diary' address, can be 'a defence against loneliness … both friend and confidant, one from whom neither criticism nor treachery need be feared.' It can also be the repository of 'thoughts that cannot be spoken aloud'. Or, as Fanny Burney put it, 'To Nobody, then, will I write my journal, since to Nobody can I be wholly unreserved, to Nobody can I reveal every thought, every wish of my heart …' Still that sense of secrecy.

Of course, there is another agenda implicit here: the assumption that women's experience differs from that of men; that their diaries reflect that difference; that they need to be chronicled separately. It risks cliché to suggest that the female diary is more inclined to introspection – or even that the women found the diary form, with its privacy and informality, its unassuming quality, less daunting than the open self-proclamation of the male-dominated autobiography.

But historically women's experience has been different to that of men. (The husband of pioneer Amelia Stewart Knight likewise faced the hardships of the Oregon Trail – though he was not eight months pregnant while doing so.) Yet anthologies not devoted specifically to women still include an alarmingly low percentage of female diarists.

Many years ago, I wrote a book about the subjects women cover in their diaries. In this country at least, women's writing was then to some degree still regarded as a second-class subject of study; but the point is that your own country was pretty much all you could study, since the barely nascent internet had not yet made texts from around the world available. (I managed, then, to include a few American texts not published here – but only because my mother happened to be visiting the USA, and was prepared to spend much of her trip in the Library of Congress.) The internet has exponentially altered that situation – but with new opportunities come new responsibilities. Something else has changed in those years, likewise for the better. Recent times have seen a growing awareness of the need for any selection of voices from the past to be as inclusive as possible.

Historically, the production (and, crucially, preservation) of diaries has, for obvious reasons, been weighted towards the literate middle and upper classes. That has, in turn, had the effect of prioritizing white women; though the situation is slowly being remedied today. I found a particular challenge in tracking down English-language or translated diaries by women of Asian origin; though I look forward to hearing from those whose work has taken them further along these lines. A disproportionate number of diaries published, moreover, are by professional writers … or else by the female connections of famous men (Sophia Tolstoy, Frances Lloyd George, Dorothy Wordsworth, Anna Dostoevsky), a fact that tells its own story.

By the same token, the list of published diaries in the shops places a particular weight on the overtly extraordinary; recorded either because the diarist enjoyed an experience they wanted to remember, or suffered one the world must never forget. (Travellers, on the one hand – and on the other victims of the Holocaust.) I have limited the use of such very specific records – yet behind the uniqueness of what is described, there often lies a depth of common sentiment. Few widowhoods are as famous as that of Queen Victoria; few suffer Anne Morrow Lindbergh's experience of the kidnap and death of her son. But the experience of grief and loss is universal.

The therapeutic qualities of diary-writing – 'journalling' – are now well known. The way women turn to their diary in times of distress may, however, present an unbalanced picture – besides offering a gloomy prospect for the diary reader! As Barbara Pym put it: 'I seem to write in it only when I am depressed, like praying only when one is really in despair.' But historically women have often had good cause to feel dissatisfaction, and the secrecy of the diary form allowed them to voice it. It may, indeed, have been the diary's prime purpose. Beatrix Potter and Florence Nightingale are only two of the women whose diary-writing ceased or changed once they had at last found their path in life; others end their diary-keeping on marriage and maternity. Oprah Winfrey in her forties took the conscious decision to stop using her journals as therapy – venting her worries about men and weight – and instead started using them to, as she puts it, 'express my gratitude'. Happily, the gratitude diary has its own long history, from the early Quaker and Dissenter diaries.

The frequency of diary-keeping greatly increased in the late seventeenth and eighteenth centuries, with the new interest in the private, as opposed to the public, identity. That gives us a lot of time to look back on – a lot of instances when we now know, unlike the diarist themselves, how their story turned out. It is impossible to read Anne Frank's plans for life after the war without the painful awareness of what actually awaited her. It is also impossible not to feel a slight smug glow when reading George Eliot's conviction that the novel on which she was working, *Middlemarch*, would never amount to anything … Sometimes experience noted in a diary would emerge later in a better-known form. Reading Louisa May Alcott's description of her sister's decline and death, one can't but think of Beth in *Little Women*, who likewise found the sewing needle grow 'too heavy'. Often an element of outside knowledge can illumine the diary itself; hence the brief biographies of principal diarists given at the back of this book.

I would urge readers to consult those biographies for another reason, also: *Secret Voices* aims to reflect the totality of experience described in women's diaries; and some of that, inevitably, travels to a dark place: suicide (Rachel Roberts); abortion (Loran Hurnscot). A look at the life stories of the diarists might provide a warning flag for those readers with particular vulnerabilities. Another word of warning: the diaries quoted here reflect the time in which they were written. As such they are bound occasionally to deploy terms no longer in use, or to display attitudes no longer considered acceptable.

The format of this book, arranged by the days of the calendar year, presents both opportunities and challenges. It excludes many famous diarists who choose not to list their entries under a particular day; as well, of course, as diarists from any part of the world not using the Western calendar. (As it is, Sophia Tolstoy and Anna Dostoevsky listed their entries according to the Julian rather than the Gregorian calendar, which Russia did not adopt until 1917.) In Britain, Jan Morris listed the entries in her 'thought diary' only as 'Day 25, Day 26'. The Australian diarist Helen Garner, known to have written every morning and every night, nonetheless chose to have her diaries published without dates: I therefore include only such entries as she has allowed to be dated by reference to external events.

Arranging entries as if through one calendar year can risk confusion. Queen Victoria mourns the death of Prince Albert in January (1862);

but marries him only in February (1840). In that particular case, I hope the basic facts of her life are sufficiently well-known; but with less famous writers, I have often tried to select their diary entries so as to tell a brief coherent story. Individual diarists may thus not be evenly distributed throughout the book, or the year.

Details like the place of writing, or the age of the writer – or the identity of other individuals mentioned – have been given only where I feel it helpful for an understanding of the text. Moreover, it has often been necessary to edit individual diary entries for length. (Vera Brittain seeing her fiancé off to the First World War runs, in the original, to seven pages, as does Susan Sontag's discussion of her mother.) I found it necessary to take a similarly free hand with the question of where to standardize punctuation and spelling; or where to maintain, for example, the use of the dash as chief punctuation point to give a sense of the era, and the breathless quality of the writer's entry.

No decision to adapt was taken without a pang; but I was sustained by one particular thought … If the end result were to send readers back to check, to explore further in the original, this anthology would indeed have served its purpose.

Sarah Gristwood, Deal, July 2023

January

'I have set myself many tasks for the year –
I wonder how many will be accomplished?
A Novel called Middlemarch …'

George Eliot, 1869

1 January

New Year's morn. 1858. Welcome in, New Year! A *perfect* day ushers thee in. I greet thee with mingled tears of joy and sorrow. I will record no *vows*, no good resolutions *this* year, – to shed, at the beginning of the *next*, bitter, repentant tears over their graves. In the secret depths of my own heart I make some vows. Oh! may God give me strength to keep them!

Charlotte Forten, 1858

A bright frosty morning! And we are both well. The servants are going to have their little treat, and we are going to see Mr and Mrs Burne Jones and carry a book for their little boy. I have set myself many tasks for the year – I wonder how many will be accomplished? A Novel called *Middlemarch*, a long poem on Timoleon, and several minor poems.

George Eliot, 1869

… i am beginning a new year in a new character. May it be worn decently yet lightly! I wish not to be rigid and fright my daughters by too much severity. I will not be wild and give them reason to lament the levity of my life. Resolutions, however, are vain …

Hester Lynch Thrale Piozzi, 1782

To day has bin a memorable day and i thank god I have bin spered to see it the day was religiously observed all the churches were open we had quite a Jubiliee in the evenin i went to Joness to a Party had a very pleasent time.

Emilie Davis, 1863 (the day the Emancipation Proclamation became official)

My beloved and I woke at seven. Found by our bed side *Petticoats and Pockets*, a new year's gift from our *truest* friends.

Eleanor Butler, 1790

Have been unable to write my Journal since the day my beloved one [Prince Albert] left us, and with what a heavy and broken heart I enter on a new year without him! My dreadful and overwhelming calamity gives me so much to do, that I must henceforth merely keep notes of my sad and solitary life. This day last year found us so perfectly happy, and now! Last year music woke us; little gifts, new year's wishes, brought in by maid, and then given to dearest Albert, the children waiting with their gifts in the next room – all these recollections were pouring in on my mind in an overpowering manner … Arthur gave me a nosegay, and the girls, drawings done by them of their dear father and me. Could hardly touch my breakfast.

Queen Victoria, 1862

Entered on another year. Happy experience emboldens us to look forward with joyful anticipations to the voyage of life; we have been hitherto in calm water indeed, and for this how thankful we should be, but we must expect some gales before we drop our anchor. May we be prepared to meet them!

Caroline Fox, 1840

What I have to write today is terribly sad. I called on Gustav [Mahler] – in the afternoon we were alone in his room. He gave me his body – & I let him touch me with his hand. Stiff and upright stood his vigour. He carried me to the sofa, laid me gently down and swung himself over me. Then – just as I felt him penetrate, he lost all strength. He laid his head on my breast, shattered – and almost wept for shame. Distraught as I was, I comforted him.

   We drove home, dismayed and dejected. He grew a little more cheerful. Then I broke down, had to weep, weep on his breast. What if he were to lose – that! My poor, poor husband!

Alma Mahler-Werfel, 1902

This is the first day of a new year; and I am not in the humour for being wished a happy one. Into the hands oh God of all consolation, into thy merciful hands which chastise not willingly I commit the remains of my earthly happiness; and Thou mayest will that from these few barley loaves & small fishes, twelve basketfuls may be gathered.

Elizabeth Barrett (Browning), 1832

2 January

———

Sick day. Lay quietly & lived in my mind where I can generally find amusement for myself. Planned Fred's wedding, took Lulu to Boston, & went on with my novel. Dr W. came as my head was bad. Said rest, food & time were all I needed A. [Anna, her sister] in p.m., Rubbed & made cosy & slept all night. Thank God for the blessing of sleep!

Louisa May Alcott, 1887

I looked with amazement at the slashing reductions in coats, dresses and suits – up to a third of the price – but, contrasting them with the 'new look' ones, they did look dated. I knew if I'd been buying I'd not have been tempted to buy out-of-date clothes and give up coupons. I am so lucky. I've no middle-aged spread and a dart each side of my corsets gives me a waist. I've a good hem on my costume and with dropping the skirt from the top to the bottom of my waist belt and putting on a velvet ribbon belt from a belt I have, I can lengthen my skirt to London length, and with my new dusty pink and altered best dress I feel quite up to date.

Nella Last, 1948

It is wrong to set out on the New Year without thinking of the great event of 1865: the American war ending with the downfall of Slavery. It is nothing short of the fulfilment of the words: 'With men it is impossible: but with God all things are possible.'

Lucy (Lady Frederick) Cavendish, 1866

… We came back from Rodmell yesterday, and I am in one of my moods, as the nurses used to call it, today. And what is it and why? A desire for children, I suppose, for Nessa's life [her sister, Vanessa Bell]; for the sense of flowers breaking all round me involuntarily. Here's Angelica – here's Quentin and Julian [Vanessa's children]. They make my life seem a little bare sometimes; and then my inveterate romanticism suggests an image of forging ahead, alone, through the night; of suffering inwardly, stoically; of blazing my way through to the end – and so forth. The truth is that the sails flap about me for a day or two on coming back. And it is all temporary: yes, let me be quite clear about that.

Virginia Woolf, 1923

3 January

———

What a day! One huge snowstorm from end to end and the thermometer at zero. I feel smothered. Even the windows are so thickly covered with snow and frost that the sensation is of being literally imprisoned. This has seemed as long as three days.

The other day I came across this sentence in a magazine.

'It is the unhappy people who keep diaries. Happy people are too busy to keep diaries.'

At the time it rather impressed me as clever, but after thinking it over I have decided that it may be epigrammatic but it is not true. To be sure, I am not exactly a happy person; but I kept a diary and enjoyed doing so when I was quite happy. Besides, if being busy made people happy I ought to be a very happy mortal. No, the epigram should have read 'It is the *lonely* people who keep diaries' – people who are living solitary lives and have no other outlet for their moods and tenses. When I have anybody to 'talk it over with' I don't feel the need of a diary so strongly. When I haven't I must have a journal to overflow in. It is a companion – and a relief.

L. M. Montgomery, 1904

Bliss and rapture.

Alma Mahler-Werfel, 1902

Yes. This diary does sound vain. But that is what it is for. To get it out of my system. I can not even pray without the little jeering thoughts saying 'Ha! Ha! Ha! Being melodramatic. Lying prone. Seeming urgent.' It's devilish to keep them down. That is one of the biggest reasons for this blabber-book. To write here and thus away all the little jibbers.

Elizabeth Smart, 1934

4 January

———

There's no reason after all why one should expect special events for the first page of a new book; still one does: and so I may count three facts of different importance; our first use of the 17 Club; talk of peace; and the breaking of my tortoiseshell spectacles. This talk of peace (after all the most important of the three) comes to the surface with a kind of tremor of hope once in three months; then subsides; then swells again. What it now amounts to, one doesn't even like to guess; at any rate, one can't help feeling something moving.

Virginia Woolf, 1918

Snow deep. A few sheep wandering about the field in great distress. One of them apparently consumptive and coughing up its poor lungs. Made my heart ache. I wish they cou'd take money, or that I cou'd relieve them in their own simple way.

Lady Eleanor Butler, 1789

Rapture without end.

Alma Mahler-Werfel, 1902

Such a beautiful day, that one felt quite confused how to make the most of it, and accordingly frittered it away.

Caroline Fox, 1848

5 January

——

… a man in a greatcoat made like a soldier's followed me down our lane & asked if I wanted a sweetheart. He was a few yards behind & I said, 'If you do not go about your business, sir, I'll send one that will help you.' I heard him say, 'I should like to kiss you.' It annoyed me only for a moment, for I felt, on coming upstairs, as if I could have knocked him down. But I ought not to have spoken, nor should, but being so near home I was at unawares provoked to it.

Anne Lister, 1820

Yesterday I read an article about blushing by Sis Heyster. This article might have been addressed to me personally. Although I don't blush very easily, the other things in it certainly all fit me. She writes roughly something like this – that a girl in the years of puberty becomes quiet within and begins to think about the wonders that are happening to her body …

… I think what is happening to me is so wonderful, and not only what can be seen on my body, but all that is taking place inside. I never discuss myself or any of these things with anybody; that is why I have to talk to myself about them.

Each time I have a period – and that has only been three times – I have a feeling that in spite of all the pain, unpleasantness, and nastiness, I have a sweet secret, and that is why, although it is nothing but a nuisance to me in a way, I always long for the time that I shall feel that secret within me again.

Sis Heyster also writes that girls of this age don't feel quite certain of themselves, and discover that they themselves are individuals with ideas, thoughts, and habits. After I came here, when I was just fourteen, I began to think about myself sooner than most girls, and to know that I am a 'person'. Sometimes, when I lie in bed at night, I have a terrible desire to feel my breasts and to listen to the quiet rhythmic beat of my heart.

Anne Frank, 1944

Turned out of doors into the street! In the anguish of my mind, I broke out into complaints; this only was my fault. I took a chaise to Leigh; my brother not being at home, dismissed it and stopped two nights. He brought me home with an intention to effect either a reconciliation or a separation. He could do neither. Mr Stock [her husband] wants me either to remain at home penniless, as an underling to his own daughter, or to be kept by anyone that will take me. I cannot agree to such a reconciliation, or such a separation, whilst he has plenty of money. I am obliged totally to withdraw myself from any domestic affairs, in obedience to my husband's orders; to live in an apartment alone; not to sit at table with the family, but to have my meat sent to me; and amuse or employ myself as I can.

When and how will this end?

Ellen Weeton, 1818

6 January

Black day. Dark, no sky to be seen; a livid sea; a noise of boiling in the air. Dreamed the cats died of *anti-pneumonia*. Heart attack 8 a.m. Awful day. No relief for a moment. Couldn't work. At night changed the position of my bed. At five o'clock I thought I was at sea tossing – for ever. N.B.

Katherine Mansfield, Ospedaletti, Italy, 1920

A sun-burst touched my face early this morning and actually coaxed me out of bed. I opened the window and exuberant greetings floated up to me from the box hedges, just as in April. Polly said the crows were cawing lustily, the thrushes and tits twittering all round. Out in the garden I saw the yellow jasmine blooming, and they tell me snowdrops and other spring flowers will appear soon. How different Scotland, with its frost and snow melting at noonday and a happy imminence of spring through the winter, is from the northern United States with the sod frozen hard and not a sign of greenness or fragrance during four or five months!

Six long notes and two short written this morning, and there are still a dozen in the offing, but my hands demanded a rest … Curiously enough, a presentiment keeps knocking away at my mind's door that I shall not much longer be able to keep at the typewriter as steadily as I have. Often my hands feel cramped or limp, which does not surprise me, as they have never been still, except in sleep, since I was two years old. They mean the world I live in – they are eyes, ears, channels of thought and goodwill. Sooner would I lose my health or even the ability to walk (and walking is among the few cherished bits of personal liberty I possess) than the use of these two hands. However, if I take proper care of them now and use other muscles not already overtasked, I shall still have the joy of working in different ways. What these ways will be I am not certain, but I shall know when I begin experimenting.

Helen Keller, 1937

Beb [her husband] was on duty so I had one of my little dinners and went straight to bed. I am in best looks. Marie Bashkirtseff is always apologetic when she makes a similar entry in her diary, but why should one be? Today I could really pass a great deal of time very happily just looking at myself in the glass. It's extraordinary how one's whole outline seems to alter, as well as complexion and eyes.

Lady Cynthia Asquith, 1917

7 January

Dashed home to change hurriedly for the Buckingham Palace reception for the Commonwealth Prime Ministers. It was an awful nuisance having to dress but the only way I could see of meeting my old friends during my frantic week. It was nice to see Indira Gandhi again: I warm to her. She is a pleasant, rather shy and unassuming woman and we exchanged notes about the fun of being at the top in politics. When I asked her whether it was hell being Prime Minister she smiled and said, 'It is a challenge.' Oddly enough, I always feel protective towards her.

Every group I spoke to greeted me as the first woman Prime Minister to be. I hate this talk. First, I'm never going to be PM and, secondly, I don't think I'm clever enough. Only *I* know the depth of my limitations: it takes all I've got to survive my present job.

Barbara Castle, 1969

I am in a very bitter state. The end of every hope and plan is that I am tied to an invalid [her husband Hubert] whom I do not love. I have tenderness for him, and pity, but there's no love, there's sometimes panic fear and sometimes hatred. Well, I conceal my bitterness. Short of finally breaking with Barny [her lover], which I cannot and will not do, for it is only he that makes this dreadful existence possible at all, I am drearily unwilling to do everything I can for this Hubert I once loved – or imagined I did.

Loran Hurnscot, 1924

… a neighbor told me she had been in a small car accident and had managed to persuade the local paper to ignore her true age (as it appears on her license) and to print her age as thirty-nine! I was really astonished by this confidence. I am proud of being fifty-eight, and still alive and kicking, in love, more creative, balanced, and potent than I have ever been. I mind certain physical deteriorations, but not really. And not at all when I look at the marvelous photograph that Bill sent me of Isak

Dinesen just before she died. For after all we make our faces as we go along, and who when young could ever look as she does?

May Sarton, 1971

A queer day. Up early, and had my bread and milk and baked apples. Fed my doves. Made May a bonnet, and cut out a flannel wrapper for Marmee, who feels the cold in the Concord snowbanks. Did my editorial work in the p.m., and fixed my dresses for the plays. L sent $50, and F $40, for tales. A. and boys came.

To Dorchester in evening, and acted Mrs Pontifex, in 'Naval Engagements,' to a good house. A gay time, had flowers, etc. Talked half the night with H. A. about the fast ways of young people nowadays, and gave the child much older-sisterly advice, as no one seems to see how much she needs help at this time in her young life.

Dreamed that I was an opera dancer, and waked up prancing.

Louisa May Alcott, 1868

8 January

———

O such a scramble of shopums as I have gone through! … I have bought velvet and cloth cloaks, a hat, flowers, a bonnet, boots and shoes, gloves, collars and cuffs, a canezon, a sealskin muff, a linsey petticoat, a set of jet, a buckle, a set of studs, a fan, a new gown, etc., etc.

Lucy (Lady Frederick) Cavendish, 1864

… My dear Brother's letter reached me with the melancholy, but not unexpected intelligence of my dearest Mother's death on the 23rd Augt last. Very thankful am I to Almighty God that she was to the very last free from pain, & although I was not permitted to be with her I bow with submission to the will of God & with a grateful heart for all his mercies humbly trusting to meet him my dear Father & all we love on earth in a better world.

Sarah Broughton, clergyman's wife and emigrant to Australia, 1837

At Marks and Spencer's I bought a peach coloured vest and trollies to match with insertions of lace. Disgraceful I know but I can't help choosing my underwear with a view to it being seen!

Barbara Pym, 1934

9 January

The President's man Jim – whom he believed in, as we all believe in our own servants – and Betsy, Mrs Davis's maid, decamped last night. It is miraculous that they had the fortitude to resist the temptation so long. At Mrs Davis's, the hired servants are mere birds of passage; first they are seen with gold galore, and then they fly to the Yankees. But I am sure they have nothing to tell. It is wasted money to the Yankees.

Mary Boykin Chesnut, Confederate States of America, 1864

Tiberio was standing with the light on in the bedroom looking out, and he'd been waiting for me for three hours. I had such a bad feeling. He calmly told me that he wanted to leave me, because he'd had enough of waiting for me all night, of me never being home because I was at the House of Commons, because I was married to the constituency and not to him …

It boils down to this: he doesn't see me, he doesn't have a life with me, and he wants a partner who is a partner, not a ghost. He is going to find out if his office can move him to Italy, and if that happens we should separate.

I have this image of me clinging to the bottom of his trousers while he's trying to shake me off.

'I don't want to live without you,' I pleaded. 'You are the most important thing in my life.'

'Oona, you're bullshitting me. I'm not the most important thing in your life. If I was the most important thing in your life you would stop working the hours you do …'

I was left choking on that really bitter pill that so many women swallow, or so many *people* actually: the choice between your job or your life …

Oona King, 2001

Is sexual attraction natural, or must it be suppressed? …

I see life without sexual love. I do not know whether this can be, but I should incline to think that it is possible. It is simpler and more comprehensible; however, not knowing where truth is, I dare not affirm this, but want to think that it is the truth.

The feeling exists. And at present it expresses itself in uncouth and misshapen forms. New ones must take their place. That is what I think.

Nelly Ptashkina (aged 15), 1919

What a day this was for me. Till the evening I was in the most anxious expectation. Fremantle made Mr French speak to Papa in the morning and as Papa did not mention one word about it to anybody at home, I concluded that he had refused. The evening my surprise and happiness were beyond expression at hearing that on the contrary Papa had given a very favourable answer. It is now decided I shall marry Fremantle, I could say much on this subject but what I must feel on this occasion is not easily expressed.

Betsey Wynne Fremantle, 1797

10 January

Look at that ugly dead mask here and do not forget it. It is a chalk mask with dead dry poison behind it, like the death angel. It is what I was this fall, and what I never want to be again. The pouting disconsolate mouth, the flat, bored, numb, expressionless eyes: symptoms of the foul decay within. Eddie wrote me after my last honest letter saying I had better go get psychiatric treatment to root out the sources of my terrible problems. I smile, now, thinking: we all like to think we are important enough to need psychiatrists. But all I need is sleep, a constructive attitude, and a little good luck.

Sylvia Plath, 1953

Still in my solitary confinement. Had a new cloak brought home, and the first thought on seeing it was, Well! I have made sure of this, however (having long wished for a Winter garment of this description, and not had it in my power to obtain it). Alas! ... how presumptuous! That very night might my soul have been required of me, disease having seized me, or fire have destroyed both it and me and all else I possessed. But Thou, O Father, hast been very merciful. Yes! although my husband makes me as it were, a prisoner in my own home, I have a Peace which he knows nothing of, a Joy which he cannot take away. Oh! That his heart would soften, and that he might repent.

Ellen Weeton, 1818

Head swimming with murderous rages again. Must keep away from people during this period as it is almost uncontrollable – never know where it will light.

Dawn Powell, 1935

Today we were sitting in front of the cabin, the whole family. Mama was picking over rice; [her brothers] Renato and Nhonhô were making bird-traps, I was darning my stockings and [her sister] Luizinha was watching us work. All of a sudden I asked, 'Why do you think we're alive? Wouldn't it have been better if God hadn't created the world? Life is nothing but work. We work, eat, work some more, and sleep, and then we never know if we're finally going to hell or not. I really don't know why we're alive. Mama said, 'What a horrible thing to say, child! What have you been studying your catechism for all this time ... ?'

Helena Morley (aged 13), 1894

11 January

Sir William Hamilton and his Lady came in the morning. It is impossible to say how civil they were, especially Lady Hamilton, she is a charming woman, beautiful and exceedingly good humoured and amiable. She took all the management of this affair, and the wedding is to be tomorrow at her own house. I never felt more miserable than I did this morning, I was almost sorry that my marriage was to take place, I feared I would not have courage to undertake so much. However I made up my mind to it. Happy I am sure to be with Fremantle, it certainly is dreadful to be obliged to leave my family …

… For the last time I shall write as Miss Wynne, what a day tomorrow is – I dread it.

Betsey Wynne Fremantle, Naples, 1797

Another sedentary day, which must however be entered for the sake of recording that the Lords have passed the Suffrage Bill [giving British women the vote]. I don't feel much more important – perhaps slightly so. It's like a knighthood; might be useful to impress people one despises.

Virginia Woolf, 1918

My birthday.

Sita Wrede has talked the doctors of her Luftwaffe hospital into taking me on to work there … The training includes first-aid under fire (in case we are posted to an airfield), etc. I have been given a Red Cross uniform, a new set of identity papers and an identity tag on which my name is engraved twice and which can be broken in two if I am 'killed in action', one half being then sent back to my 'dear ones' – rather a weird feeling.

Marie Vassiltchikov, 1945

This day began in the early hours of the morning with a long talk. Lyndon woke up, as he often does these nights, and we talked about the prospects for the years ahead. They are so fraught with danger and with decisions whose outcomes we cannot see. I am torn between two feelings. One, the healthy one, is that I should enjoy each day in this job and live it to the fullest. The other, that the end of the term is like the light at the end of a tunnel. And my advice to Lyndon is so mundane and uninspiring: stay healthy, laugh a little, remember you are as tough as other Presidents who have lived through the same or worse.

Lady Bird Johnson, White House, 1966

The old Eve in me is delighted with buying a trousseau for our nine months' journey. It is a long time since I have had a really good 'go' at clothes and I am revelling in buying silks and satins, gloves, underclothing, furs and everything that a sober-minded woman of forty can want to inspire Americans and Colonials with a due respect for the refinement of attractiveness! It is a pleasure to clothe myself charmingly! For the last ten years I have not had either the time or the will to think of it … I believe that it is a deliberate expenditure because six months ago I determined that I would do myself handsomely as part of a policy, but I daresay one or two of the specially becoming blouses are the expression of concrete vanity.

Beatrice Webb, 1898

12 January

At one o'clock we all went to Lady Hamilton's [sic] where the ceremony was performed by Mr Lambton's Chaplain. What I felt at the wedding is not to be described. Prince Augustus gave me away, Sir Gilbert Elliot, Sir William Hamilton, Mr Lambton, Colonel Drinkwater were all witnesses. We all dined at Sir William's, went to the opera in the evening and returned to the Albergo Reale …

Betsey Wynne Fremantle, Naples, 1797

The hope of peace all broken up again; once more running in every direction, as far as one can tell.

Virginia Woolf, 1918

Soon the flotilla began to roll in, some sober, some slightly whizzed, some gloriously and homerically stinkers. Everyone was delighted to see me again. There were guitars and accordions so we sang sea shanties, then everything from 'Loch Lomond' to 'Lili Marlene'. There were men lying on the floor, heaped up on bunks, dancing on the table. It was a grand party, and Hans, who was wearing my earrings, got happily drunk, but almost made a point of not showing me any special affection. I imagined he was shy in front of his new crew.

Then to my surprise, a little Norwegian Wren appeared.

'Who's that?' I asked suspiciously.

'Oh,' Hans said casually, 'that's Lieven, she's a mother to us all.'

Lucky old Lieven, I thought, wondering how many of the men there had been her lovers. She certainly didn't look the motherly type ...

Joan Wyndham, 1945

13 January

I never felt better and happier in my life than I did today. I did not choose to see anybody and the weather being horrid we could not go to see any thing of Naples so I did not go out of my apartment. The family is not so dismal and Papa in quite high spirits. Lady Hamilton came with Sir Gilbert in the evening, it is not possible to express the many civilities she has shown us as well as every other person here.

Betsey Wynne Fremantle, Naples, 1797

Dear Kitty,

Everything has upset me again this morning, so I wasn't able to finish a single thing properly.

It is terrible outside. Day and night more of those poor miserable people are being dragged off, with nothing but a rucksack and a little money. On the way they are deprived even of these possessions. Families are torn apart, the men, women and children all being separated. Children coming home from school to find that their parents have disappeared. Women return from shopping to find their homes shut up and their families gone....

... And as for us, we are fortunate. Yes, we are luckier than millions of people. It is quiet and safe here, and we are, so to speak, living on capital. We are even so selfish as to talk about 'after the war', brighten up at the thought of having new clothes and new shoes, whereas we really ought to save every penny, to help other people, and save what is left from the wreckage after the war ...

... I could go on for hours about all the suffering the war has brought, but then I would only make myself more dejected. There is nothing we can do but wait as calmly as we can till the misery comes to an end. Jews and Christians wait, the whole earth waits; and there are many who wait for death.

Yours, Anne

Anne Frank, 1943

Can we count on another twenty years? I shall be fifty on 25th, Monday week that is; and sometimes feel that I have lived 250 years already and sometimes that I am still the youngest person on the omnibus. (Nessa says she still always thinks this, as she sits down.) And I want to write another four novels; and the *Tap on the Door*; and to go through English literature, like a string through cheese, or rather like some industrious insect, eating its way from book to book, from Chaucer to Lawrence. This is a programme, considering my slowness, to last out my twenty years, if I have them.

Virginia Woolf, 1932

14 January

Ann was married to Wm. Osgood. God grant them to live in love to their lives end. She lived with us 13 years and half, and was a Faithful Servant.

Mary Woodforde, 1686

I fed the hens, put the blackouts up all over (except the dining-room, which I left till later) and made tea: a boiled egg, wholemeal bread, two tiny toasted scones from yesterday, a baked apple – and a little piece of Christmas cake for my husband. I drew the table up to the fire, and my husband's slippers were warm when he came in. I wonder if Arthur was right once when he said, 'You make home too attractive, dearie – and it's turned into your prison.' But when I look at my husband's tired face sometimes, I wonder what else I could have done.

Nella Last, 1942

Poor Alice Green! … the other evening when I was alone with her she broke down and wept bitterly in my arms. Arthur Strong, after using her money and her influence to climb into the position of Librarian to the House of Lords, marries a brilliant and beautiful Greek scholar – Eugenie Sellers. For eighteen months the poor woman has been eaten into with bitterness; when at times I have watched her unawares she has looked like a lost soul. And a certain lack of dignity and the extreme unhappiness of her expression has alienated some of her old friends, and even Society is becoming cold to her. The world gets impatient at her restless unhappiness: at fifty years of age, with a good income, distinguished position, a woman ought to settle down contentedly. But some women never grow too old to be in love, or at least to require love. And why should they?

Beatrice Webb, 1898

15 January

A new term in a new year – a golden opportunity to get a peer's heir – a worthy theological student – or to change entirely! But Oxford really is intoxicating.

Barbara Pym (aged 18), 1932

Inconstant

We sailed last night, had fair weather and pretty good wind all day. I find it quite odd to be alone here. I dare not think on those I left at Naples for it makes my heart swell with anguish, however I can make no complaints for I am as happy in my situation as it is possible to be. Fremantle is all attention and kindness. I have got a comfortable little cabin where I can do what I like. The Vice Roy and Colonel Drinkwater are a pleasant society for us.

Betsey Wynne Fremantle, 1797

… I suppose [her friend] Jos doesn't know any more about it than I do, but her words 'I hope … ' imply that people only have children when they really want to. That does make sense, but on the other hand, the way things happen in poor families makes me wonder if this is so. Last week at the X's, the mother and father were down in the dumps because they are going to have a sixth child, while the other five already don't have enough to eat. Surely, when there is no work, that is too many children for their means. But isn't it up to them, then, to decide not to have any more?

Henriette Dessaulles (aged 20), 1881

… the chestnut horse is disposed of at last. Papa sent Reynolds to the Zoological Gardens to enquire the price of cat's meat: £2 for a very fat horse, 30/- for a middling one, thin ones not taken as the lions are particular. However he is sold to a cab owner along the road for £15.

Beatrix Potter (aged 15), 1882

16 January

It is strange how even in a land where scarce a thing is growing, a sudden benediction comes, and lo, the spring is there.

So it was yesterday morning, or at least it was so to me, for I went for the first time these three weeks out from among the brown houses of the town to see the Moongod's temple, now fully excavated and already abandoned. I had meant to try the hour's ride, but Abdulillah stepped providentially out of space from his green-tasselled car and offered to take me. Sayyid 'Ali came; Qasim seized his white coat with the gilt buttons and leaped in: the Mansab's son boarded us in the High Street, and I snatched up little Husain, who was the only infant about, for a joy-ride: he was far too overcome to say a word of thanks, but in silence turned his face towards us at intervals from the seat in front, with an expression of such ineffable ecstasy that that alone seemed like the springtime of the world …

Freya Stark, Hureidha, Arabia, 1938

All the morning, preparing clean stays, covering the steel busk, etc. & putting by my hoard, forty-four pounds & Tib [Isabella Norcliffe] owes me six, which will make fifty. I never was so rich before.

Anne Lister, 1819

But oh these resilient sunny mornings! The lemon trees, the tall poinsettias and hibiscus and residential palms! He gives me back my love of the world, my medicinal, alchemical love that can convert everything into food for the soul and senses. I am happy. I go to him at lunchtime with two lettuces and a basket of strawberries under my arm. I see the tall palms with fat trunks, the dark untidy garden and the little hut that is his studio. Such underground tunes singing in my head! And the things said and unsaid hardly have a difference, so little do they burst or break the surface in issuing forth.

Elizabeth Smart, 1940

My brother came with a view to assist, if in his power, to put an end to the unhappy state in which Mr Stock and me were. It was done. My hopes are not very sanguine; but should this peace be of short continuance, or should it be more lasting than before, may I bear it meekly …

Ellen Weeton, 1818

17 January

A.'s [her husband's] birthday. He is nervy over his birthday just as Doria and I are. Today I felt oh! the nothing done; all the effort and waste of small creative powers, and nothing to leave behind. Is that why people want children? But I want the glory of living, and not to live by proxy, even through a child.

Ivy Jacquier, 1922

I fear my diary has got very behindhand. The last three weeks have been so busy and happy that I have not had the opportunity for writing things down. C. [her married lover David Lloyd George; Chancellor of the Exchequer] returned from Wales on Dec 29th and from then till now I have been with him at W. H. [Walton Heath, Lloyd George's home], coming up every day to town, and going back in the evening. It has been like an idyll, but alas! came to an end yesterday when the family returned from Criccieth, & I returned home. The longer we are together, the more our love and affection seem to increase, so that it is all the more difficult to part. But we have resolved not to be miserable at parting, for 'my true love hath my heart, & I have his' and happy memories will buoy us up till 'the next time' ….

Frances Stevenson, 1915

I had ridden over late in the morning, when the workmen had gone. No one was available to lead the donkey, till the small Muhammad, who has the beautiful mother, saw me and leaped at the chance of missing school …

Sick men came running as we went: peasants came up to shake hands and greet my reappearance: an old man spurring along sold me a bronze spear from Mekka [sic]. It was pleasant to be alive again at last in the friendly open world … When I reached our door my heart was giving some trouble, and I have had to rest it and see people from my bed again.

Freya Stark, 1938

When Henry [Miller] telephones me, wants to see me, the world begins to sing again, the chaos crystallizes into one desire – all the heavings, fermentations, constellations are soldered by the rich sound of his voice.

I run upstairs in my kimono and add five pages to the dream book. I obey only instinct, senses, and they are subjugated by Henry. I am afloat again. Children. What are children? Abdication before life. Here, little one, I transit a life to you of which I have made a superb failure. No. N. What a female I am! Even children. I must have been tired last night. *Allons donc.* Pull yourself together, you fake artist, you …

The other day, Hugh [her husband] took me to a hotel room to fuck me – playing at an adventure. 'You whore, you, you whore.' He loved the strangeness of it, and for a moment as I touched his body it seemed like a stranger's body – but it was a joyless game for me. I'm physically obsessed by Henry. I'm afraid I'm a faithful female, all in all!

Anaïs Nin, 1933

18 January

A strange empty day. I did not feel well, lay around, looked at daffodils against the white walls, and twice thought I must be having hallucinations because of their extraordinary scent that goes from room to room. I always forget how important the empty days are, how important it may be sometimes not to expect to produce anything, even a few lines in a journal. I am still pursued by a neurosis about work inherited from my father. A day when one has not pushed oneself to the limit seems a damaged damaging day, a sinful day. Not so! The most valuable thing we can do for the psyche, occasionally, is to let it rest, wander, live in the ever-changing light of a room, not try to be or do anything whatever.

May Sarton, 1971

Another skip, partly due to my writing a long letter to Nessa, which drained up some of the things I should have said here. But I like this better than letter writing. On Thursday and Friday we worked away at printing. Unvarying cold and gloom, which turns now to rain, now to snow. This is the Hell of the year. We seem to mark time in the mud.

Virginia Woolf, 1918

… I received a message from my uncle, requesting to see me. I called upon him, and he offered me an asylum at his house, should I ever want one. He had heard how I had been situated lately, and was then ready, he said, to take me in. I told him that a kind of reconciliation had taken place; that his offer, notwithstanding, had released my mind from an anxious burthen; for I did not know where to go when turned out before. At the same time, I would do all that was in my power to avoid being placed in such a situation again. I had ever striven to act as a wife ought to do; in the same way, I would endeavour to continue. I could not promise more.

Ellen Weeton, 1818

Dined with Mr and Mrs P. We talked of the wrongs and suffering of our race. Mr P. thought me too sensitive. – But oh! how inexpressibly bitter and agonizing it is to feel oneself an outcast from the rest of mankind, as we are in this country! To me it is *dreadful, dreadful*. Were I to indulge in the thought I fear I should become insane. But I do not *despair*. I will not *despair*; though *very* often I can hardly help doing so. God help us! We are indeed a wretched people. Oh, that I could do *much* towards bettering our condition. I will do *all*, all the *very little* that lies in my power, while life and strength last!

Charlotte Forten, 1857

To Nan's in p.m., to take care of her while Papa and Freddie went to C[oncord]. The dear little man so happy and important with his bit of a bag, six pennies, and a cake for refreshment during the long journey of an hour.

We brooded over Johnny [her sister's baby] as if he were a heavenly sort of fire to warm and comfort us with his sunny little face and loving ways. She is a happy woman! I sell my children, and though they feed me, they don't love me as hers do.

Louisa May Alcott, 1868

In writing a diary all the most important things get left out. Only the decorations get mentioned and the shape of the building is taken for granted. Far the greatest pleasure I have almost every day of my life is simply being with R. [her husband Ralph], or, when I'm not with him, from remembering everything to tell him afterwards. In some ways the outer bleakness created by the war has intensified this very great happiness.

Frances Partridge, 1940

19 January

The cold increases, the snow is getting deep, and I hear the Thames is frozen over very nearly, which has not happened since 1814.

Queen Victoria, 1838

Nothing but sensuousness seducing me, cajoling me, muffling me up in lazy luxury. The will to work is a faint idea, not an urgent immediate one. It is pleasant – no, it would be pleasant, but for the feeling underneath of time flying, of waste, of unaccomplishment, and the story of The Talents. This is the fight against the powerful, the irresistible, the compelling monster Sex.

Elizabeth Smart, 1934

I said to my husband, 'Have you never thought of leaving me?' I said it jokingly, but he considered it very seriously and said, 'No – why should I? I would have everything to lose.' I said, 'Tell me then – what do you consider my greatest attraction for you?' I didn't expect him to say, 'Your beauty', but did think he would say, 'Because you are such a good cook' or at least something 'positive'. Instead he said, 'Because you are such a comfortable person to live with.' I felt all flat feet and red flannel – as others see us!

Nella Last, 1946

20 January

I've fussed more about food and its values and looks since war finished than I'm sure I did all the war years, and watched over my husband's health more. Perhaps it's because so many people I know have cracked up and, if they have not died, have seemed to go all to pieces. This morning when the sea birds came over in screaming clouds, he came upstairs and said, 'You should come and see your pitiful pensioners', and I said 'Tip those boiled scraps in the bucket, under the crab-apple tree. If you put it by the rockery the gulls gobble all, and the rest don't get a chance.' He said, 'Well, I never thought to see birds fight over boiled potato peelings. They flapped round me head till I felt their wings brush me. I'm glad you don't like to see things hungry' – and he smiled at me. I said, 'Ah well, you said I was "comfortable to live with". I suppose you referred to me feeding you.' He said, 'I don't know why you feel so snippy about me saying that. I meant to say there was comfort and peace wherever you were, and I think it's the best compliment that could be paid to a woman.' I suppose it is, but it's the demanding women who get most fun!

Nella Last, 1946

Oh God, grant my prayer! Preserve my voice; should I lose all else I shall have my voice. Oh God, continue to show me Thy goodness; do not let me die of grief and vexation! I long so much to go into society. Time passes and I make no progress; I am nailed to the same place, I who would live, live by steam, I who burn, who boil over, who bubble with impatience!

'I have never seen anyone in such a fever of life,' said Doria of me.

Marie Bashkirtseff (aged 15), 1876

The fortnight in bed was the result of having a tooth out, and being tired enough to get a headache – a long dreary affair, that receded and advanced much like the mist on a January day. One hour's writing daily is my allowance for the next few weeks; and having hoarded it this morning, I may spend part of it now, since I am much behindhand with the month of January. I note however that this diary writing does not count as writing, since I have just reread my year's diary and am much struck by the rapid haphazard gallop at which it swings along, sometimes indeed jerking almost intolerably over the cobbles. Still if it were not written rather faster than the fastest typewriting, if I stopped and took thought, it would never be written at all; and the advantage of the method is that it sweeps up accidentally several stray matters which I should exclude if I hesitated, but which are the diamonds of the dustheap.

Virginia Woolf, 1919

… At times I feel quite anxious in looking forward to another confinement, but Willie needs a companion and I ought to be willing to give him one. Yet at times the thought will come over me that I may bring into the world a deformed child. And if I should? May not mercy mingle with this judgement? May not such a trial be the very thing I need to teach me humility and patience? God knoweth.

Caroline Healey Dall, 1849

21 January

I am astonished more and more at the stupid extravagance of the women. Mrs H. (who gains her living by keeping a boarding house) has spent, she says, at least £60 on hair dyes in the last ten years. All the ladies, even little girls, wear white powder on their faces and many rouge. All wear silk dresses in the street and my carmelite and grey linen dresses are so singular here that many ladies would refuse to walk with me. Fashion rules so absolutely that to wear a hat requires great courage.

Barbara Leigh Smith Bodichon, New Orleans, 1858

Driving to Falmouth, a pig attached itself to the cortège and made us even more remarkable than usual. Piggy and Dory (the dog) scampering on side by side, and playing like frolicsome children, spite of all we could do to turn the incipient Bacon back his former path in life.

Caroline Fox, 1849

C. [Lloyd George] is not very well today. He has been working very hard, but personally I think he is suffering from too much 'family'. He was very upset on Monday because not one of them had remembered that it was his birthday on Sunday … 'They take me for granted', he said to me rather bitterly.

Frances Stevenson, 1915

It's a terrible thing when the person you love says they don't like you any more; not even they don't love you, but they don't like you. So that's why I think I'm close to a mental breakdown. He says to me what they all say, 'You're a politician, I don't believe a word that comes out of your mouth. You'll never change.' I feel that I try really hard to be a better person. I feel I try as hard as it's possible to try, but either I'm not trying hard enough, or what I'm trying to do is impossible.

I arrive at the surgery, and I'm thinking, 'Don't cry, don't cry …'

Oona King, 2001

22 January

Got a snow-slide on my bonnet, so made another in the p.m., and in the evening to the Antislavery Festival. All the old faces and many new ones. Glad I have lived in the time of this great movement, and known its heroes so well. War times suit me, as I am a fighting *May*.

Louisa May Alcott, 1868

My thirty-third birthday! Just sent off the first instalment of my first book. Working hard and working well – one day goes like another. Breakfast at 8, work from 8.30 to 11.30, a few minutes' turn, then read to Father for one hour. Lunch, cigarette, one hour or so walk, a sleep, read 4.30, work till 7.30. Supper, cigarette, letter-writing or dictating (if I am not too tired) and then to bed at 10 o'clock … Mrs Thompson, little Miss Darling, Neale, Don and the cat – occasional letters from men friends – and my own thoughts fill up the intervals of work. But in spite of my 33 years I feel younger than I have ever done before, except that I feel horribly 'independent', absolute mistress of myself and my circumstances – uncannily so. 'Men may come and men may go, but I go on for ever!'

Beatrice Webb, 1891

I feel so useless tonight – always a sign of nervous tension with me. I feel as if my efforts are so tiny and feeble – so little to help all the trouble and pain in the world. I'll have two aspirins tonight to try and sleep, for when I don't sleep it makes my wretched bones worse and makes the pain in my back unbearable. I sat quietly casting my knitting and feeling half-wild with nerves, when my little dog got up from where he was lying and peered up at me with his blinding old eyes, as if he knew I was unhappy.

Nella Last, 1940

Took tea with Mrs Ball, and met Mrs Morris and Mrs Walker. Mrs Morris is a woman of peculiarly amiable disposition, and fascinating simplicity of manner, combined with good sense. How unfortunately she has married; the only child of her parents, and having a handsome fortune, it is all squandered away most unaccountably by a hog of a husband, and she now toils amidst a numerous flock of fine-looking boys and girls, like a galley slave. Mrs Walker, a shop-keeper in Holland, is a woman of such strange manners, that I would never be surprised to hear she was become deranged. She is greatly to be pitied. The anxiety of business, and a family of 5 or 6 children to support, will be too much for her. I admired most of her sentiments, they appeared so correct; but the nervous, twitching manner she had, almost forced a smile even from pity's self.

Ellen Weeton, 1824

23 January

I forgot to mention yesterday that Clergy the ancient Valet de Chambre of the poor French King arrived here and dined with us ... He gave us many details on that unfortunate Royal family. Louis [XVI] died with great courage and never showed a moment's weakness. His neck being so fat his head did not fall at the first stroke and he was heard to scream. The Queen had been kept in such piggishness during a great while that she was quite an eskalleton [sic] when she was killed. All her members trembled. Mde Elizabeth on the contrary was mild and calm and looked as fresh as a rose.

Betsey Wynne Fremantle, 1796

I have caught myself wishing an old long-forgotten wish that I had been born of the rougher sex. Women are very dependent here, and give a great deal of trouble; we feel our weakness more than anywhere else. This, I cannot but think, has a slight tendency to sink us, it may be, into a more natural and proper sphere than the one we occupy in over-civilized life ...

Anne Langton, Canada, 1838

Began to poultice Raven's [her son's] neck again with white bread and White Lylys and grounsell.

Mary Hardy, 1787

24 January

Sara Sophie Jacquier Skinner, born at 2.20 a.m., much better than losing an appendix.

Dr Moore-Ede was a gem; I enjoyed the experience.

Ivy Jacquier, 1922

'Hello, do you want to see him?' He didn't make any lengthy preparations, but picked up the animal, turned him over on to his back, deftly held his head and paws together and the lesson began. 'These are the male organs, these are just a few stray hairs, and that is his bottom.' The cat did another half turn and was standing on his white socks once more.

If any other boy had shown me 'the male organs,' I would never have looked at him again. But Peter went on talking quite normally on what is otherwise such a painful subject, without meaning anything unpleasant, and finally put me sufficiently at ease for me to be normal too. We played with Moffi, amused ourselves, chattered together, and then sauntered through the large warehouse towards the door …

… I wasn't quite my usual self for the rest of the day though, in spite of everything. When I thought over our talk, it still seemed rather odd. But at least I'm wiser about one thing, that there really are young people – and of the opposite sex too – who can discuss these things naturally without making fun of them.

Anne Frank, 1944

And this day there was none that dined here nor visited me, so I spent the day in hearing some chapters read to me and in preparing myself to receive the Holy Sacrament of Bread and Wine which I intend, God willing, to receive with my family.

Lady Anne Clifford, 1676

25 January

There. It's happened. I'm flying to New York. It's true … Usually, travelling is an attempt to annex a new object to my universe; this in itself is a fascinating undertaking. But today it's different: I feel I'm leaving my life behind. I don't know if it will be through anger or hope, but something is going to be revealed – a world so full, so rich, and so unexpected that I'll have the extraordinary adventure of becoming a different me.

Simone de Beauvoir, 1947

New York. Writing nights steadily until two and three o'clock, and finding that I get more done by these uninterrupted midnight hours than a day of half-interrupted work.

Dawn Powell, 1932

I remembered how this day was 52 years [ago], in the withdrawing Room chamber at Knole House in Kent as we sat at dinner, had my first Lord and I a great falling out …

Lady Anne Clifford, 1676

I feel so much lighter to-day and can move more easily in bed and the nurse who arrived two days ago thinks that before Sunday the little thing will have arrived. We have just returned from dinner at the German Embassy; [Count Paul Graff Wolff] Metternich included Poppets in the invitation: he arrived here to-day from Newlands. I drove him and [her

44

son] Hansel about this afternoon; the precious little boy goes to Shelagh at Eaton to-morrow, I shall miss him dreadfully, but please God when I see him again I shall have a strong healthy little baby-brother (or sister) to show him. Patsy comes tomorrow.

My guardian spirit helps me, as it does *so often*, even prompting me what to do and say at critical times.

Princess Daisy of Pless, 1905

26 January

I want one. After this book-year, after next-Europe-year, a baby-year? Four years of marriage childless is enough for us? Yes, I think I shall have guts by then ... I will write like mad for 2 years – and be writing when Gerald and or Warren 2nd is born, what to call the girl? O dreamer. I waved, knocked, knocked on the cold window glass and waved to Ted moving out into view below, black-coated, black-haired, fawn-haunched and shouldered in the crisp-stamped falling snow. Fevered, how I love that one.

Sylvia Plath, 1958

A battle against depression, routed today (I hope) by clearing out kitchen; by sending the article (a lame one) to N. S.: and by breaking into *Pointz Hall* two days, I think, of memoir writing. This trough of despair shall not, I swear, engulf me. The solitude is great. Rodmell life is very small beer. The house is damp. The house is untidy. But there is no alternative. Also days will lengthen. What I need is the old spurt. 'Your true life, like mine, is in ideas.' Desmond [MacCarthy] said to me once. But one must remember one can't pump ideas. I begin to dislike introspection.

We are going to Cambridge for two days. There's a lull in the war. Six nights without raids. But Garvin says the greatest struggle is about to come – say in three weeks – and every man, woman dog cat even weevil must girt their arms, their faith – and so on. Yes, I was thinking; we live without a future. That's what's queer, with our noses pressed to a closed door.

Virginia Woolf, 1941

Whatever turn events may take, whatever may happen in Russia, nothing can stop the march of time. The years will pass, I shall grow up and enter life. What do I need then? Education and knowledge.

Whatever I neglect now I shall have to pay for later. What I mean by this is that my studies represent to me my very life, the greatest part of my interests, and that is why I am so anxious about their fate.

And after all my ego stands in the first place: events and all the rest only occupy the background. My own life obscures them …

Nelly Ptashkina (aged 14), 1918

For no reason at all I hated this day as if it was a person – its wind, its insecurity, its flabbiness, its hints of an insane universe.

Dawn Powell, 1938

27 January

Raven [her son] much as usual, began taking antimony and sarsaparilla.

Mary Hardy 1787

Miss Edith Bernal Osborne dined; her sister has just married the Duke of St Albans; she has been living in Italy for some years alone as she cannot stand her parents. In about a fortnight she is going to marry what Jack calls her policeman (Mr Blake) – a man in the Irish Constabulary. She is extremely handsome, has her hair cut short & a moustache as big as Jack's.

Mary, Lady Monkswell, 1874

Oh my God! I am a mother!

George Frederick Evans, named after my dad and Harry's [her husband Harold Evans], was born two months early at two o'clock on Sunday morning. I am so not ready for this and in my cocky, breezy, I-amsuperwoman way, I never dreamed anything bad could happen with our baby. I am humbled by the awful swift cycle of events and feel there is an admonition in it. This is life. This could have been death. I have only seen my son for five minutes in the incubator. He is four and a half pounds. Trying to conjure up a maternal bond but actually feeling as if I have been in a car crash. But then, this morning, shuffling slowly in my gown with an IV attached, I went to visit him in the preemie unit with Harry …

It was all so unreal, so utterly unlike what I had hoped for or planned. Now we wait and pray that the fluttering creature in the warm light box will make it and be the sturdy little boy, the little Harry of our dreams. Please, God, please let him be all right.

Tina Brown, 1986

28 January

———

Dear Kitty,

I ask myself this morning whether you don't sometimes feel rather like a cow, who has had to chew over all the old pieces of news again and again, and who finally yawns loudly and silently wishes that Anne would occasionally dig up something new.

Alas, I know it's dull for you, but try to put yourself in my place, and imagine how sick I am of the old cows, who keep having to be pulled out of the ditch again. If the conversation at mealtimes isn't over politics or a delicious meal, then Mummy or Mrs Van Daan trot out one of the old stories of their youth, which we've heard so many times before …

Anne Frank, 1944

I was quite miserable all the morning as the three Mariners were punished and flogged along side of every ship, some men flogged likewise on board.

Betsey Wynne Fremantle, 1797

I shall not remember what happened on this day. It is a blank. At the end of my life I may want it, may long to have it. There was a new moon: that I remember. But who came or what I did – all is lost. It's just a day missed, a day crossing the line.

Katherine Mansfield, 1920

29 January

———

Adieu to all that's dear, to all that's lovely. I am parted from my Life, my Soul! my Piozzi: *Sposo promesso! Amante adorato! Amico senza equale* ['Promised spouse, adored lover, friend without equal']. If I can get Health and Strength to write my Story here, 'tis all I wish for now! Oh Misery! The cold Dislike of my eldest daughter I thought I might wear away by Familiarity with his Merit, and that we might live tolerably together or at least part Friends, but No: her Aversion increased daily, & She communicated it to the others; they treated me insolently, and him very strangely – running away whenever he came as if they saw a Serpent: and plotting with their Governess, a cunning Italian how to invent Lies to make me hate him, and twenty such narrow Tricks. by these means the notion of my partiality took air … I wrote my Lover word that my Mind was all distraction, and bid him come to me the next Morning my Birthday. 27 Jan. mean Time I took a Vomit, & spent the Sunday Night in Torture not to be described – my Falsehood to my Piozzi, my strong affection for him; the Incapacity I felt in myself to resign the Man I so adored, the Hopes I had so cherished, inclined me strongly to set them all at Defiance, and go with him to Church to sanctify the Promises I had so often made him – while the Idea of abandoning the Children of my first Husband, who left me so nobly provided for, and who depended on my Attachment to his Offspring, awakened the Voice of Conscience, and threw me on my Knees to pray for *his* Direction who was hereafter to judge my Conduct ….

Hester Lynch Thrale Piozzi, 1783

The nurse says the baby *must* arrive to-night or to-morrow, I am sure I wish it would; it is weary work waiting and I dread the whole performance. For the second time the King [Edward VII] has told people I am doing far too much, I ought to be quiet. Last night he told Metternich. I wish people would mind their own business. And anyway, what does His Majesty know about it! He and the Queen sent me each a pretty Christmas present.

Princess Daisy of Pless, 1905

Cutting curl papers half an hour … Arranging & putting away my last year's letters. Looked over & burnt several very old ones from indifferent people … Burnt … Mr Montagu's farewell verses that no trace of any man's admiration may remain. It is not meet for me. I love, & only love, the fairer sex & thus beloved by them in turn, my heart revolts from any love but theirs.

Anne Lister, 1821

30 January

… The excitement of hearing about the advance into Germany puts us into a frenzy of impatience, and I am well aware of wanting to forge along through time as quickly as possible, looking forward each day to evening. And then to the start of a new day, and so on. I said to R. [her husband Ralph] how much I deplored this scrabbling through our lives.

'Yes, I want to get to the end of the story,' he said. F.: 'What? To old age, decrepitude – the tomb?' R.: 'Yes' (in a serio-comic voice), the tomb – that's where I want to get.' 'And separation from me!' I cried. 'Don't you realise that's what it'll be, even if we are lucky enough to die at the same moment – the end of all our happiness together!' '*Don't*,' said R. … And he rushed from the room leaving me in tears.

Frances Partridge, 1945

The sixties are marvellous years, because one has become fully oneself by then, but the erosions of old age, erosion of strength, of memory, of physical well-being have not yet begun to frustrate and needle. I am too heavy, but I refuse to worry too much about it. I battle the ethos here in the USA, where concern about being overweight has become a fetish. I sometimes think we are as cruel to old brother ass, the body, as the Chinese used to be who forced women's feet into tiny shoes as a sign of breeding and beauty. 'Middle-aged spread' is a very real phenomenon, and why pretend that it is not? I am not so interested in being a dazzling model as in being comfortable inside myself. And that I am.

May Sarton, 1975

My life seems to have drained away. My darling baby had two days of getting steadily worse till yesterday, when his oxygen needs began to decrease. Then he got jaundice and I couldn't bear to see more tubes and plasters all over his tiny, struggling body in the incubator. But today, the improvements continued and I felt so shattered by the emotion of it all, I just sat in front of his glass container in the preemie unit and cried. This evening, to my joy, he is breathing on his own …

I want to enter a new period of calm in which all the energy goes into loving Georgie. The world is upside down. When I opened my eyes on Tuesday morning, I saw the Challenger shuttle explode before our eyes on TV. The crew had become so real to me. I cried and cried.

Tina Brown, 1986

… I have never stooped to underhand measures to accomplish any end and I will not begin at this late date by doing that that my soul abhors; sugaring men, weak, deceitful creatures, with flattery to retain them as escorts or to gratify a revenge, & I earnestly pray My Father to show me the right & give me the strength to do it because it is right, despite temptations. I shall pray for Mr G. & all the others who have formed themselves in a league against a defenseless girl …

Ida B. Wells, 1866

31 January

What makes daily life so agreeable in America is the good humour and friendliness of Americans. Of course this quality has its reverse side. I'm irritated by those imperious invitations to 'take life easy', repeated in words and images throughout the day. On advertisements for Quaker Oats, Coca-Cola, and Lucky Strike, what displays of white teeth – the smile seems like lockjaw. The constipated girl smiles a loving smile at the lemon juice that relieves her intestines. In the subway, in the streets, on magazine pages, these smiles pursue me like obsessions. I read on a sign in a drugstore, 'Not to grin is a sin.' Everyone obeys the order, the system. 'Cheer up! Take it easy.'

Simone de Beauvoir, 1947

The last day of this month! This evening I have been reading to G. [her partner George Henry Lewes] some entries in my note-book of past times in which I recorded my *malaise* and despair. But it is impossible to me to believe that I have ever been in so unpromising and despairing a state as I now feel. – After writing these words, I read to G. the Proem and opening scene of my novel [*Romola*] and he expressed great delight in them.

George Eliot, 1862

Mrs Davis gave her 'Luncheon to Ladies' on Saturday. Many more persons were there than at any of those luncheons which have gone before. We had gumbo, ducks and olives, *suprème de volaille*, chickens in jelly, oysters, lettuce salad, chocolate cream, jelly cake, claret cup, champagne, etc., …

Today, for a pair of forlorn shoes, I gave eighty-five dollars … Mr Pettigrew says: 'You take your money to market in the market basket and bring home what you buy in your pocketbook'.

Mary Boykin Chesnut, 1864

February

'My dearest Albert put on my stockings for me. I went in and saw him shave; a great delight for me.'

Queen Victoria, 1840

1 February

There was a letter from Roland [her fiancé] which disturbed me somewhat. He has found out that the 4th Suffolk Regt. want three more officers for the front at once. He is going – or rather has offered himself to-day – as one of them. He is so obviously anxious to go that I do not know what to think or wish. For his sake & in consideration of what I might feel if he did not want to go I am glad, but for my own sake, which is regulated by what it wants rather than by what it ought to want, I would like him to stay. Somehow I feel he may succeed this time in his attempts ...

Vera Brittain, 1915

Fremantle attacked me for some nonsense or other I am too inanimate, but we were very good friends at last. I see that very little is required to make him uneasy and must be still more on my guard.

Betsey Wynne Fremantle, 1797

My writing career becomes an increasing problem. I have written in all directions in the last year, with the result that nothing is finished. Even the vignettes I have done are to no purpose but spraying out on all sides. I cannot let myself get flabby this way, particularly since I never felt better, more alive, keyed up to impressions in my whole life. No excuse except diffused personal life which, if it gets too much in my way, should be sacrificed to my original intent.

Dawn Powell, 1935

The 'cold snap' which has been snapping all the week is abating somewhat. I have been in such a state of 'freezation' ever since it began that now when I find myself gradually thawing and revivifying, the sensation has all the charm of novelty.

L. M. Montgomery, 1902

2 February

Homosexuality – The mutual mistrust from the start: don't deny it's there, it *is*. Except perhaps at the very start, when one is eighteen. But after 30 or so, it is there. Love can never take a straight, hard, fast course, running to the other, growing stronger day by day. One's relationship in bed improves, we are easier around the house together, but even in this greater ease lies the danger that she is 'getting on her feet' now, and may no longer need me in ten days. That is because we suspect that such relationships are based only on need, selfishness, anyway. And now we are only 30 days old, in this new relationship of admitting we love each other.

Patricia Highsmith, 1954

Went to Confession at the Servite – Father Carato, *again*, three Hail Marys. While I was kneeling in front of the altar saying my penance, I suddenly thought of G.[erhardt] kissing me and a kind of delicious stabbing pain ran through my stomach, so sharp and strong that I winced.

I was walking back past the dairy towards Milborne Grove, thinking about kissing and whether I would like it better next time, when the door of the Artists' Café burst open and a hand shot out, pulling me into the murky interior, which smelt of stale cooking fat and garlic. It was Gerhardt! I felt quite faint with the excitement of seeing him again so suddenly.

Joan Wyndham (aged 18), 1940

This long slow dying is no doubt instructive, but it is disappointingly free from excitements: 'naturalness' being carried to its supreme expression. One sloughs off the activities one by one, and never knows that they're gone, until one suddenly finds that the months have slipped away and the sofa will never more be laid upon, the morning paper read …

A little while ago we had rather an amusing episode with the kind and usually understanding [Dr] Tuckey, who was led away into assuring me that I would live a good bit still – I was terribly shocked and when he saw the havoc that he wrought, he reassuringly said: 'but you'll be comfortable, too,' at which I exclaimed: 'Oh I don't care about that, but boo-hoo, it's so *inconvenient*!' and the poor man burst into a roar of laughter. I was glad afterwards that it happened, as I was taken quite by surprise, and was able to test the sincerity of my mortuary inclinations. I have always *thought* that I wanted to die, but I felt quite uncertain as to what my muscular demonstrations might be at the moment of transition … 'twould be such a bore to be perturbed.

Alice James, 1892

… Poor Lady Anne Butler has been extremely ill. She was brought to Bed of Twins. The Boy is dead. She was in labour three days and very little hopes of her life. About nine days after, being pretty well for that time, fell ill of a Fever and is not yet perfectly recovered.

Lady Eleanor Butler, 1789

3 February

I progress slowly. These queer blobs beneath me are not my own feet yet. Being sick is a horrid way to spend your money. Alice brought me all her cherished Chinese lilies and her Christmas cactus. I just revelled in their perfume all night.

Emily Carr, 1937

Last night I was again plunged into despair. His [her husband, Leo Tolstoy's] temperature went up to 37.8. It was a terrible night: at three in the morning he had another morphine injection, but it did not relieve his agony and insomnia. I was alone with him till five. Seryozha and Doctor Altschuler came in twice.

After I had lifted Lyovochka [Tolstoy] up in the bed and had attended to him all night without once sitting down, he squeezed my hands and stroked them tenderly, saying: 'Many thanks, darling,' and 'Sonya, I have exhausted you.' And I kissed his forehead and hands and said it gave me great pleasure to look after him, if only to relieve his sufferings a little.

Sophia Tolstoy, 1902

The Lord's Day.

After private prayers I did eat my breakfast, and then dressed the sores that I had undertaken: after, I went to the Church: after, I prayed privately and then dined: in the afternoon I went again to church: after I came home I read of the testament, and wrote notes in it and upon [theologian William] Perknes, and then went about the house and, at my accustomed hour, Came to private examination and prayer, and then to supper: after to the repetition and, when I had dressed some sores, I went to private prayer and so to bed.

Lady Margaret Hoby, 1599

4 February

Thinking so much these days about what it is to be a woman, I wonder whether an ingrained sense of guilt is not a feminine characteristic. A man who has no children may feel personally deprived but he does not feel guilty, I suspect. A woman who has no children is always on the defensive.

May Sarton, 1975

The Gov. set off from hence in a sleigh with 6 officers & 20 soldiers for the Mohawk Village on the Grand River where Capt. Brant & 20 Indians are to join him & guide him by the La Tranche River to Detroit, no European having gone that track & the Indians are to carry Provisions.

The Gov. wore a fur Cap tippet & Gloves & maucassins [sic] but no Great Coat. His servant carried two Blankets & linen. The other Gentlemen carried their Blankets in a pack on their Back.

Elizabeth Simcoe, Niagara, 1793

I was sent for to Trutsdall to the travail of my Cousin Ison's wife, who that Morning was brought to bed of a daughter: the same day, at night, I heard of a fish that was taken up at Yarmouth, 53 foot long and 23 broad.

Last Margaret Hoby, 1602

I would like ... I don't really know what I would like! Not to die like Madame Y., but to sleep for a long, long time and be transported into a higher realm where I would understand myself and everything else. As it is, I'm completely confused.

Henriette Dessaulles (aged 15), 1876

5 February

This morning the ocean seemed all sun, and I wished I could sing as we walked. Truly a golden thread of poetry runs through the daily routine on this ship ... When we left Havre, I solemnly declared to Polly, hand on heart, that I was going to diet, but the dinner to-night – mushroom soup, fish melting in the mouth, meat smothered in juices I had not dreamed of, and crèpe Suzette – knocked over my good intentions like ninepins! ...

Helen Keller, 1937

Late this afternoon in the House someone said to me, 'Have you heard the news? Margaret Thatcher has swept to the top in the leadership poll.' I fear that I felt a sneaking feminist pleasure. Damn it, that lass *deserves* to win.

Barbara Castle, 1975

I went to the Pagets somewhat guiltily. This comes of borrowing other people's pets. Miss Paget has an infinite number of guinea-pigs. First I borrowed and drew *Mr Chopps*. I returned him safely. Then in an evil hour I borrowed a very particular guinea-pig with a long white ruff, known as *Queen Elizabeth* … this wretched pig took to eating blotting paper, pasteboard, string and other curious substances and expired in the night.

I suspected something was wrong and intended to take it back. My feelings may be imagined when I found it extended, a damp – very damp disagreeable body. Miss Paget proved peaceable, I gave her the drawing.

Beatrix Potter, 1893

6 February

Mr Bartell came to see Raven [her son] laid 2 little costick plasters to his neck to open the sores.

Mary Hardy, 1787

What a wonderful day [her fifteenth birthday]! I've been pampered and coddled to my heart's content. I was given nice presents, but what meant even more to me was that I felt loved. Mama was so affectionate; Aunt Leman gave me another volume of Dickens, dear Papa gave me music.

Henriette Dessaulles (aged 14), 1875

… Today I wasn't in the best of moods. A little disappointed in myself. I went to visit Miep [Fernandes, best friend], who didn't go to school because she wasn't well. A friend of theirs has been arrested. We're all supposed to register, we can't postpone it any longer, and I guess we'll get a 'J' stamped on our papers. Anyway. Whatever happens, happens. I don't want to think about it too much. Letter from Guus [sic; her brother], dated December. He's so happy there, he's turning into a real American … He describes all sorts of domestic appliances, butter, tinned goods, advertisements, the bright lights, etc. and we meanwhile sitting here in the dark, simply drooling over his description of the good life …

Edith Velmans, Holland, 1941

7 February

To the hut for two marvellous days. The sky was grey and the woods were dim, but that did not matter. And yet again, we quarrelled. My period was due and at present I'm not in the mood to take risks. He [her lover Barny] was angry and bitter. But presently I was in his arms again, and his bitterness passed, and there was a new world.

Loran Hurnscot, 1924

Eliza Dunstan died today. It was such a child's deathbed, so innocent, so unpretending. She loved to hold her father's hand, he, poor fellow, kneeling by her in silent agony. She thought none could nurse her so well as father. Her spirit was most tenderly released. It is a wonderful thought, that sudden total change of hers. Has Heaven its Infant Schools? Who can tell?

Caroline Fox, 1844

Talked … of the Marriage Ceremony; my being a little agitated and nervous; 'Most natural,' Lord M.[elbourne] replied warmly; 'how could it be otherwise?' Lord M. was so warm, so kind, and so affectionate, the whole evening, and so much touched in speaking of me and my affairs. Talked of my former resolution of never marrying. 'Depend upon it, it's right to marry,' he said earnestly; 'if ever there was a situation that formed an exception, it's yours; it's in human nature, it's natural to marry; the other is a very unnatural state of things; it's a great change – it has its inconveniences: everybody does their best, and depend upon it you've done well; difficulties may arise from it,' as they do of course from everything.

Queen Victoria, 1840

This morning there was again a heavy raid. I sat it out in the cellar ward where the badly wounded lie. This is not much help. As one hears every bomb whistling down and feels every explosion. On such occasions I make a point of sitting with the worst cases, as when one sees how helpless *they* are, one feels stronger oneself.

Marie Vassiltchikov, Vienna, 1945

A heavenly day! Walked under spring sun, and then, in a little open sleigh, swept merrily through Brighton and Brookline, our hearts chanting aloud the beauty of God's world. In so mild an air such a drive is next to the exhilaration upon a good steed. All the houses were decorated with clothes taking the air, often festooned under the drawing room windows! Did no work today of any kind. The sun pronounced it a holiday and we could not gainsay it …

Fanny Longfellow, 1844

8 February

I behaved very foolishly towards Fremantle caused him much uneasiness and made myself very unhappy, certainly not intentionally I was very angry with myself afterwards but it was too late, all for a trifle and nonsense.

Betsey Wynne Fremantle, 1797

My husband has just gone out: a little shopping, a letter to throw in the box. I often go to the window to watch him leaving. He always looks up, we send each other smiles and kisses. The people going by and the taxi-drivers who are always there watch us and must say to themselves: how those two love each other. And in the end they are right. I'd detest him so much if I didn't have a huge fondness for him!

Liane de Pougy, 1937

How can anybody believe that hell is reserved for a future life? We get it right along in this world on the instalment plan and I have had a good stiff dose of mine this past week in the shape of a wretched, persistent little ailment – nothing serious enough to justify laying up but a half-and-half sickness that left me able to do what I had to do but poisoned the doing of it until I could have cried – and did cry – for sheer discouragement. This week has seemed as long as three. I'm a little better today but far from well yet and have to crawl around with misery just sticking out of my eyes.

L. M. Montgomery, 1902

… Funny about friends, you want them frightfully, but you can't find any to fit. Nothing in you and them that answers each other, only commonplaces – weather conditions, ailments or food – beyond that, blank. They slam the door of their innards and you slam the door of yours …

Well, today has been a day of lead. Why are there days when yeast, gunpowder and champagne are lifeless and you are brown and sagging as a rotten apple, days when one *longs* for somebody with their whole soul? Somebody that they never met or knew or saw …

Emily Carr, 1935

9 February

A sharp rime frost very fine day. Mr Bartell came to see Raven [her son]. We began to apply hemlock to his neck instead of poultice. He continues much as yesterday.

Mary Hardy, 1787

… We go up to Heaven and down to Hell a dozen times a day – at least, I do. And the discipline of work provides an exercise bar, so that the wild, irrational motions of the soul become formal and creative. It literally keeps one from falling on one's face.

That is one way to keep alive in self-made solitary confinement. I have found it useful also these past days to say to myself, 'What if I were not alone? What if I had ten children to get off to school every morning and a massive wash to do before they got home? What if two of them were in bed with flu, cross and at a loose end?' That is enough to send me back to solitude as if it were – as it truly is – a fabulous gift from the gods.

May Sarton, 1971

Just before Harriet [Milne] went, happening to talk a little to her in the complimentary style, M– [Mariana Lawton] & Eli [Eliza Belcombe] remonstrated. M– & I talked about an hour after we got into bed. A very little would make M– desperately jealous. Speaking of my manners, she owned they were not masculine but such was my form, voice & style of conversation, such a peculiar flattery & attention did I shew, that if this sort of thing was not carried off by my talents & cleverness, I should be disgusting. I took it all in good part. Vowed over & over, constantly, etc., and M– gave me a good kiss.

Anne Lister, 1820

Was unhappy all the morning as I saw I had given F.[remantle] real cause to be angry with me however I was better explained and we were friends again.

Betsey Wynne Fremantle, 1797

10 February

Got up at a ¼ to 9 – well, and having slept well; and breakfasted at ½ p 9. Mamma came before and brought me a Nosegay of orange flowers. My dearest kindest Lehzen [Louise, governess and adviser] gave me a dear little ring … Had my hair dressed and the wreath of orange flowers put on. Saw Albert for the last time alone, as my Bridegroom …

The Ceremony was very imposing, and fine and simple, and I think ought to make an everlasting impression on every one who promises at the Altar to keep what he or she promises. Dearest Albert repeated everything very distinctly. I felt so happy when the ring was put on, and by Albert. As soon as the Service was over, the Procession returned as it came, with the exception that my beloved Albert led me out. The applause was very great ...

As soon as we arrived [at Windsor] we went to our rooms; my large dressing room is our sitting room; the 3 little blue rooms are his ... After looking about our rooms for a little while, I went and changed my gown, and then came back to his small sitting room where dearest Albert was sitting and playing; he had put on his windsor coat; he took me on his knee, and kissed me and was so dear and kind. We had our dinner in our sitting room; but I had such a sick headache that I could eat nothing, and was obliged to lie down in the middle blue room for the remainder of the evening, on the sofa, but, ill or not, I never, never spent such an evening ... He called me names of tenderness, I have never yet heard used to me before – was bliss beyond belief! Oh! this was the happiest day of my life!

Queen Victoria, 1840

The raids are getting worse. This is the third one in as many days ... my nerves (which are bad enough as it is as a result of all those raids I lived through in Berlin) are not improving and when the bombs start crashing here in Vienna as well, I am pretty shaken each time.

Marie Vassiltchikov, 1945

Of the many times in which I have commenced writing a journal, one reason or other has prevented its continuance, or at least thrown upon it that check, which diminishes the pleasure of writing, and renders the matter less interesting. If nobody is ever to read what one writes, there is no satisfaction in writing; and, if any body does see it, mischief ensues. So I will not write a journal, but brief notes of such things as I conceive may be amusing, without incurring danger to myself or others.

Lady Charlotte Bury, 1811

11 February

When day dawned (for we did not sleep much) and I beheld that beautiful angelic face by my side, it was more than I can express! He does look so beautiful in his shirt only, with his beautiful throat seen. We got up at ¼ p. 8. When I had laced I went into dearest Albert's room, and we breakfasted together. He had a black velvet jacket on, without any neckcloth on, and looked more beautiful than it is possible for me to say …

Queen Victoria, 1840

I wonder why I never seem to know people. It makes one wonder whether one is presentable. It strikes me it is the way to make one not.

Beatrix Potter, 1896

As I stood bung-eyed at the stove, over the breakfast frying-pan in came Wilde for the chicken pail and burst out, 'Newbury was bombed yesterday'. 'No! Was there much damage? Anyone killed?' 'Yes, quite a few. A school and a church were hit.' It turned out to be exactly true, and some eighteen people were killed. If this had happened earlier in the war people would have stopped sending their children to school in Newbury. Now it's as if being bombed by the Germans was one of the normal hazards of life, like being run over by a motor car, and there was no use trying to avoid it. Probably it's more realistic than the earlier reaction.

Frances Partridge, 1943

Mr Cubit from N. Walsham to see Raven [her son], staid [sic] here all night. Raven very bad but came down to dinner.

Mary Hardy, 1787

12 February

Oh how shall I write it. My poor Raven died this morning abt. 5 o'clock. Sent for Bro. Raven from Whissonsett, he came even 4 [i.e. at 4 in the evening] and staid all night.

Mary Hardy, 1787

But I am forgetting, after three days, the most important event in my life since marriage – so Clive [Bell] described it. Mr Cizec has bingled [shingled] me. I am short haired for life. Having no longer, I think, any claims to beauty, the convenience of this alone makes it desirable. Every morning I go to take up [the] brush and twist that old coil round my finger and fix it with hairpins and then with a start of joy, no I needn't. In front there is no change; behind I'm like the rump of a partridge. This robs dining out of half its terrors.

Virginia Woolf, 1927

I think of my Mary [her daughter] from day to day, and mean immediately to make another attempt to see her, let Mr Grundy treat me as he may. I think he means well upon the whole, but Mr Stock has taken so much pains to prejudice his mind against me, that he is influenced to obey Mr S's tyrannical directions much more decidedly than he ought if he were really a Christian; which I hope he is, almost.

Ellen Weeton, 1824

13 February

My dearest Albert put on my stockings for me. I went in and saw him shave; a great delight for me.

Queen Victoria, 1840

The house is full of spring flowers, valentines. There is no month when I can imagine spring flowers being more of a delight. Yesterday the trees were sheathed in ice and it is bitterly cold; so the freshness, the aliveness of daffodils and iris and tulips indoors is quite overwhelming. Even the rich green leaves and the scent in this frozen odorless world seem like marvels.

May Sarton, 1971

First time I've had the heart to write here for weeks. A lousy green depressing cold. Cried again with the old stone-deep gloom with R. B. [therapist Ruth Barnhouse] yesterday. She said I don't work as well [when I feel] so bad. I think I'm going to get well and then I feel I can't; need to be punished. Get a job, in Cambridge, somewhere in a 10 day limit. I dream of bookstores, Design Research. That would be something …

We are fools. The alarm on, we shower and rise. Five hours from seven to twelve is all we need for writing. She says: you won't write. This is so, not that I can't, although I say I can't.

Sylvia Plath, 1959

I awoke at four o'clock with a desperate head, the darling of my heart arose, got me some warm water which gave me a momentary relief, but it returned with greater violence and continued till three, during which time my beloved Sally never left me for a single moment. At three we arose, but I grew ill again yet determined to struggle against it. Read for three hours. Loud storm all day. Frequent showers.

Lady Eleanor Butler, 1788

14 February

Valentine's Day. I'm sitting on a runway in Saudi Arabia. I'm not supposed to be here. Bangladesh Airlines – Biman – took a wrong turn ...

Oona King, 2004

No valentines but during the morning as I sat at the sewing machine, Alan Maclean rang from Macmillan saying that they would *love* to publish the novel [*Quartet in Autumn*]. Can hardly believe it can be true but he said he would confirm by letter (with 8½p stamp).

Barbara Pym, 1977

I rush down to the front door to check the post. No deluge of valentine cards, unless they have all gone to the Opera House. There was just one waiting for me at Barons Court (I'm not even sure it was a valentine) with a cryptic message: 'Is she kind as she is fair? For beauty lives with kindness.' It surely can't be from anyone at work, as they would realise that in truth I'm much kinder than I am fair. Generally, in rehearsal, I'm not fair at all. I turn up looking like an old dog.

Deborah Bull, 1998

An anxious night. It's a long time since I felt so weak and exhausted as I do today. My heart is weak again and I am short of breath ...

As for Lyovochka [Tolstoy], I simply don't know what to think: he eats less and less, his nights are worse and worse, he talks more and more quietly. I don't know whether this weakness is temporary or terminal. I keep hoping, but today matters have again taken a gloomy turn.

How I should love to look after him patiently and gently to the end, and forget all the old heartaches he has caused me. But instead I cried bitterly today for the way he persistently scorns all my love and concern for him. He asked for some sieved porridge, so I ran off to the kitchen and ordered it, then came back and sat beside him. He dozed off, the porridge came and when he awoke I quietly put it on a plate and offered it to him. He then grew furious and said that he would ask for it himself, and that throughout his illness he had always taken his food, medicines and drinks from other people, not me. (Although when someone has to lift him up, go without sleep, attend to him in the most intimate ways and apply his compresses, it is, of course, me whom he forces mercilessly to help him.) With the porridge, however, I decided to employ a little cunning, so I called Liza to him and sat down in the next room; and the moment I had gone he asked for the porridge, and I began weeping.

This little episode summarises my whole difficult life with him. This difficulty consists of one long struggle with his *contrary spirit*. My most reasonable and gentle advice to him has always met with protest.

Sophia Tolstoy, 1902

My third hyacinth bloomed the a.m., a lovely pink. So I found things snug, and had a busy day chasing – – who dodged. Then I wrote my tales. Made some shirts for my boys, and went out to buy a squash pie for my lonely supper. It snowed, was very cold. No one paid, and I wanted to send some money home. Felt cross and tired as I trudged back at dusk. My pie turned a somersault, a boy laughed, so did I, and felt better. On my doorstep I found a gentleman who asked if Miss A. lived here. I took him up my winding stair and found him a very delightful fly, for he handed me a letter out of which fell a $100 bill. With this bait Mr B. lured me to write 'one column of Advice to Young Women,' as Mrs Shaw and others were doing. If he had asked me for a Greek oration I would have said 'yes,' so I gave a receipt, and the very elegant agent bowed himself away, leaving my ''umble' bower full of perfume, and my soul at peace.

Thriftily taking advantage of the enthusiastic moment, I planned my article while I ate my dilapidated pie, and then proceeded to write it with the bill before me. It was about old maids. 'Happy Women' was the title, and I put in my list all the busy, useful, independent spinsters I know, for liberty is a better husband than love to many of us. This was a nice little episode in my trials of an authoress, so I record it.

So the pink hyacinth was a true prophet, and I went to bed a happy millionaire, to dream of flannel petticoats for my blessed Mother, paper for Father, a new dress for May, and sleds for my boys.

Louisa May Alcott, 1868

15 February

This morning my good friend Mrs Custance sent her Coach for me to make her a Morning Visit, which I did and was happy to find her in good spirits notwithstanding the Dear Soul was not able to move in her Bed nor have not for these seven Weeks, and it is greatly feared that she will not be able to sit up in her Bed these two Months to come. Her complaint is strain across her Loins which happened when she was brought to Bed [i.e. gave birth]. Last Friday was the first Day of her seeing Company. She was very glad to see me and I keep up my Spirits as well as I could tho' it was with difficulty that I refrain'd from tears at seeing my good friend in such a Melancholy situation.

Nancy Woodforde, 1792

… We spent the morning listening to the King's funeral [George VI]. Good things were – the muffled Westminster bells: the iron-chain noise of the feet of the ratings and the troops (just like Great Eye's beach after storm) and the ripple of the horse-hoofs. Big Ben tolling once a minute for each year (56) of the King's life; above all, at Paddington & at Windsor, the pipe-playing … The Archbishop of Canterbury, belling like a ram, prayed that the King might not be suffered to fall into the torment of eternal life – shows how much he believes in it. I never say water when I mean wine, or Bach when I mean Handel. It all petered out very oddly.

Sylvia Townsend Warner, 1952

We both went up to London this afternoon; L.[eonard] to the Library, and I to ramble about the West End, picking up clothes. I am really in rags. It is very amusing. With age too one's less afraid of the superb shop women. These great shops are like fairies' palaces now. I swept about in Debenhams and Marshall's and so on, buying, as I thought, with great discretion. The shop women are often very charming, in spite of their serpentine coils of black hair. Then I had tea, and rambled down to Charing Cross in the dark, making up phrases and incidents to write about. Which is, I expect, the way one gets killed. I bought a ten and elevenpenny blue dress, in which I sit at this moment.

Virginia Woolf, 1915

Qualities that turn me on (Someone I love must have at least two or three):
1. Intelligence
2. Beauty; elegance
3. Douceur ['gentleness, sweetness']
4. Glamor; celebrity
5. Strength
6. Vitality; sexual enthusiasm; gaiety; charm
7. Emotional expressiveness, tenderness (verbal, physical, affectionateness)
One great discovery in the last years (embarrassing) has been how much I respond to 4…

Susan Sontag, 1970

I have been much delighted today by the manly rescue of a fugitive slave by about 100 colored people. Seizing a favorable hour, they broke into the court room, where the slave was confined, and with no weapons but their fists, and in a perfectly good humored way – bore him off, without opposition …

Caroline Healey Dall, 1851

16 February

It seems I cannot love moderately or even singly, and I look for a mother in men and women the moment they reveal a regard. On the Coast I sought a great sea-rocking mother in the indifferent ocean who never rocked me. Moreover, being always over-avid, I demand from those I love a love equal to mine, which, being balanced people, they cannot supply. If only my neighbors across the road so far had not been a succession of medical people whose life's profession was Looking After, and if only I were not the grand look-after-ee of all time ... the thing's fantastic. Yet when K. [her husband Keith] came back from Home Guard in the evening he managed to mother me, pulling me into his bed. 'You mustn't cry like that,' he said.

Sylvia Ashton-Warner, 1941

... Sherman was at Orangeburg, barely a day's journey from Columbia, and he left a track as blackened as a fire in the prairies.

So my time had come too. My husband urged me to go home. He said Camden would be safe enough, that they had no spite to that old town as they have to Charleston and Columbia. Molly too. She came in, weeping and wailing, wiping her red-hot face with her cook's grimy apron. She said I ought to go among our own black people on the plantation. They would take care of me better than anyone else.

So I agreed to go.

Mary Boykin Chesnut, Confederate States of America, 1865

Last night was *dreadful*. I couldn't sleep – I seemed burning up with strange nervous pulsations, and I thought around and around in a circle of misery. The night was so cold that I couldn't bear my face above the clothes and the physical discomfort aggravated the nervous disorder.

When the days on which I feel better come I look back with wonder to these miserable sensations and marvel that I could not overcome them. But the fact remains that I cannot, try as I will and do. I have been dosing myself with emulsion all winter but though I am gaining a little in flesh I cannot see that it is helping my nerves any. A talk with [her cousin] Frede Campbell if I could get it would do them more good than all the drugs in the world.

My gray cat 'Daffy' has just come in and climbed up on my knee. I don't know what I'd do without him, the big gray furry fellow. He is three years old and the mere touch of his soft sides and sleek head is a comfort to me. But Daffy can't talk and I just want somebody – sealed of the tribe – to talk with and to. *You* can't talk, old journal, who have gone through so much with me, but you are a help for all that. It is wonderful what a relief it is to write this stuff out.

L. M. Montgomery, 1909

17 February

M– [Mariana Lawton] loves me. Certainly her heart is wholly mine. If I could have allowed her twenty or thirty pounds a year in addition to what she had, she certainly would not have married. But what could she do on her allowance of only thirty pounds a year? Passed an affectionate hour or two.

Anne Lister, 1820

It was curious to reflect that in my own life there was a time, & in other lives the time is still, when it was perfectly possible to spend a day reading Proust without a jaw abscess & a swelled face as ticket of admission.

Sylvia Townsend Warner, 1952

And this 17th day in the afternoon about three o'clock did my Cousin Mr Richard Musgrave oldest son to my cousin Sir Philip Musgrave, and his Lady and their daughter, who is their only child, come in their coach hither from Edenhall, and I had them into my Chamber, and kissed my said Cousin and his wife and the child and also their gentlewomen and I gave to my Cousin, wife and child each of them a gold Ring, and after they had stayed a while they went away. And this day did my Servant, Mr Thos. Strickland, and his man, Lancelot Machell, ride from his own house near Kendal called Garnett House towards Appleby whither they came that night to gather my Candelmas Rents, and he lay in the Barron's Chamber there and his man in the Musty Chamber. And to-day I had one or two very ill fitts [sic]. Yet I slept well in the night, thank God.

I went not out of my house nor out of my Chamber to-day.

Lady Anne Clifford, 1676

18 February

Some of my good friends remembered me extensively in the burlesque valentine line as I have received this time no less than half a dozen, some by hand, some by post, and some from the schoolchildren …

Ida B. Wells, 1886

Our Mansab has issued an order that spangles, sequins, cowrie shells and all such ornaments are to be abolished from the wardrobes of Hureidha. Consternation fills every harim. The ladies with sighs are snipping from their new dresses, just finished for the feast, the stars they wear so gracefully in the middle of their backs, swaying as they walk. And the sadness is that *we* are responsible for the tragedy. It is the sight of *our* dowdy clothes that inspires dress reform in the heart of the Mansab … It almost makes one wish to dress like the Archaeologist in trousers, which no-one would copy.

Freya Stark, 1938

Teaching in Infant School. By way of realising a lecture on affection and gratitude to parents, I asked each of the little class what one thing they had done for their mothers that morning; and I confess I felt humbled and instructed to discover that one of these tiny creatures had worked some pocket-handkerchief, another lighted the fire, another helped to lay the breakfast, whilst most of them had taken part in tending the baby whilst mother was busy.

Caroline Fox, 1846

I am 46 years living today and very pleased to be alive, very glad and very happy. Fear and pain and despair do not disappear. They only become slowly less and less important. Although sometimes I still long for a simple orderly life with a hunger sharp as that sudden vegetarian hunger for meat.

Audre Lorde, 1980

We received a letter from the good Mary my Sister that poor woman has been obliged to retire to a convent being so ill treated in her family. This new[s] gave us all a great deal of Sorrow and we much long to know What obliged the young woman to take such a rash resolution.

Betsey Wynne Fremantle, 1793

19 February

We received all the particulars of Mary's separation with her husband. Her late husband wrote himself and has not got one thing against our good Sister ... The reason of Mary's quitting that family is that Silvestro her brother in law was in love with her and she was used very ill in that cursed house – Cunning false Italians. The weather was horrid and I could not walk out at all. We were very uneasy on our Sisters account but the letters we had were a great consolation for us as we see that her conduct and behaviour is not at all to blame.

Betsey Wynne Fremantle, 1793

... All through the weekend the stress was on Food – what we were going to eat next, or what a good meal we had just eaten, and I couldn't help feeling that sometimes too much attention is paid to this admittedly very important subject. However they went off saying they had never had such delicious *food* – so I hope they enjoyed themselves.

Frances Partridge, 1943

I woke up early this morning and when I opened the shutters the full round sun was just risen. I began to repeat that verse of Shakepeare's: 'Lo, here the gentle lark weary of rest', and bounded back into bed. The bound made me cough – I spat – it tasted strange – it was bright red blood. Since then I've gone on spitting each time I cough a little more. Oh, yes, of course I'm frightened. But for two reasons only. I don't want to be ill, I mean 'seriously', away from J. J. is the first thought. 2nd, I don't want to find this is real consumption, perhaps it's going to gallop – who knows? – and I shan't have my work written. *That's what matters.* How unbearable it would be to die – leave 'scraps', 'bits'... nothing real finished'.

Katherine Mansfield, 1918

I had not been here two days when I felt the violent effects of a cold I caught by sleeping in a damp Room at the Rapide Plat ... I was obliged tonight to throw off most of the wrappings I had bound about my eyes & head & go to a Ball given by the Inhabitants of the Province to the Gov., people came forty miles to it in Carrioles. I was really so ill I could scarcely hear or see & possibly neglected the very persons I meant to be most civil too.

Elizabeth Simcoe, Quebec, 1795

N.B. Lying in bed, even in discomfort or pain, I find in myself a very definite compliance towards inactivity, retirement from life, a quiet sofa'd old age. I cannot say that these last five days have been agreeable; but my God, they have been congenial.

Sylvia Townsend Warner, 1952

20 February

Dear Doctor: I am feeling very sick. I have a heart in my stomach which throbs and mocks. Suddenly the simple rituals of the day balk like a stubborn horse. It gets impossible to look people in the eye: corruption may break out again? Who knows. Small talk becomes desperate …

So there. With bike at the repair shop, gulped down coffee-with-milk, bacon and cabbage mixed with potato, and toast, read two letters from Mother which cheered me quite a bit … She also was encouraging about teaching. Once I started doing it I wouldn't feel so sick. That frozen inertia is my worst enemy; I get positively sick with doubt. I must break through limit after limit: learn to ski (with Gordon & Sue next year?) and perhaps teach at an army base this summer. It would do me a hell of a lot of good. If I went to Africa or Istanbul, I could do articles about the place on the side. Enough romance. Get to work.

Sylvia Plath, 1956

Peaceful night so far. Only one mild air raid. Have been reading a textbook on tropical diseases in preparation for my foreign draft, which is such a long time in coming. But the book rather puts me off! In India and China there's a disease called Kala-azar which sounds horrific …

… We will be inoculated against cholera and yellow fever, so I hope to escape agonizing cramps, 'rice-water' stools, collapse and death from the former; and convulsions, with a 25 per cent mortality from the latter.

But what about pneumonic plague? Fatal within a few days. Or typhus, which according to the book, is a disease not of hot climates but of 'lousy populations', transmitted by lice or fleas. Having survived German bombs, how ironical it would be to be killed by a Chinese louse or an Indian flea.

Is a foreign draft really worth the risk?

And what are the advantages?

So far I've not got beyond sun, bananas – have not seen the latter for the last three years – and perhaps a wider outlook on life.

Eve Williams, VAD, 1944

Why should he, why should any man, have the right, the power, to send me to bed disgruntled? Are the real and steadfast things of life, then, the static inanimate things, like the long shadow of a streetlamp on the deserted pavement?

Elizabeth Smart, 1936

21 February

Stopped with Henry for dressmaker ... I have outgrown my wedding dress, and it will no longer cover one beating heart only! O Father, let the child but be as happy, and far better, than the mother and I pray for no other boon. Feel sometimes an awe and fear of myself, a fear that my heart is not pure and holy enough to give its life-blood, and perhaps its nature, to another. What an awful responsibility already is upon me! God alone knows how much my thoughts and temper may mould the future spirit. Let me strive to be all truth and gentleness and heavenly mindedness, to be already the guardian-angel of my child ...

Fanny Longfellow, 1844

In the last weeks I have had chicken pox! And proceeded to pass it on to C.[harles, her husband] and little Anne. It is such an unlovely disease. You feel unloved and miserable and grouchy. And at night, not sleeping, the anguish becomes mental – I tossed and tossed in the conflict of the book, trying to explain and defend.

Then C. had it, up and downstairs with trays, food all wrong, orders not carried out. 'I don't ask very much!' The baby crying and miserable and not eating and I getting tireder and tireder.

At the end of it I feel as if I had been living in a hair shirt for weeks. A hair shirt is not agony – not suffering really – just a hair shirt. In fact this whole year has been a hair shirt. The trouble with a hair shirt is that it makes you feel so awfully *good* – as though you are entitled to a little wickedness. You feel as though you had atoned for all your sins and even for a few you hadn't committed! It is a lucky thing there are no temptations in my path (Satan hasn't done right by me!). Although I am beginning to feel that I am so 'good' that if I saw a temptation, I would turn and run the other way.

The first day in town I had my hair done and bought a wild 'come-hither' hat with two Renoir full-blown roses burning off the front of it. It almost satisfied my urge for wickedness.

Though C. said it was dreadful – the hat.

Anne Morrow Lindbergh, 1941

22 February

———

Before I was out of my bed did I pare off the tops of the nails of my fingers and toes, and when I was up I burnt them in the chimney of my chamber, and a little after in this same chamber of mine did George Goodgion clip off all the hair of my head, which I likewise burnt in the fire, and after supper I washed and bathed my feet and legs in warm water, wherein beef had been boiled and bran. And I had done none of this to myself since the 13th of December that George Goodwin cut my hair for me in this chamber of mine. God grant that good may betide me and mine after it.

I went not out of my House nor out of my Chamber today.

Anne Clifford, 1676

Must guard against the curious forms death takes. The bereaved suddenly must *hate* someone as if that person was to be punished for still being alive. I find myself schizying around hating, loving, etc., to fill in the strange numbness [after her husband's death]. I do know I could not have gone on in my desperate duties much more, and for a year or two or more have often stopped in [the] street with my bundles and wondered if I was about to drop dead.

Dawn Powell, 1962

… Spent afternoon and evening with Benjamin Jones in their happy little home at West Norwood. They live on £400 and are as happy as others on £4,000. Three boys and a girl; have taken measures to prevent others from coming, and advise others to do so … The question of Neo-Malthusianism [which advocated population control] is coming to the fore; the underground growth of it is unquestioned; the open discussion of it is every day more permitted. I see it practised by men and women who are perfectly pure. I cannot see any *reason* against it; yet my moral instinct is not with it.

Beatrice Webb, 1888

So, I am not going to have a baby after all. Felt in really deep mourning – so surprised, and so disappointed. I had become far advanced in sentimentality and now I feel the ground knocked from under my feet as far as plans go. I must reconstruct my life. I must try and find a second string to my cinema bow.

Lady Cynthia Asquith, 1918

23 February

Last night four women sat at my dining-room table in the candlelight: one in her forties; one in her thirties; Mary, sixteen; and I, fifty-three. We walked warily and rather sadly around the fact that no one was going to look after us but ourselves. The idea of being protected by men dies hard. We had all (except perhaps Mary) given up the feeling that such protection is our *right*. But we all, in varying degrees, decreasing with age, cherished some small hope of the idyllic warmth of male shelter. I have come, even so recently as within the last month, to the verge of preferring to look after myself. This is partly because it begins to seem financially possible. *Arundel* XIV sold yesterday. *Summer Sentinel* is out on approval. The University of Maryland has invited me to lecture. I have been paid by the Baltimore Museum of Art and by the University of South Carolina.

The crux of the matter seems to me to be the true danger of emotional dependence ... The only viable relationship between a man and a woman seems to me to be a relationship of peers.

Anne Truitt, 1975

This must be the 26th February 23rd I have lived through: over a quarter of a century of Februaries, and would I could cut a slice of recollection back through them and trace the spiralling stair of my ascent adultward – or is it a descent? I feel I have lived enough to last my life in musings, tracings of crossings and recrossing with people, mad and sane, stupid and brilliant, beautiful and grotesque, infant and antique, cold and hot, pragmatic and dream-ridden, dead and alive. My house of days and masks is rich enough so that I might and must spend years fishing, hauling up the pearl-eyed, horny, scaled and sea-bearded monsters sunk long, long ago in the Sargasso of my imagination ... We walked out about seven into the pleasant mild-cold still night to the library: the campus snow-blue, lit from myriad windows, deserted. Cleared, cleansed, stung fresh-cheeked chill, we walked the creaking-cricking plank paths through the botanical gardens and while Ted delivered thesis and book I walked four times round the triangle flanked by Lawrence House, the Student's Building and the street running from Paradise Pond to College Hall, meeting no one, secretly gleeful and in control, summoning all my past green, gilded gray, sad, sodden and loveless, ecstatic, and in-love selves to be with me and rejoice ...

Sylvia Plath, 1958

24 February

Lighted the fires & clean'd the hearths. Clean'd no boots. Swept & dusted the dining room. Wash'd myself and got the breakfast up. Clean'd away after & wash'd up. Got a letter to say my Aunt Ellen was dead. I expected it quite, for a dog came in yesterday morning and howl'd piteously. I couldn't help crying, & feeling it, for she is my mother's sister & has been kind to me always – I try not to cry, it makes my head ache so. I shall put some crape on my black straw bonnet & frock & Sarah has given me an old dress of Mrs Foster's I can wear. I wrote to my sister Ellen & told her about it. Clean'd the knives. Made the fires up & got dinner ready. Laid the kitchen cloth. Clean'd away after & clean'd the hearth & tables. Wash'd up in the scullery & had tea. Clean'd myself & did my bonnet up wi' the crape. Got supper ready & clean'd the kitchen cloth. Clean'd away after. Rubb'd Mrs Smith's foot again & then to bed.

Hannah Cullwick, 1863

I opened a tin of pineapple, and one of sliced peaches, and made jelly. After taking enough to make a nice helping with custard for tea, I set the fruit in the jelly, and I'll open a tin of cream tomorrow. It's only a small tin, which I saved for last Christmas, but there will be a wee dab for us all. I feel quite excited at a full table again, with laughing people round it.

All was so happy and gay; and then when Cliff [one of her two sons] went out, my husband and I had one of our rare quarrels. A chance remark started it … *His* boy, indeed! He has never taught, cared for, spanked or tried to understand either of them – or *ever* thinks of writing to them – and is not always interested enough in their letters to listen if I read them.

Pent-up feelings and 'wrongs' rushed over me, and before I could get hold of myself again, I'd got in a few punches below the belt …

Nella Last, 1942

25 February

It is now half-past seven in the morning. I have clipped my toenails, drunk a mug of genuine Van Houtens cocoa, and had some bread and honey, all with what you might call abandon. I opened the Bible at random, but it gave me no answers this morning. Just as well, because there were no questions, just enormous faith and gratitude that life should be so beautiful, and that makes this a historic moment, that and not the fact that we are on our way to the Gestapo.

Etty Hillesum, Holland, 1942

Went to a psychiatrist this morning and like him: attractive, calm and considered, with that pleasant feeling of age and experience in a reservoir; felt, Father, why not? Wanted to burst out in tears and say Father, Father, comfort me …

… Sometimes I feel so very stupid, yet, if I were, would I not be happy with some of the men I've met? Or is it because I'm stupid that I'm not; hardly. I long for someone to blast over Richard [Sassoon, her lover]; I deserve that, don't I, some sort of blazing love that I can live with. My God, I'd love to cook and make a house, and surge force into a man's dreams, and write, if he could talk and walk and work and passionately want to do his career. I can't bear to think of this potential for loving and giving going brown and sere in me. Yet the choice is so important, it frightens me a little. A lot …

Sylvia Plath, 1956

My spirits have risen into youthfulness. It is rare for me to feel youthful but just now I do! and am looking forward to my month in London …

Begin investigation of docks …

Beatrice Webb, 1887

From the most delicious dreams I woke to the most delicious smell of England – and even (wafted from afar) London. I got up and stood to look at Plymouth in the foggy dawn, damp, misty, nothing but a rich suggestion. And then the suns of departure, change, anticipation. It was rich and warm to lie in bed dreaming of things to come, warm, smelling the mixed smells of the beloved land after the sea, having a pleasantly cool damp nose from the fog.

Nothing happened in the day at all, but I was supremely happy waiting.

Elizabeth Smart, SS *Ranpura*, 1937

26 February

The air had been full of snow for some time. Back home, I felt a New Englander's joy in the light, soft, virgin snow-mounds on the privet hedges and white festoons on the vines at the front door. The flakes are big, and will be gone by tomorrow or Sunday; but a beautiful snowstorm like this is unforgettable, especially to one who wearies of hard pavements and brick buildings in the city during winter.

Helen Keller, 1937

The knock on the door at night. Utter silence. A triple knock at first, then too short a pause before another knock comes, cautious and yet insane because there is a horrible effort to be polite in this knock, a horrible persistence at the same time, and utter madness directing it. 'And one suddenly remembers, the door is unlatched …

Patricia Highsmith, 1954

A small note after a large orgy. It is morning, gray. Most sober, with cold white puritanical eyes: looking at me. Last night I got drunk, very very beautifully drunk, and now I am shot, after six hours of warm sleep like a baby, with Racine to read, and not even the energy to type; I am getting the dt's. Or something.

Sylvia Plath, 1958

27 February

———

Very early on Wednesday morning a large group of us were crowded into the Gestapo hall, and at that moment the circumstances of all our lives were the same. All of us occupied the same space, the men behind the desk no less than those about to be questioned. What distinguished each one of us was only our inner attitudes …

… I am not easily frightened. Not because I am brave, but because I know that I am dealing with human beings and that I must try as hard as I can to understand everything that anyone ever does. And that was the real import of this morning: not that the disgruntled young Gestapo officer yelled at me, but that I felt no indignation, rather a real compassion, and would have liked to ask, 'Did you have a very unhappy childhood, has your girl-friend let you down?' Yes, he looked harassed and driven, sullen and weak. I should have liked to start treating him there and then, for I know that pitiful young men like that are dangerous as soon as they are let loose on mankind. But all the blame must be put on the system that uses such people. What needs eradicating is the evil in man, not man himself.

Something else about this morning: the perception, very strongly borne in, that I cannot hate others …

Etty Hillesum, Holland, 1942

Dearest Kitty,

From early in the morning till late at night, I really do hardly anything else but think of Peter. I sleep with his image before my eyes, dream about him and he is still looking at me when I am awake ...

But how and when will we finally reach each other? I don't know quite how long my common sense will keep this longing under control.

Yours, Anne

Anne Frank, 1944

28 February

Tomorrow is that extra day that comes only every four years, and something great should be done with it. Susan [Sherman, author and editor] will be here, and that in itself is a celebration.

May Sarton, 1992

Perhaps it is rather unfortunate that it is only when I am in a certain soul-searching-self mood – the egoist to the extreme – that the need for this diary is so urgent. For success doesn't need a confessor, and neither does a dull contentment ...

Elizabeth Smart, 1934

Still snow. There's no doubt it's a practically unmitigated nuisance. Mr Blow [the snow] arrived in the evening – a real ghost of one's past. When I was a child he was *the* Key to Heaven; now he makes me sleepy – alas! Bateman came to dinner, very typical. Papa went away in the morning, rather mortified by my defeating him in a jigsaw puzzle race. No particular news of the Verdun battle. I suppose thousands are dying each minute.

Cynthia Asquith, 1916

Returned this morning to our cottage and never enjoyed it more, coming from the stupid dull town. St Gratiem and Captain de Wyl, and General Horneck called, I spent the whole day and evening tête-à-tête with Fremantle, it was cold and we wrote letters till supper time. I never thought of the Ball, last year I should have been distressed and miserable to finish the carnaval in my room but now I am never so happy as alone with Fremantle and have not the least desire to enjoy any other pleasure.

Betsey Wynne Fremantle, 1797

29 February

At half past four drove in an open landau and four with Arthur, Leopold, and Jane C.[hurchill], the Equerries riding. We drove round Hyde and Regent's Parks, returning by Constitution Hill, and when at the Garden Entrance a dreadful thing happened … It is difficult for me to describe, as my impression was a great fright, and all was over in a minute. How it happened I knew nothing of. The Equerries had dismounted, [John] Brown had got down to let down the steps, and Jane C. was just getting out, when suddenly someone appeared at my side, whom I at first imagined was a footman, going to lift off the wrapper. Then I perceived that it was someone unknown, peering above the carriage door, with an uplifted hand and a strange voice, at the same time the boys calling out and moving forward. Involuntarily, in a terrible fright, I threw myself over Jane C., calling out, 'Save me,' and heard a scuffle and voices! I soon recovered myself sufficiently to stand up and turn round, when I saw Brown holding a young man tightly, who was struggling …

… It is to good Brown and to his wonderful presence of mind that I greatly owe my safety, for he alone saw the boy rush round and followed him! When I was standing in the hall, General Hardinge came in, bringing an extraordinary document which this boy had intended making me sign! It was in connection with the Fenian prisoners!

Queen Victoria, 1872

Isabella [Norcliffe] went down to read prayers this afternoon. She drinks a bottle a day, all but two glasses that my uncle & aunt take. The latter leaves the room at luncheon to let her take three or four glasses, but I am to be sure to take no notice of this. What a shame Tib should do so. She goes into the dining-room about seven in the evening to have a glass of wine & sends for George or Cordingley to get it. She shall not come here again soon if I can possibly help it.

Anne Lister, 1824

... Sick for the first time in nine years but didn't miss a day of teaching; not that I felt puritanically bound to teach but (I think) I wanted to see if I could impersonate myself. ... I seem to have been successful. Went out to dinner with two other couples Saturday night, in even worse condition (the disease wasn't infectious) and impersonated myself again. A fascinating experience.

What is illness ... ? Retreat from the world. Descent into the self. A totally different consciousness. All values upset, all emotions altered.

Joyce Carol Oates, 1976

March

'We have had a thaw – a really, truly thaw. Oh, the joy
of it! I feel like a prisoner released.'

L. M. Montgomery, 1905

1 March

I couldn't sleep for excitement – at last something new is going to happen to me!

Got to Jo's café soon after ten, and found he had been up early, scraping down an old canvas, and hadn't even had time to wash or shave. Luckily he didn't seem to expect me to pose in the nude …

… Soon my arms got cramped and I began to droop visibly, owing to lack of sleep. Before I knew what was happening, Jo had put down his palette and was bearing down upon me. ' You're tired my lovely, my precious petling! Wouldn't you like to take a rest?'

What happened after that was so quick and unexpected that I had no time to protest. My neck and shoulders were bare, and Jo was covering them with kisses. I could feel the unshaven bristles rasping against my skin. To my amazement, I felt a great shiver of pure delight run through me, rather like the way I felt in church when I was thinking about Gerhardt.

Well, I thought, I'm not going to be so stupid the second time round, so this time when I saw Jo's face looming over me, blue stubbly chin and rather thick sensuous lips pouting for a kiss, I decided to shut my eyes and bear it. Actually it wasn't as bad as I had expected. In fact I even found myself responding a little, kissing him back. A pity he smelt of garlic.

Just as things were beginning to get hectic the doorbell rang furiously. It was the dustman. Jo said, 'This pisshole is just one damn thing after another,' and went to the back door. By the time he had disposed of the dustman the atmosphere of passion had somewhat evaporated and so we resumed the sitting.

Joan Wyndham (aged 18), 1940

Old Uncle Lloyd died last night. D. [Lloyd George] is very upset and will be until after the funeral has taken place. It is a great strain for him, coming at this time. He will miss the old man very much, and he says I am his only devoted friend now – that I shall have to fill the old man's place. God knows I shall try. D. needs so much someone who will not hesitate to give him everything, & if necessary to give up everything, & whose sole thought & occupation is for him. Without that it is hopeless to try and serve him.

Frances Stevenson, 1917

Too tired to write Diary last night. Better today. Set off up the road last night, and that awful howl began. It felt like a violent internal pain which rose and fell – but inexorable. I knew it would rise again and again before it died away. It has not gone through me like that for a long time. Last Monday, I was told that fourteen bombs fell on Peckham in four minutes. Only small ones – but to anyone listening to those Swishes – I know just what it means. Peckham is the second worst district for bombing. Presumably the worst is Dockland. The woman who described it to me said the shops had no one to sell to – everyone had gone.

Winifred Vere Hodgson, 1941

I wish I could write out my sensations at this moment. They are so peculiar and so unpleasant. Partly Time of Life? I wonder. A physical feeling as if I were drumming slightly in the veins: very cold: impotent: and terrified. As if I were exposed on a high ledge in full light. Very lonely. Very useless. No atmosphere round me. No words. Very apprehensive. As if something cold and horrible – a roar of laughter at my expense were about to happen. And I want to burst into tears, but have nothing to cry for. And I cannot unfurl my mind and apply it calmly and unconsciously to a book. And my own little scraps look dried up and derelict. And I know that I must go on doing this dance on hot bricks till I die.

Virginia Woolf, 1937

2 March

Up the road last night just as a Second Warning went. Could hear the German plane zooming very near over my head, and the road seemed very long. Great flashes filled the sky – the guns boomed out … I knew the shrapnel would begin to fall, so hastened my steps and fell up the little flight of steps to the front door. Once in the porch I watched in case incendiaries fell – and I must run back to Sanctuary. Guns again and again, then ping, ping – down came the shrapnel.

A nice restful Sunday. Took Mrs Ellis of Chichester into Kensington gardens. She had not been to London for thirty years – and remembered it last with horse buses! Her son is a pilot in R.A.F., so I felt it my duty to look after her for the sake of what he was doing for us.

Winifred Vere Hodgson, 1941

… I was very happy to hear that Mrs Custance had turned in her Bed on Wednesday for the first time since her illness, and that she had turn'd two or three times since, but with great pain. She offered me a beautiful Rose which Mrs Branthwaite brought her out of their hothouse but I would not take it on any account … Betty walked with me and she carried my New Gown and Apron which I showed to Mrs Custance, both of which she admired very much indeed as did Mr Custance likewise.

Nancy Woodforde, 1792

A bustle of moving – read *Corinne* – I and my baby go about 3 – S.[helley] and Clara [Claire Clairmont] do not come till six – [Thomas Jefferson] Hogg comes in the evening.

Mary Shelley, 1815

3 March

Nurse my baby – talk & read *Corinne* – Hogg comes in the evening.

Mary Shelley, 1815

A dribbling of visitors and rain drops. A nice long visit from Mr Prescott, fresh as a rose. Prof. L. [Longfellow] in p.m. and a dripping walk with Emmeline …

Fanny Longfellow, 1840

… How strange it is that in the huge machine of life, past, present and future, there should be a fourteen-year-old girl who is sitting and writing all kinds of stupid things about her small soul, which to her seems something immense, and that she occupies herself so seriously with something which is really small and of no consequence … How strange is this abstraction; how strange the isolation of my little life in comparison with that other which is so immeasurably big.

Nelly Ptashkina (aged 14), 1918

4 March

Read, talk, and nurse – S.[helley] reads the *Life of Chaucer* – Hogg comes in the evening and sleeps – …

Mary Shelley, 1815

Since he [her brother William] has left me (at ½ past 11) it is now two I have been putting the Drawers into order, laid by his clothes which we had thrown here there and everywhere, filed 2 months' newspapers and got my dinner 2 boiled eggs and 2 apple tarts … I transplanted some snowdrops – the Bees are busy – WM has a nice bright day. It was hard frost in the night. The Robins are singing sweetly. Now for my walk. I *will* be busy, I *will* look well and be well when he comes back to me. O the Darling! Here is one of his bitten apples! I can hardly find it in my heart to throw it into the fire ...

Dorothy Wordsworth, 1802

... I have seen a Negro woman sold upon the block at auction. I was walking. The woman on the block overtopped the crowd. I felt faint, seasick. The creature looked so like my good little Nancy. She was a bright mulatto, with a pleasant face. She was magnificently gotten up in silks and satins. She seemed delighted with it all, sometimes ogling the bidders, sometimes looking quite coy and modest; but her mouth never relaxed from its expanded grin of excitement. I dare say the poor thing knew who would buy her. My very soul sickened. It was too dreadful. I tried to reason, 'You know how women sell themselves and are sold in marriage, from queens downwards, eh? You know what the Bible says about slavery, and marriage. Poor women, poor slaves.'

Mary Boykin Chesnut, 1861

... For tea, I made thick wholemeal toast and, when it was done, put on a layer of sliced cheese and a dusting of cayenne pepper, and cooked it under the grill till it was frothy and golden. My husband said suddenly, 'What did that old gypsy say to you – and that Hindu fortune-teller at Wembley – "No man who had loved you would ever forget you", wasn't it?' I laughed and said, 'Something like that. Fancy you remembering it!' His answer surprised me, for he said quietly, 'I'm remembering a lot of things, my love – more than you realise,' and then he patted my hand and said, 'Not only warm slippers and a cheery smile, either, you know.'

Nella Last, 1942

5 March

This is the anniversary of our landing in this Colony, and 12 years has made such an alteration in everything here that a comparison would be very amusing, say, 'Sydney in the year 1816', and 'Sydney in the year 1826', or we will take a less period and say 1817 – the year in which the Bank of N.S. Wales was established: ... by the end of the year it is believed there will be three Banks, three newspapers and three steam engines – Bob Howe [editor of the *Sydney Gazette*] says ADVANCE AUSTRALIA but this is advancing with rapid strides.

Christiana Brooks, Australian settler, 1826

Still more and more snow. I am weary of God's crude practical joke.

Lady Cynthia Asquith, 1916

Outside it is a milky world, snow driving past the windows in horizontal waves. Drifts pile up under the high wind. But I am truly in Heaven. There are charming 'February' daffodils out in a pale green pot on my desk, tulips on the mantel a subtle apricot color veined in yellow with dark purple hearts. I have lighted the fire in here because the wind creeps in and I feel the chill. I have Beethoven sonatas (*Pastoral* and *Les Adieux*) on the record player. And now to work!

May Sarton, 1971

Quiet week-end for the raids. Some think it is the moon. Americans and ourselves pounding Germany all week, and I cannot believe they have planes free to come here. Anyway, whatever the reason – God be praised.

My first oranges. Lady in next flat queuing up, so kindly took my ration book and got me three lovely ones. She waited three quarters of an hour. We have seen orange peel in the street – most refreshing even to look at it.

Winifred Vere Hodgson, 1944

6 March

Last night was frightful. Agony in his body, his legs, his soul – it was all too much for him, and what grieved me most was that he let slip how bad he felt and cursed the fact that he had got better. 'I can't imagine why I recovered, I wish I'd died.'

He was sunk in apathy all day. I sat with him as usual, but slipped off to the side wing for the first time to play a few of my favourite pieces … But now I mustn't even do this.

Sophia Tolstoy, 1902

My birthday! – My thoughts will go to the past – the past – to the ever ever beloved [her mother] – My happy days went away with her! – If I were to count up every happy hour since, how few they wd. be! – But there is no use in all this! The tears which I am shedding at this moment are as vain – as if they were smiles! – In another year, where shall I be – & what shall I have suffered? – A great deal I dare say – and my heart appears to be giving way even now.

Elizabeth Barrett (Browning), 1832

This evening I had the cutting news that my second boy was in rebellion at the College at Winton, where he and all his Companions resolved not to make any verses, and being called to be whipped for it several of them refused to be punished, mine among the rest. Some of them did submit, among which was Cousin John Woodforde, and if the others do not, they must be expelled. God I beseech thee subdue their stubborn hearts, and give them grace to repent and accept of their punishment due to their fault, and let them not run on to ruin, for Christ's sake.

Mary Woodforde, 1687

Find my baby dead …

Send for Hogg – talk – a miserable day – in the evening read *Fall of the Jesuits* – Hogg sleeps here.

Mary Shelley, 1815

7 March

Why do I not write my diary any more? I shall so like to re-read it later … and for 'Petrouska, i.e. or Sara Sophie'. For to her turn all my thoughts … I think to myself if she is like me (and sometimes I feel I hold myself in my arms) – these many years of diary will help. I was not kissed and stroked enough … never enough. She shall have all that. When back from visits she shall be tucked up in bed. And the tangible word: 'Oh! I am excited at having you again, Petrouska' shall be said literally. We are all bound by thongs of reserve. She still seems so near to me I could cry when she does … and often it is as if the crying was in my inside. She is nearly an obsession. I dream of her at night. Love is a load: love is heavy. When I look back on the nine months of carrying 'Petrouska' they seem suffused with health, creativeness, imagination …

Ivy Jacquier, 1922

Ran down to see Father, who has had a slight apoplectic attack. He lies in his bed in a state of complete apathy. His life can no longer be a pleasure to him or to those around him; it would be merciful if he should be taken. But the breaking of the tie would be sad, inexpressibly sad to a lonely life like mine. Still, I long for a complete holiday which his death would enable me to take … I must not let myself get morbid over it. I must check those feelings which are the expression of physical instinct craving for satisfaction; but God knows celibacy is as painful to a woman (even from the physical standpoint) as it is to a man. It could not be more painful than it is to a woman.

Beatrice Webb, 1889

Yesterday my dear Husband went to Winton about Jack [her son], and I have received this afternoon a letter from him which gives me hopes he has now humbled himself for which I from the bottom of my heart give most humble thanks to Almighty God ...

Mary Woodforde, 1687

8 March

Finish Rinaldini – talk with Shelley – in very bad spirits but get better – sleep a little in the day – in the evening not – Hogg comes – he goes at ½ 11. – Clary has written for Fanny but she does not come.

Mary Shelley, 1815

Just back from L.[eonard]'s speech at Brighton. Like a foreign town: the first spring day. Women sitting on seats. A pretty hat in a teashop – how fashion revives the eye! And the shell-encrusted old women, rouged, decked, cadaverous at the teashop. The waitress in checked cotton.

No: I intend no introspection. I mark Henry James's sentence: Observe perpetually. Observe the income of age. Observe greed. Observe my own despondency. By that means it becomes serviceable. Or so I hope. I insist upon spending this time to the best advantage. I will go down with my colours flying. This I see verges on introspection; but doesn't quite fall in. Suppose I bought a ticket at the Museum; biked in daily & read history. Suppose I selected one dominant figure in each age & wrote round & about. Occupation is essential. And now with some pleasure I find that it's seven; & must cook dinner. Haddock & sausage meat. I think it is true that one gains a certain hold on sausage & haddock by writing them down.

Virginia Woolf, 1941

... Work is the best of narcotics, provided the patient be strong enough to take it.

Beatrice Webb, 1885

9 March

Dined at Mrs W. Fremantle's to meet Lady Cave. These ladies say I shall very soon be brought to bed. I am exceedingly well had the monthly nurse in the house.

Betsey Wynne Fremantle, 1798

Read & talk – still think about my little baby – 'tis hard, indeed, for a mother to lose a child – Hogg and C.[harles] C.[lairmont] come in the evening – C. C. goes at 11. Hogg stays all night – Read Fontenelle *Plurality of Worlds*.

Mary Shelley, 1815

Harry Hopkins says 'No more zippers' in *Reader's Digest*. Oh, thank you, Brother Hopkins! I have ruined a slip, a pair of flannel trousers, and a zipper when the zipper gets caught in the slip. Thank God the zipper era is over! I always did hate them – cold, slippery, metallic things – never could trust them. They never hold when you want them to. They are rigid when you want them to ease a little. No resilience, no charm, no texture. Take a button, now, you know where you are. It holds till death, but it will give, too, humanly, if you gain a half an inch. Besides, the feel of a button – so friendly and comfortable, warm to touch.

C.[harles] comes back late and is cross because I say I won't be able to get to the trailer tomorrow. I have to make the formula. He says with three people in the house, can't one of them make the formula, wash the bottles, do the routine? He says I get caught up in routine, in which he is right. But I always feel it's cowardly of me, or lazy, shirking, to do only the nice part of taking care of the children. I have a kind of missionary zeal about doing all the dirty jobs, too. C. says he never knew anyone who made such symbolism out of picayune jobs.

Anne Morrow Lindbergh, 1943

I have felt very low this morning & have been inclined to it all the day on account of this being the fifth anniversary of M–'s [Mariana Lawton] marriage, but I have driven off the remembrance as well as I could by constant occupation. Just before tea I talked to my uncle & aunt & walked about in the drawing room. Indeed, I began dancing when by myself & got into a heat.

Anne Lister, 1821

What a desolate, despairing, exquisite thought, that one cannot live without loving someone. What a more desperate thought, that one cannot create anything without this inspiration!

Patricia Highsmith, 1944

10 March

The day after tomorrow Marianne will be six months old. I wish I had begun my little journal sooner, for (although I should have laughed at the idea twelve months ago) there have been many little indications of disposition &c. already; which I cannot now remember clearly. I will try and describe her *mentally*. I should call her remarkably good tempered; though at times she gives way to little bursts of passion or perhaps impatience would be the right name. She is also very firm in her own little way occasionally; what I suppose is obstinacy really, only that is so hard a word to apply to one so dear. But in general she is so good that I feel as if I could hardly be sufficiently thankful, that the materials put into my hands are so excellent, and beautiful. And yet it seems to increase the responsibility. If I should misguide from carelessness or negligence! *willfully* is not in a mother's heart. From ignorance and errors in judgement I know I may, and probably shall, very often. But oh Lord I pray thee to lead me right (if it be thy will) and to preserve in me the same strong feeling of my responsibility which I now feel. And you too my dearest little girl, if when you read this, you trace back any evil, or unhappy feeling to my mismanagement in your childhood forgive me, love!

Elizabeth Gaskell, 1835

Mrs Wood the charwoman was to dinner – she's cleaning upstairs for Mary this week. She laughs at me for having my frocks so short & she's very particular not to get dirty over cleaning. I'm sure she despises me for being so black & even *she* wears gloves & all her children too when they goes out. And the poor woman's sorry they won't let her little boy wear gloves at the Orphan School where some lady got him into. She's very particular how herself & children look, still she doesn't mind going to ladies a-begging. Her husband was a coach-man only, so it's extremely disgusting of her to be so proud & particular.

Hannah Cullwick, 1863

11 March

I woke in great pain this morning, continued poorly all day, but minded it as little as possible. To my no small happiness and everybody's surprise I was brought to bed by seven o'clock in the evening of a boy, before Dr Savage had time to come, the nurse delivered me. A small child but a sweet boy.

Betsey Wynne Fremantle, 1798

This last fortnight has been too dreary and unhappy to write of. I am down here to recover from the effects of it. My people have been trying to separate us – trying to make me promise that I will give up his love, the most precious thing of my life. They do not understand – they will never understand – they do not see that our love is pure and lasting – they think I am his plaything, & that he will fling me aside when he has finished with me – or else they think that there will be a scandal and that we shall all be disgraced. I know they are fond of me, and think it is for my good that they are doing this, but I have always held different ideas from theirs, & it was bound to come to this, or something akin to this, sooner or later. I am willing to pay dearly for my happiness, but I will not give it up …

… In addition to distress of mind, I have been ill, which increased my misery. Finally C. [Lloyd George] insisted that I should come down here & have absolute rest for a few days, & be free from worrying surroundings. I agreed to this all the more willingly as I could see that C. was making himself ill through worrying about me – several times I thought he was on the point of breaking down; but he has been better since I have been down here & have shown signs of recovering.

I do not think I can ever repay him for his goodness to me the last fortnight or three weeks. He has been husband, lover & mother to me. I never knew a man could be so womanly & tender. He has watched and waited on me devotedly, until I cursed myself for being ill & causing him all this worry. There was no little thing that he did not think of for my comfort, no tenderness that he did not lavish on me. I have indeed known the full extent of his love. If those who idolise him as a public man could know the full greatness of his heart, how much more their idol would he be! And through it all he has been immersed in great decisions appertaining to this great crisis [the First World War], until I have trembled for his health, & loathed myself for causing him trouble at this time.

Frances Stevenson, 1915

12 March

I do not greatly admire Miss Pickford, nor have I ever behaved to her as if I did … I feel that I have jumped too soon to conclusions with Miss Pickford, but 'tis no matter. Time will set all right. She has not dignity enough for me. Till I get M– or someone else, I do believe I shall never know how to conduct myself to ladies. I am always getting into some scrape with them.

Anne Lister, 1823

A very fine morning. We went to see Mr Clarkson off. Then we went up towards Easedale but a shower drove us back. The sun shone while it rained, and the stones of the walls and the pebbles on the road glittered like silver. When William [her brother] was at Keswick I saw Jane

Ashburner driving the cow along the high road from the well where she had been watering it. She had a stick in her hand and came tripping along in the Jig step, as if she were dancing – Her presence was bold and graceful, her cheeks flushed with health and her countenance was free and gay. William finished his poem of the singing bird. In the meantime I read the remainder of Lessing. In the evening after tea William wrote Alice Fell – he went to bed tired with a wakeful mind and a weary Body. A very sharp clear night.

Dorothy Wordsworth, 1802

Creativeness … at least capacity to make my life is with me again. So not banished by having a baby? I feel more intelligent this year than ever before. I suppose 32 is the hey-day?

Ivy Jacquier, 1922

Pottered. In evening went to Revivalist meeting at Allawah. Oh hell.

Miles Franklin, 1933

13 March

S.[helley] H.[ogg] and C.[lary, Claire Clairmont] go to town – net, & think of my little dead baby – this is foolish I suppose yet whenever I am left alone to my own thoughts & do not read to divert them they always come back to the same point – that I was a mother & am so no longer – Fanny comes wet through – she dines & stays the evening – talk about many things – she goes at ½ 9 – cut out my new gown …

Mary Shelley, 1815

… This is the most feverish overworked political week we've had yet. Hitler has his army on the Rhine. Meetings taking place in London. So serious are the French that they're – the little intelligence group – is sending a man to confer here tomorrow: a touching belief in English intellectuals. Another meeting tomorrow. As usual, I think, Oh this will blow over. But it's odd, how near the guns have got to our private life again. I can quite distinctly see them and hear a roar, even though I go on, like a doomed mouse, nibbling at my daily page.

Virginia Woolf, 1936

… the statement that every *genius* is more closely connected to the dead philosophers than to the living members of his family circle. It is rather a naïve conclusion … living geniuses, until they have thrown off their mortal envelope and passed into history with their works, are created to consume the entire existence of the apparently uncomprehending members of their family circle.

For a *genius* one has to create a peaceful, cheerful, comfortable home; a *genius* must be fed, washed and dressed, must have his works copied out innumerable times, must be loved and spared all cause for jealousy, so that he can be calm; then one must feed and educate the innumerable children fathered by this genius, whom he cannot be bothered to care for himself, as he has to commune with all the Epictetuses, Socrateses and Buddhas, and aspire to be like them himself.

And when the members of his family circle have sacrificed their youth, beauty – everything – to serve this genius, they are then blamed for *not understanding* geniuses properly – and they never get a word of thanks from the geniuses themselves, of course, for sacrificing their pure young lives to him, and atrophying all their spiritual and intellectual capacities, which they are unable to nourish and develop due to a lack of peace, leisure and energy.

I have served a *genius* for almost forty years. Hundreds of times I have felt my intellectual energy stir within me, and all sorts of desires – a longing for education, a love of music and the arts … And time and again I have crushed and smothered all these longings, and now and to the end of my life I shall somehow or another continue to serve my *genius*.

Sophia Tolstoy, 1902

This morning we had a letter from Sam [her son] wherein he expresses a great deal of dullness and indisposition to his studies, and a desire to change the air if his Father think fit to see if it would do him good. Now we are in a strait which way to incline. We beg direction of thee, O All wise and Almighty God what to do, and beseech thee to satisfy our Child to submit to which ever shall be presently concluded on for him.

Mary Woodforde, 1687

14 March

I reflected tonight on the changes the war had brought. I always used to worry and flutter round when I saw my husband was working up for a mood; but now I just say calmly, 'Really dear, you *should* try and act as if you were a grown man and not a child of ten, and if you want to be awkward, I shall go out – ALONE!' I told him he had better take his lunch on Thursday, and several times I've not had tea quite ready when he has come in, on a Tuesday or Thursday, and I've felt quite unconcerned. He told me rather wistfully I was 'not so sweet' since I'd been down at the Centre, and I said, 'Well! Who wants a woman of fifty to be sweet, anyway? And besides, I suit *me* a *lot* better!'

Nella Last, 1940

My little boy begins to suck very nicely and I am not at all troubled with my milk, he is a charming child and never cries. Got up for half an hour in the afternoon. Our house was broken open last night. John heard the noise and called the watchman: I fortunately heard nothing of it.

Betsey Wynne Fremantle, 1798

My dear [sister] Beth died at three this morning, after two years of patient pain. Last week she put her work away, saying the needle was 'too heavy,' and having given us her few possessions, made ready for the parting in her own simple, quiet way. For two days she suffered much, begging for ether, though its effect was gone. Tuesday she lay in Father's arms, and called us round her, smiling contentedly as she said, 'All here!' I think she bid us goodbye then, as she held our hands and kissed us tenderly. Saturday she slept, and at midnight became unconscious, quietly breathing her life away till three, then, with one last look of the beautiful eyes, she was gone.

A curious thing happened, and I will tell it here, for Dr G. said it was a fact. A few moments after the last breath came, as Mother and I sat silently watching the shadow fall on the dear little face, I saw a light mist rise from the body and float up and vanish in the air. Mother's eyes followed mine, and when I said, 'What did you see?' she described the same light mist. Dr G. said it was the life departing visibly.

For the last time we dressed her in her usual cap and gown, and laid her on her bed, — at rest at last. What she had suffered was seen in the face, for at twenty-three she looked like a woman of forty, so worn was she, and all her pretty hair gone.

On Monday Dr Huntington read the Chapel service, and we sang her favorite hymn. Mr Emerson, Henry Thoreau, Sanborn, and John Pratt, carried her out of the old home to the new one at Sleepy Hollow, chosen by herself. So the first break comes, and I know what death means, – a liberator for her, a teacher for us.

Louisa May Alcott, 1858

15 March

I had finished my breakfast when the letters came – one from Roland [her fiancé] which had been sent on from Somerville. He has obtained his wish at last, and is off to the front in about 10 days' time. He has been given a transfer to the 7th Worcestershire Rgt – Territorials – which is on the point of going abroad & is short of two officers. This news was not unexpected but is none the less a terrible shock to me. I can hardly realise that the moment has come at last which ends my peace of mind until the war is over – that in a few days' time the individual so very dear to me will have gone to those regions of bloodshed and death, perhaps – nay, probably – never to return. The worst of it is he wrote to me at College thinking I was going down on Monday & trying to arrange a meeting in London that day. He says he can't possibly go to the front without seeing me, & certainly I could never let him go without saying goodbye, however sad it is to do so. But the letter was delayed & now I don't know where he is or where to write to him.

Later. I was getting ready for bed this evening when a telephone message – which with a kind of presentiment I had been half expecting all day – came for me from Roland in London. The beloved voice made me shiver with apprehension, thinking of the time when I should hear it no more. He tells me he is going to the front – not in ten days' time – but on *Saturday.* I said I supposed he wanted me to say I was glad about what had happened but I was not even going to pretend to. He only laughed. Telephoning is very unsatisfactory & there was such a noise going on I could scarcely hear anything. However I went to Mother & Daddy & announced my intention of going to London to say goodbye. They demurred a little at first but gave in sooner than I expected.

Vera Brittain, 1915

He [Klimt] took my skirt on his knee, and himself washed the stain out of my petticoat. Both his legs and mine were hidden under the skirt, and inevitably they touched. Although I kept withdrawing – for I consider such behaviour vulgar – I did so with reluctance and was overcome by such a strange, sweet sensation [by the physical contact with the man I loved]. My goodness, what I'm writing here is madly sensual, but I've promised always to write the full truth – regardless of myself or my neighbours – so I'm writing things down that cause blood to rush to my cheeks. *There's nothing else I can do …*

Can one love a man who's so unscrupulous? Yes, unfortunately. – Artists are rarely people of integrity.

Alma Schindler (Mahler-Werfel), 1899

16 March

I talked a good deal about Roland to Mother who was quite sympathetic & seemed anxious to find out just how much he had 'made love to me' & seemed surprised to find how little he had done so obviously … Nevertheless she wants to go up to town with me when I go to say goodbye – because I have not been well, not because she does not trust Roland.

Vera Brittain, 1915

Lunched at 'Thirty'. We all talked about the enduring power of love. Some of those present said that love goes in a man when the woman becomes middle-aged. I said that it often amazed me to see how love endured, though I admitted that in a certain class – the prosperous commercial class, no man, whatever his age, has any use for a woman, even for her company, after she is, say, forty. That is one of the things that strikes me in one circle I frequent. The moment you know a man at all well, he confides to you quite frankly what a bore he finds his wife's friends – that being a man of sixty talking of women between forty and forty-five.

Marie Belloc Lowndes, 1912

I made Jack Foster's acquaintance when I first arrived, but he has been away a good deal. He is very homely & wears shockingly old fashioned clothes, checked pantaloons for instance. – On the other hand, his blood is blue, his connections splendid, his manners excellent: he is polite, kind, attentive, jolly, amusing, & 23. What is more, he has never said or done anything that jarred me in the least. We had a very nice time together at the tableaux, & he was very attentive. After that I saw him occasionally, & about three weeks ago, he made me a present of a beautiful alligator, about eight inches long, & just the right size. When I first got him, every one announced that he would die; I said he should not, we have fed him on raw beef & he is more lively than ever. I have named him Jack, & shall take him home.

Julia Newberry (aged 16), 1870

Mother her most fiendish. She is the most infernal devil I know with her tongue. Nothing will stop her.

Miles Franklin, 1933

Is it cold-blooded to write truthfully of one's relationship to a man? If one tells anything one should tell all … All the small *affaires de coeur* of past years I have left unmentioned, simply because they have not interested me. The commonplaces of love have always bored me. But Joseph Chamberlain with his gloom and seriousness, with the absence of any gallantry or faculty for saying pretty nothings, the simple way in which he assumes, almost asserts, that you stand on a level far beneath him and that all that concerns you is trivial; that you yourself are without importance in the world except in so far as you might be related to him: this sort of courtship (if it is to be called courtship) fascinates, at least, my imagination …

I don't know how it will all end. Certainly not in my happiness … If I married him I should become a cynic as regards my own mental life. I should become *par excellence* the mother and the woman of the world intent only on fulfilling practical duties and gaining practical ends. And that, Mary would say, is a consummation devoutly to be wished for.

Beatrice Webb, 1884

17 March

May I never forget the impression William Savery [a preacher] has made on my mind, as much as I can say is, I thank God for having sent at least a glimmering of light through him into my heart, which I hope with care, and keeping it from the many draughts and winds of this life, may not be blown out, but become a large brilliant flame, that will direct me to that haven, where will be joy without a sorrow, and all will be comfort.

Elizabeth Fry (aged 17), 1798

I can't think of anything except something horrible I have had to do, getting the warble fly maggots out of the cattle, oh god it was filthy. The chap came to licence Timo [the bull]...said he had warble flies and pressed an awful maggot out of his back, I was nearly sick. Duncan says not to worry too much, they all have them …

Naomi Mitchison, 1944

William went up into the orchard and finished the Poem … I went and sate with W. and walked backwards and forwards in the orchard until dinner time – he read me his poem. I broiled Beefsteaks. After dinner we made a pillow of my shoulder, I read to him and my Beloved slept – I afterwards got him the pillows and he was lying with his head on the table when Miss Simpson came in. She stayed [to] tea. I went with her to Rydal. No letters! A sweet Evening as it had been a sweet day, a grey evening, and I walked quietly along the side of Rydal Lake with quiet thoughts …

Dorothy Wordsworth, 1802

18 March

Slept with M– in Anne's room upstairs over the drawing-room … Little tiff with Tib … Said lying in bed & taking snuff did not suit me & she knew it. Answer; I never found fault with M–, & proceeded to it. It was a pity I let her marry. M– advised me last night to tell Tib every now & then that she did not suit me & not to let her dwell so on the idea of our living together … Told Louisa I should not like to be long in the same house with M– & Tib. Lou is sure I like M– the best.

Anne Lister, 1820

Went to see Dr S. today. He is kind and efficient but so brisk that one wonders if one had a psychological problem how much time he would be able to give it. In this connection – the doctor's surgery is crowded but the vicar's study is empty. And there could be a sort of rivalry between them when it comes to dealing with life's difficulties.

Barbara Pym, 1977

I have just been brought through a sharp little attack of bronchitis, and feel bound to record my sense of the tender mercy that has encompassed me night and day. Though it may have been in part my own wilfulness and recklessness that brought it on, that and all else was pardoned, all fear of suffering or death was swallowed up in the childlike joy of trust: a perfect rest in the limitless love and wisdom of a most tender Friend, whose Will was far dearer to me than my own … I had before been craving for a little more spiritual life on any terms, and how mercifully this has been granted! and I can utterly trust that in any extremity that may be before me the same wonderful mercy will encompass me, and of mere love and forgiving compassion carry me safely into Port.

Caroline Fox, 1866

Dance matinée of the Camera Club … breezed through my first and only quadrille with Kl[imt].

Today we talked everything over seriously, and he told me it would never be possible for him to marry me – that he was fond of me all the same. Never had we spoken in greater seclusion and solitude than in the midst of the dancers in that salon. Never had I felt sadder than in the inner circle of that waltz. Never. –

After that quadrille, we all went home. We were with Dr Henneberg – anyway, I couldn't have danced with anyone else.

Alma Schindler (Mahler-Werfel), 1899

19 March

Dream that my little baby came to life again – that it had only been cold & that we rubbed it before the fire & it lived – I awake and find no baby – I think about the little thing all day – not in good spirits – Shelley is very unwell – read Gibbon. Charles Clairmont comes. Hogg goes to town till dinner-time. Talk with C. C. about Skinner St – they are very badly off there –I am afraid nothing can be done to save them –

Mary Shelley, 1815

Whatever the future may bring – whether it be the sorrow I fear more than anything on earth, or the joy which now I scarce dare dream of, much less name – as long as I have memory & thought, I shall not forget today & yesterday. My beloved one [her fiancé Roland Leighton] has been here and departed again, & now indeed I may see his dear face never more. I cannot write about it much …

I asked him if he thought it better to have seen the possibility of great joy that could not be realised as yet, perhaps never, or if he thought it better to keep one's peace of mind & never see. He said he thought the first was better, & I agreed with him, agreed it was better to suffer & try to be strong over it than never to have risen to the point where suffering becomes possible. I do feel indeed like one standing at the entrance of the Promised Land – or like one who has been permitted to gaze upon it from the mountain tops without being allowed to enter. Sometimes I have wished I had never met him – wished that he had not come to take away my impersonal attitude towards the war, and made it a cause of personal suffering to me as it is to thousands of others. But yet, if I could choose never to have met him I would not …

… There is not after all much more to be said. I was tired & slept but my night was restless & disturbed with dreams, & so, as he told me in the morning, was his. We had breakfast alone together as previously arranged, and had no time to be long over it …

… I shall never forget the look of the station so early on that cold bright March morning … As the train was almost due to start I got up

into the railway carriage to say goodbye to him … He held my hand &
looked at me without a word. For a moment I wished he would have
kissed me: many men would have done so and it would hardly have been
a liberty at that solemn moment. But afterwards I was glad that he had
not done so, but had remained characteristic of himself up to the last
… Then there was a slight bustling on the platform & the train began
to move. We clasped hands once more as it was going &, though I was
trying to train my mind into realising that probably this was indeed a
final farewell, at the last I could only bring myself to say 'Au revoir.'
He said it too & dropped my hand, then remained leaning out of the
window looking sadly at me as I stood motionless watching the train
until it disappeared altogether and where it had been there was nothing
but the merciless sunlight shining on the rails. I hate public exhibitions
of emotion, but if I could have burst into tears then & there I should
have been glad, I felt so stunned & cold as I turned & walked slowly out
of the station.

Vera Brittain, 1915

This morning I returned from three happy, if busy, days at Cambridge.
On Monday I gave the Keynote Speech at a conference on 'Sexing the
Liturgy' held at the university's Faculty of Divinity in St John street.
I thought the title a little odd; I associate sexing with chickens …

I pointed out that Christianity is both an historical and a patriarchal
religion. It was a Jewish patriarch, St Paul, who was chiefly responsible
for extending the Judeo-Christian Inheritance to non-Jews. Christ
Himself taught us to call God 'Abba, Father'. I see a difficulty, at least
for myself, in accepting such changes as 'mother' or 'Sister'. This is surely
to substitute one stereotype for another; since God is spirit He can have
no gender. Even as a young child I never pictured God as a benevolent
Father Christmas sitting in a white nightdress on a heavenly throne.

P. D. James, 1998

20 March

The details of today were anything but pleasant; the result, however, is very satisfactory. We got Sally Jordan to come and give her assistance, and we ladies were as busy as the servants, rubbing furniture, etc. Not, however, busier than we have been on a like occasion at Bootle [i.e. in England]. Here, indeed, we may make a comparison in favour of this much-abused country. You lose no respect by such exertions. In Mount Pleasant, where our establishment was very small, we used occasionally at busy times to make our beds. On one occasion a housemaid, receiving her dismissal, was inclined to retaliate by a little insolence and told us we were certainly no ladies, or we should not make beds. Here one of our domestics would be surprised, and perhaps think herself a little ill-used if, in any extra bustle, we should be sitting in our drawing room ...

Anne Langton, Canada, 1840

Bloomington, Indiana

Our family, consisting of father, mother, two brothers and one sister, left this morning for that far and much talked of country, California. My father started our wagons one month in advance, to St Joseph, Missouri, our starting point. We take the steamboat at New Albany, going by water to St Joe ... The last hours were spent in bidding good bye to old friends. My mother is heartbroken over this separation of relatives and friends. Giving up old associations for what? Good health, perhaps. My father is going in search of health, not gold. The last good bye has been said – the last glimpse of our old home on the hill, and wave of hand at the old Academy, with a good bye to kind teachers and schoolmates, and we are off. We have been several days reaching New Albany on account of the terrible condition of the roads. Our carriage upset at one place. All were thrown out, but no one was hurt. We were detained several hours on account of this accident. My mother thought it a bad omen and wanted to return and give up the trip.

Sallie Hester (aged 14), on the California Trail, 1849

Yesterday a nadir of sorts. Woke up to cat's early mewling around six. Cramps. Pregnant, I thought. No such luck. After a long 40 day period of hope, the old blood cramps and spilt fertility. I had lulled myself into a fattening calm and this was a blow … I'd like four in a row. Then dopey, and the cramps all day.

Sylvia Plath, 1959

21 March

———

The alligator died last night, a most untimely death, & from no apparent cause; I feel dreadfully about it, & especially so, because I did not paint his picture as I might have done … All the nice people have left, & the house is full of strange faces, & flashy young ladies. Sister has a frightful cold.

Julia Newberry (aged 16), 1870

Spring!

An exceedingly quiet, mauve gray day in the city, after a wonderful day yesterday with Roberto (Robert L. Allen). We worked & puttered about the house until 2.00 and then went to Oakland for a walk half way around the lake. Just being out in the warm sun was heavenly. I was knocked out by it, though, and took a nap at Robert's apartment afterward. Very quiet & colorful & cozy there, I must say!

Then home – after an early dinner and grocery shopping in Rockridge, which I like very much – and the last half of *The Women of Brewster Place*, which was beautiful & moving. I must send a telegram to Oprah.

And how are you? My trusty confidant? I write less and less in you. And even now I'm aware that just from writing half a page, my fingers hurt. Is it early arthritis? Anyway, I find I have little to say, though much has happened …

Alice Walker, 1989

Finished this morning *The Mill on the Floss*, writing from the moment when Maggie, carried out of the water, thinks of her mother and brother. We hope to start for Rome on Saturday, 24th.

Magnificat anima mea! [*Magnificat anima mea Dominum:* my soul doth magnify the Lord]

The manuscript of *The Mill on the Floss* bears the following inscription:

'To my beloved husband, George Henry Lewes, I give this MS of my third book, written in the sixth year of our life together, at Holly Lodge, South Field, Wandsworth, and finished 21st March 1860.'

George Eliot, 1860

… I went to buy clothes today and was struck by my own ugliness. Like Edith Sitwell I can never look like other people – too broad, tall, flat, with hair hanging. And now my neck is so ugly.

Edith Sitwell came to tea: transparent like some white bone one picks up on a moor, with sea water stones on her long frail hands which slide into yours much narrower than one expects like a folded fan …

Virginia Woolf, 1927

22 March

I am glad to go home, & yet sorry to leave this interesting spot; it is a queer place, & its charm lies in being queer. It will be horrid when they have a railroad, more hotels, & a bridge instead of a Ferry … I shall always be grateful to St Augustine, for being here has saved me from several months, of nasty cold wet weather, shut up in a house in New York.

Julia Newberry (aged 16), Florida, 1870

Mrs Simpson came unexpectedly at 9 … told M– this morning she could not bear me, that I was the only woman she was ever afraid of. Wondered how anyone ever got acquainted with me. Mentioned my deep-toned voice as very singular. The girls said they were afraid of me but could like me because M– did.

Anne Lister, 1820

… K. [her husband] examined my face as though he were seeing it for the first time.

'It may not be apparent,' I said, 'but I love you and you come first in the world with me, before everything before anybody. You and the children. My family and home are more to me than my work. If it came to the choice it would be my work that went overboard. No doubt I've appeared to be a failure in the home but that is not indicative. Do you feel I've failed you in the home?' I called on all my courage to ask this question which could draw a devastating answer. He put out two cups and saucers. 'Well, it has crossed my mind that you shouldn't have married.'

Catastrophe! 'But I've been a good mother! Look at me all through my babies. How I stuck to them on the Coast.'

'Yes. But what I mean is that a person, any person, with your inclinations should not marry. You should have gone on with your work. Marriage has sidetracked you.'

Desperately on the defensive, 'I wash and dress the little boys in the morning, and Jonquil. I feed them.'

'I know. What I mean is that people like you with talents and ideas should be undisturbed by marriage.'

'Ah … but you see! I wouldn't have had these desires at all if I hadn't married. When I didn't teach and had no babies, I hardly lifted a brush. Hardly did a thing. The *need* to study, to do, to make, to think, *arises* from being married. I need to be married to work …'

Sylvia Ashton-Warner, 1942

23 March

Another year older. I have just filled in a survey on the tube and noticed that I have moved one box further in the great pigeon holing of life. I can no longer tick the 25–34 age bracket. I've moved into the 35–44 bracket. How did that happen? Last time I looked I was 21.

Deborah Bull, 1998

The little crises multiply themselves, and we steer the course of our marriage with nothing but a deep love. There was the night when Hugh [her husband] realised, not without bitterness, that he was becoming the typical 'businessman' we both hate. The work being more difficult, and Hugh feeling many more responsibilities, he has given not only his time to it, but his soul …

… He will come home as usual, tired, obsessed by the bank, asking me from habit rather than from interest: 'What have you done today, little Pussywillow?' and without waiting for an answer he will tell me about the success of his last suggestion to the management about the carelessness of one of the stenographers, about the resignation of a man in his department, about the lost folder and the interesting talk with a French business genius.

I understand now the spirit that pushes some married women to embrace an inane social life, to spend their afternoons in a club playing bridge, to 'go around' with other men. They are accused of selfishness because meanwhile the poor husbands are killing themselves with work. They have no right to kill themselves with work. By doing that they kill all the living beauty of marriage – the companionship, the united enjoyment, the united growth.

Only the love of writing and reading keeps me home, but even then I feel the longing for companionship. Twice a day, once before my mirror and once before my desk, I ask myself, 'What is the use?' It is in vain that I seek a more exalted 'raison d'être'. All humanity, fame, cannot replace the insatiate desire of a woman in love with her young, ideal and chosen companion. He is trying to come back. I am waiting.

Anaïs Nin, 1925

We have had a thaw – a really, truly thaw. Oh, the joy of it! I think even the hearts half century dead over there in the graveyard must have throbbed in unison with the great heart of spring. There are bare spots in the fields – they are not so beautiful as the white drifts but oh, so dear to see for their promise. I feel like a prisoner released. There are mountains of snow yet – but spring is coming. I could clap my hands for joy – I *did* clap them tonight up on the hill and laughed aloud for sheer gladness of heart. All at once life seemed beautiful again. I felt as if I could run, dance, sing with delight, like a child.

L. M. Montgomery, 1905

24 March

———

Betty and I set off on a Walk to Weston but was prevented from proceeding on my Journey by Rain, which was a great disappointment to me as I wish'd very much to have spent an Hour or two with poor Mrs Custance in her Melancholy situation. Mrs England sent me a nice Pot of Honey for which my Uncle gave James Atterton a Shilling. Had my Carlton House Magazine would have come at the beginning of this Month. Rcd of John Priest the following ingredients for a Diet Drink. Senna 2 oz 8d. Sassafras 2 oz 2d. Guiacum 6d. Jalp 1 oz 4d. Saffron 4 oz one Shilling. Rhubarb one Shilling. Maiden Hir 3d. Sweet Fennel sed 1 oz 2d. Anniseeds 1 oz 1d. Creme Tartar ½ oz 1d. For the above paid four Shillings.

Nancy Woodforde, 1792

We are now at the 24th of March, 1856, and from this point of time, my journal, let us renew our daily intercourse without looking back. Looking back was not intended by nature, evidently, from the fact that our eyes are in our faces and not in our hind heads. Look straight before you, then, Jane Carlyle, and, if possible, not over the heads of things either, away into the distant vague. Look, above all, at the duty nearest hand, and what's more, do it. Ah, the spirit is willing, but the flesh is weak, and four weeks of illness have made mine weak as water. No galloping over London as in seven league boots for me at present. To-day I walked with effort one little mile, and thought it a great feat; but if the strength has gone out of me, so also has the unrest. I can sit and lie even very patiently doing nothing.

Jane Carlyle, 1856

What is this feeling between Mother and me? It is a kind of feeling of dislike and distrust which I believe is mutual. And yet it ought not to be! She has always been the kindest and best of mothers, though in her manners she is not over-affectionate. She is such a curious character I can't make her out. She is sometimes such a kind, good affectionate mother, full of wise judgement and affectionate advice, and at other times the spoilt child comes out so strong in her. But whatever she is, that ought not to make the slightest difference to my feeling and behaviour towards her ...

Beatrice Webb (aged 15), 1873

25 March

Paul [her brother] went to France last week. I went home for the weekend, and was glad I did so, as Mamma was very upset about it. She is quite sure he will never come back. She is very bitter as to the disappointment that one's children bring ... Poor Mother! She cannot realise, & I fear she never will, that parents cannot control their children's lives forever – that children exist for their own and the next generation, and not for that of their parents, which is past. However, it is hopeless to argue with her: but I fear she will never be happy unless she takes a wider view.

Frances Stevenson, 1915

This evening came Waddie from London and brought me word of Mr Hoby's health: but all things may not concur, for in this Life we must have Gaul as well as Honey: but blessed be god that tourneth all things Unto good to his Children.

Lady Margaret Hoby, 1604

Dined in Bry. Sq. … very pleasant indeed, music evening. Sat betw. Messrs. Bryce and Gaskell, female suffrage the staple of our talk.

Mary Gladstone, 1884

I came up on Sunday after a leisurely day in bed with Zelie [Duvauchelle]. She's such a sweet lover! I'm so fortunate. She's *so* the young masculine to my Great Mother. I had this insight about myself: That I've always loved the young masculine. And have loved men who carried, embodied, it until they began to lose it. In their thirties and Robert [L. Allen] in his forties, men seem (some of them) to begin a slide into the old feminine, which isn't the same energy as the Great Mother, perhaps because they're men. The Great Mother's attribute, like that of the Empress, is abundance, fecundity, plenty. Lush Life. Nurturing but in a reciprocal way, usually.

Alice Walker, 1998

26 March

I'd sent no diary to M. [Massa] but I was so delighted that I was going to see him in the evening & I got off after my days work & went on the platform at Ludgate Hill to meet him. I miss'd sight [of him] & he went down the stairs, & I waited a minute thinking he was not come. But I found M. down stairs & that he was cross with me about the diary & we was very dull all the evening. I wash'd his feet & rubb'd 'em & did the usual jobs, washing the brushes &c., & came away in time for prayers, & feeling that I really must write more, for it is not life to me at all if M. isn't nice with me.

Hannah Cullwick, 1871

Had to leave at six to go to Sadler's Wells with Rowena. During the interval we had cocoa and Welsh rarebit at the Angel Café, while Rowena told me about her 'uncle' and how nice sex is. She says it's the best indoor recreation she has yet discovered, particularly in the afternoon which is the only time he can get away from his wife. She says it's like an old

French song which just goes on and on, and I really ought to try it. I asked her what she did to prevent herself from getting pregnant, and she said there are things called Volpar Gels which are quite effective, but the best thing is to go to the Marie Stopes clinic and get a Dutch cap.

I told her all about Gerhardt and Jo, and she said it sounded very boring and rather decadent. Of course I'm not decadent at all really, I only wish I was.

Joan Wyndham (aged 18), 1940

I was over to the traps today and fox has been in cold oil Can traps and trap was sprung but didn't hold fox and this morning about 11 o'clock I sew [sic] a Polar bear on the ice, and I sew three foxxes one with trap on her food, and I haul one load of sled and saw four cuts of log and chop wood, and we look at knight's legs [explorer Lorne Knight, other remaining member of the Wrangel Island Expedition team] my! they are skinny and they has no more blue spots like they use to be. And I pretty near finish my black belt.

Ada Blackjack, 1923

Took the steamboat *Meteor* this evening for St Joe. Now sailing on the broad Ohio, floating toward the far West.

Sallie Hester (aged 14), 1849

Easter Sunday: grim, cold, snowing, altogether forbidding, but delightful here inside. HAVE FINISHED 'Cybele'. And feel spotless as a lamb.

Joyce Carol Oates, 1978

27 March

ADDRESSED TO A CERTAIN MISS NOBODY

Poland Street, London, March 27

To have some account of my thoughts, manners, acquaintances and actions, when the hour arrives in which time is more noble than memory, is the reason which induces me to keep a Journal. A Journal in which I must confess my *every* thought, must pen my whole heart! But a thing of this kind ought to be addressed to somebody – I must imagine myself to be talking – talking to the most intimate of friends – to one in whom I should take a delight in confiding, and remorse in concealment – but who must this friend be? to make choice of one in whom I can but *half* rely, would be to frustrate entirely the intention of my plan. The only one I could wholly, totally confide in, lives in the same house with me, and not only never *has*, but never *will*, leave me one secret to tell her. To *whom*, then, *must* I dedicate my wonderful, surprising and interesting Adventures? – to *whom* dare I reveal my private opinion of my nearest relations? my secret thoughts of my dearest friends? my own hopes, fears, reflections, and dislikes? – Nobody!

To Nobody, then, will I write my Journal! since to Nobody can I be wholly unreserved …

Fanny Burney (aged 15), 1768

Mr C. took Nero out with him tonight, and half an hour after he opened the door with his latch-key and called in, 'Is that vermin come back?' Having received my horrified 'No!' he hurried off again, and for twenty minutes I was in the agonies of one's dog lost, my heart beating up into my ears. At last I heard Mr C.'s feet in the street; and, oh joy! heard him gollaring [sic] at something, and one knew what the bad little something was. Ach! we could have better spared a better dog.

Jane Carlyle, 1856

I shall be glad when Sidney [her husband] retires, as the lonely life down here, with the alternative of days and nights in London (equally lonely during the day, and with the discomforts of the little flat and the noise and bustle of the streets), beginning to prey on my nerves, and might end in a bad breakdown. I am beginning to feel the helplessness of old age, which with me is masked by will-power and physical activity. To other people I feel in full possession of my faculties, but in my own consciousness I am depressed and dazed: memory fails me and I worry about this thing and that ...

Beatrice Webb, 1931

28 March

A lamentable falling off. Had my few remaining locks clipped short at Douglas's. Droughty. My hair nearly all came off since I was ill. Now that the sheep is shorn, I may say without pride that I have seldom seen a more beautiful head of hair than mine. Last summer it was very thick and within about four inches of my knees, being more than a yard long.

Beatrix Potter (aged 18), 1885

While driving through the palm trees on the way back from the beach in Puerto Rico in January 1963, just a week or so before my first New York exhibit was due to open, I had a moment of purest panic. I saw clearly that I could have lain low, snug in my marriage and motherhood, and I most profoundly wished that I had. No one would have faulted me. There would not even have been much loss of face, as I had rarely let on that I was doing anything beyond being a housewife. As I eased the car over the sandy ruts, I thought to myself how pushy I had been in aiming to do anything more. It seemed incredible to me that in a short while I would have to face the public gaze. Every fiber shrank.

I feel something like that now ...

Anne Truitt, 1975

I dread the dictatorship of loneliness, the collaboration compelled because that's all there is. The mind and sometimes the heart have rejected someone, weighed him ever as a loss in every way – but the empty hour forgives this and once again your splendid wings are clipped, the proud neck choked.

Dawn Powell, 1962

Put on my best dress for the Cabinet official photo and hoped the tiredness wouldn't show too much. As it was cold the chairs had been set out in the upstairs reception room at No. 10, instead of outside. We had all been given a set place and Shirley [Williams] and I found ourselves on the two outside seats of the semi-circle. 'You wait till the women of the movement learn about this,' Shirley called out to Harold [Prime Minister Harold Wilson]. 'Not to worry, Shirley,' I called back, 'We can do a pincer movement on him. His days are doomed.' Harold just grinned but I hope he was a bit embarrassed.

Barbara Castle, 1974

29 March

Leopold came to my dressing-room, and broke the dreadful news to me that my good, faithful [John] Brown had passed away early this morning. Am terribly upset by this loss, which removes one who was so devoted and attached to my service and who did so much for my personal comfort. It is the loss not only of a servant, but of a real friend.

Queen Victoria, 1883

What shall I think of that's liberating and freshening? I'm in the mood when I open my window at night and look at the stars. Unfortunately it's 12.15 on a grey dull day, the aeroplanes are active, Botten is to be buried at 3. Well I recur what shall I think of? The river. Say the Thames at London Bridge; and buying a notebook; and then walking along the

Strand and letting each face give me a buffet. For we're up in London on Monday. Then back here I'll saunter … oh yes and we'll travel our books round the Coast – and have tea in a shop – and look at antiques, and there'll be a lovely farmhouse – or a new lane – and flowers – and bowls with L. and May coming and asparagus, and butterflies. Perhaps I'll garden a little oh and print, and change my bedroom furniture. I'm inducing a state of peace and sensation feeling – not an idea feeling. The truth is we've not seen spring in the country since I was ill at Asheham – 1914 – and that had its holiness in spite of the depression. I think I'll also dream a poet-prose book, perhaps make a cake now and then …

Virginia Woolf, 1940

Am labouring with my paper on the Lords' Report, have been for the last three weeks. Stuck in the middle; oppressed with a constant headache and sick to death of grappling with my subject. Was I made for brain work? Is any woman made for a purely intellectual life? Then the background to my life is inexpressibly depressing – Father lying like a log in his bed, a child, an animal, with less capacity for thought and feeling than my old pet, Don … One longs for release and yet sickens at the thought of this weary desire for the death of one's father.

Beatrice Webb, 1890

30 March

Loneliness. I lie and read politics with a heavy cold. A. [her husband] rushes back from a meeting, rushes out to dinner, I resume the thread of my thoughts. Tonight I say to myself I will get a very good nurse and travel, leaving 'Petrouska'. And to think that I probably would not have the guts to travel and develop along my own lines while A. is so busy. Also to be always happy would not suit me. These miserable days help me in reality to concentrate …

Ivy Jacquier, 1922

... [Mama] does not intend taking Mary and me out this year, she says she is tired of it. In fact we are evidently *de trop* in this establishment. I suppose one ought to marry. It would be horrid even if one could, to marry someone one don't care a bit about, but I suppose one must come to that. It is sad, when one thinks of all one's dreams, working together for some noble aim in perfect concord, but one soon gets *disillusionnée*, especially when one is *de trop* everywhere, and it doesn't mend matters to write sentiment in middling French and English mixed.

Ellen Peel, 'A Victorian Young Lady', 1887

Dreadfully raw, disagreeable day. Very unwell with the worst cold I've had. It *stupefies* me. Who sh'ld come in, all in a shiver, but Mr Pierce. Had a good long talk with him, over the fire, during which took occasion to ask him about that speech [against coloured missionaries]. He emphatically denies ever having made it. Talked a long time on the subject and the result is that we are good friends. I'll allow myself to like him now; – which is very much easier than *disliking* him, *Je vous assure* ...

Charlotte Forten, 1863

31 March

At 4.0 I had a short letter from Roland. They have received their final orders now, & left Maldon at 6.30. They may either wait in the docks a day or two or cross over to France to-night. He says he cannot realise that he may be in a trench in a very few hours, & gives me as a parting injunction 'Think of me to-morrow night – & after.' Need he have told me!

Vera Brittain, 1915

Mrs Earle to tea, joined by [the cleric] E. B. O.[ttley], funny talk on love in marriage and women's positions and duties. The latter stayed on and we went on to morals.

Mary Gladstone, 1884

I ought to have left Hu [her husband] long ago, before it became impossible. Last week he was vilely insulting – said he would like to bring an action against [her lover] Barny for debauching me – that I had become absolutely vicious, had a vicious look, I disliked all normal people, and led the life of a person with a secret vice. His mind is a positive sink of jealous hysteria. But I can't treat him only with pity. These outbursts terrify me.

He had had bad news; the lung would not collapse, and Dr Westerleigh had told him he would get rapidly worse if he could not get his resistance back. This I suppose was the cause of his hysteria. I am deadly sorry for him as he lies there and sees his resistance going – but when he shouts insults at me I can only feel shattered and long to be out of his presence. What remains of our relations is a very terrible thing. He knows he can rely on my pity to answer his claims as far as I can, to bring the things he needs, to visit him (and be shouted at), even to take a house and nurse him if he wants it – he knows I can't answer him as one would a normal man: 'Oh, go to hell.' I'm in a horrible position. There's no strength like that of a weak man.

Loran Hurnscot, 1924

The first issue of my *VF* [*Vanity Fair*] is on the newsstands at last! …

Entertainment Tonight came to film me in the office and I was feeling so glum with all the staff problems and anxiety about the reader reaction to April that I mistakenly ran off at the mouth and now am in terror they will run the damning segment. Usually I bang on about America the Beautiful, but this time I heard myself say, 'At first I thought I had to go carefully so as not to offend the aunties in Ohio, but now I feel if they don't want to read us, too bad.' What was I thinking?

'Ohio,' John Heilpern said, as we sat, with freezing feet from the ice storms raging outside, waiting for the curtain to rise on *Death of a Salesman*, 'is a pretty fucking enormous place to kiss off, Teen. In fact most presidents have found they can't win an election without it.' We both fell into a depressed silence …

Tina Brown, 1984

April

'*Very sad news was received this morning of the murder of the President.*'

Emilie Davis, 1865

1 April

Well, the beginning of the fourth month and a donkey, then *two* donkeys eating the cabbages in the garden. (April Fool.) Felt very weary and aching all over …

Barbara Pym, 1943

Remembered the excitement of the April Fool's Days of my childhood and felt sadly 'grown up'. I sent a message to Michael [her second son] to say I had grown a moustache in the night and he crept into my room full of apprehension. I also revived my old joke of inking a face on my knee and pretending it was a baby – to the huge delight of the three children. All three rabbits have died. Michael says 'They lived as long as they could'. I read *Black Beauty* to him in the hall while David and Martin [her nephews] did a puzzle and Evan continued his desultory reading …

Lady Cynthia Asquith, 1918

Today is the anniversary of my husband's birthday and inevitably it is a day for memory to take hold. It was an unpropitious day to be born, provoking in childhood the inevitable jokes and teasing. Connor would have been seventy-eight today and I am trying to picture him, like me stiffer in his walk, his strong fair hair now a thatch of grey. I know that he was glad to die and I never mourned him in the sense of wishing that it had not happened. I still miss him daily, which means that no day goes by in which he doesn't enter into my mind: a sight which he would have relished, a joke which he would have enjoyed, something seen or read which could be shared with him, the reiteration of familiar gossip, opinions, prejudices, which are part of a marriage. And then there is the success and prosperity in which he never shared and which could have made such a difference to his comfort, and the grandchildren he longed to see but never did.

P. D. James, 1998

Sid [Sidonie Houselander] and Mummy stayed over at the Grail House last night, so was alone in London for the first time since the blitz started. Went up to Sid's bedroom and read all her juicy books about psychopaths and sexual abnormalities and the symbolism of dreams. There was one by Kraft Ebbing that got me so excited that I remembered something Leonard told me and took a candle from the little altar. Now I suppose I'm completely beyond the pale as far as the Church is concerned.

Joan Wyndham (aged 19), 1941

After private prayers I did eat and was busy about dyeing of stuff till dinner time, saving I had some Conference with John Brown unto whom I gave the best advice I Could; after, I prayed and then dined: after, I was busy as I was before times and so, at 5 o'clock, I went to private meditation and prayer: After I went to supper, then to public prayers, and then to bed.

Lady Margaret Hoby, 1600

2 April

Oh bliss! The dear soft glorious air again: exit snow, exit frost, exit the last remains of chilliness, but pouring rain all day. I adventurously took pudding and barley-water to the Pratt child; which is recovering from croup, as none but a poor child would at 6½: warm, green, and delicious.

Lucy Lyttleton (Lady Frederick Cavendish), aged 17, 1859

Today, we're undertaking a long journey. The bus leaves at nine in the morning and will reach Jacksonville at two at night. This is an 'express' that makes only two or three stops. They sell sandwiches and Coca-Cola on board; the seats have movable backs, and at night everyone lights a little individual lamp, as in airplanes. And the steward encourages us, plotting our position from time to time, announcing the next stop and explaining the landscape. We're travelling through Louisiana, Mississippi,

Alabama, and Florida. The branches of the delta are as vast as lakes; they glisten in the sun, and the Gulf of Mexico is as blue as a honeymoon dream. Palm trees, cacti, azaleas, flowing cities, tropical forests with thick vegetation ...

And throughout the day the great tragedy of the South pursues us like an obsession. Even the traveler confined to a bus and waiting rooms cannot escape it. From the time we entered Texas, everywhere we go there's the smell of hatred in the air – the arrogant hatred of whites, the silent hatred of blacks. At the stations the respectable, badly dressed lower middle-class matrons stare with envious anger at the pretty black girls in bright dresses and joyful jewelry, and the men resent the nonchalant beauty of the young black men in light suits. American niceness has no place here. In the crowded line outside the bus, the blacks are jostled. 'You aren't going to let that Negress go in front of you,' a woman says to a man in a voice trembling with fury.

Simone de Beauvoir, 1947

One needs to be frantically spoilt and adulated after a baby. And one is not.

Ivy Jacquier, 1922

D. [Lloyd George] & I had hardly seen each other last week, so we drove down to Walton on Saturday to lunch, & had two hours of bliss together. D. saw I was rather down & lonely, & it was sweet of him to suggest it, for he was very tender & kind & bucked me up again. I feel as though I ought not to mind when he is busy & cannot pay me very much attention, but I suppose I am only human and I get depressed. But he soon puts me right again.

Frances Stevenson, 1917

3 April

To love one's child is as painful and has all the vulnerability of being in love. This sort of passionate protectiveness hurts one. One has no outlet; to hug tight ... for this Sally is too tiny.

Ivy Jacquier, 1922

M– [Mariana Lawton] said, very sweetly & with tears at the bare thought, she could never bear me to do anything wrong with ... anyone in my own rank of life. She could bear it better with an inferior, where the danger of her being supplanted could not be so great. But to get into any scrape would make her pine away. She thought she could not bear it. I never before believed she loved me so dearly & fondly. She has more romance than I could have thought & I am satisfied ... I thought of its being my birthday, but let it pass without notice. How time steals away! What will the next year bring to pass? May I improve it more than the last!

Anne Lister, 1820

Contrary to my usual custom, I will for once write more fully about the food because it has become a very difficult and important matter, not only here in the 'Secret Annexe' but in the whole of Holland, all Europe and even beyond.

In the twenty-one months that we've spent here we have been through a good many 'food cycles' – you'll understand what that means in a minute. When I talk of 'food cycles' I mean periods in which one has nothing else to eat but one particular dish or kind of vegetable. We had nothing but endive for a long time, day in, day out, endive with sand, endive without sand, stew with endive, boiled or *en casserole*: then it was spinach, and after that followed swedes, salsify, cucumbers, tomatoes, sauerkraut, etc., etc.

For instance, it's really disagreeable to eat a lot of sauerkraut for lunch and supper every day, but you do it if you're hungry ...

Anne Frank, 1944

… Sleet storm, blizzard, everything covered (again) with snow. Wind all night long. Bits of ice thrown against the windows, crackling tinkling noises, small explosions. Another Ice Age is upon us …

Joyce Carol Oates, 1975

4 April

It is not possible that he [George Baker] will not return. I sit here on one elbow hourly expecting his tight peremptory tap on the door. Each time the inefficient jangle of the elevator gets into motion, I start up. Will this monster stop at my floor and disgorge my miracle? I hurry back from a half-finished walk up the street. Are there any telegrams? Has there been a phone call? Is the red Buick parked a little way down the street? I see a car with a tall radio aerial — this is the grass of hope that grows indomitably over my eyes.

For to say he will not and never come is to throw myself into the whirlpool and to deliver my mind into madness and my dear my unborn child into a flood of blood and death. This I cannot do nor will my watchful protectors [protectress?] allow it. She sends me a thousand desperate instincts which make me hurry up and down streets, scrutinize magazines and become absorbed feverishly in the irrelevant price of gramophones.

I will not think of these things now. I have no time. When I have washed these stockings I will. When I have written these letters of thanks, or sewn on a button, I will. – meticulousness showers me with the skill of Penelope to do small precise tasks I bungled before – buttonholes and frills for collars. For dear God, I must not think now for I cannot cry here. The walls are too thin.

Elizabeth Smart, 1941

Fine. wrote letters. To town at 11. Shopping. Dress &c. Felt well. Oil bath. Slept well. Pay Miss J. Chop.

Louisa May Alcott, 1887

Heard to-day that there has been another fugitive arrested. There is to be a trial. God grant that the poor man may be released from the clutches of the slavehunters. Mr P.[utman] has gone down. We wait anxiously to hear the result of the trial. How long, oh, how long shall such a state of things as this –last?

Charlotte Forten, 1859

While Mr Per was fixing my hair, Lynda Bird, who had been watching TV, came flying into my room crying: 'Dr King's been shot!' Quieting down a little, she told us that Martin Luther King, about to lead a march in Memphis tomorrow, had been shot on a motel balcony, and was on his way to the hospital.

From that moment on the evening assumed a nightmare quality. A few moments later Lynda came in and said, 'Mama, he's dead!' Everybody's mind began racing off in its own direction, as to what this would mean – to racial violence in our country, to the work of so many who were trying to bring us together – how far would it set us back?

There I sat with an elaborate hairdo, in my elegant, festive, flame-colored chiffon, ready for the Democratic Dinner, which was already in progress. But the hands of the clock had stopped, and we were in a strange sort of suspended state …

Lady Bird Johnson, 1968

5 April

I was up early after a restless night. I went into Lyndon's room for coffee. He was still firm in his feeling that I should go [escorting a press trip to Texas] …

Sometime during the day I took my compact out to powder my nose. It crashed to the floor. I picked it up and opened it and the glass was shattered into a hundred tiny fragments. An involuntary chill went through me. Somehow, it was part of the dark undercurrent of the day. Underneath the sunshine and bright excitement and genuine interest there was a sense of expectancy of we knew not what, almost foreboding.

In the backyard of the museum there was a tent, with German pastries and hot steaming coffee, served by anxious hostesses. It had been a long time since brunch on the plane and I was ravenous, as I always am on these trips. But there were hands to shake, and thanks to bestow, and greetings to familiar faces across the crowd …

I finally got to bed around one o'clock after a day that ran the full gamut of emotions, against the background of mounting turbulence, while the whole nation seemed to be straining at its seams. And yet, I had a queer sense of ambivalence. Though I was right in the middle of it, because of my husband's job and the presence in Washington of all my family, I, myself, seemed removed and encased in a different world. Here we were just hearing about events and reading about them as though they were happening on the moon.

Lady Bird Johnson, 1968

The 5th my Lord went up to my closet and said how little money I had left contrary to all they had told him. Sometimes I had fair words from him and sometimes foul, but I took all patiently, and did strive to give him as much content and assurance of my love as I could possibly, yet I told him that I would never part with [her lands in] Westmorland upon any condition whatever.

Lady Anne Clifford, 1617

I read *Airmen and Aircraft* quite late into the night as a calming influence! All that is a kind of stabilizer to me now. First, of course, because Colonel L.[indberg] is '*le seul saint devant qui je brûle ma chandelle*' ['the only saint before whom I burn my candle'] (how incongruous that is!) – the last of the gods. He is unbelievable and it is exhilarating to believe in the unbelievable. Then because all that world is so tremendous, new and foreign to me, I could not get further from myself than in it.

It is so incomprehensible that it gives me a tremendous thrill to comprehend the smallest glimmer of it.

It is, though, amusing to read the requirements – and quite sad – for an aviator. They are comically so opposed to anything I have:

'Instantaneous co-ordination between his muscles and thoughts.

Good eyesight.

The ability to withstand great physical and mental strain.

Never become stampeded by unforeseen difficulties.

A complete lack of fear while in the air …'

Anne Morrow Lindbergh, 1928

6 April

(Maundy Thursday)

All leave stopped as from midnight tonight. I suppose as the most important moment in history is about to arrive, one should not mind small personal restrictions of freedom. But I do! I was going on leave next week.

Eve Williams, VAD, 1944

Today I noticed with surprise how my hair is frosting – all the dark sleekness seems to have gone. I realised, too, how much I have changed – grown older – in the last year. Hitler has done what illnesses and operations have failed to do, and in a short time too. I turned and studied my husband, and seemed to see suddenly how he also had aged. I mentally reviewed a few friends and my colleagues at the Centre. However happy we are in our work and efforts, all look older and as if we are feeling the strain. Yet we have had no hardships or the horrors of bombings. I thought of my own inner fears and dreads, of hurting thoughts that whirled and whirled inside my head and felt like broken glass, so brittle and sharp, of my anxiety for my boys. I thought of all the pictures that came before my eyes when storms blew or on cold raw nights. I pictured terror and fear in the big cities, and thought of how I'd lost my life-long love of the sea and rolling, tossing waves – it made me think of shipwrecked men in little boats, of men left to drown when their ships were attacked by submarines. If I have had my own private hells, so must others, and mine have often been the result of too vivid an imagination – some poor women had sons and husbands at Dunkirk and in the Navy at sea. No wonder we look older. Harry in Australia said my snaps that were taken last summer looked so different. He said, although we had not altered much in some ways, our eyes had such a 'different expression'.

Nella Last, 1941

Wrote & sewed. L. [her niece Louisa] & H. H. in a fuss for L. is saucy. Needs more freedom & she shall have it. A fine active girl shut up too much with quiddly old people. I know how she feels.

Louisa May Alcott, 1887

Breakfasted at the palace. Had I any occupation under the sun, I would prefer it to that of waiting upon this royal lady [Caroline of Brunswick]; but having none, I am glad of this one, unsuited as it is to my taste in every way.

Lady Charlotte Bury, 1815

7 April

My days pass so pleasantly and uneventfully but really with nothing accomplished. I have done so little writing this year. But writing is not now quite the pleasure it used to be. I am no longer so certain of a glorious future as I used to be – though I still feel that I may ultimately succeed. Perhaps I need some shattering experience to awaken and inspire me, or at least to give me some emotion to recollect in tranquillity. But how to get it? Sit there and wait for it or go out and seek it? Join the ATS [women's territorial army] and get it peeling potatoes and scrubbing floors? I don't know. I expect it will be sit and wait. Even the idea of falling violently in love again (which is my idea of an experience!) doesn't seem to be much help in the way of writing. I seem to have decided already the sort of novels I want to write. Perhaps the war will give me something. Perhaps the Home Front novel I am dabbling with now will get published. Perhaps …

But women are different from men in that they have so many small domestic things with which to occupy themselves. Dressmaking, washing and ironing, and everlasting tidying and sorting of reliques. I think I could spend my whole day doing such things, with just a little time for reading, and be quite happy. But it isn't really enough, soon I shall be discontented with myself, out will come the novel and after I've written a few pages I shall feel on top of the world again.

Barbara Pym, 1940

I am wretched. How true is that Russian expression – 'To have a cat in one's heart'. It is true there is a cat in my heart. It is always inexpressibly difficult for me to believe that a man whom I like should be capable of not loving me.

Pietro has not come …

Marie Bashkirtseff (aged 15), 1876

Breakfast with [Thomas Jefferson] Hogg – go to the British Museum – see all the fine things – ores, fossils, statues divine &c., &c. – return – read *Rokeby* – dine – go upstairs to talk with S.[helley] – read & finish *Rokeby*.

Mary Shelley 1815

8 April

It was a mixed dance of Fleet Air Arm and RAF, a very pukka affair … Hans and I did a wildly improvised eightsome and an even wilder schottische – my suspender-belt bust in the middle of it (front suspenders only, thank God – so I carried gamely on, like a plane on one engine).

About midnight I began to feel a bit tired so took two Benzedrine which kept me nicely sober in spite of gin, crème de menthe, rum and Algerian wine!

We got a lift home with the band, me sitting on the saxophonist's knee, and they dropped us off at Ness Bank. From there we strolled down to the Islands and found an old summerhouse which is only used at weekends.

Hans pulled me down onto the dusty floor. We could hear a clock with a lame tick beating irregularly from behind a locked door. Hans's face, pale in the moonlight, as if underwater, with eyes like worn grey stones – so beautiful!

'My God, Joanie, it's wonderful to be with you again,' he said. 'I'm so happy when I hold you in my arms like this.'

All the moodiness and harshness of earlier days had vanished and I realised that most of his bad temper had been simply because he was aching to go to bed with me again – how stupid of me not to have realised it earlier!

I took his seed in my mouth and drank it. It tasted strange like bitter almonds. Hans said it was the nicest thing anyone had ever done to him in his life.

Joan Wyndham, 1944

No! This is the solution. Don't say meekly and despondently, '*I* have nothing in common with *Colonel L.*,' but flippantly and arrogantly say, '*Colonel L.* has nothing in common with *me*!'

Anne Morrow Lindbergh, 1928

… I am obsessed with a foolish idea that I have no time to stop and write, or that I ought to be doing something serious. Even now, I pelt along feverishly, thinking half the time, but I must stop and take Grizzle out; I must get my American books in order; the truth is, I must try to set aside half an hour in some part of my day, and consecrate it to diary writing. Give it a name and a place, and then perhaps, such is the human mind, I shall come to think it a duty, and disregard other duties for it.

Virginia Woolf, 1925

Operated on one case of appendicitis with inadequate anesthesia, I had only a few meager vials of Novocain to give the soldier, but he never groaned once during the entire procedure. He even smiled to encourage me. Seeing that forced smile on his lips withered by exhaustion, I empathized with him immediately.

Even though his appendix had not ruptured, I was very sorry to find an infection in his abdomen. After a fruitless hour of searching for the cause, I could only treat him with antibiotics, insert a catheter, and close the wound. A whirl of emotions unsettled me: a physician's concern and a comrade's compassion and admiration for this soldier.

Brushing the stray hair back from his forehead, I wanted to say, 'If I cannot even heal people like you, this sorrow will not fade from my medical career.'

Dang Thuy Tram, South Vietnam, 1968

9 April

My 'blues' are mostly due to brain-fag and the irritation of countless, ceaseless little worries. I write and study the greater part of the day. Then I'm tired of it and want something wholly different for a change – a cheerful chat, a drive, or any little diversion like that, and in winter especially it is very rarely forthcoming. Consequently, thrown back on myself, on my wearied brain and tense nerves, I get limp and flabby and blue.

… Things will be better in summer – they always are. And I know they can't be mended by complaining. I never do complain anywhere but in this journal. I daresay it has saved me from some alarming outbreaks elsewhere.

It is really beginning to look a little like spring. There have been some thaws and there are a few bare spots. I have been cheering myself up by planning out and ordering some new spring toggery and in getting ready to think of a garden by and by … God intended people for his human flowers but left their choice of raiment to themselves. And a very poor choice some of them do make, it must be confessed! One is almost tempted to think it would have been better if he had let them *grow* their clothes like the roses and the tulips.

L. M. Montgomery, 1904

I have been cutting open a pair of my new shoes, lacing them up, and concealing the lacing with a row of little bows down the front. If the novel appearance attracts attention, and I am asked if such is the fashion, I shall say I have just got them from England.

Anne Langton, Canada, 1839

STARTED FROM HOME about 11 o'clock and traveled 8 miles and camped in an old house; night cold and frosty.

Amelia Stewart Knight, on the Oregon Trail, 1853

I believe my *oldest Friend* [her monthly cycle] is at last going to leave me, & that will probably make a Change in my Health, if not induce the Loss of it for ever. an odd thing has been observable on the Occasion, & merits Notice.

When I was a Girl of ten Years old perhaps, the Measles attacked & put me in some Danger – leaving at their Departure a small red swelling on my Cheek, which my Mother called the Measle-Mark, & it remained there till the *Change of life* [menarche; the first period] took it quite away. That very Mark is now upon this second *critical Change* returned – nor do I, nor did I *then* feel any other very *material* Alteration from the coming or going of Youth.

I am now exactly 50 Years old I think, & am possessed of great Corporal Strength blessed be God, with ability to endure Fatigue if necessary.

Hester Lynch Thrale Piozzi, 1791

10 April

I and the rest forcibly fed last night. Some of us very ill. I, personally, feel fairly fit.

Olive Walton, suffragette, Aylesbury Prison, 1912

At one o'clock in the afternoon, I took a walk to St. Helen's to meet my little darling again [her daughter Mary]; an unusual trepidation and anxiety seized me as I went …

Bye and bye Miss Jackson, the head teacher, came past, and the whole train of boarders; my anxiety confused my sight, and I could not recognize my Mary …

We were soon at Chapel, and I determined on entering, that I might enjoy the sight of my child another hour. Miss Jackson directed me to the Pew next Mary's. During service, Mary became very faint; poor child! I know thy feelings are harassed. One of the young ladies, apparently about 14, looked at me with a peculiar degree of compassion …

I took leave of Mary at the Chapel door, timid and spiritless, afraid of going to too great lengths; yet Mary's indisposition would well have justified me in going part of the way homeward with her. I have repented ever since that I had not; but I have not the spirit of a mouse.

Ellen Weeton, 1825

For a night and a day I worried about Sang's operation. I was so happy to see him sit up this afternoon. His face bore deep lines of pain and fatigue, but a smile slowly bloomed on his fragile lips when he saw me. His hands cupped over mine, a touch filled with warmth and trust.

Oh, you young, brave wounded soldier, my love for you is as vast as it is deep: it's physician's compassion for her patient; it's a sister's love for her sick brother (we're the same age, you and I); and in admiration, it is a love special beyond others.

Dang Thuy Tram, South Vietnam, 1968

These past few months, I have stopped thinking of my life in terms of a man, stopped holding up in front of me some secret myth of union. And accepted head-on my capacity to live well on my own …

Kathleen Collins, no year

11 April

Good Friday. So shut in by clouds, and everything so dark and depressing, today might have been modelled on the first Good Friday. My husband said, as it looked so unpromising, he would like to do a bit of gardening, and I rested and read until lunch. It was easily prepared, for I made the vegetable soup yesterday, and opened a wee tin of pilchards, heated them and served them on hot toast. They were only 5½d., and yet were a better meal than two cod cutlets costing at least 2s ...

I packed up tea, greengage jam in a little pot, brown bread and butter, a little cheese and a piece of cake each, and we set off after lunch ...

Nella Last, 1941

Morn & eve we have that tube stuck down our throats and noses. This even. 7 of our number, who are very ill, were moved either to the hospital or else released.

Olive Walton, suffragette, Aylesbury Prison, 1912

On Easter Saturday afternoon I went out on my own to see *Boogie Nights*. Got home, he doesn't call out, I go into his workroom, lights on but he's not there. The whole flat is empty but lit – unheard of. I stand in his room. On the table a few sheets of folded A4. Oh no. Another letter. Shaking hands, racing eyes. In the bin another folded sheet. I expect his key at any moment. Bundling up the papers I run downstairs and sit on the hotel fence under the streetlight and read them properly ...

I pour myself a gin and tonic. I sit at the table near the window. I feel intensely tiny, and flat. Like something run over by a car and left on the bitumen.

Halfway through the gin he comes in the front door, whistles gaily and calls out.

'Don't bother to be cheerful. I read the letter. You betrayed me. You report to her about me. You've been lying to me. Won't you ever stop lying?'

He sits down, white, facing me, takes my non-gin hand in both of his. He appears devastated. He doesn't defend himself. I can't even cry. I sit there and drink and between long silences I say things, horribly feeble, I can hardly push a thread of voice out of myself.

'You move out. Why should I be the one to move out? You find somewhere else to sleep. I'm sleeping in our bed. Go to her. Stay at her place. This is my home and you've ruined everything. I'm trying to think of someone I can stay with. I'm all smashed up inside. I need to be looked after but I can't think of anyone.'

'I'll look after you,' he says, in a small voice. 'I'll be glad to look after you, if you'll let me.'

I lie on the couch in a foetal position: 'I've got no dignity left.'

'I'm the one with no dignity,' he says.

Helen Garner, 1998

I could have occupied myself with race all these years. The climate was certainly ripe for me to have done so. I could have explored myself within the context of a young black life groping its way into maturity across the rising tide of racial affirmation. I could have done that. After all, I'm a colored lady. My father died a somewhat broken colored death. My mother ended it all at my birth. And my second mother practiced a far too studied gentility. But I didn't do that. No, I turned far inside, where there was only me and love to deal with. I turned far inside till I could measure every beat of love – love living on sex, love emptied of sex, love scratching and screaming in jealousy, love neglected until it turned itself into a life so solitary there was almost no way out. Instead of dealing with race I went in search of love … and what I found was a very hungry colored lady.

Kathleen Collins, no year

I suggested 'The Cheshire Cheese' for lunch, not bombed. We poked our way up an alley. No lunches on Sunday. We opened a sliding door and saw the sanded floor and wooden settles. It looked expensive and no place for me. But we found 'Ye Old Cock Tavern' in the Strand. Sort of 16th C. Inn. Old prints round the walls, a painting of Dickens, glass cupboards of old china and an ancient fireplace. Built in 1549. We had fish and potatoes and Xmas pudding. Not much of anything, but we enjoyed ourselves. 3/- [three shillings] each.

Walked through the devastated Temple ...

Winifred Vere Hodgson, 1943

12 April

Spring began suddenly this morning. R. and Burgo [her husband Ralph and their son] went out to hunt for plovers' eggs, and I wandered out later to join them. The warm air softly embraced me as I walked; this and the trees bursting with purple-brown buds combined together to thaw the frozen corners of my brain.

'Ah, here's the spring!' and then along comes Hitler's spring offensive, and a house built on the flimsiest cards, and not even believed in, comes toppling down. Yet I feel both more detached and more fatalistic than I did last year. Indeed no time has been harder to bear, it seems to me, than the Norwegian campaign. I contrive to live much more within our magic Ham Spray circle, R., Burgo, me, the cats, the garden. Yet there lies beneath my pleasure in all that – and it is real pleasure – an implicit acceptance of the fact that we probably possess it all only for a little time, that it is a life with no future, that we are sailing along in a boat which has a hole in the bottom.

Frances Partridge, 1941

Home for Easter. Had a holiday time spring-cleaning! Tried to cope with the mice. Spoke my mind to the cat. It is disgraceful that all the Cats have joined some sort of Pacifist Organization. To keep a cat in these awful days of food scarcity – and then have to catch the mice yourself ... it is a bit thick. I explained this to our animal.

Winifred Vere Hodgson, 1942

Hair cut – much too short. The woman asked me if I was still in school, which should have alerted me: she thought I was much younger than I am. Now I have an ideal haircut for a fourteen- or fifteen-year-old. Unfortunately I will be thirty-nine in two months.

Joyce Carol Oates, 1976

Had the mantua-maker. The ground covered with snow. Walked to T. Wilkinson's and sent for letter. The woman brought me one from William [her brother] and Mary [his wife]. It was a sharp, windy night. Thomas Wilkinson came with me to Barton, and questioned me like a catechizer all the way. Every question was like the snapping of a little thread about my heart – I was so full of thought of my half-read letter and other things. I was glad when he left me. Then I had time to look at the moon while I was thinking my own thoughts.

Dorothy Wordsworth, 1802

13 April

May ever as bright a sun and such warm, genial influences rest upon this day, a day ever precious to our hearts, for it is the anniversary of the birth of all our happiness, of a certain evening party at Mrs Norton's, of a certain talk in a window-seat which broke the spell of long separation and silence. O Father! for what a year of infinite joy do we thank thee with voiceless but overflowing hearts! Make us worthy to deserve another like unto it!

Fanny Longfellow, 1844

Nobody hurt, after all. How gay we were last night. Reaction after the dread of all the slaughter we thought those dreadful cannons were making such a noise in doing. Not even a battery the worse for wear.

Fort Sumter has been on fire. He [Union Army Major Anderson] has not yet silenced any of the guns, or so the aids – still with swords and red sashes by way of uniform – tell us. But the sound of those guns makes regular meals impossible …

Not by one word or look can we detect any change in the demeanour of these Negro servants. Lawrence sits at our door, as sleepy and as respectful and as profoundly indifferent. So are they all. They carry it too far. You could not tell that they even hear the awful noise that is going on in the bay, though it is dinning in their ears night and day. And people talk before them as if they were chairs or tables, and they make no sign. Are they stolidly stupid, or wiser, than we are, silent and strong, biding their time.

Mary Boykin Chesnut, Confederate States of America, 1861

Roosevelt is dead. A New Zealander, Sister Irvine, says she thinks it is more of a tragedy than if it was Churchill. Personally I would rather have Churchill alive than Roosevelt.

Still sitting in the mess and waiting …

Eve Williams, VAD, 1945

14 April

Here I am settled in my Plan of Economy, with three Daughters, three Maids and a Man: my Lover is leaving England, and I wait here patiently for my own Release: living if possible on 1000£ Pr. Ann [per annum] that I may save Money enough to pay my Debts, and fly to the Man of my heart …

My daughter does not I suppose much delight in *this* Scheme, but why should I lead a Life of delighting her who would not lose a shilling of Interest, or an Ounce of Pleasure to save my Life from perishing? when I was near losing my Existence from the Contention of my Mind, and was seized with a temporary Delirium in Argylle Street, She and her two eldest Sisters laughed at my distress, and observed to dear Fanny Burney – that it *was monstrous droll: She* could scarcely suppress her indignation.

Hester Lynch Thrale Piozzi, 1783

Quite cold. Little ewes crying with cold feet. Sixteen wagons all getting ready to cross the creek. Hurrah and bustle to get breakfast over. Feed the cattle. Hurrah boys, all ready, we will be the first to cross the creek this morning. Gee up Tip and Tyler and away we go the sun just rising. Evening – We have traveled 24 miles today and are about to camp in a large prairie without wood. Cold and chilly; east wind. The men have pitched the tent and are hunting something to make a fire to get supper. I have the sick headache and must leave the boys to get it themselves the best they can.

Amelia Stewart Knight, 1853

When I took off my mourning, the watchers watched me very exactly, 'but they whose hands were mightiest have found nothing': so I shall leave the town, I hope, in a good disposition towards me, though I am sullen enough with the town for fancying me such an amorous idiot that I am dying to enjoy every filthy fellow. God knows how distant such dispositions are from the heart and disposition of H.L.T.

Hester Lynch Thrale Piozzi, 1782

15 April

I have always thought it would be unwholesome for me to attempt to write a diary. I'm sure it will make me think my life drab and strain after sensation to make copy for my autobiography. I shall become morbidly self-conscious and a valetudinarian about my career, so I shall try not to be un-introspective, and confine myself to events and diagnoses of other people. In any case I am entirely devoid of the gift of sincerity, and could never write as though I were really convinced no other eye would ever see what I wrote. I am incurably self-conscious. This impromptu resolution sprung from an absurd compact I made with Duff Cooper that we would both begin a diary at the same moment, and bind each other over to keep it up. He has given me this lovely book – but instead of inspiring, it paralyses me and makes me feel my life will not be nearly sufficiently purple.

Lady Cynthia Asquith, 1915

Very sad news was received this morning of the murder of the President [Lincoln] the city is in deep mourning we had a meeting of the association.

Emilie Davis, 1865

When we were in the woods before Gowbarrow park we saw a few daffodils close to the water side. We fancied that the lake had floated the seeds ashore and that the little colony had so sprung up. But as we went along there were more and yet more and at last under the boughs of the trees, we saw that there was a long belt of them along the shore, about the breadth of a country turnpike road. I never saw daffodils so beautiful. They grew among the mossy stones about and about them, some rested their heads upon those stones as on a pillow for weariness and the rest tossed and reeled and danced and seemed as if they verily laughed with the wind that blew upon them over the lake, they looked so gay ever dancing ever changing.

Dorothy Wordsworth, 1802

A few months ago I heard that Mr Muriel, our doctor, had said that both Evelyn and I had got a monomania and that was the love of men! It seems a dreadful thing for him to have said, and still more so as I am certain he was not mistaken, though I think Evelyn's monomania is restricted to curates only! Sometimes I feel afraid when I think how desperately, how awfully, wicked I am ...

Margaret Fountaine (aged 20), 1883

16 April

I have been thinking that I am a shirker. I have dodged publicity, hated write-ups and all that splutter. Well, that's all selfish conceit that embarrassed me. I have been forgetting Canada and forgetting women painters. It's them I ought to be upholding, nothing to do with puny me at all. Perhaps what brought it home was the last two lines of a crit in a Toronto paper: 'Miss Carr is essentially Canadian, not by reason of her subject matter alone, but by her approach to it,' I am glad of that. I am also glad that I am showing these men that women can hold up their end. The men resent a woman getting any honour in what they consider is essentially their field. Men painters mostly despise women painters. So I have decided to stop squirming, to throw any honour in with Canada and women. It is wonderful to feel the grandness of Canada in the raw, not because she is Canada but because she's something sublime that you were born into, some great rugged power that you are part of.

Emily Carr, 1937

The 16th my Lord & I had much talk about these Businesses, he urging me still to go to London to sign & seal [the surrender of her ancestral lands], but I told him that my promise was so far passed to my Mother & to all the world that I would never do it, whatever became of me and mine.

Lady Anne Clifford, 1617

The doct. begins to feed us three times a day. It is a shame. We have fine tussles before they get us tied into the chair! Feel very low-spirited today.

Olive Walton, suffragette, 1912

17 April

Decided to Postpone the fair very fine Day everyone seems to Partake of the solemnity of the times.

Emilie Davis, 1865

Dear Kitty,

Do you think Daddy and Mummy would approve of my sitting and kissing a boy on a divan – a boy of seventeen and a half and a girl of just under fifteen?...

... What would my girlfriends say about it if they knew that I lay in Peter's arms, my heart against his chest, my head on his shoulder and with his head against mine!

Oh, Anne, how scandalous! But honestly, I don't think it is; we are shut up here, shut away from the world, in fear and anxiety, especially just lately. Why, then, should we who love each other remain apart? Why should we wait until we have reached a suitable age? Why should we bother?

Anne Frank, 1944

Said to [Lord Melbourne] how dreadful it was to have the prospect of torment for many years by Mama's living here, and he said it was dreadful, but what could be done? She had declared (some time ago) I said she would never leave me as long as I was unmarried. 'Well then, there's that way of settling it,' he said. That was a schocking [sic] alternative, I said.

Queen Victoria, 1839

[Actress] Miss Ellen Terry's complexion is made of such an expensive enamel that she can only afford to wash her face once a fortnight, and removes smuts in the meantime with a wet sponge. The Crompton Potters know someone who knows her well.

Beatrix Potter (aged 16), 1883

… we have got our privileges back. What a victory! How lovely bread is.

Olive Walton, suffragette, 1912

18 April

Hu [her husband] has told Dr Westerleigh of my relation with Barny [her lover] … Hu has now seen a nerve specialist, who said that worry over it had contributed to his loss of resistance. Hu told him he was sure I wouldn't give the man up, even if I knew it had a bad effect on him. Of course the wretched man can only give a partial account, because he fancies I love him – God knows why – he daren't confess to himself that only pity has prevented me from breaking away from him finally, long ago. So because I am sorry for him, and because he thinks I have wronged him, I must leave the cottage and the hills and my love, and return to domestic slavery to a bad-tempered invalid who will do nothing but shout and bluster at me. But unless and until my relation with Barny comes of itself to an end, I shall not give him up. I've thought and thought, tried to look at it all in a dozen ways. But the simple cruel fact remains that I can't give up a man I love for a man I hate.

Loran Hurnscot, 1924

Home again to Paris in the ivory-colored room, sobered by a return to wifely duties and equally dutiful letters and at the same time stirred by Hugh's [her husband] augmented fervor and devotion. But as he says, we did not need to be separated to be certain of what we mean to each other. He did confess that he was distressed by his unmended socks, and that he could not find his pipe or his slippers or his cuff links, and that a wife, from a practical point of view, was a very necessary object.

Anaïs Nin, 1925

19 April

I regret that entries about T. & I are so skimpy. When things are going well & they mostly do, I don't think of writing. There is a very prosaic peace, and a very steady intense passion. She is so beautiful to me. Yesterday, just because her dark skin looks so ravishing in cobalt blue, I put on sheets of that color – & there she lay in a bed of cobalt blue, her dark eyes shining, her skin glowing, her beauty absolute. So absolute I sometimes feel my love is worship. We kiss & kiss some more, and somehow the distances have not destroyed any of our closeness while making us more conscious of its preciousness.

Alice Walker, 1993

At 8.30am I went downstairs from our bedroom to the loo, opened the door, and saw two bright eyes staring at me from the lavatory pan. It was a sweet little baby rabbit sitting at the bottom of the pan, with its nose and ears just above the water line! I was shaken to the core! I shut the door and went back upstairs to Ted [her husband], asking him seriously, 'Do you think I could possibly have DTs?' … I shall never go to the lavatory again without remembering it sitting there. The dramas of the countryside are endless.

Barbara Castle, 1975

This was a day that made me reflect very seriously as I accomplished my seventeenth year and I must own I think it prodigiously old as it is not far from twenty. This made me spend a very dull birthday as at the bottom of my heart I was very sad to think I was beginning the eighteenth year of my life and that till now I had wasted my time in a very foolish way but I took resolutions to begin to be more applied to things that will be of more use to me in future and to enjoy life as it is very short. I was quite Philosophical and mean to remain it.

Betsey Wynne Fremantle, 1795

'What can minister to a mind diseased?' Why, sunshine. The sun has been shining for a week, the snow is almost gone and lo, life is a friend once more – not the shrewish old hag who has been scolding and rating me all winter but a young laughing comrade ready to run hand in hand with me in pursuit of worthwhile.

Besides, I've been gardening a bit and nobody can do *that* and be morbid. To potter with green growing things watching each day to see the dear new sprouts come up, is to take a hand in creation. How we all love to create! It is a little bit of the divine in us.

L. M. Montgomery, 1904

20 April

Easter Day & the Twentieth of April being Sunday, I invited my new Tenant, his Wife and His Two Children to dinner: and the first Time I ever saw her; she was full of Care, about her Lying In, But I bid her Leave those things to God, For I saw Death in her Face; that night she Rode home to Winch[combe?], And died the Next Day, being Easter Monday.

Elizabeth Freke, 1712

Happiness is to have a little string onto which things will attach themselves. For example, going to my dressmaker, or rather thinking of a dress I could get her to make, and imagining it made – that is the string, which as if it dipped loosely into a wave of treasure brings up pearls sticking to it. And my days are likely to be strung with them. I like this London life in early summer – the street sauntering and square haunting, and then if my books were to be a success, if we could begin building at Monks [House], and put up wireless for Nelly [the Woolfs' cook], and if – if – if. But really what I should like would be to have three pounds to buy a pair of rubber soled boots, and go for country walks on Sundays.

Virginia Woolf, 1925

The 20th being Easter day my Lord & I and Tom Glenham and most of the Folk received Communion from Mr Ran, yet in the afternoon my Lord & I had a great falling out, Matthew [a servant] continuing still to do me all the ill offices he could with my Lord. All this time I wore my white Satin Gown and my white Waistcoat.

Lady Anne Clifford, 1617

I'm sitting on my bed, with a sunburnt face and aching knees [after an all-day bike ride]. Apart from that, everything is normal ... except my state of mind. I need cheering up a little. You've got to admit it's a little upsetting when you enter a small village, and you see a sign: JEWS ARE NOT WELCOME HERE. There was a little café in Wilnis that we walked into on the first day. Nice people. They had a sign too but they kept it hidden in a cupboard ... They'd refused to hang it up. We saw similar signs in other villages. Oh well.

Edith Velmans, Holland, 1941

21 April

Ted [her husband] and I were sitting by the telly listening to the six o'clock news when there suddenly was Enoch Powell, white-faced and tight-lipped, delivering his Wolverhampton speech on immigration. As we listened to his relentless words – 'I see the Tiber running with blood' – intense depression gripped us. I knew he had taken the lid off Pandora's box and that race relations in Britain would never be the same again. This is certainly a historic turning point, but in which direction? I believe he has helped to make a race war, not only in Britain but perhaps in the world, inevitable.

Barbara Castle, 1968

I was[h?] today and haul load of wood And then chop wood didn't go out to the traps. And when I come in and build the fire knight started to cruel with me [sic]. I cann't count the times he started to cruel at me every time he say something against me. He says Black Jack [her abusive ex-husband] was good man and was right in everything and was right to treat me mean. And saying I wasn't good to him he never stop and think how much it's hard for women to take four mans place [the three other expedition members had left to seek help], to wood work and to hunt for some things to eat for him and do waiting to his bed and take the shut [shit?] out for him. And he menitions [sic] my children, and saying no wonder your children die you never take good care of them he just tear me pieces when he menition my Children that I lost. This is the worst life I ever live in this world. Thought it is hard enough for me to wood work and trying my best in everything and when I come home to rest here a man talk against me saying all kinds of words against me then what could i do. When I can't get meat he says I wasn't trying to save he. And he say he was going to write to Nome people to fix me up then what could I do. Though I was hungry myself for meat and trying my best we both have no witness. If knight happen to die what will I do here in this island all alone he is lying in his bed since feburay 9th and now April 21st he is looks very skiny. And its longtime yet we might see ship come. Well God knows everything.

If I be known dead, I want my sister Rita to take Bennett my son, for her own son and look after every things for Bennett she is the only one that I wish she take my son don't let his fathar [sic] Black Jack take him, if Rita my sister live. then I be clear.

Ada Blackjack, 1923

I feel weaklier every day, and my soul also is sore vexed – Oh how long! I put myself in an omnibus, being unable to walk, and was carried to Islington and back again. What a good shilling's-worth of exercise!

Jane Carlyle, 1856

Cloudy and very dark the funeral Prossion [sic] Pass though tomorrow I have not been out to day I am tired of the St. Vincent was up this evening he is so full of business.

Emilie Davis, 1865

… The beginning of a film [*Sense and Sensibility*] is like watching a huge newborn centipede trying to get up on its hundred legs and go for a walk. Keeps tripping up until it's worked out how to coordinate. Any film will take two to three weeks to get into its stride – some never do. I think the key is good communications.

A care package arrived from Columbia Pictures: dressing gown, slippers, bath-pillow, blanket. A care package. Half expected a Zimmer frame (one of those balancing frames you get given when you're old and wobbly). Very kind. Caring, even.

Roast beef and a square of chocolate for lunch. Very yang. I keep tripping over my frock and swearing.

Emma Thompson, 1995

22 April

… Yesterday was wiped out by the cramps and drug-stitched stupor of my first day of the curse, as it is so aptly called. Do animals in heat bleed, feel pain? Or is it that sedentary bluestockinged ladies have come so far from the beast-state that they must pay by hurt, as the little mermaid had to pay when she traded her fish tail for a girl's white legs?

Sylvia Plath, 1958

My nature is like a strong wilful ship; unless I keep it occupied it gives me endless trouble. Lately I have allowed it free play and must have a struggle with it, before I can again have peace. Can I begin this struggle bravely and instantly? What is the use of drifting, unless indeed I half desire to be where the current of my own feeling will bring me? And there is the trouble. My own mind is not made up. I have been meditating over the question [a possible proposal from Joseph Chamberlain] for five months, have done little else but think about it; now I am no nearer solving it … Looking back on the whole affair, I confess to myself that my action and thought have been wanting in dignity and nicety of feeling. I have *chattered* about feelings which should be kept within the holy of holies.

The only excuse has been the extraordinary nature of the man and his method and the interest which public position lends his personality. But now I can make a fresh start; force my thoughts from their dwelling-place of the last five months, and devote myself vigorously to my duties and to the nature and true development of my own nature,

Amen …

Beatrice Webb, 1884

Quite a tolerable morning in Avonmouth. I was back in Bristol at lunchtime and bought a utility brassière which makes me look a *very fine shape*, not at all like 'this English lady'.

Barbara Pym, 1943

23 April

The 23rd, Lord Clanricarde came hither. After they were gone my Lord & I and Tom Glenham went to Mr Lune's House to see the fine Flowers that is in the Garden. This night my Lord should have lain with me but he & I fell out about matters.

Lady Anne Clifford, 1617

Evening – It has been raining hard all day; everything is wet and muddy. One of the oxen missing; the boys have been hunting him all day. Dreary times, wet and muddy, and crowded in the tent, cold and wet and uncomfortable in the wagon. No place for the poor children. I have been busy cooking, roasting coffee, etc. today, and have come into the wagon to write this and make our bed.

Amelia Stewart Knight, 1953

My fellow blood transfusers talk about the prison camps. That really seems to have got under the skin of even Carradale [site of her Scottish farm]. I keep on saying that when some of us talked about concentration camps three years before the war the people who talk about them now wouldn't listen. One just can't quite imagine the quality of hell it must be in Berlin. I suppose Hitler and Goering will either get themselves killed or commit suicide. I hope they won't be martyrs anyhow!

Naomi Mitchison, 1945

The coffin and hearse was beautiful this morning went down to see the President but could not for the crowd.

Emilie Davis, 1865

24 April

I got to see him after waiting two hours and a half it was certainly a sight worth seeing very Pleasant.

Emilie Davis, 1865

The 24th my Lord went to Sen'oak [Sevenoaks] again. After supper we played at Burley Break upon the Green. This night my Lord came to lie in my chamber.

Lady Anne Clifford, 1617

I get stimulation out of even the dullest people. Being amusing for them is like practicing the piano when you are sure no one is listening. You can be freer, attempt bolder things, and often succeed.

Patricia Highsmith, 1942

Birds are nesting – each tree is a noisy green musical box. Today I bump into the beauty with the Peke a second time. I admire the Peke. She says he is called Michelin, because of his rolls of loose skin. Walking on the

Common with another person is rather like having one's hair washed, or sitting behind a taxi driver: there is no eye contact, so people tend to talk about themselves more than they would normally.

Jilly Cooper, 1974

25 April

I was very indifferent all day and safe delivered of a little girl soon after five o'clock.

Betsey Wynne Fremantle, 1804

The reading in which I find most relaxation is religion. It seems to rest my brain and refresh my spirit … And yet I cannot bring my faith and my practice into line with the Christian religion. I cannot acquiesce in the claims of Christianity. I should love to worship with others and to feel the support and the charm of a regular and definite ritual. But directly I hear the words in which Christians clothe their religious aspirations my intellectual sincerity takes alarm. I am not even attracted by their God, whether in the Jewish or the Christian version.

Beatrice Webb, 1902

I am one day up and down another. Have been a long way down today, and now my head feels empty and I am nothing in particular. Will things never settle? Is this being grown-up? If I could have seen my mind as it is now, when I left Dalguise [House, their Scottish holiday home] I should not have known it.

Beatrix Potter (aged 16), 1883

26 April

The day I Left my house my daughter Came Rudely In to my Chamber and Told me I Owed her husband Fifty pounds and Twenty pounds (when he now owes me Above Five thousand pound) and they had of me here above three hundred ... In Which Time their youngest son lay two month dying of the small Pox, Who infected Four of my servants of Which one of Them died. I will not say more than from such another Time Good Lord deliver me & make thankful to God.

Elizabeth Freke, 1712

St Andrew's by the Wardrobe has gone – but that was some time ago. I wonder if they will reroof them [London's churches] after the war – if there is anything left of the walls and any of us left to do the work! It is amazing, however, how well our nerves keep on the whole. If we are bombed then they go a bit; but if we survive the night, we come up bright and smiling the next morning, very keen to exchange notes on the adventures of the night.

Winifred Vere Hodgson, 1941

... Moira told me an amusing story of Lady Wolverton. The latter, thinking the time had come to economise, got into a bus. She sat beside a woman who kept loudly sniffing and she asked her aggressively if she hadn't got a handkerchief. The woman replied: 'Yes, but I never lends it in a bus.'

Lady Cynthia Asquith, 1917

Sidney Webb, the socialist, spent Sunday here ...

I am not sure as to the future of that man. His tiny tadpole body, unhealthy skin, lack of manner, Cockney pronunciation, poverty, are all against him. He has the conceit of a man who has raised himself out of the most insignificant surroundings into a position of power – how much power no one quite knows … A London retail tradesman with the aims of a Napoleon! A queer monstrosity to be justified only by success. And above all a loop-hole into the socialist party; one of the small body of men with whom I may sooner or later throw in my lot for good and all.

Beatrice Webb, 1890

27 April

St Joe. Here we are at last, safe and sound. We expect to remain here several days, laying in supplies for the trip and waiting our turn to be ferried across the river. As far as the eye can reach, so great is the emigration, you see nothing but wagons. This town presents a striking appearance – a vast army on wheels – crowds of men, women and lots of children and last but not least the cattle and horses upon which our lives depend.

Sallie Hester (aged 14), 1849

Yes, that'll be nice – to sit out of doors and drink, in some French town, away from all this. Coronation impending. But on the 7th we're off.

Virginia Woolf, 1937

I saw my darling Lorenzo [Henry Harvey] today. Just a fleeting glimpse of his profile – but so divine. His hair is more auburn, and his skin lovely, pale brown with a faint flush.

Barbara Pym (aged 19), 1933

The station dance. Great excitement, everyone hoping to get off with a pilot. Wings, of course, are the thing; if you don't have wings you don't stand a chance, but the men turned out to be dreadful, all mechanics and technical chaps. The hut was small and crowded, boiling hot and smelling of Brylcreem and sweat.

We had a bet in our hut to see who could get the most – I got five, each one worse that the last, and a date for tea at the Regal, which I ought to keep but can't, because our hut is being kept in over the ST [sanitary towel] scandal.

Samantha is laid up with a sprained ankle. She fell over a slagheap running away from a mechanic after the dance last night.

Joan Wyndham (aged 19), 1941

28 April

——

Was our Late gracious Queen [Elizabeth I] buried at Westminster, in that sort as became so great a prince.

Lady Margaret Hoby, 1603

The 28th was the first time the Child put on a pair of Whalebone Bodice. My Lord went a hunting the Fox and the Hare.

Lady Anne Clifford, 1617

Once more there is a question which gives me no peace: 'Is it right? Is it right that I should have yielded so soon, that I am so ardent, just as ardent and eager as Peter himself? May I, a girl, let myself go to this extent?' There is but one answer 'I have longed so much and for so long – I am so lonely – and now I have found consolation' …

Am I 14? Am I really still a silly little schoolgirl? Am I really so inexperienced about everything? I have more experience than most; I have been through things that hardly anyone of my age has undergone. I am afraid of myself, I am afraid that in my longing I am giving myself too quickly. How, later on, can it ever go right with other boys? Oh, it is so difficult, always battling with one's heart and reason; in its own time, each will speak, but do I know for certain that I have chosen the right time?

Anne Frank, 1944

I attended the sectional meetings and dinner of the British Academy, of which I have been elected the first woman member ... Mother would have been more gratified ... Her daughter the perfected Blue Stocking! and her own lifelong absorption in book-learning amply justified – her ambition brought to fruition in one of the ten children whom she had, at the cost of her own career as an intellectual, brought into the world. Bless her.

Beatrice Webb, 1932

I realize now how deeply I needed this physical rest. I have buried away my puritan detestation of idleness. I am enjoying this most pleasant medicine prescribed to me, enjoying the long, sunny, unfilled hours, the dozing in the early afternoon. And a joyous accent added to my lady's existence: I bought, after long months of privation – no, years – in one day, a black silk coat, a lavender hat, a handbag, a small umbrella and perfume!

Anaïs Nin, 1925

Mother is not well today & spoke to me, quite oddly about my Journal. It is absurd to keep one, it is never anything but a tissue of lies! After the painful talk was over, I could not help thinking that a Journal must always be true in one sense. If not true to facts & if the character appears in it gracefully draped, the untruth & the drapery reveal the starkness stalking beneath. I sent a message to Edwd – [a fugitive slave] tonight through one of the Committee of Safety, for I dared no longer delay – bidding him to go to Canada as soon as possible – for he was watched.

Caroline Healey Dall, 1851

29 April

Oh ever to be remembered day. Lorenzo spoke to me! I saw him in the Bod[leian Library] and felt desperately thrilled about him so that I trembled and shivered and went sick. As I went out Lorenzo caught me up – and said 'Well, and has Sandra finished her epic poem?' – or words to that effect … I was almost completely tongue-tied.

Barbara Pym (aged 19), 1933

The Embassy gave an Easter supper, which took place after mass, two hours after midnight … I did not produce at all the effect I wished. Laferrière [her dressmaker] came late, and I was obliged to put on a dress that fitted badly. I had to improvise a chemisette; it was a low-necked dress, and had to be altered. On my dress depended my temper; on my temper, my manner and the expression of my face – everything, in fact.

Marie Bashkirtseff (aged 17), 1878

Cool and pleasant; saw the first Indians today. [Her daughters] Lucy and Almira afraid and run into the wagon to hide. Done some washing and sewing.

Amelia Stewart Knight, 1853

Since I last wrote, I have led rather a remarkable life; so surprisingly followed after by the great, and others, in my Newgate concerns; in short, the prison and myself are becoming quite a show, which is a very serious thing in many points. I believe, that it certainly does much good to the cause, in spreading among all ranks of society, a considerable interest in the subject; also a knowledge of Friends [Quakers] and their principles; but my own standing appears critical in many ways … Lady Harcourt, who most kindly interested herself in the subject, took me with her to the Mansion House, rather against my will, to meet many of the Royal Family at the examination of some large school. Amongst the rest, the

Queen was there. Much public respect was paid to me, and except the Royal Family themselves, I think that no one received the same attention. There was quite a buzz when I went into the Egyptian Hall, where one to two thousand people were collected …

Elizabeth Fry, 1818

30 April

I was very happy thinking about Lorenzo and the funny way he talked and everything. I had that kind of gnawing at the vitals sick feeling if that describes it at all – that is so marvellous … I couldn't eat any supper – but drank a glass of water – amazing what love will do!

Barbara Pym (aged 19), 1933

Having waited for 2 or 3 days for fair weather, that I might walk over to Parr Hall to see my little daughter once more before I went to London, I set out this day at 10 o'clock. The morning was fair and bright, but the wind blew quite a hard gale, and I had great difficulty in forcing my way through it, for it blew right in my face. I had for some weeks been rather weak and indisposed, and, on setting out today, almost despaired of accomplishing so long a journey on foot; but a mother's heart can do great things … I staid with her until 4 o'clock, and then returned home, less fatigued with a 12 or 14 mile walk than might have been expected.

Ellen Weeton, 1824

We're going to tour the neighborhood that Paul Morand calls 'the ghetto' and the Americans call 'the East Side.' As we walk through the teeming streets, I feel transported to Central Europe … Buyers and sellers bargain vehemently; much of the merchandise is marked down, but it seems to be of good quality. Here and there, there's a dazzling display window with long satin or taffeta evening dresses in vivid colors, shimmering with sequins – rich dresses for poor women. I imagine that singers and hostesses at second-rate nightclubs come here to shop. In the more modest shop windows there's more genuine merriment: hand-painted ties decorated with horses and naked women, and I would like to know who buys those flowered underpants or those briefs with purple stripes.

Simone de Beauvoir, New York, 1947

The true luxury of early success is that it allows you to be conceptual about the rest of your career ...

I retreat to Quogue [on Long Island] to think about it all. The power life roars along with all the real thoughts, fears buried or put indefinitely on hold. I want more time to contemplate, but I can't seem to live any other way. I feel panic when I stop. I am an action junkie. My best hope for peace is when I am with G. [her son].

At the PEN dinner Vartan Gregorian grabbed Harry [her husband Harold Evans] and urged him to come teach at Brown. 'It's so wonderful,' he said to Harry, 'being safe with my books in academia instead of watching ladies not eat their lunch at Le Cirque.' I am sure he's right, but journalists like us find it hard to be out of the arena.

Tina Brown, 1989

May

'I am working at the laboratory all day long, it is all I can do; I am better off there than anywhere else.'

Marie Curie, 1906

1 May

I slept late, didn't remember it was May Day till 10 in the morning, then dashed up to the roof with the red flag [for international socialism], to find the halyard broken. Got the ladder from the stables, Rosemary [her assistant] climbed it and with great difficulty caught the end as the wind blew it – and a plane came down to practise on us just as she was doing it. Got the flag fixed …

Naomi Mitchison, 1941

It is so good to see the sky again blue: sunshine after two weeks of cold and rain. It was like a heavy blanket and weighed you down. Now that *blue* – I am walking in it! Blue and white clouds. It is too good to believe – I have to keep looking at it from sheer joy. I feel as though I were wearing it.

Anne Morrow Lindbergh, 1928

Upon the 1st I cut the Child's strings from her Coats and made her use tags alone, so she had 2 or 3 falls at first but had no hurt with them.

Lady Anne Clifford, 1617

Of course, *the* American woman is a myth. In America there are about eighty million individuals of the female sex … Yet since everyone in America talks about it, especially men, there must be some truth to this myth. I'm often aware of referring to it myself.

… I'd imagined that women here would surprise me with their independence. 'American woman,' 'free woman' – the words seemed synonymous. At first, as I've said, their dress astonished me with its fragrantly feminine, almost sexual character. In the women's magazines here, more than in the French variety, I've read long articles on the art of husband hunting and catching a man. I've seen that college girls have little concern for anything but men and that the unmarried woman is much less respected here than in Europe.

... Their demanding, defiant attitude is proof that American women are not really on equal flooring with men. They feel contemptuous often with good reason, of the servility of Frenchwomen, who are always ready to smile at their men and humor them. But the tension with which they twist around on their pedestal conceals a similar weakness. In both cases, through docility or arbitrary demand, man remains king: he is essential and woman is inessential. The praying mantis is the antithesis of the harem girl, but both depend on the male.

... The result is that relations between the sexes are a struggle. One thing that was immediately obvious to me when I came to America is that men and women don't like each other. Women can barely survive, except in relation to men.

Simone de Beauvoir, New York, 1947

I have now appointed three days a week to attend at the counting-house.

If an angel from heaven had told me twenty years ago that the man I knew by the name of *Dictionary Johnson* should one day become partner with me in a great trade, and that we should jointly or separately sign notes, drafts, &c., for three or four thousand pounds of a morning, how unlikely it would have seemed ever to happen! Unlikely is no word tho', – it would have seemed *incredible*, neither of us then benign worth a groat, God knows, and both as immeasurably removed from commerce as birth, literature and inclination could get us ...

Hester Lynch Thrale Piozzi, 1781

2 May

Pleasant evening; have been cooking, and packing things away for an early start in the morning. Threw away several jars, some wooden buckets, and all our pickles. Too unhandy to carry. Indians came to our camp every day, begging money and something to eat. Children are getting used to them.

Amelia Stewart Knight, 1853

The 2nd, the Child put on her first coat that was laced with Lace, being
of Red Bays [baize].

Lady Anne Clifford, 1617

They've announced on Hamburg radio that Hitler is dead! Berlin has
surrendered to the Russians.

As soon as we came off watch we all piled into cars and set out for the
nearest pub, with Oscar, Pandora and I crammed into Dizzy's car.

When we had drunk so many toasts that we could hardly stand,
someone took over the piano and we sang till closing time. The whole
pub turned out to shout goodbye. The ride home was a nightmare – we
went tearing through the night, whooping and singing, with screeching
brakes and screaming horns. Then three times round the WAAF Mess,
howling like wolves – according to custom – and when we reached the
RAF Mess we found it practically ablaze.

Joan Wyndham, 1945

We have a week of vacation. Mother takes me aside.

'My child. There's something I have to tell you.'

I answer, 'Mother, if you have something to tell me, do it quickly. Tell
me.'

But her words are like a death sentence.

'I'm afraid you may have been to school for the last time.'

My eyes go wide. I look up at her. 'How can you say something like
that? These days you can't live without an education. Even a peasant
needs knowledge to ensure good harvests and to farm well.'

Mother insists. 'Your brothers and you add up to three children to be
sent to school. Your father is the only one earning money, and it's not
enough.'

I'm frightened. 'Does this mean I have to come home to work?'

'Yes.'

'And my two brothers?'

'Your two brothers will carry on with their studies.'

I protest. 'Why can boys study and not girls?'

Her smile is tired. 'You're still little. When you grow up you'll understand.'

No more money for school this year. I'm back in the house and I work the land in order to pay for my brothers' education. When I think of the happy times at school, I can almost imagine myself there. How I want to study! But my family can't afford it.

I want to go to school, Mother. I don't want to work at home. How wonderful it would be if I could stay at school forever!

Ma Yan (aged 13), 2001

3 May

Have I told you that Moffi has disappeared? Simply vanished – we haven't seen a sign of him since Thursday of last week. I expect he's already in the cats' heaven, while some animal lover is enjoying a succulent meal from him. Perhaps some little girl will be given a fur cap out of his skin. Peter is very sad about it.

Since Saturday we've changed over, and have lunch at half-past eleven in the mornings, so we have to last out with one cupful of porridge; this saves us a meal. Vegetables are still very difficult to obtain: we had rotten boiled lettuce this afternoon. Ordinary lettuce, spinach and boiled lettuce, there's nothing else. With these we eat rotten boiled potatoes, so it's a delicious combination!

… I have often been downcast, but never in despair; I regard our hiding as a dangerous adventure, romantic and interesting at the same time. In my diary I treat all the privations as amusing …

… I am young and I possess many buried qualities; I am young and strong and am living a great adventure; I am still in the midst of it and can't grumble the whole day long. I have been given a lot, a happy nature, a great deal of cheerfulness and strength. Every day I feel that I am developing inwardly, that the liberation is drawing nearer and how beautiful nature is, how good the people are about me, how interesting this adventure is. Why, then should I be in despair?

Anne Frank, 1944

After dinner I was writing to Aunt Charles, and on running upstairs for more paper, I was startled to find myself spitting blood. It proved to be only from the throat, but I, for half an hour, took it entirely as a signal of death, and shall, I believe, often look back with satisfaction to the solemn quietness which I felt at that time. I finished Aunt Charles's note, and then lay down alone, and felt altogether rather idle about life, and much disposed to be thankful, or at any rate entirely submissive, whatever might be the result.

Caroline Fox, 1843

4 May

Complications are setting in; the illness is affecting the brain. I'm worried and pray for the little darling [her sister Rosalie] whom I love so much. I remember how enthralled I was when they first took me over to the blue cradle to show her to me. She was so delicate, so tiny that I couldn't believe it was a real baby. It was the first one I'd ever seen ... I wasn't like this with the others. I do love them, but with nothing like the feelings I have for this little girl who suffers so much now without my being able to do anything.

Henriette Dessaulles (aged 16), 1877

A night of terror, and there are few windows left in the district! – or roof tiles! Land mines, incendiaries and explosives were dropped, and we cowered thankfully under our indoor shelter. I've been so dreadfully sick all day, and I'm sure it's sheer fright, for last night I really thought our end had come. By the time the boys come I'll be able to laugh about it. Now I've a sick shadow over me as I look at my loved little house that will never be the same again ... I'll never forget my odd sensations, one a calm acceptance of 'the end', the other a feeling of regret that I'd not opened a tin of fruit salad for tea – and now it was too late! ...

The birds sang so sweetly at dawning today – just as the all-clear sounded and people timidly went round looking at the damage. I wonder if they will sing as sweetly in the morning – and if we all will hear them. Little sparrows had died as they crouched – from blast possibly. It looked as if they had bent their little heads in prayer, and had died as they did so. I held one in my hand: 'He counteth the sparrow and not one falleth that He does not see' – Poles, Czechs, Greeks, all sparrows.

Nella Last, 1941

War is almost over. Mussolini dead, Hitler possibly dead and Berlin in Russian hands.

Eve Williams, VAD, Brisbane, 1945

5 May

Report that war was over. Then report that it was not.

Eve Williams, VAD, 1945

I got to M. [Massa] by ½ past six. He sat on my lap again & we'd another nice talk. I've so much to say about Miss O. [her employer] & my work & going out of errands & that. It was wet & windy, but I don't care for that to get out. Massa took me down to look at the empty kitchen below, & ask'd me if I shd like to live down there. Of course I said yes – anywhere to be at home & with him. I got the dinner & wash'd up. Did the usual jobs after & was late getting back, ½ past 10, & Miss Otway was angry.

Hannah Cullwick, 1872

To die is a word which is easily said and written, but to think, to *believe* that one is going to die soon? Do I really *believe* it? No, but I *fear it.*

It is of no use trying to hide the fact; I am consumptive. The right lung is much damaged, and the left one has also become slightly diseased in the last year ... There's no hope of getting well, it looks as if I were taking too gloomy a view, but no, it is the simple truth. But there are so many things to do besides these cauterisations! I do them all. Cod-liver oil, arsenic, goats' milk. They have bought me a goat.

This may lengthen my life, but I am lost.

Marie Bashkirtseff (aged 25), 1884

The shock of my life today. This little tiny constant pain in my heart, the X-ray and Dr Witt says, is a tumor or cyst over it and between the lungs. Nothing to worry about, he says, just a question of waiting. And waiting for what? ... I walked down Madison Avenue not looking in shops for the first time because I thought it extravagant to buy or even want things for so short a while. It doesn't matter what the corpse wears.

Later I realized what he said had already been true many months – and nothing had happened. Nothing probably would.

Dawn Powell, 1933

Another wasted day. To be with Mother a purgatory. Terrible old woman.

Miles Franklin, 1933

6 May

How is it these high-heeled ladies who dine out, paint and pinch their waists to deformity, can racket about all day long, while I who sleep o'nights, can turn in my stays, and dislike sweets and dinners, am so tired towards the end of the afternoon that I can scarcely keep my feet? It is very hard and strange, I wonder if it will always be so?

Beatrix Potter (aged 18), 1885

The Hampton Estate has fifteen hundred Negroes on Lake Washington, in Mississippi; but neither Wade nor Preston, that splendid boy, would lay a lance in rest, or couch it – which is the right phrase? – for the sake of slavery. They hate slavery as we do. Someone asked: 'then what are they fighting for?' 'For southern rights, whatever that is! And they do not want to be understrappers forever for those nasty Yankees'...

A telegram says we repulsed the enemy at Williamsburg. Oh, if we could drive them back to 'their ain countree!'

Mary Boykin Chesnut, Confederate States of America, 1862

7 May

We commemorate the sixteenth anniversary of the victory at Dien Bien Phu, that historic victory which broke the French colonial invaders.

Sixteen years have passed, but blood still flows and bones still break in this country. The South has been at war for twenty-five years. Oh, my country! Twenty-five years immersed in fire and bullets, we are still strong. We will persevere and be courageous and hold our heads high and take the offensive. Blood soaks each of our steps on this road of struggles! Is there any country on earth that has suffered as much as ours? And are there any people who have fought as courageously, persistently, and tirelessly as we have?

This afternoon, everyone goes down to the plains. I don't know if they will make it through. The enemy shells the road with their artillery. Perhaps my comrades are still at Xoi slope ... My heart burns with choking worries, sadness, and hatred.

Dang Thuy Tram, South Vietnam, 1970

The news is bad. She's [her sister Rosalie] very sick. Dear Lord, aren't You going to make her better? Perhaps she is dying. But that's an unbearable thought, why have You given her to us if You are going to take her away so soon? Could it be that God is capricious – like us?

Henriette Dessaulles (aged 16), 1877

I rose early. I had to bake bread, tidy up and go down to town for my groceries – and Cliff came in unexpectedly for lunch. When I went downtown, all the shops had got their rosettes and tricoloured button-holes in the windows; and Redman's, the multiple grocer's, had ladders out and men putting up lengths of little pennants and flags. There seemed a curious expectancy about, but to my many enquiries for M[ass] O[bservation] about, 'What will you do on V.E. Day?' I got disappointing answers: 'I don't know' and 'What *is* there to do?' were the two chief ones …

Steve [a visiting neighbour] pooh-poohed the idea that V.E. Day would come tonight. I said, 'It *might* have been announced in a programme' – and I put the wireless on at five minutes to nine o'clock. We agreed that, if Stuart Hibbard said, 'The King will speak in approximately one minute's time', we *would* have missed an announcement – and smiled at each other when it proceeded normally. Then, when he said so unemotionally that tomorrow was to be the V.E. Day, and that Churchill was to speak at three o'clock, we just *gazed* at each other, and Steve said, 'WHAT a flop! What a *FLOP*!' We could none of us believe our hearing … We felt no pulse quicken, *no* sense of thankfulness or uplift, of any kind. Personally, I've felt more thrilled on many occasions by news on the air. At intervals, Steve chanted, 'But what a flop' as if fresh angles had struck him. I'd heard people say, 'I'll kneel down and pray if it's in the street when I hear it', 'I know I'll cry my eyes out', 'I'll rush for that bottle I've kept – open it and get tight for the first time in my life', and so on. I rose placidly and put on the kettle and went through to prepare the salad. I looked on my shelf and said, 'Well, dash it, we *must celebrate somehow* – I'll open this tin of pears', and I did.

Nella Last, 1945

My Pierre [her dead husband], I think of you without end, my head is bursting with it and my reason is troubled. I do not understand that I am to live henceforth without seeing you, without smiling at the sweet companion of my life.

For two days the trees have been in leaf and the garden is beautiful. This morning I looked at the children there. I thought you would have found them beautiful and that you would have called me to show me the periwinkles and the narcissus in bloom. Yesterday, at the cemetery, I did not succeed in understanding the words 'Pierre Curie' engraved on the stone. The beauty of the countryside hurt me, and I put my veil down so as to see everything through my crepe.

Marie Curie, 1906

8 May

We were all fairly unsteady by the time we left Soho and headed for Piccadilly, fighting our way slowly through the crowds towards Whitehall, where we heard Churchill was appearing. Everyone was singing the old songs, 'Roll Out the Barrel'. 'Bless 'em All', and 'Tipperary', and dancing in circles. At one point I got whirled away into the dance by a group of Polish airmen and I thought I was lost forever, but managed to keep one eye on the beacon of Sid's bright red hair. As I fought my way back, one of my shoes came off and had to be abandoned.

We linked arms and slowly made our way towards Whitehall – when we got there we were packed in like sardines. Everybody was singing 'Why are we waiting?' and 'We want Winnie' [Winston Churchill] – a few people fainted but suddenly all the floodlights came on, sirens wailed and there he was on the balcony making the V sign, just like on *Pathé Gazette*.

He made a wonderful speech but I don't remember very much of it except for the bit where he said 'Were we downhearted?' and we all yelled, 'No!' Then we sang 'Land of Hope and Glory' and I think we all cried – I certainly did. It was one of the most exciting moments of my life.

Limped home with my stockings in ribbons, the whole sky ringed with searchlights.

Joan Wyndham, 1945

Papers full of *Lusitania*. They think 1,500 have been drowned, amongst them Sir Hugh Lane. It shows vividly how one's standards have altered – in fact, how out of drawing everything is. Very nearly as big a disaster as the *Titanic*, which loomed so large in one's life for months, and this is merely an incident, so full has one 'supped of horrors'. It will, however, arouse great rage, and one wonders how America will take it.

Lady Cynthia Asquith, 1915

Icy wind and driving rain – we all got soaked coming back to lunch. I made curry for supper. Later in the evening, cutting dreary sandwiches for work tomorrow, I let myself go for perhaps half an hour. But one always has to pick oneself up again and go on being *drearily splendid*.

Barbara Pym, 1943

This month is Called a *tender* one – It has proved so *to* me – but not *in* me – I have not breathed one sigh, – felt one sensation, – or uttered one folly the more for the softness of the season. – However – I have met with a youth whose Heart, if he is to be Credited, has been less guarded – indeed has yielded itself so suddenly, that had it been in any other month – I should not have known how to have accounted for so easy a Conquest.

Fanny Burney, 1775

Quite uncertain for this summer, I am afraid there is a chance of going back to Dalguise [their Scottish holiday home]. I feel an extraordinary dislike to this idea, a childish dislike, but the memory of that home is the only bit of childhood I have left … Everything was romantic in my imagination. The woods were peopled by the mysterious good folk. The Lords and Ladies of the last century walked with me along the overgrown paths, and picked the old fashioned flowers among the box and rose hedges of the garden.

Half believing the picturesque superstitions of the district, seeing my own fancies so clearly that they became true to me, I lived in a separate world. Then, just as childhood was beginning to shake, we had to go, my first great sorrow. I do not wish to have to repeat it, it has been a terrible time since, and the future is uncertain, let me keep the past. The old plum tree is fallen, the trees are felled, the black river is an open hollow, the elfin castle is no longer hidden in the dark glades of Craig Donald Wood.

Beatrix Potter (aged 17), 1884

9 May

Zelie [Duvauchelle] & I need a break from each other but in such a good way! We've been together constantly for weeks, months, and it's been so *real*. Now it is just time for solitude …

Zelie helps me realize I can live on very little & still be happy. And so I seem to be losing some of my *shack* fear.

Alice Walker, 1998

… Phyllis [Bentley] to my delight appeared looking really nice in a very pretty black & silver dress that revealed to me the fact that she had a quite beautiful figure. After the oranges and greens of the previous days, & Winifred [Holtby]'s remarks about her clothes being terribly provincial & all hung about with beads & things, it was a pleasant surprise; also her face seemed better looking as on Saturday I hinted gently how becoming her horn-rimmed spectacles were, & she thereafter abandoned the pince-nez & stopped looking like a school-mistress.

She looked animated too, and happily expectant, like a pleased child.

Vera Brittain, 1932

I've just seen her. She is resting quietly. She is so pretty, so exquisitely pretty but for whom and for what? For the grave – oh, it's horrible! Yes, I know about the angels and heaven, I know about them. But all I see is the tomb and … the parting.

Henriette Dessaulles (aged 16), 1877

10 May

After tea we had a long talk about masturbation. Leonard approves of it and gave me the reasons why. He says everybody masturbates, it's perfectly normal and a pleasurable way of getting satisfaction when other means are impossible. Just as it was getting interesting and I was going to ask him how it was done, another artist conchie rushed in waving a newspaper. 'They've invaded Holland and Belgium!' he panted.

So there it is. We looked at one another. The war had really started. Things seemed to be moving so fast ...

Joan Wyndham (aged 18), 1940

A filthy day, very wet and stormy. But I wore my fur-lined boots and took an extra jersey. Now I can see how people get eccentric.

Barbara Pym, 1943

Very polite sentimental note from Mrs Scanlan with a present of the most beautiful Tree in Seaweed elegantly arranged. Storm very unpleasant. We set up the eolian harp in the Pantry window. Had a sublime and delightful effect.

Lady Eleanor Butler, 1789

... I will not, *cannot*, go back to the narrowness of my husband's '*I* don't want anyone else's company but yours – why do *you* want anyone else?' I looked at his placid, blank face and marvelled at the way he had managed so to dominate me for all our married life, at how, to avoid hurting him, I had tried to keep him in a good mood, when a smacked head would have been the best treatment. His petulant moods only receive indifference now. I *know* I speak sharply at times, I *know* I'm 'not the sweet woman I used to be' – but then I never was! Rather was I a frayed, battered thing, with nerves kept in control by effort that at times became too much, and 'nervous breakdowns' were the result. No one would ever give me one again, *no* one. I've begun to take a 'so far and no further' attitude with that crab of a Cliff [her son]. He must not let illness be an excuse to be rude, discourteous and downright disagreeable. I've told him so very plainly – *and* a few other things.

Nella Last, 1945

Just returned from Burghclere where I spent the weekend with Mary – The country is perfect there, especially at this time of year. Nothing could be more beautiful or more full of peace. All the family are dears, but the girls are brought up in a strict old-fashioned way. Mary, even though married, being still practically treated as a school-girl. She was telling me of the way in which they have been brought up, in such ignorance of the world, that she on her marriage day knew absolutely nothing of what was expected from a wife to her husband on marriage. The consequence was that she was frightened & unhappy, & the revelations which came to her that day did not tend to make the first 48 hours of their wedding go as smoothly as would have been the case had she been more prepared … Mary herself has not changed an atom since we were at college. It seems only yesterday that we were idling on the river playing the fool or indulging in college gossip. It seemed altogether as though I had been in a pleasant dream for two whole days, & woke up this morning to the realities of things in a train from Newbury to London.

Frances Stevenson, 1915

11 May

The D. H. Lawrences arrived at one o'clock and we went out on a bus and had lunch at a filthy little shop … The Lawrences were riveted by the freakishness of John [her son], about whom they showed extraordinary interest and sympathy. The ozone had intoxicated him and he was in a wild, monkey mood – very challenging, just doing things for the sake of being told not to – impishly defiant and still in his peculiar, indescribable detachment. We all went out with the children till their bedtimes and then we returned to our lodgings about five minutes away, had a short rest, and then a dinner of whiting and cold chicken – Lawrence and I had bought asparagus, and so on, on the way home from the station. We had delightful dinner talk.

I find them the most intoxicating company in the world. I never hoped to have such mental pleasure with anyone … His talk is so extraordinarily real and living – such humour and yet so much of the fierceness and resentment which my acquiescent nature loves and covets. He is a Pentecost to one, and has the gift of intimacy and such perceptiveness that he introduces one to oneself. I have never known such an X-ray psychologist.

Lady Cynthia Asquith, 1915

12 May

The 12th I began to dress my head with a roll without a wire.

I wrote not to my Lord because he wrote not to me since he went away. After supper I went with the Child who rode the piebald nag that came out of Westmorland with Mrs –.

Lady Anne Clifford, 1617

Today I am thirty – the age Christ began his mission. Now no more childish things. No more love. No more marriage. Now Lord let me think only of Thy Will, what thou willest me to do. Oh Lord. Thy Will, thy Will.

Florence Nightingale, 1850

I was to the traps today nothing at all. And I chop wood and haul wood and I took out some stuff from store shed. And I fry one biscutt for knight thats all he eat for 9 days he don't look like he is going to live very long. if I happen to live untill ship comes Oh thank a living tru God.

Ada Blackjack, 1923

The baby's body [that of her son, kidnapped some weeks before] found and identified by skull, hair, teeth, etc., in woods on Hopewell-Mount Rose road. Killed by a blow on head. They think he was killed immediately with intention of hiding all evidence. They took the sleeping garment off him to use to extort money …

Everything is telescoped now into one moment, one of those eternal moments – the moment when I realized the baby had been taken and I saw the baby dead, killed violently, in the first flash of horror. Everything since then has been unreal, it has all vanished like smoke. Only that eternal moment remains. It *was* then and it *is* now.

I look on it now as a police case, a murder case, and I am interested in it as such and can and *have* to ask and talk about it. Soon it will be personal, but I do not face it yet.

I feel strangely a sense of peace – not peace, but an end to restlessness, a finality, as though I were sleeping in a grave.

It is a relief to know definitely that he did not live beyond that night. I keep him intact somehow, by that. He was with me the last weekend and left loving me better than anyone. I know that. But all that is merely selfish and small.

But to know anything definitely is a relief. If you can say 'then he was living,' 'then he was dead,' it is final and finalities can be accepted.

Anne Morrow Lindbergh, 1932

13 May

Greg [Wise]: 'Very energetic this morning.'
   Morag: 'Nothing that a syringe of horse sedative won't cure.'
   Overheard later:
   Kate [Winslet]: 'Oh God, my knickers have gone up my arse.'
   Alan [Rickman]: 'Ah. Feminine mystique strikes again.'

Emma Thompson, 1995

Met John [her son] at Dr Shuttleworth, the specialist recommended by Miss Weisse. John answered above his average. The doctor disquieted me on the whole. He said, 'You can't go by looks', and there *might* be indubitable intelligence permanently without control. I feel cold terror about John now more and more often. It is just because the word 'stupid' is so inapplicable and because of a strange completeness about him as he is, that makes one despair of any reason why he should ever change. Oh God, surely nothing so cruel can really have happened to me myself? I must just hope and wait and hope.

Lady Cynthia Asquith, 1916

He has already been dead a hundred years.

A long sleepless night but calm with C. [her husband Charles] sitting beside me every hour, and I could see it all from a great distance …

Then a long day when everything personal flooded back over me, a personal physical loss, my little boy – no control over tears, no control over the hundred little incidents I had jammed out of sight when I was bargaining for my control.

C. to Trenton – the cremation – the blanket. C. going through that – even in the brief news account – is unbearable.

I am glad that I spoiled him that last weekend when he was sick and I took him on my lap and rocked him and sang to him. And glad that he wanted me those last days …

Impossible to talk without crying.

Immortality perhaps for the spark of life, but not for what made up my little boy.

Anne Morrow Lindbergh, 1932

I admit to some content, some closing of a chapter, and peace that comes with it, from posting my proofs today: I admit – because we're in the third day of 'the greatest battle in history'. It began (here) with the 8 o'clock wireless announcing, as I lay half asleep, the invasion of Holland and Belgium. Apple blossom snowing in the garden. Churchill exhorting all men to stand together. 'I have nothing to offer but blood and tears and sweat.' Duncan saw an air battle over Charleston – a silver pencil and a puff of smoke. Percy has seen the wounded arriving in their boots. So my little moment of peace comes in a yawning hollow. But though L.[eonard] says he has petrol in the garage for suicide should Hitler win, we go on. It's the vastness, and the smallness, that make this possible.

Virginia Woolf, 1940

14 May

One of the village girls has been led into evil: such a rare thing in this parish, that it is extra horrible.

Lucy Lyttleton (Lady Frederick Cavendish), 1859

My little Pierre, I want to tell you that the laburnum is in flower, the wistaria, the hawthorn and the iris are beginning – you would have loved all that.

I want to tell you, too, that I have been named to your chair [the professorship of physics at the Sorbonne], and that there have been some imbeciles to congratulate me on it.

I want to tell you that I no longer love the sun or the flowers. The sight of them makes me suffer. I feel better on dark days like the day of your death, and if I have not learned to hate fine weather it is because my children have need of it.

Marie Curie, 1906

About three weeks ago, I paid a very satisfactory visit to the Duchess of Kent, and her very pleasing daughter, the Princess Victoria. William Allen went with me. We took some books on the subject of slavery, with the hope of influencing the young princess in that important cause. We were received with much kindness and cordiality … I had long felt an inclination to see the young princess, and endeavour to throw a little weight in the right scale, seeing the very important place that she is likely to fill. I was much pleased with her, and think her a sweet, lovely and hopeful child.

Elizabeth Fry, 1830

The 14th the Child came to lie with me, which was the first time that ever she lay all night in a bed with me since she was born.

Lady Anne Clifford, 1617

Evening – Women's Freedom League Jubilee dinner at First Avenue Hotel … [Nancy Astor] mentioned in her speech that though it seemed unfair that an American woman & not one of the English pioneers shd be the first woman M.P. to enter the House [of Commons], she had certain 'disagreeable qualities' wh. were very necessary in the first woman Member. Doubtless she was right – American women have a freedom from inferiority complex, & hence a quality of being unsnubbable, very seldom found in English women with their long tradition of repression & inferiority.

Vera Brittain, 1935

15 May

Immediately after dinner, I set off to St. Helen's to see my Mary [her daughter] once more … my little darling held my hand and we gave each other many an affectionate squeeze. Tears were in Mary's eyes; bless[ed] tender-hearted child … I then took leave, an affectionate leave, of my Mary, possibly for the last time! When she found that I stood in the road looking after her, she continued turning her dear face to the last moment, as she walked on to the house. When the hedge intervened, she continued jumping up to look again at me, and again. At last, she quite disappeared. Oh, what hearts of stone those are that can separate mother and child. I got home, weary and depressed. 12 miles.

Ellen Weeton, 1825

We talked fully, emotionally, for the first time. I am glad he [her murdered son] did not live beyond that night. He was such a gay, lordly, assured little boy and had lived always loved and a king in our hearts. I could not bear to have him baffled, hurt, maimed by external forces. I hope he was killed immediately and did not struggle and cry for help – for me.

Anne Morrow Lindbergh, 1932

… She said one of the strange things she had noticed was the amazing position now attained by young unmarried girls. She spoke as if men valued youth to a very peculiar and exceptional degree, far more so than was the case, say, thirty, forty or a hundred years ago. Then, the affairs which married people in society had, were with one another – the girls played no part at all. Now men, both married and single, no longer quite young, delight in the society of girls. They like their conversation and their fresh point of view. I told her that I did not agree. I thought it was true of a small group of girls but quite a small group who, though unmarried, were very much in the world knowing all that went on, able to talk of politics and all the things that the ordinary married woman in that set is interested in. I do not think the sort of man to whom she referred would at all care for the unsophisticated country girl, however nice, fresh and intelligent.

Marie Belloc Lowndes, 1912

16 May

I got my permit to fly from Liverpool to Belfast today, so now I can really make plans. I feel so excited about going, especially when I'm going by air. It will cost about £7, I think, and then there will be little expenses. I took £10 out of the bank, after all, I'm not going to buy a new costume so my extra holiday is my own affair. When I felt the surge of joy run through my veins, I thought surprisedly that I'm not as old as I thought, that it's rather the monotony of life that tires and ages me.

By Gad, if I won the Sweep my poor husband would get a shake up. I'd try anything once! I always drilled it into the boys it was all the things

I hadn't done and nothing I'd done that grieved me as I got older. Ill health, little nervy and giving way too easily about any little change all combined to make me walk sedately, but if I had the chance I know I still love travel and change as much as ever, and that dullness breeds dullness in me.

Nella Last, 1947

More dressing up, this time to make history. I am the first woman apart from royalty to dine as the Treasurer's guest at the Honourable Society of Gray's Inn. Dingle, my host, has told me I have got to put on my full dibs. Guests are introduced into the dining-hall with almost as much ceremonial as at the Guildhall banquet. Everyone else was in white tie and decorations, the students in the hall in subfusc. So I made quite a stir as I swept in in my green bouffant and my topazes, the successor in guest terms, they tell me, to Queen Elizabeth I and Queen Elizabeth II, and trying to look the role ... What tickles me is how much men adore this kind of ceremonial. They are far more play actors at heart than women are.

Barbara Castle, 1968

Paris. I dreamed all night of Rupert Brooke [the poet: dead in the First World War]. And today as I left the house he was standing at the door, with a rucksack on his back and his hat shading his face ...

I crossed and recrossed the river and leaned over the bridges and kept thinking we were coming to a park when we weren't. You cannot think what a pleasure my invisible, imaginary companion gave me. If he had been alive it would never have possibly occurred; but – it's a game I like to play – to walk and talk with the dead who smile and are silent, and *free*, quite finally free. When I lived alone I would often come home, put my key in the door, and find someone there waiting for me. 'Hullo! Have you been here long?'

I suppose that sounds dreadful rubbish.

Katherine Mansfield, 1915

17 May

Anniversary today of my son's birth he is thirty-one. I longed passionately for a girl because of the dresses and the long curly hair. My son was like a little living doll given to a small girl. I was very proud and forgot all my sufferings. Yet destiny was determined to make me a pitiful mother; all of life drew me, all the different countries called me away.

My Marco, who was not loved enough and who didn't love me enough! The last three years we understood each other better, drew closer.

My God, thank you for awakening me under the spur of pain ... [Marco had been killed, as an airman during the First World War]. I thank you for all that I have suffered, which made me truly my Marco's mother.

Liane de Pougy, 1920

Drove down to Clapton and Snaresbrook in Mrs, Lloyd Lindsay's carriage. First to the cholera orphanage at Clapton. We went upstairs, and a door being opened, out tumbled a swarm of tiny 5 and 3 and 2-year-old boys, as fresh and clean as pinks, all with outstretched arms to be taken up and hugged; climbing on one's back, clinging round one's neck, and chattering all at once. It was too pretty! The Convalescent Home very flourishing, with 10 charming recovering men in it; and oh, such tea and bread and butter!

Lucy (Lady Frederick) Cavendish, 1867

This melancholy second Sunday since my irreparable loss [the death of her husband] I ventured to church. I hoped it might calm my mind and subject it to its new state – its lost – lost happiness. But I suffered inexpressibly; I sunk on my knees, and could scarcely contain my sorrows – scarcely rise any more! but I prayed – fervently – and I am glad I made the trail, however severe. *Oh, mon ami! mon tendre ami!* if you looked down! if that be permitted, how benignly will you wish my participation in your blessed relief!

Fanny Burney, 1818

18 May

On the 4th of April I broke a blood-vessel and am now dying of consumption, in great suffering, and may not live many weeks. God be merciful to me a sinner.

God be praised for giving me such excellent parents. They are more than any wishes could desire, or than any words can sufficiently praise. Their presence is like sunshine to my illness.

Emily Shore (aged 19), 1839

I thought I would lead him and teach him and now he has gone first into the biggest experience in life. He is ahead of me. Perhaps when I have to go through it I will think of him – my gay and arrogant child going into it – and it will not seem so terrifying, so awesome, a *little* door.

They talk and talk, conferences, discussions. But I am so tired of the talking. What difference does it make now? '*Why* Tuesday night?' 'What happened to the diapers?' To reconstruct his murder, to try to understand. I will never climb out of this hell that way.

Anne Morrow Lindbergh, 1932

19 May

I'm shameless in bringing raffle books out … I don't wonder at my husband being surprised – when I contrast the rather retiring woman who had such headaches, and used to lie down so many afternoons with the woman of today who can keep on and *will not think*, who coaxes pennies where once she would have *died* rather than ask favours, who uses too bright lipstick and on dim days makes the corners turn up when lips will not keep smiling. Mrs Waite used to be *horrified* at my 'painted mouth', till one day she said thoughtfully, 'It would not be a bad idea if we all bought a lipstick and got little Last to show us how to paint a smile.'

Nella Last, 1940

… Evening falls on New York – my last evening. This country so often irritates me, and now I'm torn apart to be leaving. In the past few days, several people have asked me, 'Do you like America?' and I've gotten into the habit of answering, 'Half and half,' or 'Fifty-fifty.' This mathematical evaluation doesn't mean much; it only reflects my hesitations. Hardly a day has passed that I haven't been dazzled by America; hardly a day that I haven't been disappointed. I don't know if I could be happy living here; I am sure I'll miss it passionately.

Simone de Beauvoir, 1947

Monday was the Princess of Wales's birthday. I went to pay my respects … Princess Charlotte was rather gracious to me. Her legs and feet are very pretty: her Royal Highness knows that they are so, and wears extremely short petticoats. Her face would be pretty too, if the outline of her cheeks was not so full …

Lady Charlotte Bury, 1813

Told we would have Red Cross armlets, also civilian identity cards in case of German parachute landings. I fail to see how they are going to help.

Eve Williams, VAD, 1944

20 May

After he had finished peeing he sat down again and started teaching me words like bugger, fuck, cunt, cock, etc., which he thinks should not be thought of as vulgar but should become part of the English language.

After he had gone on about this for quite a long time with the air of an Oxford don, he moved his chair nearer to me and said, 'I'm being terribly curious, and I suppose your friends would think me either silly or a cad to speak to a young girl like this, but have you ever thought that you would like to indulge in certain erotic practices other than mere face to face copulation?'

I told him that quite honestly I didn't know there were any, which is probably why I had never thought about it. Leonard looked rather taken aback, but went on to describe, with scholarly enthusiasm, how a woman could lie on top of a man or sit astride him, or how she could kneel upright with a man coming in behind, or how they could do it standing up, or the woman could lean back over a table.

'But of course,' he went on, 'it's more difficult for a woman to come in those attitudes than when you're face to face – do you follow? I'll demonstrate if you like?'

'Oh no – thank you very much, I'd really rather you didn't – what does come mean?'

Leonard stared at me in amazement. 'An orgasm, of course. My goodness, I keep forgetting how young you are.' ...

Leonard believes that any normally attractive man can get any woman in the end if he is patient and soft with her. I looked at Leonard's skinny legs and decided it wasn't true.

Joan Wyndham (aged 18), 1940

In the morning Dick [her husband] went back to London; we would both have liked some assurance that we would be seeing each other again: and in at least tolerable circumstances. It was less dramatic, less moving perhaps, than when he went to London from Glasgow Central the Wednesday of Munich, or when he went back from Campbeltown by air last September, But it was more depressing. I am alone now for the first time for some weeks; the last time I was alone, in March, none of this [the active phase of the war] had happened. One hardly listened in, one could forget for hours. I feel sick this evening; I have a kind of pressure at the back of my head, the same I used to get as a child after [a] frightening nightmare.

Naomi Mitchison, 1940

Church at 8 and 11.30. All my worst thoughts seem to be brought up to the surface on such occasions – like a poultice drawing the poison out of a boil perhaps – !

Barbara Pym, 1934

21 May

We had two deaths in our train within the past week of cholera – young men going West to seek their fortune. We buried them on the banks of the Blue River, far from home and friends. This is a beautiful spot. The Plains are covered with flowers. We are now in the Pawnee Nation – a dangerous and hostile tribe. We are obliged to watch them closely and double our guards at night. They never make their appearance during the day, but skulk around at night, steal cattle and do all the mischief they can. When we camp at night, we form a corral with our wagons and pitch our tents on the outside, and inside of this corral we drive our cattle, with guards stationed on the outside …

Sallie Hester (aged 14), 1849

Amelia [Earhart] landed in Ireland!

Last night I went into His closet, opened the door, a flood of warmth. His blue coat on a hook, his red tam, his blue Dutch suit, the little cobweb scarf we tied around his neck. I opened the suitcase and went over each suit. His two wrappers hung on a hook and a pair of white shoes and his bunny bedroom boots. In the pockets of his blue coat I found a shell, a 'tee', and his red mittens. It was like touching his hand. In the drawers I found all the Hansel and Gretel set he played with that last day and the little pussycat I pushed in and out of a little toy house for him. It delighted him so. It gave me a pang of happiness to find it again. Oh, it was so good to feel that intimacy of that memory. It was grief; but it was my own boy – real, alive in my memory, not a police case. I gave Mother the shell and the tee.

C.[harles] and I talked about the feeling of insecurity in life. Never, never will I dare say of him, *You are mine* or, *I have you* now. While we speak, things change – slip from us …

Perhaps one can count only on the present instant or on eternity – nothing in between. These raindrops and … the planets.

Anne Morrow Lindbergh, 1932

I spent a horrible night. I dreamt I lived in a decent house that had a bathroom, kitchen, pantry and even a maid's room. I was going to celebrate the birthday of my daughter Vera Eunice. I went and bought some small pots that I had wanted for a long time. Because I was able to buy. I sat at the table to eat. The tablecloth was white as a lily. I ate a steak, bread and butter, fried potatoes, and a salad. When I reached for another steak I woke up. What bitter reality! I don't live in the city, I live in the favela. In the mud on the banks of the Tietê River. And with only nine cruzeiros. I don't even have sugar, because yesterday after I went out the children ate what little I had …

I found a sweet potato and a carrot in the garbage. When I got back to the favela my boys were gnawing on a piece of hard bread. I thought: for them to eat this bread they need electric teeth.

I don't have any lard. I put meat on the fire with some tomatoes that I found at the Peixe canning factory. I put in the carrot and the sweet potato and water. As soon as it was boiling, I put in the macaroni that the boys found in the garbage. The favelados are the few who are convinced that in order to live, they must imitate the vultures. I don't see any help from the Social Services regarding the favelados. Tomorrow I'm not going to have bread. I'm going to cook a sweet potato.

Carolina Maria de Jesus, 1958

22 May

Washed the windows so the summer sun could shine in. And – after two of Ginnie's [Virginia Kent Catherwood] APAC pills, with a swimming brain – worked with clarity on 'Mrs Afton.' My hellish story! So – read, slept for 15 minutes, everything was wonderful! Met Ginnie at the bistro. She was very downcast, silent, complaining. And when we finally began discussing our relationship, I said (although we were both angry) that it was the first time we were actually discussing something. How can one understand women?

Patricia Highsmith, 1947

Today I'm sad. I'm nervous. I don't know if I should start crying or start running until I fall unconscious. At dawn it was raining. I couldn't go out to get any money. I spent the day writing. I cooked the macaroni and I'll warm it up again for the children. I cooked the potatoes and they ate them. I have a few tin cans and a little scrap that I'm going to sell to Senhor Manuel. When João came home from school I sent him to sell the scrap. He got 13 cruzeiros. He bought a glass of mineral water: two cruzeiros. I was furious with him. Where had he seen a favelado with such highborn tastes?

The children eat a lot of bread. They like soft bread but when they don't have it, they eat hard bread.

Hard is the bread that we eat. Hard is the bed on which we sleep. Hard is the life of the favelado.

Carolina Maria de Jesus, 1958

Woke up at four, so came down and joined a very successful soldier party. Huge whist drive in which Papa, Evan, and Mr Balfour took part. I won the booby prize. My last night on [nursing] duty – uneventful, except that the heat was so appalling that we sat with our tongues hanging out, and I was very tired and sleepy. Sister Orde went off early leaving me in charge. Had it not been that I am returning in a fortnight, I should have felt very sad at leaving the hospital – as it is, bedtime is rather a pleasant prospect. I have loved it, to an extent that puzzles me. I quite understand one's liking for the human interest side of it and the absorbed, feverish desire to satisfy Sister and please the men, but I rather wonder why one enjoys the sink, tray, Lysol, bustle side of it quite so much.

Lady Cynthia Asquith, 1918

I am working at the laboratory all day long, it is all I can do: I am better off there than anywhere else. I conceive of nothing any more that could give me personal joy, except perhaps scientific work – and even there, no, because if I succeeded with it, I could not endure you not to know it.

Marie Curie, 1906

... The situation is extremely dangerous, with the constant threat of attack. The enemy has stealthily moved closer to our meeting place without our knowledge. Focused on cutting trees and laughing, we only know their presence when a highlander charges in to warn us that the enemy is right by our side. We evade their sweeping operation. Fortunately, we handle the emergency well, otherwise they would have killed us with their gunships, artillery, and infantry. Even in the madness, we are still able to be cheerful. The smiles have not vanished from these young faces. Each night in the small house, we hang our hammocks close together and tell jokes. It's hard to be serious with all the laughter ...

What makes me cheerful? Is it the affection of everyone, of Phuong, Ton, Hao, Hang, Minh, brother Ky ... and of this whole happy family?

Dang Thuy Tram, South Vietnam, 1970

23 May

Nightmares. Almost inevitable. And the baby wriggling terrifically all night. I am thinking much less about this baby than I ever did about the others; I haven't made little she-plans about it as I did with the others; the future is black fogged ahead of one; all one can cultivate is acceptance ...

The 6 o'clock news, with the fighting at Boulogne and capture of Abbeville was a bit of a shock. I remember so well going through Abbeville when Dick [her husband] was wounded when I went out as next of kin. I began to worry a lot about him and Denny [her eldest son] in London and the others at school. Winchester is very near Southampton. I looked at the map, to see just how far all the children's schools were from Boulogne ...

Naomi Mitchison, 1940

D. [Lloyd George] & I had a long talk. I know [Sir Albert] Stern would marry me if I gave him the slightest encouragement & if he thought I would leave D. It is great temptation in a way for although I don't love him we are good friends & I know he would be very kind to me. It would mean a title & wealth, whereas now I may find myself old & friendless and having to earn my own living, if anything should happen to D. People will not be so anxious to marry me in 10 years' time. On the other hand I know I should not be happy now away from D. & no-one else in the world could give me the same intense & wonderful love that he showers on me. He was very sweet about it, & says he wants to do what is best for me. But I can see that he would be unhappy if I left him, so I promised him I would not.

Frances Stevenson, 1919

After prayers I went again to the New College organ recital. I have come to the conclusion that music awakens the usually dormant physical side of my emotions. When I am listening to music it is always the touch, the voice, the physical embrace of the beloved that I long for. I ache more then for the feel of his hand over mine and the glance of his eyes when I look into his, than at any other time. And I dream of my imagined children ...

Vera Brittain, 1915

24 May

Once, in Venice, we were standing on a bridge, staring into the black canal (it was night-time), in front of us the magnificent arch of the Bridge of Sighs. We were leaning on the parapet, Kl[imt] standing at my side, the others further off. Suddenly I could feel Kl's fingers pulling, tearing at my collar. As I was leaning on the stone, the neckline tightened. Before I could realize what he was about, everyone moved on, and we had to start walking too, but further behind. As was his wont, he pinched my arm, whispering:

Silly girl, Alma, I could have put my hand on your heart – easily.

A cold shiver went through me, my heart missed a beat. He wanted to feel my breasts! Or did he want to see how fast my heart was beating? The former would have been lechery, the other love – unfortunately I'm *sure* it was the former.

Alma Schindler (Mahler-Werfel), 1899

Today is my 18th birthday! How old! and yet how far am I from being what I should be. I shall from this day take the firm resolution to study with renewed assiduity, to keep my attention always well fixed on whatever I am about, and to strive to become every day less trifling and more fit for what, if Heaven will it, I'm some day to be! ... The Courtyard and the streets were crammed when we went to the Ball, and the anxiety of the people to see poor stupid me was very great, and I must say I am quite touched by it, and feel proud which I always have done of my country and of the English Nation.

Queen (then Princess) Victoria, 1837

Again my old birthday returns, my eighty-first! God has been very merciful and supported me, but my trials and anxieties have been manifold, and I feel tired and upset by all I have gone through this winter and spring ...

The number of telegrams to be opened and read was quite enormous, and obliged six men to be sent for to help the two telegraphists in the house. The answering of them was an interminable task, but it was most gratifying to receive so many marks of loyalty and affection.

Queen Victoria, 1900

Rose at five. The sun was shining brightly through my window, and I felt vexed with myself that he should have risen before me; I shall not let him have that advantage again very soon. How bright and beautiful are these May mornings! ...

Charlotte Forten, 1854

25 May

D. told me this morning that he had definitely made up his mind that he could not let me leave him. So that is final, & I am very glad. I need not worry about it any more. It would be very foolish to spoil for material prospects the most wonderful love which ever happened …

Frances Stevenson, 1919

Began my early morning readings. This is my day: tea at 6 o'clock, study from 6 to 8 o'clock. Notes and chat till 11; Father till lunch. 3.30 to 5.30 study. Then a delightful walk or ride: supper, cigarette with Father; saunter in the moonlight or starlight; to bed at 10 o'clock. An alternation of vigorous study and dreamy restfulness – of sleep, exercise, food (including in food the delicious and well beloved cigarettes!) and the enjoyment of natural beauty …

Beatrice Webb, 1889

Man can never know the kind of loneliness a woman knows. Man lies in a woman's womb only to gather strength, he nourishes himself from this fusion, and then he rises and goes into the world, into his work, into battle, into art. He is not lonely. He is busy. The memory of the swim in amniotic fluid gives him energy, completion. The woman may be busy too, but she feels empty. Sensuality for her is not only a wave of pleasure in which she has bathed, and a charge of electric joy at contact with another. When man lies in her womb, she is fulfilled, each act of love is a taking of man within her, an act of birth and rebirth, of child-bearing and man-bearing.

Anaïs Nin, 1932

26 May

———

… We went to the great party at the Foreign Office in the evening … The Princess of Wales looked graceful & delicious in a lovely grey silver gown which undulated over the stairs. Her hair most beautifully done with a splendid diamond tiara, with great emeralds in it, put on in exactly the right place. What a convenience it must have been to her all these years to be so good looking.

Mary, Lady Monkswell, 1894

Why nothing to read in the outpatients at the Radcliffe [Infirmary]? Must we be content with our thoughts?

Barbara Pym, 1977

I feel so miserable. I haven't felt like this for months; even after the burglary I didn't feel so utterly broken. On the one hand the vegetable man [arrested for harbouring Jews], the Jewish question, which is being discussed minutely over the whole house, the invasion delay, the bad food, my disappointment in Peter; and on the other hand, Elli's engagement, Whitsun reception, flowers, Kraler's birthday, fancy cakes and stories about cabaret, films and concerts. That difference, the huge difference, it's always there; one day we laugh and see the funny side of the situation, but the next we are afraid, fear, suspense and despair staring from our faces …

Miep sent us a currant cake, made up in the shape of a doll, with the words 'Happy Whitsun' on the note attached to it. It's almost as if she's ridiculing us; our present frame of mind and our uneasiness could hardly be called 'happy.' The affair of the vegetable man has made us more nervous, you hear 'shh, shh' from all sides again, and we're being quieter over everything. The police forced the door there, so they could do it to us too! If one day we too should … no, I mustn't write it, but I can't put the question out of my mind today. On the contrary, all the fear I've already been through seems to face me again in all its frightfulness …

Again and again I ask myself, would it not have been better for us all if we had not gone into hiding, and if we were dead now and not going through all this misery, especially as we should no longer be dragging our protectors into danger. But we recoil from these thoughts too, for we still love life; we haven't yet forgotten the voice of nature, we still hope, hope about everything. I hope something will happen soon now, shooting if need be – nothing can crush us *more* than this restlessness. Let the end come, even if it is hard; then at least we shall know whether we are finally going to win through or go under.

Anne Frank, 1944

27 May

——

… There were a couple of spare wooden horses from the merry-go-round flaring their nostrils in one corner, and lots of smelly old sacks on the floor. We made them into a pile and sank down on them, the pungent dust rising around us. He kissed me for ages, much longer than my other boyfriends usually do, and soon I was longing for him to make love to me.

I knew, of course, that ultimately it would be disappointing – there would come a point when I would go dead and nothing would happen – so what happened next was a complete surprise.

He was inside me and kissing my breasts at the same time when I suddenly felt the most extraordinary sensation as if an electric current had been switched on, turning my whole body into a radiant powerhouse of sexual expectation. It was as though someone had mended a fuse in a dark room and all the lights had blazed on. For the first time I felt totally at home inside my own skin – not watching myself any longer from outside, I was really there, relaxed and letting go. My mind went dead, but my body was running away with me, and as our movements became faster and stronger it was like the long ride down from Flichity Inn, freewheeling all the way – look, no hands! – laughing and shouting with surprise and pleasure as I finally relaxed into joy.

Joan Wyndham, 1945

I feel weaker every morning, and I suppose am beginning to sink; still I can at times take up my pen. I have had my long black hair cut off. Dear papa wears a chain made from it. Mamma will have one too.

Emily Shore, 1839

Henry [Wadsworth Longfellow] took his sunset row on the river. Sat at window and followed the flashing of his oars with my eyes and heart. He rowed round one bend of the river, then another, now under the shadow of the woods and now in the golden sunlight. Longed to be with him and grew impatient for wings he looked so far away. How completely my life is bound up in his love – how broken and incomplete when he is absent a moment, what infinite peace and fullness when he is present. And he loves me to the uttermost desire of my heart. Can any child excite as strong a passion as this we feel for each other?

Fanny Longfellow, 1844

Shooting Willoughby carrying Marianne up the path. They did it four times. 'Faster,' said Ang [Lee, the director]. They do it twice more. 'Don't pant so much,' said Ang. Greg [Wise], to his credit, didn't scream. The image of the man carrying the woman is horribly effective. Male strength – the desire to be cradled again? Had sage discussion with John Jordan (focus puller, very gentle) over the barrel of the lens about allowing all those politically incorrect desires their head. I'd love someone to pick me up and carry me off. Frightening. Lindsay [Doran, producer] assures me I'd start to fidget after a while. She's such a comfort.

Emma Thompson, 1995

28 May

Did we smoke? Heaven forbid the unholy thought! I am an old-fashioned woman and hate these mannish ways. But I would whisper a small truth in the reader's ear. Let men beware of the smoking woman. For the pretty dress and the sweet-smelling cigarette unite the outward tokens of a woman's sympathy and a man's ease. I would urge earnestly on the defenders of man's supremacy to fight the female use of tobacco with more sternness and vigour than they have displayed in the female use of the vote. It is a far more fatal power.

Beatrice Webb, 1886

I am leading a cluttered life these days ... Clutter is what silts up exactly like silt in a flowing stream when the current, the free flow of the mind, is held up by an obstruction. I spent four hours in Keene yesterday getting the car inspected and two new tyres put on, also finding a few summer blouses. The mail has accumulated in a fearful way, so I have a huge disorderly pile of stuff to be answered on my desk. In the end what kills is not agony (for agony at least asks something of the soul) but everyday life.

The immense value of a love affair is, of course, that it burns up the clutter like the trash it is. When X and I first met life was nothing but a long hymn of praise ...

May Sarton, 1971

I whipped him with a little strip of whalebone, but with no effect. While smarting he called out 'Yes, yes Mamma, I will be good, I will reckon,' but the next moment returned the same resolute look, and 'No, I will not reckon.'

After about half an hour spent thus, I did not know what to do, feeling I had got into a contest which I must win ... I found Alick as firm as ever, whipped him again and tied him to the bed post. I was glad to see such resolution in his character and afraid to break his spirit. Yet I could not give up ... Darling child, with what cost to myself I punished him! I think he was subdued, not merely exhausted, but I am by no means sure I took the right method. Perhaps had I left him for longer time in the first instance, I might have avoided the conflict. Perhaps had I prayed more fervently God would have made him yield. For one thing I am most thankful, that he was not the slightest estranged from me, but on the contrary clings more than ever to his 'own dear mamma'.

Honoria Lawrence, colonial administrator's wife, India, 1842

29 May

Mr B.[uller] says nine-tenths of the misery of human life proceeds according to his observations from the institution of marriage. He should say from the demoralisation, the desecration, of the institution of marriage, and then I should cordially agree with him.

Jane Carlyle, 1856

Beached – or shoaled? Shoaled I think. Life has been complete hell for weeks. For example Mother took a notion that she could not see …

I said now some literary men do good work when drunk, and Nature does not care whether a man depletes himself by an excess of industry or worry or an excess of alcohol: the result is sometimes similar. So, despite being bemused by fatigue, distracted & tormented beyond using intelligence or generating inspiration, I'll write on & on & see what happens …

Miles Franklin, 1938

I was much better. I made bread and a wee Rhubarb Tart and batter pudding for William [her brother]. We sate in the orchard after dinner. William finished his poem on Going for Mary. I wrote it out. A sweet day. We nailed up the honeysuckles, and hoed the scarlet beans.

Dorothy Wordsworth, 1802

30 May

Rose very early and was busy until nine o'clock; then, at Mrs Putnam's urgent request, went to keep store for her while she went to Boston to attend the Anti-Slavery Convention. I was very anxious to go, and will certainly do so to-morrow; the arrest of the alleged fugitive will give additional interest to the meetings, I should think …

Charlotte Forten, 1854

The Council, it would seem, by a General Order in this week's Gazette, are quite tired of the applications for *female* servants being addressed to them, and it is now simply specified that families who are in want of female servants may be supplied from the prisoners lately arrived in the Ship *Lady Rowena* describing what sort of servants are wanted, and which application is to be addressed in writing to the Principal Superintendant [sic] of Convicts.

Christiana Brooks, Australia, 1826

Last spring was another piece of the fall and winter before, a progression from all the pain and sadness of that time, ruminated over. But somehow this summer which is almost upon me feels like a part of my future. Like a brand new time, and I'm pleased to know it, wherever it leads. I feel like another woman, de-chrysalised and become a broader, stretched-out me, strong and excited, a muscle flexed and honed for action.

Audre Lorde, 1980

Bells ringing all Day on account of Mrs Custance coming down Stairs for the first time since Christmas … Finished working my double Handkerchief.

Nancy Woodforde, 1792

31 May

The oculist said to me this afternoon: 'Perhaps you're not as young as you were'. This is the first time that has been said to me, and it seemed to me an astonishing statement. It means that one now seems to a stranger not a woman, but an elderly woman. Yet, although I felt wrinkled and aged for an hour, and put on a manner of great wisdom and toleration, buying a coat, even so, I forgot it soon; and became 'a woman' again.

Virginia Woolf, 1929

To him who waits, all things come! My aspirations may have been eccentric, but I cannot complain now, that they have not been brilliantly fulfilled. Ever since I have been ill, I have longed and longed for some palpable disease, no matter how conventionally dreadful a label it might have … they sent for Sir Andrew Clark four days ago. And that blessed being has endowed me not only with cardiac complications, but says that a lump that I have had in one of my breasts for three months, which has given me a great deal of pain, is a tumour, that nothing can be done for me but to alleviate pain, that it is only a question of time, etc. This with a delicate embroidery of 'the most distressing case of nervous hyperaesthesia' added to a spinal neurosis that has taken me off my legs for seven years; with attacks of rheumatic gout in my stomach for the last twenty, ought to satisfy the most inflated pathological vanity.

Alice James, 1891

I feel that this month I have conquered my Panic Bird. I am a calm, happy and serene writer. With a pleasant sense of learning and being better with every story …

I feel in a rug-braiding mood today. Very sleepy, as after a good lovemaking, after all that writing this week. My poems are so far in the background now. It is a very healthy antidote, this prose, to the poems' intense limitations.

A happier sense of life, not hectic, but very slow and sure, than I have ever had. That sea, calm, with sun bland on it. Containing and receiving all the reef, narrow straits in its great reservoir of peace.

Sylvia Plath, 1959

June

'It's an odd idea for someone like me to keep a diary.'

Anne Frank, 1942

1 June

Thank God, dear Emma's troubles are all over, and a fine little boy was born yesterday at 9 o'clock. It is nice to have this to enter in the same Vol. of journal which has the account of the sad disappointment 2 years ago. Now she has everything in the world. I feel rather heart-pinched in the lessening of our own hopes; but it is the only thing wanting to us, and one ought to be full of thankfulness.

Lucy (Lady Frederick) Cavendish, 1868

It has been raining all day long and we have been travelling in it so as to be able to keep ahead of the large droves. The men and boys are all soaking wet and look sad and comfortless. (The little ones and myself are shut up in the wagons from the rain. Still it will find its way in and many things are wet; and take us all together we are a poor looking set, and all this for Oregon. I am thinking while I write, 'oh, Oregon, you must be a wonderful country.' Came 18 miles today.)

Amelia Stewart Knight, 1853

To any one who has not been there, it will be hard to understand the enormous relief of [the doctor's] uncompromising verdict, lifting us out of the formless vague and setting us within the very heart of the sustaining concrete. One would naturally not choose such an ugly and gruesome method of progression down the dark Valley of the Shadow of Death, and of course many of the moral sinews will snap by the way, but we shall gird up our loins and the blessed peace of the end will have no shadow cast upon it.

Having it to look forward to for a while seems to double the value of the event, for one becomes suddenly picturesque to oneself, and one's wavering little individuality stands out with a cameo effect and one has the tenderest indulgence for all the little *stretchings out* which crowd in upon the memory. The grief is all for K.[atharine] and H.[enry] who will *see* it all, whilst I shall only *feel* it, but they are taking it of course like archangels, and care for me with infinite tenderness and patience. Poor dear William with his exaggerated sympathy for suffering isn't to know anything about it until it is all over.

Alice James, 1891

I awakened feeling dull … The weather is neither cheerful nor depressing. It makes me restless. The trees are tossed by gusty, fantastic wind. The sun is hidden. If I put on my dressing gown I am too hot, if I take it off I am cold. Leaden day in which I shall accomplish nothing worthwhile. Tired and apathetic brain! I have been drinking tea in the hope that it would carry this mood to a climax and so put an end to it.

George Sand, 1837

2 June

I said a great deal to Campbell, as much as I could and dared, but was often interrupted, by others coming up to us, my want of courage, and his own evident wish to avoid an explanation – How painful it is for a Woman to talk on such a Subject! – I am sure that I likewise put him in pain, Walter unluckily dragg'd him away to Mrs Greville's Masquerade just as I should have got him to speak – However I went so far as to beg he would soon make up his mind and tell me his determination when he had – But did he understand me? – God alone knows! – it makes me quite miserable – but it was necessary that I should speak – W. came home at about four o'clock – I was tired, dull and unhappy –

Eugenia Wynne (Campbell), 1806

We are very quiet now a days & if I only felt well it would be very pleasant. – I get up late & paint in my Studio for two or three hours, have dinner read lounge around, play on the piano & then about five drive up the Park & down Wabash Ave: with plenty of painting and hysterics in between.

Julia Newberry (aged 16), 1870

Happiness overwhelms me. Twenty-three days at Yaddo [the artists' colony]. My life is regular, pleasant, healthful on the obvious plane. (And how often and where, in the past eight years, since I lived with my parents, have I been able to say this?) On the less obvious plane, it restoreth my dignity, my self-confidence, it enables me to complete what I have never completed, that child of my spirit, my novel, and give it birth.

Patricia Highsmith, 1948

3 June

Well! here have I, with the grace of God and the assistance of good friends, completed – I really think very happily – the greatest event of my life, I have sold my brewhouse to Barclay, the rich Quaker, for 135,000l., to be in four years' time paid. I have by this bargain purchased peace and a stable fortune, restoration to my original rank in life, a situation undisturbed by commercial jargon, unpolluted by commercial frauds, [un]disgraced by commercial connections. They who succeed me in the house have purchased the power of being rich beyond the wish of rapacity, and I have procured the improbability of being made poor by flights of the fairy, speculation. 'Tis thus that a woman and men of feminine minds always – I speak popularly – decide upon life, and chuse certain mediocrity before probable superiority ...

Hester Lynch Thrale Piozzi, 1781

I have altered – that is new written my Will to day; & left the Estate unentailed, to my eldest Daughter & her heirs for ever: only charging it pretty heavily with Legacies which however she will now be empowered to pay by selling the Estate if She pleases, and what signifies in entailing it on People who have already more than does them good? if I cannot Live to enjoy my Estate with the husband of my Choice, they may take it that please – I care not.

Hester Lynch Thrale Piozzi, 1783

Yesterday morning William walked as far as the Swan with Aggy Fisher. She was going to attend upon Goan's dying Infant. She said 'There are many heavier crosses than the death of an Infant', and went on, 'There was a woman in this vale who buried 4 grown-up children in one year, and I have heard her say when many years were gone by that she had more pleasure in thinking of those 4 than of her living Children, for as Children get up and have families of their own their duty to the parents 'wears out and weakens'. She could trip lightly by the graves of those who died when they were young, with a light step, as she went to Church on a Sunday.'

Dorothy Wordsworth, 1802

We were assail'd with tiresome visitors all the mor[nin]g – Campbell to my surprise and sorrow never came near me – Before we went out to an early dinner at Mrs Bankes, I wrote to explain my meaning of last night, and to ask for a decision, which he can no longer deny me – my heart breaks, when I think that now the die is cast and that we shall perhaps part for ever … I returned miserable, sick at heart, and overcome to find that Campbell had sent no answer – when shall I know my fate – Mrs Bankes takes great interest in the whole affair, and spoke to me with all the kindness of a mother on the subject – But if I love him, can anything make me amends for his loss!

Eugenia Wynne (Campbell), 1806

4 June

I had a Letter, from Campbell this morning which cost me many tears, and I repented most heartily that I had not followed my own inclinations and feelings on the subject, but yielded to the solicitations of others – I have plainly offended him – he however answered all my questions and it is as plain that he does not intend to marry me unless he obtains some situation.

Eugenia Wynne (Campbell), 1806

I wonder if I shall burn this sheet of paper like most others I have begun in the same way. To write a diary, I have thought of very often at far & near distances of time: but how could I write a diary without throwing on paper my thoughts, all my thoughts – the thoughts of my heart as well as of my head? – and then how could I bear to look on *them* after they were written? Adam made fig leaves necessary for the mind, as well as for the body. And such a mind as I have! So very exacting & exclusive & eager & head long – & strong & so very very often *wrong*!

Elizabeth Barrett (Browning), 1831

At nine my beloved and I went to the dressing-room, the air being cold. We got a fire intending to write. Finished a letter to Lady Dungannon, and her letter to which ours was an answer lying on the Table we threw it in the fire. It blazed violently, and the flames communicating to the Soot the Chimney instantly took fire and roared internally with the most fearful noise Imaginable. Our agony at this is not to be described. We sent to the Village for assistance … When all was over they removed their Ladder, ropes, Pails, etc. We rendered them plentiful potations of Beer. They drank our Health, wished us long life and health. After returning thanks to the Almighty for our great deliverance we composed ourselves to rest, the Village clock striking two.

Lady Eleanor Butler, 1788

5 June

It seems [the doctor] said that although I might die in a week or so, I might also live some months. This is a strain, as Katharine says I have looked 'prepared' for a week, and I am sure I shall not be able to keep that up for some months ...

Alice James, 1891

I sate out of doors great part of the day and worked in the garden – had a letter from Mr Jackson, and wrote an answer to Coleridge. The little birds busy making love, and pecking the blossoms and bits of moss off the trees; they flutter about and about, and thrid [sic] the trees as I lie under them. Molly went out to tea, I would not go far from home, expecting my Brothers. I rambled on the hill above the house, gathered wild thyme, and took up roots of wild columbine.

Dorothy Wordsworth, 1800

A fine morning – I went with Rupert [Gleadow] up to Boars Hill – we went into a wood and sheltered from the showers under trees. He was very Theocritean and loving. I got a wee bit sick of it – but tried to please him as I was determined to treat him as kindly as possible as he'd Schools [exams] on the 9th.

Barbara Pym (aged 20), 1932

6 June

Mr Churchill is back and we are relieved. We began to be anxious when the Air Liner was attacked. Definitely the Germans thought he might be on it. They have never attacked these planes before. But to lose Leslie Howard is grievous. I heard him on the Brains Trust, as well as seeing him in *Pygmalion, Romeo and Juliet*, and surely he was Ashley in *Gone with the Wind?* I am sure he cheered the others up in those awful moments before they fell into the sea – or at least comforted them. They must all have been killed instantly.

Winifred Vere Hodgson, 1943

Dear Kitty,

'This is D-day,' came the announcement over the British Radio and quite rightly, 'This is *the* day.' The invasion has begun! ...

Oh, Kitty, the best part of the invasion is that I have the feeling that friends are approaching. We have been oppressed by those terrible Germans for so long, they have had their knives so at our throats, that the thought of friends and delivery fills us with confidence!

Now it doesn't concern the Jews any more; no, it concerns Holland and all occupied Europe. Perhaps, Margot says, I may yet be able to go back to school in September or October.

Anne Frank, 1944

Why does one marry? Am I glad? I have exchanged an agitated family life for an intensely quiet and an if-not-boring-why-not present, where I meet no-one, live in an ugly little house and eat plain food in dread of the servant leaving me. So lonely I doubt if I can draw, or read, or write letters here.

Ivy Jacquier, 1921

After fifteen years of marriage & more or less continuous companionship, the experience of being alone is a very enlightening one. The *aloneness* awakens in me memories of similar times, similar emotions, many years ago. A very strong continuity of personality, then: I recognize myself as a girl seamlessly existing within my present self (a woman who will be thirty-eight on the 16th of June). It's nonsense, as I have always believed, to imagine that one's personality changes very much over the course of years. It expands, that's all.

Joyce Carol Oates, 1976

7 June

When I was a girl my dream was to become a man to defend Brazil, because I read the history of Brazil and became aware that war existed. I read the masculine names of the defenders of the country, then I said to my mother:

'Why don't you make me become a man?'

She replied:

'If you walk under a rainbow, you'll become a man.'

When a rainbow appeared I went running in its direction. But the rainbow was always a long way off ...

Carolina Maria de Jesus, 1958

Wrote a good luck letter to Lorenzo [Henry Harvey] . Quite prosaic and hearty – but oh – what wouldn't I have liked to say – still I knew it would be a mistake. Nor did I want Jockie and Barnicot to know any more about the state of my heart!

Barbara Pym (aged 18), 1933

Fyodor [Dostoevsky; the novelist, her husband] said to me today that I am 'good', that I was 'good,' that I was devoid of sin ... My darling!! I do not deserve all this praise and am not nearly so good as he makes out, but I love to hear him say it ...

Anna Dostoevsky, 1869

Friday I sate before breakfast & thought of my despair – this day twelve months, June 7, 1849 I made that desperate effort, the Crucifixion of the sin, in faith that it would cure me. Oh what is Crucifixion – would I not joyfully submit to Crucifixion, Father, to be rid of this? But this long moral death, this failure at all attempts at cure. I am in just the same state as I was last June. I think I have never been so bad as this last week. When Plato's plane tree, when riding in the Academy, when living intercourse with these dear Hills could not recall my attention to actual things. And I thought, when I was 30 I should be cured. 8 months since the last incentive to sin, & not a day has passed without my committing it.

Florence Nightingale, Egypt, 1850

8 June

If man injures man, the injured has a great portion of power to defend himself, either from natural strength of body, of resolution, of the countenance of many of his fellows, or from the laws; but when man injures woman, how can she defend herself? Her frame is weaker, her spirit timid; and if she be a wife, there is scarce a man anywhere to be found who will use the slightest exertion in her defence; and her own sex cannot, having no powers. She has no hope from law; for man, woman's enemy, exercises, as well as makes those laws. She cannot have a jury of her peers or equals, for men, every where prejudiced against the sex, are her jurors; man is her judge. Thus situated, thus oppressed, she lives miserably, and by inches sinks into the grave. This is the lot not merely of a few, but of one half, if not two thirds of the sex!

Ellen Weeton, 1825

I know now I am driven to this impasse over and over again, and faced with the same outcome, the physical possession: and that I am interested not in the physical possession but in the game, as Don Juan was, the game of seduction, of maddening, of possessing men not only physically but their souls, too – I demand more than the whores.

Already today I was satanically pleased when Artaud said, 'I have divined that [René] Allendy loves you. Do you still love him?' I refused to answer his question. Quite definitely, today I felt classified, categorized as a species of seductress not often encountered. I play not only with sex but with souls, imaginations. A whore is an honest whore. I seduce men's bodies and souls, and I play with serious, sacred things. As Henry said once, I love sacrilege. I am a new kind of enchantress ... I entered

Allendy's life; I bit a morsel of it; I tasted it, barely touched it. I brushed against him and I passed on. And, oh, the bitterness of the man so tricked by my unseizableness. And now I step warily into [Antonin] Artaud's fantastic regions, and he, too, lays heavy hands on me, on my body, and like the mandragora at the touch of human hands, I *shriek*.

Anaïs Nin, 1933

9 June

Our wedding day. I cannot write about it. I can only look backwards with loving regret, and forward with bright but trembling hope. We were married in Westminster Abbey, by Uncle Billy, and came here [Chiswick] about 4 o'clock, into peaceful summer loveliness and the singing of birds.

Lucy (Lady Frederick) Cavendish, 1864

… I went to Mrs Jenkinson, she having sent me word that her husband and C.[ampbell]. were returned – how it made my heart beat to hear that! – I went most anxious to know how C. would behave towards me – He came up to me in the most good humoured manner and shook hands – ashamed and happy, I know not how I had the appearance of coldness – he reproached me with it – but we ended up by making it up and being better friends than ever … I shall not be surprized, if he takes it into his head to be *the Master* when we marry – but I shall willingly yield to him, and shall not quarrel for that.

Eugenia Wynne (Campbell), 1806

Super news of the invasion …

The excitement here has worn off a bit; still, we're hoping that the war will be over by the end of this year. It'll be about time too! Mrs Van Daan's grizzling is absolutely unbearable; now she can't any longer drive us crazy over the invasion, she nags us the whole day long about the bad weather. It really would be nice to dump her in a bucket of cold water and put her up in the loft.

Anne Frank, 1944

When we read of the battles in India, in Italy, in the Crimea, what did we care? It was only an interesting topic, like any other, to look for in the paper. Now, you hear of a battle with a thrill and a shudder. It has come home to us. Half the people that we know in the world are under the enemy's guns. A telegram comes to you and you leave it on your lap. You are pale with fright. You handle it, or dread to touch it, as you would a rattlesnake, or worse; for a snake could only strike you. How many, many of your friends or loved ones this scrap of paper may tell you have gone to their death.

Mary Boykin Chesnut, Confederate States of America, 1862

10 June

I have discovered that I cannot burn the candle at one end and write a book with the other.

Life without work – I would commit suicide. Therefore work is more important than life.

Katherine Mansfield, 1919

Coleridge came in with a sack-full of Books etc. and a Branch of mountain ash. He had been attacked by a cow … Mr Simpson drank tea. William [her brother] very poorly – we went to bed latish. I slept in sitting room.

Dorothy Wordsworth, 1802

No letter from Allela [Cornell], but a card from [Ruth] Bernhard. Mother here to paint my bookcases. And she said I mustn't become like Cornell, crying every night, wanting to be 'pretty,' but not doing anything about it. She also used the word lesbian. Wrote to Allela, although I was far too tired. Am still happy and full of hope.

Patricia Highsmith, 1943

11 June

Smeared all over the papers' front pages again. And the memory of my boy wiped out in this avalanching crime. Nothing found out yet in spite of conclusions jumped at ...

... Out to Port Washington, Falaise. Honeysuckle, the sea very calm, small ripples, smooth patches that reflect the gold of the sky. And the Guggenheims very calm and cool and generous and, thank God, conversation about broad world problems ...

I feel as though their world were secure, as though dreadful things could never happen in it, because they have faith in it. As though ours were toppling, anything could happen, because we have lost faith in it. As though once you had lost your faith you were vulnerable and nothing you did could stop evil and sorrow and misery from pouring in.

Anne Morrow Lindbergh, 1932

My father is dead.

The telegram was received this morning at ten o'clock, that is to say just this instant. My aunt and Dina downstairs were saying that mamma must come back at once without waiting for the funeral. I came up here, very much moved, but not crying. But when [her maid] Rosalie came to show me the arrangement of a dress, I said to her, 'It is not worth while Monsieur is dead,' and I began to cry without restraint. Am I guilty of any wrongs against him? I don't think so. I have always tried to be amiable ... but at such a time one always feels guilty of something ...

Marie Bashkirtseff, 1883

Drank far too much last night and woke at 5.30 a.m. Could've gone on drinking all night. Quite grateful for a hangover, it provides a bit of peace. Walked on to my balcony completely naked last night and took the couple that have moved into the suite next door slightly by surprise. Walked back in calmly affecting insouciance and then bit all my pillows, one after the other.

Emma Thompson, 1995

12 June

This part of the Mountain is said to abound with Rattlesnakes, & why I did not meet them in these unfrequented places I know not. I gathered a great many plants, Green gave them all names, and I stopped at his House to write them down ... Madder, toothache plant, a beautiful species of fern, Sore Throat weed, Dragon's blood, Adam & Eve or ivy blade, very large, which heals Cuts or burns, droppings of beach [sic], enchanter's nightshade, Dewberrys, Wild Turnip which cures a cough – it is like an Arum.

They prepared me some refreshment at this House, some excellent Cakes baked on the coals, Eggs, a boiled black squirrel, tea & Coffee made of Peas which was good, they said Chemists Coffee was better. The sugar was made from black Walnut Trees which looks darker than that from the Maple, but I think it is sweeter.

Elizabeth Simcoe, Canada, 1796

... Totally alone all day – not even a wrong number on the telephone to break my solitary confinement.

Miles Franklin, 1949

One works for the far future with children: probably for after one's death: certainly for when they have children ... I remember seeing in the one written page of this very book Mother gave me to use, the line she had left: 'I am always very lonely.' What bores women are with their loneliness!

Ivy Jacquier, 1922

13 June

Went with the Mills to the Anti-Slavery Meeting at Exeter Hall, and had capital places assigned to us. It was so immensely crowded, and at eleven we were all ordered to take off our hats, as Prince Albert and an illustrious train appeared on the platform. The acclamations attending his entry were perfectly deafening, and he bore them all with calm, modest dignity, repeatedly bowing with considerable grace. He is certainly a very beautiful young man, a thorough German, and a fine poetical specimen of the race.

Caroline Fox, 1840

The gnats kept Arabel & me & half the house besides up half the night: witness my swelled finger – witness this *eccentric* writing. I will *gnat* sleep in that room again, until the weather changes.

Elizabeth Barrett (Browning), 1831

On June 7 Miss Fawcett came out *above* the Senior Wrangler in the Cambridge mathematical Tripos. This caused a great stir throughout the cultivated world. I never saw Bob [her husband] more moved as one of his most intimate beliefs is the inferiority of the female brain where mathematics are concerned. He has a perfect right to this belief after having been married to me for 17 years, for I can just get through the household accounts & the yearly budget and *no more*.

... I used to care so very much for the 'Women's Cause'. Whether it is that the women who endeavour to lead it sicken me, or that my interests and joys are bound up in one man and three boys I do not know ... The real reason why I have ceased to care for it is that I have lived, surrounded by stronger characters than myself who have not cared, &, being reduced for so many years to less than half rations of health & strength, I have kept any small energy I might possess for more immediate use. Every woman feels 2 inches taller for this success of Miss Fawcett, aged 22.

Mary, Lady Monkswell, 1880

Man knows himself necessary to woman.

He has therefore acquired an almost fatuous self-confidence. And the majority of women, whether from cupidity, or sex need, or vanity, have so much at stake in their love for men that they allow men to arrogate to themselves a despotic power over their lives.

When for any one of these reasons her tyrant becomes indispensable, woman faces the double problem of holding her tyrant and lightening her yoke. There is but one means of achieving these two ends, and that is by the basest sort of flattery. Submission, loyalty, tender care and devotion a man takes for granted. He ceases to value them because they are given him for nothing. Unless he receives all these from a woman he will not deign to bother with her at all.

She must do more for him. She must prostrate herself before him ...

George Sand, 1837

14 June

My goodness what a lovely summer!

Through my window I can see the moon in the clear sky. It is still and silent, and the air is caressing and delightfully warm. I have been spending almost all my time outside with nature; I go swimming and in the evenings I water the flowers and go for walks. My beloved Tanya [her daughter] is staying here with her husband, with whom I am becoming reconciled since she loves him so ...

Sophia Tolstoy, 1902

How I like things to be done quietly and without fuss. It is the fuss and bustle principle, which must proclaim itself until it is hoarse, that wars against Truth and Heroism. Let Truth be done in silence till it is forced to speak,' and then should it only whisper, all those whom it may concern will hear.

Caroline Fox, 1843

Yesterday I went to register … I said I did social and secretarial work. She entered me as a Welfare Worker. Was I full time? My reply – Very much so! She did not think I should be called before Christmas. Met another of my age group coming out. She said pathetically: 'They have put me down as unemployed – and I am looking after my aged Mother and have other responsibilities, and have done so for years. I don't know what she would do without me.' I told her not to worry – they would only take her for part time work.

Winifred Vere Hodgson, 1942

15 June

As I sat so quiet and still, a question in a Mass Observation questionnaire that I'd done this morning came back into my mind – about the war's effect on 'sex'. Speaking personally, I could only say that, at fifty-one, sex questions answered themselves, war or no war; but I began to think back to when I was a girl – and after all, that's not such a very great while since …

… A woman was expected – and brought up – to obey, and we had not got far from the days of Victorian repression: men expected to be masters in matters widely to do with sex. No woman was ever expected to be out, for instance, when her husband came in for a meal. Gosh, how I've nearly broken my neck to race home in time to brew the tea and pour it – even though the rest of the meal was laid ready. No woman was let go on holiday alone …

… Now I sense a different spirit. One never sees the pub doors disgorge groups of fuddled soldiers, with harpies hanging on to their arms or waiting outside. Everything in respect of sex is altering – when I think of naughty old men I knew, engaging front seats at a music-hall we had then, because they could see the girls' knees when they danced! And when I think of what they could see of the 'female form divine' on a country walk – well, I chuckle.

Nella Last, 1941

I wonder if it's because I haven't been able to poke my nose outdoors for so long that I've grown so crazy about everything to do with nature? I can perfectly well remember that there was a time when a deep blue sky, the song of the birds, moonlight and flowers would have never kept me spellbound. That's changed since I've been here …

Alas, it has had to be that I am only able – except on a few rare occasions – to look at nature through dirty net curtains hanging before very dirty windows. And it's no pleasure looking through these any longer, because nature is just the one thing that really must be unadulterated.

Anne Frank, 1944

At 1.30 a.m. Mother knew me, at 3.30 she went into coma & passed at 1.30 p.m.

Miles Franklin, 1938

16 June

The woods about the waterfall veined with rich yellow Broom. A succession of delicious views from Skelleth to Brathay. We met near Skelleth a pretty little Boy with a wallet over his shoulder – he came from Hawkshead and was going to 'late' a lock [seek a measure] of meal. He spoke gently and without complaint. When I asked him if he got enough to eat he looked surprized and said 'Nay'. He was 7 years old but seemed not more than 5.

Dorothy Wordsworth, 1800

I have suffered a great deal since I have been sick but never more than during this last trip – The journey to Geneva was fearful also! Once there I rallied again; we sent for the celebrated Dr Binet, whom we liked very much … He said first that I had developed bodily & mentally much too fast and now I have to make up for it, by perfect quiet of mind & body. I am not allowed to read anything serious, or have any kind of lesson. I think the whole time & that I cant help; I wanted to know German as well as I know French, which could only be done by my going to school in Dresden; but they say I mustn't think of such a thing as taxing my brain any more, & that this lazy, idle stupid, dull life is the only thing for me. As soon as I begin to fail in one place we must leave it & go to another. – I can draw & paint though whenever I have a good day, & no one knows the pleasure it gives me … If I were obliged to earn my living, I might make a name for myself that would last, but situated as I am, it is more likely that I shall live a comfortable life, & die & be forgotten.

Julia Newberry (aged 17), 1871

17 June

I have sunk very low. I emptied tea leaves out of the window.

Barbara Pym, 1943

How strange it was that within the same day I should have under my roof the successful & extremely intelligent woman novelist of 37 crying bitterly because (it amounts to that) she hadn't had a man, & at the other end of the intellectual scale the little housemaid of 20 crying just as bitterly because she had. I decided that on the whole it was probably far more bearable to be Dorothy [the maid] …

Vera Brittain, 1932

I find myself once more immersed in the gaieties of a London season, in which I had thought I should never again participate. But my young orphan niece, a girl of great beauty, and not less amiable than beautiful, and very dear to me, is the object which induces me to seek such scenes. At first a few of my old acquaintants were amazed when they discovered my altered and aged face in the gay crowds … I must confess the old stagers, who have without intermission gone on living in constant dissipation, look less aged than those who have been absent for some years, on their return to the world. Not one of my contemporaries appears to be half as old as I am … I will not look worse than they. I have a great mind to begin again wearing rouge, and get a new 'front,' and grow young. Yet I shrink from assuming youth now that it is gone. I cannot buy a young heart …

Lady Charlotte Bury, 1819

After dinner, Papa unfortunately walked *after* me out of the room … The consequence of this was a critique on my down-at-heel shoes; & the end of that, was my being sent out of the drawing-room to put on another pair. So while Anne is mending the only pair I have in the world, I am doing my best to write nonsense and catch cold without any.

Elizabeth Barrett (Browning), 1831

18 June

Discovery: that love is not all in life even for women. I say it again and again and to sleep drew out a chart. If we faced love as men do we would be happier. As episodes, accesses. Life is not meant for love alone. We are hipped by the old saws of women about life turning on love, etc., etc. *Je veux surmonter ma fémininité.* Love is not the whole of life. One ought to use men as they do us, as a means of experience to more knowledge. (Not more men because one is fairly monogamous.) To realise what A.'s [her husband] given me for instance. A fuller life, more established, more rounded … and then be self-supporting, a person, not a wife.

Ivy Jacquier, 1922

I walked slowly along the street, staring across it at the houses. I came to the corner, to a dark little park called Bedford Square. On three sides of it, more rows of neat, narrow brick houses, these much more beautiful and beautifully cared for. I sat on a park bench and stared at the houses. I was shaking. And I'd never in my life been so happy.

All my life I'd wanted to see London. I used to go to English movies just to look at streets with houses like those …

Charing Cross is a narrow, honky-tonk street, choked with traffic, lined with second-hand bookshops. The open stalls in front were piled with old books and magazines, here and there a peaceful soul was browsing in the misty rain.

We got out at 84 …

… I started back downstairs, my mind on the man, now dead, with whom I'd corresponded for so many years. Half-way down I put my hand on the oak railing and said to him silently:

'How about this, Frankie? I finally made it.'

Helene Hanff, 1971

Dusk falls, the light dying slowly behind the distant range. The roaring of jet fighters and scout planes has ceased. The forest in the evening is terrifyingly quiet. Not a single bird chirps. Not a human voice. There is only the murmur of the stream and the song from a transistor radio. I don't notice the song title. I am caught in the melody, as smooth as a rice field in the evening fog. Suddenly I forget everything, forget the heavy mood that has settled on me for the past few days …

Dang Thuy Tram, South Vietnam, 1970

19 June

What a divine night it is – I have just returned from Kentish Town – a calm twilight pervades the clear sky – the lamp like moon is hung out in heaven & the bright west retains the dye of sunset – If such weather would continue I should again write – The lamp of thought is again illumined in my heart – & the fire descends from heaven that kindles it – Such, my loved Shelley now ten years ago – at this season – did we first meet – & these were the very scenes. That churchyard with its sacred tombs was the spot where love first shone in your dear eyes – My own love – we shall meet again …

I feel my powers again – & this is of itself happiness – the eclipse of winter is passing from my mind – I shall again feel the enthusiastic glow of composition – again as I pour forth my soul upon paper, feel the winged ideas arise, & enjoy the delight of expressing them – study and occupation will be a pleasure and not a task – & this I shall owe to sight & companionship of trees & meadows flowers & sunshine –

I have been gay in company before but the inspiriting sentiment of the heart's peace I have not felt before tonight – and yet, my heart's own, never was I so entirely yours – in sorrow and grief I wish sometimes (how vainly) for earthly consolation, at a period of pleasing excitement – I cling to your memory alone – & you alone receive the overflowings of my heart – Beloved Shelley – Goodnight – One pang will seize me when I think – but I will only think that thou art where I shall be, & conclude with my usual prayer, from the depths of my soul I make it – May I die young! –

Mary Shelley, 1824

The position of the unmarried woman – unless, of course, she is somebody's mistress, is of no interest whatsoever to the readers of modern fiction. The beginning of a novel?

Barbara Pym, 1972

20 June

I was awoke at 6 o'clock by Mamma, who told me that the Archbishop of Canterbury and Lord Conyngham were here, and wished to see me. I got out of bed and went into my sitting-room (only in my dressing-gown), and *alone*, and saw them. Lord Conyngham then acquainted me that my poor Uncle, the King was no more, and had expired at 12 minutes p. 2 this morning, and consequently that I am *Queen* ...

Since it has pleased Providence to place me in this station, I shall do my utmost to fulfil my duty towards my country; I am very young and perhaps in many, though not in all things, inexperienced, but I am sure, that few have more real good will and more real desire to do what is fit and right than I have.

Queen Victoria, 1837

Have entered the fiftieth year of my reign and my Jubilee year. I was upset at the thought of those no longer with me, who would have been so pleased and happy, in particular my beloved husband, to whom I owe everything, who are gone to a happier world.

There were beautiful and most kind articles in *The Times*, *Standard* and *St James's*. I don't want or like flattery, but I am very thankful and encouraged by these marks of affection and appreciation of my efforts.

Queen Victoria, 1886

It's an odd idea for someone like me to keep a diary; not only because I have never done so before, but because it seems to me that neither I – nor for that matter anyone else – will be interested in the unbosomings of a thirteen-year-old schoolgirl. Still, what does that matter? I want to write, but more than that, I want to bring out all kinds of things that lie buried deep in my heart.

Anne Frank, 1942

I have been and am battling depression. It is as if my life were magically run by two electric currents: joyous positive and despairing negative – which ever is running at the moment dominates my life, floods it. I am now flooded with despair, almost hysteria, as if I were smothering. As if a great muscular owl were sitting on my chest, its talons clenching and constricting my heart. I knew this fresh life would be harder, much harder, than teaching – but I have weapons, and self-knowledge is the best of them. I was blackly hysterical last fall beginning my job: The outside demands exacted my blood, and I feared. Now, a totally different situation, yet the same in emotional content. I have fourteen months 'completely free' for the first time in my life, reasonable financial security, and the magic and hourly company of a husband so magnificent ... big, creative in a giant way, that I imagine I made him up – only he offers so much extra surprise that I know he is real and deep as an iceberg in its element. So I have all this, and my limbs are paralyzed ... there is no outer recalcitrant material to blame for snags and failures, only the bristling inner recalcitrance: sloth, fear, vanity, meekness.

Sylvia Plath, 1958

Today there is only enough rice left for an evening meal. We cannot sit and watch the wounded soldiers go hungry. But if one of us goes out, there is no guarantee she will be safe or that she can come back. There are too many dangers on the road. And if two of us go, leaving one behind, what can she do alone of something happens? Even without thinking about the remote possibilities, this rain in front of us is difficult enough. If it starts pouring in earnest how can one person manage? She can't cover the shelter in advance because of the danger of being spotted by airplanes. Still, in the end, two of us must go.

Dang Thuy Tram, South Vietnam, 1970

Two days later, on a jungle trail, Dang Thuy Tram was shot dead by an American patrol.

21 June

We afterwards went to Mrs Jenkinson's where I had appointed Campbell to meet us, and there I experienced what I can hardly bear to think of now and what I hope he may never make me feel again – He had an air of triumph, and a sort of flow of *false spirits* like a person who is doing wrong, who knows it, and yet *cannot help* doing it – He was going to meet Mrs S. at a Concert, and left me at cards notwithstanding the pressing entreaties of everyone present – I alone did not dare say one word because I knew, *why* he was so anxious to go – but I felt so mortified, so hurt and so wretched, that the tears actually ran down my cheeks – but he did not see it, and went to ratify his vanity at the expense of my heart – Vanity is his prevailing fault and he cannot resist this abominable woman – I could not sleep and cried all night – to be thus slighted by a Man whom I love with so much sincerity and tenderness and to be slighted for an unworthy object, who at best can only feel a whim for him, is too much for me to bear –

Eugenia Wynne (Campbell), 1806

Meanwhile my husband and I grow nearer to each other each hour of the day. A beautiful pact, marriage. Personal love and tenderness, community of faith, fellowship in work, a divine relationship. The one and only drawback – a doubt whether happiness does not stupefy life with its inevitable self-complacency. As days and months fly by, and little is done, one wonders whether one is unduly apathetic or simply lazy …

Beatrice Webb, 1893

Left camp and started over the Black Hills, sixty miles over the worst road in the world. Have again struck the Platte [River] and followed it until we came to the ferry. Here we had a great deal of trouble swimming our cattle across, taking our wagons to pieces, unloading and replacing our traps. A number of accidents happened here. A lady and four children were drowned through the carelessness of those in charge of the ferry.

Sallie Hester (aged 14), 1849

22 June

Did three pages on the novel. Tired to death but work out of sheer nervous desperation, weight of responsibility, necessity for making plans about Jojo [her troubled son] this fall, making money for these plans. I can't see or think about anything else …

Thinking it over, no great woman writers ever raised kids, did they? All the 'charming' lady literati have had charming children but then they write magazine trash. Women seem to me the greatest opportunists. The most unscrupulous artist in the world – they turn any genius they have into money without a pang – whereas the man artist, supporting his family by distortions of his genius, never ceases to bemoan his lost ideal.

Dawn Powell, 1931

Noon: Finish scene with Alan [Rickman].

Me: 'Oh! I've just ovulated.'

Alan (long pause): 'Thank you for that.'

Emma Thompson, 1995

Great news at last! Germany has invaded Russia – and we shall see what they can do about it. The Russians have not been too nice to us in the past, but now we have to be friends and help one another ... I ran across the landing to tell Mrs Watkins and beg her to come. She leapt out of bed and padded across with bare feet to hear that Goebbels had been talking at 5 a.m. – and the whole thing was underway ...

It has been a sweltering day – my room is like an oven. Mrs Fisher came and we made for the Park ... We watched all the sights of the Park. One couple well-known for bringing their Siamese cat for a walk ... though this time the little creature was draped around the man's neck, quite happy. Then the man who brings the green parrot – he was there.

Tonight have heard Mr Churchill. Says we have just reached the 4th climacteric of the war. One was the defection of France. 2nd: defeat of the Germans by the R.A.F. over England. 3rd: passing of the Lease-Lend Act, and the 4th: entry of Russia into the war. He had already notified the Russians we should support them as much as they wanted us to.

Winifred Vere Hodgson, 1941

Dined with Mary Herbert – a particularly successful and delightful party ... Every woman was looking her best. Why does that sometimes happen?

Lady Cynthia Asquith, 1917

23 June

... Fyodor went off to the Rooms taking with him some thalers and fifteen ducats; but he promised not to play, and not to stay here long. I stayed in and sewed some hooks on my dress, as well as mending my coat, and generally putting my clothes to rights. I was terribly depressed and full of fear, I don't know exactly why, but I could scarcely bear it. I didn't want to see anyone or go anywhere, but only to lie in the dark room and not move. At the end of three hours Fyodor came back and told me he had lost all the money he had taken with him ... Poor Fyodor, he is fearfully depressed. There's no help for it, however, and we still have forty-five ducats.

Anna Dostoevsky, 1867

I have had a visit from my beloved, my kindest Father – and he came determined to complete my recovery by his goodness. I was *almost* afraid – and *quite* ashamed to be alone with him – but he soon sent for me to his little Gallery Cabinet – and then, with a significant smile that told me what was coming, and made me glow to my very forehead with anxious expectation, he said 'I have read your Book [*Evelina*], Fanny – but you need not blush at it. – It is full of merit – it is really extraordinary.' – I fell upon his Neck with heart-beating emotion, and he folded me into his arms so tenderly that I sobbed upon his shoulder – so delighted was I with his precious approbation ... I had written my little Book simply for my amusement; I printed it, by the means first of my Brother, Charles, next of my Cousin, Edward Burney, merely for a frolic, to see how a production of my own would figure in that Author like form: but as I had never read any thing I had written to any human being but my sisters, I had taken it for granted that They, only, could be partial enough to endure my compositions. My unlooked for success surprised, therefore, my Father as much as my self –

Fanny Burney, 1778

At breakfast this morning, Bummy [her aunt] proposed that I shd. go to see [her neighbour] Mr Boyd in the evening ... I wd. not go tomorrow or any day if I did not believe in my heart that he really does like to have me with him.

Elizabeth Barrett (Browning), 1831

24 June

How kind and amiable Captain Fremantle is. He pleases me more than any man I have yet seen. Not handsome, but there is something pleasing in his countenance and his fiery black eyes are quite captivating. He is good natured, kind, and amiable, gay and lively in short he seems to possess all the good and amiable qualities that are required to possess everybodies heart the first moment one sees him.

Betsey Wynne Fremantle, 1796

Wednesday, And Midsummer day the 24 of June, being very Ill by A violent fit of the Colic, I Attempted my going out [of London] In hopes of A Little quiet (having had none In six months before) and Being Quite Tired out, and my son apprehending my death Near, Came in the Coach down with me, tho' I begged the Contrary of him, and by God's Great mercy to me I Came home in my own Coach In five days.

Elizabeth Freke, 1712

O happy, happy day! No letter this morning as I ate peaches and cream, but there was one this evening when I got home. Airmail!!! It was pale red – the stamp – and I laid it on the carpet till I had taken a shower and dusted the house, poured some rum, lit a cigarette – and finally – four yellow pages – all about the cat painting, and on the last page – last line, she wrote: My love Pat really – Allela [Cornell]. And my heart soared once more! I'll keep the letters – (four) of course. Forever.

Patricia Highsmith, 1943

'I don't feel towards you as if you were my daughter.'

  'I don't feel as if you were my Father.'

  'What a tragedy. What are we going to do about it? I have met *the* woman of my life, the ideal, and it is my daughter! I cannot even kiss you as I would like to. I'm in love with my own daughter!'

'Everything you feel, I feel.' …

With a strange violence, I lifted my negligee and I lay over him.

'*Toi, Anaïs! Je n'ai plus de Dieu!*'

Ecstatic, his face, and I now frenzied with the desire to unite with him … undulating, caressing him, clinging to him. His spasm was tremendous, of his whole being. He emptied all of himself in me … and my yielding was immense, with my whole being, with only that core of fear which arrested the supreme spasm in me.

Then I wanted to leave him. Still, in some remote region of my being, a revulsion. And he feared the reaction in me. I wanted to run away. I wanted to leave him. But I saw him so vulnerable … this flight, I would not hurt him with. No, not after the years of pain my last rejection had caused him. But at this moment, after the passion, I had at least to go to my room, to be alone. I was poisoned by this union. I was not free to enjoy the splendor of it, the magnificence of it. Some sense of guilt weighed down on my joy and continued to weigh down on me, but I could not reveal this to him. He was free – he was passionately free – he was older and more courageous. I would learn from him. I would at last be humble and learn something from my Father!

Anaïs Nin, 1933

25 June

An inexpressibly sad day to me, I looked again for letters but finding none, went with a depressed spirit in search of strawberries … While I read Ernest the Seeker, I could not help thinking, what a mistake it is in the Protestant Church that it does not provide for its broken-hearted members. How much happier for me, if when Mr Dall left [to preach in Calcutta, against Caroline's wishes], I could have gone into some retreat, approved by my own friends, where I could have been useful to others, & not separated from my children, have educated them in the best manner, without pecuniary anxiety. But our church is no mother to her desolate children and I have not a friend on earth whom I dare ask to share the whole burden of my soul.

Caroline Healey Dall, 1855

... We still have twenty-five gold pieces left, but Fyodor has taken another five to-day, which only makes twenty, really. As he was going out he asked me to be ready by the time he came back, that we might go to the post together. Directly he had gone, I began to feel incredibly afraid. I was almost certain he would go and lose all the money he had with him, and then come back again in that terrible state. Several times I burst into tears, and was quite beside myself, but when Fyodor came home, I asked him with the utmost calmness: 'Have you lost?' 'Yes,' he said, distractedly, and once again cursed his own weakness. With much emotion in his voice he assured me how he loved me, how I was a splendid woman, and he was not worthy of me. Then he implored me to give him more money.

Anna Dostoevsky, 1867

There is one thing has struck me in this tedious crisis, and that is the confidence with which everyone – except the Radicals – looked on the Queen. Say what they like, it is a great thing to have someone at the head of the kingdom, who, unlike a president, is not dependent for place on either party.

Beatrix Potter (aged 18), 1885

Re-read my diaries of 1875, 1876, and 1877. I complain in them of I know not what; I have aspirations towards something indefinite. Every evening I felt sore and discouraged, pending my strength in fury and despair in trying to find *what to do*. Go to Italy? Stop in Paris? Get married? Paint? What was to be done? If I went to Italy I couldn't be in Paris and I wanted to be everywhere at once!! What vigour there was in it all!!!

As a man I should have conquered Europe. Young girl as I was, I wasted it in excesses of language and silly eccentricities. Oh, misery!

Marie Bashkirtseff, 1884

The poor Queen's [Victoria] terrible fault in remaining (or indeed being) at Balmoral has given rise to universal complaint, and much foul-mouthed gossip. She is travelling up tonight.

Lucy (Lady Frederick) Cavendish, 1866

26 June

Monday evening June 26th 1937 A bit past 4 o'clock Charlotte working in Aunt's room, Branwell reading Eugene Aram to her – Anne and I writing in the drawing room – Anne a poem beginning 'Fair was the evening and brightly the sun' – I Augusta Almeda's life 1st V. 1 – 4th page from the last – fine rather coolish thin grey clouds but sunny day Aunt working in the little room the old nursery Papa gone out Tabby in the kitchen – the Emperors and Empresses of Gondal and Gaaldine preparing to depart [Gondal was the Brontës' imaginary world] … All tight and right in which condition it is hoped we shall all be this day 4 years …

Emily and Anne Brontë, 1837

The baby's room was still and peaceful, the big French windows wide open, just the same secure intimate room it was in that other world. I left the door open.

This place does not suggest crime now, but I realize here intensely what I am realizing at Englewood more and more: that the new baby will not make any difference to me in this feeling I have for Charlie. I thought vaguely it would be different after the baby came, but it won't be at all. It won't change things. I'll miss him just as much. The feeling for the new baby will grow up separately, a lovely, different thing, alongside of this feeling. I'll live with that always, always all my life, only it will be perhaps easier to live with because more and more separate from my daily life. I don't want it to be otherwise.

Anne Morrow Lindbergh, 1932

I was taking walk over to little Island and I found three see gall [sic] eggs in one nest. and I cook them for my lunch I take tea and Saccharine I had a nice picknick all by myself. [Knight had died on the 23rd.]

Ada Blackjack, 1923

27 June

Nothing particular occurred during the week. I still continued very sick and became so weak that I could scarcely sit up. About 6 o'clock this morning I felt very unwell and had the Doctor and Mrs Davies called up, and a little after six *Mary-Jane* was born. She was so very small that I was inclined to think she was born a month too soon, but the Doctor thought it was owing to my having been so very sick.

At 9 o'clock Mr D. baptized our little girl and gave her the name of Mary Jane. After my confinement I never was in the least sick, and should have been up in a day or two but that the weather was exceedingly stormy, and the Ship was very much tossed. Mr D. was so very unwell that he almost thought he should not survive the passage.

Sarah Docker, curate's wife and emigrant to Australia, aboard the Adams,
1828

The locals have arranged a pilgrimage to Lourdes. All Brittany took part. The sister of my cook, Marie, wanted to go. She prayed for me and asked that my wishes be granted. She came back yesterday, and no later than that same evening I got a telegram from an agency saying: 'Found firm buyer [for the family home] who sees solicitor tomorrow, drop all discussions.' A little miracle! Coincidence, the sceptics say. Me, I prefer to believe in miracles. Is not every being's existence a miracle in itself?

Liane de Pougy, 1926

28 June

… I then again descended from the Throne, and repaired with all the Peers bearing the Regalia, my Ladies and Train-bearers to St Edward's Chapel, as it is called; but which, as Lord Melbourne said, was more unlike a Chapel than anything he had ever seen; for what was called an Altar was covered with sandwiches, bottles of wine, etc., etc. The Archbishop came in and ought to have delivered the orb to me, but I had already got it, and he (as usual) was so confused and puzzled and knew nothing and – went away. Here we waited some minutes; Lord Melbourne took a glass of wine, for he seemed completely tired. The Procession being formed, I replaced my Crown (which I had taken off for a few minutes), took the Orb in my left hand and the Sceptre in my right, and thus loaded, proceeded through the Abbey – which resounded with cheers …

Queen Victoria, 1838

I *like* the life I lead – working here & just going to M.[ass] when I can of a Sunday, & a chance time to clean of a weekday when I can get leave now & then, oftener of course if I could – better even I think than a married life. For I never feel as if I *could* make up my mind to that – it's too much like being a *woman*.

Hannah Cullwick, 1871

The people generally remark, as I pass along, how much I am like a man. I think they did it more than usual this evening. At the top of Cunnery Lane, as I went, three men said, as usual, 'That's a man' & one axed 'Does your cock stand?' I know not how it is but I feel low this evening. I don't think quite so much of Miss Browne but still too much … I wish I could get her out of my head.

Anne Lister, 1818

29 June

I am a descendant of slaves. I came from nothing. No power. No money. Not even my thoughts were my own. I had no free will. No voice. Now, I have the freedom, power, and will speak to millions every day – having come from nowhere. I would be a fool to give up *The Oprah Winfrey Show*. I must figure out a way to make it work. To surround myself with people who are enthusiastic, who want to do it, who are not burned out, who understand the worth of this extraordinary time and opportunity to change people for the better.

Oprah Winfrey, 1997

I am home all day because I got monthly and I fix bed and I went after a seal she was up between from end of sandspit before she went down and when I came back after trying to get that seal I fixed the back sight and shot target and I hit where I aiiam [aiming]...

Ada Blackjack, 1923

I have never seen anyone with such a capacity for making a place uncomfortable as Mrs Lloyd George. Her meanness forces the household to economise in coal & food, & everything that makes for comfort. The servants would be a disgrace to any house, & the PM is rightly ashamed of them. But it is no use his protesting – he says he gave that up long ago, because it had no effect & only caused unpleasantness.

Frances Stevenson, 1919

… In the present ridiculous state of society the chances are as in my case that I literally only beheld Bob twice in morning costume, i.e. not at a party, before I was engaged to him. I will not complain of the bridge that has carried me over, but absurd & mistaken in the extreme are the laws of the intercourse between unmarried men & women.

Mary, Lady Monkswell, 1874

I spent an agonizing morning in the midst of suspense and anxiety – Bankes call'd after his conference with Campbell, whom he persuaded to write to his Father to settle on him £700 per annum and to enable him to settle upon me and my children the Estate which it appears his Father is at liberty to sell during his Life time – Unless the Father agrees to this Bankes advises me not to think of the match …

Eugenia Wynne (Campbell), 1806

30 June

What would it be like to live in a world where it is always June? Would we get tired of it? I daresay we would, but just now I feel that I could stand a good deal of it if it were as charming as today.

But that is the *outside* world. Inwardly, I have been as a ravening wolf!

I had a 'white night' last night. I don't often have them. I generally have a firm enough grip on myself to choke back all premonitory symptoms and go to sleep like a philosopher. But last night – somehow – the floods overwhelmed me. Gods, how I felt!

I couldn't sleep – didn't sleep until dawn. Every trouble I ever had came surging up with all its old bitterness – and all my little present-day worries enlarged themselves to tenfold proportions and flew at my throat. Life seemed a horrible, cruel, starving thing and I hated it and wished I were dead. I cried bitterly at sheer heart sickness and loneliness. Anything like that wrings the stamina out of me. I never can stop half way in an emotion. I must sound the deeps every time and sometimes they are like to drown me. I am a hundred years older than I was yesterday …

L. M. Montgomery, 1902

This is the last day of June and finds me in black despair because Clive [Bell] laughed at my new hat, Vita [Sackville-West] pities me, and I sank to the depths of gloom … Clive suddenly said, or bawled rather, what an astonishing hat you're wearing! Then he asked where I got it. I pretended a mystery, tried to change the talk, was not allowed, and they pulled me down between them, like a hare, it was very forced and queer and humiliating. So I talked and laughed too much. Duncan [Grant] prim and acid as ever told me it was utterly impossible to do anything with a hat like that. And Leonard got silent, and I came away deeply chagrined, as unhappy as I have been these ten years; and revolved it in sleep and dreams all night; and today has been ruined.

Virginia Woolf, 1926

The 30th still working and being extremely melancholy and sad to see things go so ill with me and fearing my lord would give all his land away from the Child.

Lady Anne Clifford, 1617

Have just been much put about by discovering I had unbeknown pulled off my wedding-ring for the very first time. Made my Fred put it on again, as I remember Mamma used to make Papa.

Lucy (Lady Frederick) Cavendish, 1867

July

'My poor Journal! how dull, unentertaining,
uninteresting thou art! – oh what I would give
for some Adventure worth reciting!'

Fanny Burney, 1768

1 July

I don't know how to write about this awful day. I didn't expect Beb [her husband Herbert Asquith] till 2.30, so had arranged to lunch with my grandmother. Was back soon after two, ran into the room in high spirits. Beb said, 'I'm afraid there's bad news', and gave me an opened letter from Papa. 'The worst is true about Ego [Hugo Charteris]. The officer prisoners of Angora certify that he was killed at Katia … I don't know how Letty [Ego's wife] will be told. It is very cruel and we must all help each other to bear it.'

Oh God – Oh God, my beautiful brother that I have loved so since I was a baby – so beautiful *through* and *through*! Can it be true that he'll never come back? At first I could only think of Letty, just the blank horror of that gripped me …

Letty was alone with the children, playing the piano to them. Papa went up – I waited downstairs. The music stopped and I heard a gay 'Hulloa', and then silence. I rushed up and found Letty clinging to Papa. It's indescribable – it was just like somebody in fearful, unimaginable, physical pain …

Marjorie came in, perfectly self-controlled and bracing – spoke to Letty as you would to a housemaid being vaccinated. 'Now, now Letty – come, come'. At last we got her to go upstairs and carried her to her room …

Cynthia Asquith, 1916

I have been addicted of late to growing faint after breakfast. I do not much mind it myself, only that it alarms papa and mamma. Poor papa is so anxious about me, that one would think every cough I utter is my death-knell.

I suppose I am never to be strong again …

Emily Shore (aged 18), 1838

At times when I see such silly waste in shop windows, I think it's a pity there are no women in the War Cabinet … It's getting easy to recognise the haves and have-nots now – womenfolk I mean – by the wearing of silk stockings and frequent trips to the hairdresser's. I think silk stockings and lovely soft leather gloves are the only two things I envy women for. I can dodge or contrive dresses and, as I'm light on my feet, my shoes last a long time with care, but there is such an uplift about seeing one's feet and legs so sleek and silky, or in peeling off a pair of lovely leather-smelling gloves. My hands are small squarish paws, with knotting fingers, but my feet and legs are my one beauty and, when I have the choice of a birthday or Christmas present, I like to choose silk stockings – or if it will run to it, new shoes.

Nella Last, 1940

At length I have been able to arrange my affairs, so as to be free to leave England, and go where I like … The sun is gaily shining: it withdrew for a moment, as we slowly glided out of the harbour at Dover; for a moment, too, a cloud of tender regret for what might have been, stole across my mind; but the recollection that it is not, quickly resumed its power, and a feeling of pride and pleasure succeeded, that I was going to new scenes which would occupy and change the current of my thoughts. Perhaps, like a person excited by fictitious means, I may sink hereafter; but the present moment is buoyant with renovated hope.

Lady Charlotte Bury, 1814

2 July

Ghastly awakening. She [Letty] began moaning in her sleep, 'Don't let me wake up to this ghastly day – I don't want to wake up'. She said, 'I've had such a wonderful dream. I dreamt that he was there.' Then the full realisation came back to her: 'Oh God, make me mad – make me mad, if I can't die!' 'Come back to me for just one minute my sweet Ego, just to tell me how to bear it, I can't bear it without you …'

The agony of one's impotence to help. I'm not the right person for her – not spontaneous enough, too self-conscious. A sense of their utter futility makes the words die in my throat …

Beb and I had early dinner and then he went away to Brighton. Not till I was left alone did I feel the full pain for myself – Letty's had parried it. It burst upon me now and I was in Hell.

Cynthia Asquith, 1916

Tonight we had our annual dinner with the Windsors. The party was chiefly American and included Mrs Donahue, the colossally rich Woolworth woman who pays for a great deal of the Windsors' life. She is the mother of the homosexual Donahue for whom the Duchess conceived such a notorious passion two or three years ago, and during which she became rude, odious and strange. One had the impression that she was either drugged or drunk. She spent all her time with the effeminate young man, staying in nightclubs till dawn and sending the Duke home early: 'Buzz off, mosquito' – what a way to address the once King of England! Finally Donahue's boy-friend is alleged to have told him 'It's either her or me', and so he chucked the Duchess.

Cynthia Gladwyn, political hostess, 1956

LONDON. We rode. A runaway man and horse, we heard, came full tilt against the Prince of Wales, who was riding with the Princess and the Queen of the Belgians, and knocked him clean over, horse and all. He rode home, and dined out this evening; so I suppose he is not much hurt ...

Lucy (Lady Frederick) Cavendish, 1866

3 July

Came upstairs at 6 to prepare for the bleeding … In bed at 7.40. The leechwoman Jane Protheroe came upstairs immediately & put 12 leeches on my back, from the bottom to 5 or 6 inches upwards. It was 1¾ hour (9½) before the last leech was taken off & I was *very* much tired of lying so long in one position. The blood drawn by the midway leeches (one in particular on the left side) was *very* black & thick, the woman said. The blood of the topmost leeches was the best.

Anne Lister, 1823

For over a year I've been longing for death, for an end to the pain and torment Barny [her lover] has caused me, and in a blank indifferent way I even hope for more final calamities as another spur to drive me on to make an end. My period is five days overdue – it's possible that I conceived, that night at the hut – well, and if I have? The one overwhelming reason for dying.

Loran Hurnscot, 1926

Fyodor can never stay long at rest in one place, and now asked me if there was nothing he could go and get. He is as pleased as Punch, these days, to go out and shop, and has quite taken it off my shoulders. I told him we were in need of cheese, oranges and a lemon. He went off, promising not to go to roulette, however strong the temptation. A long time went by, and the tea was brought in, but no Fyodor, so that I began to think he had not been able to get the better of his desire and had gone to play, after all. At last he appeared, with his pockets crammed full of every conceivable thing. First of all he handed me out the cheese, oranges, and lemons, and then produced a bottle the contents of which puzzled me greatly. Whatever could it be? Why, of course, my favourite relish – *ryzhiki*! Was there ever such a man! What other husband in the world would have found *ryzhiki* for his wife in Baden-Baden? Really it is an achievement on his part never to be forgotten! Then he produced some bilberries from his pocket that he had also discovered here, then caviar, then some French mustard – in short, all the things I like best! Wasn't it sweet of him, and haven't I the dearest husband in the world?

Anna Dostoevsky, 1867

4 July

———

It is the 4th of July. Mrs Bush has invited me to do a literacy campaign event with her – I've said no. Better George should spend money on education, food & shelter for America's children than that I collude with his wife in the pretense that reading comes before eating.

Now to strike at least a *few* of the weeds from the garden!

Alice Walker, 1990

Had a divine weekend at Chequers, though Megan [Lloyd George's daughter] rather troublesome, turning up just before lunch on Sunday resented things being in my hands & was very cross and rude. Everyone noticed how bad-tempered she was. Her frivolous life is taking from her charm and looks. No one seems to have any control over her or to be responsible for her comings & goings. She just goes wherever she pleases & does what she likes – avoids her father when she has something else to do and resents finding me there when she condescends to turn up.

Frances Stevenson, 1921

…I went after the [seal] that was right in front of camp and I got the rifle already and wait for him to put his head up and rifle was already hammer was ready so I look for some thing and move around boom it went and seal went dow and I stand up and say fourth of juy. I was surprised rifle boomm so I had my fourth of July.

Ada Blackjack, 1923

Georges loves Littlest! Littlest loves Georges! Crack, it has happened. Is it worse than cancer?

Georges admitted it this morning, then Littlest, summoned, came in very pale. I've told myself for a long time that something was bound to happen.

Georges is so much younger than I am, he has given me eighteen years of happiness ... I must think! We're facing a common situation, after all. I don't want to take it too tragically and anyway love will find the way! If it's true love it will bend us to its laws. If it's a passing fancy it will pass. Yes but ... I've a difficult nature. I don't yet know how I'm going to react, behave to them or myself ... Georges is hooked, but he insists that he adores me and can't do without me. My great happiness – splendid, complete, pure – is finished.

Liane de Pougy, 1926

Slept all right, with Dial, a few contractions in the night but not many. Pretty nervous and worried by morning: also rather frightened, more for the baby than for myself. However Dr Hunter was extremely nice. Says it is perfectly O.K., and that it does sometimes take days with an induction. We also talked about schools, housing, etc., and about Ruth and Denny [her son and his fiancée] and the difficulties of a woman being able to work and also be married. But it is a nuisance to have these days with nothing to do in them, as I have everything tidied up; one is bound to concentrate more on oneself, which is so stupid, more than ever now.

Naomi Mitchison, 1940

5 July

I could not walk ... on account of fridging [sic] the leech-bites, which itched exceedingly all the while I was downstairs, the minute I was unemployed ... Sent for a blister today, at Suter's.

Anne Lister, 1823

All these ancestors and centuries, and silver and gold, have bred a perfect body. She [Vita Sackville-West] is stag like, or race horse like, save for the face, which pouts, and has no very sharp brain. But as a body hers is perfection. So many rare and curious objects hit one's brain like pellets, which perhaps may unfold later. But it's the breeding of Vita's that I took away as an impression [from Vita's ancestral home], carrying her and Knole in my eye as I travelled up with the lower middle classes, through slums.

Virginia Woolf, 1924

Just then the air raid siren went off. We hailed a taxi and persuaded the driver to take us to Ruthven's studio. As soon as I'd sunk into my seat Dylan [Thomas] smothered me in wet beery kisses, his blubbery tongue forcing my lips apart. It was rather like being embraced by an intoxicated octopus. I tried to tell myself that I was being embraced by a great poet but it was a relief when the taxi finally stopped.

Joan Wyndham, 1943

Rose at six. Showery all night. Heavy clouds. We shall have more rain I fear. Got two plates of cherries, one white and the other the Orleans cherry, for breakfast. Got a bundle of Moss Rose buds. Threw them in a careless manner over the Library table, which had a beautiful effect.

Lady Eleanor Butler, 1788

6 July

Went to Miss North – ordered black linen dress. I walked to Bruton Street, meeting Diana and Katharine on the way. I am looking so ghastly that people stare at me in the street. Soon I shall be too tired to think or feel.

Lady Cynthia Asquith, 1916

I noticed a very funny note in the kitchen from old Kate who 'does' for my mother. 'Madam,' it said, 'had one [bomb] at the top of our street. I was shot out of my bed. It was gastley, all night digging. Today I am nearly a cripple, I can hardly walk. I think it must be rumatism. I am breaking up. The butcher has run out of sausages.' My mother's note for today simply said, 'Dear Kate, so glad you are still alive. I think we will have Welsh Rarebit tonight.'

Joan Wyndham, 1943

Those English fans who invited me to dinner are a charming couple, they live in Kensington in a mews … in a charming little stable which, they explained to me cheerfully, is so hot all summer they get out of it as soon after supper as possible. In winter they freeze without heat and suffocate with it.

Across the street from them is Agatha Christie, just as comfortably situated and a lot older.

Demented.

Helene Hanff, 1971

… If I had anyone to help me through, I might yet have had this baby – a part of me wants it. But single-handed, I know that all reason is against it, and there is only some foolish instinctive thing in me that clamours – ignoring the obvious catastrophe it would be – to give life to Barny's child and mine.

Loran Hurnscot, 1926

I went into the Cabin for the first time since my confinement, and looked so well that the Captain said he should scarcely have known me for the same person. We were this day about 90 miles from Cape Finisterre.

Sarah Docker, emigrant to Australia, aboard the *Adams*, 1828

7 July

4th to 7th

I had better get this over. The induction began to work about 1.30 on the 4th; by 3.15 I had vomited, etc., had a very severe shivering fit, and was beginning to have very adequate first stage pains. I was however very glad it had started. By 6 they were quite severe, and shortly afterwards I asked for some kind of dope. I had scopolamine and morphine, on the strict understanding that these would have no effect on the baby. After a quarter of an hour I got drowsy, had another injection, and all but the worst pains clouded over. I think I had another later, but my time sense is uncertain, and I remember little until two or three violent pains, which appeared to me to be second stage; I said that the head was breaking through and I wanted some chloroform at once. I was right and the final stage was over in a few minutes, before Dr Cameron had arrived, even. I awoke to hear them say I had a lovely little girl; I said that was right, that was what I wanted. I asked several times, was she all right. They said yes, and I think I thought so, as they had worked on her for some time and thought she was breathing all right; I just saw her and kissed her. The rest of the night – it was then after 2 o'clock, I lay, uncomfortable but happy, mostly listening to her small noises, but thinking they were not very loud …

The septum of the heart had not closed properly. It would not have made any difference if she had been ten days later at full term. If she had lived it could not have been for more than a few months or years of a very wretched kind of existence. It was just one of those things which do happen. It was excessively hard to face. No one was to blame. Nothing could at any point have been done …

… The silly thing is that I realise perfectly that much worse things are happening at this minute to thousands of people (and indeed have done so for a long time), but one cannot generalise as simply as that. I at least cannot change pain into love. And all the little things hurt, hurt, hurt, and there is nothing to be done. Nor is it fair to speak about them to others; nor indeed, would the others understand one's minding so much. But she was part of me, and wanted, all these months, and warm, and one said what a nuisance, but lovingly, and now the whole thing is ended: the love has no object. I had dreamt so often of the sweet warmth and weight of a baby at my breasts and now my bound breasts ache. If I get at all drowsy I begin to expect someone to bring the baby in, and that's hell. One has to keep awake.

Naomi Mitchison, 1940

My back very sore but would have no more dressing with ointment. Sponged it well with cold water. Put a dry piece of linen next it & dressed … In the evening … bathed my back with urine with my hand, having first sponged it with cold water, & put a little tallow on.

Anne Lister, 1823

Yes, a mother – a real mother – that must be 'the someone' I dreamt about last night. Well, as far as that's concerned it's all over. I may as well lock up my heart with everything in it because the [step]mother I have finds me a bother, she hardly speaks to me, I feel I'm in her way like a little nuisance. Could it be that I am the cause of her coldness? I know I have a lot of faults. Even though I feel things deeply, I'm shy and reserved and undemonstrative. Perhaps she doesn't know how I long for a sign of love from her. Oh! this summer I would like to be friendly and affectionate to her – but I'm afraid, and when I reach out to her and she rejects me, I always feel bruised – as if someone has stepped on my heart …

Henriette Dessaulles (aged 14), 1875

10.15 p.m. Off home. Finished on Take 5 of Slate 550. A shot of Alan cantering against the sunset. The camera is inside a large gyroscopic white sphere, hung off the end of a small crane attached to a truck. Quite by accident I got a place on the back of the truck and witnessed the final take of the shoot go down, followed by the sun. Then we ate hamburgers and rubbery chips and drank champagne and there was much love around. People very moved. Lindsay and Laurie cried. I just grinned from ear to ear all evening. All within Elinor's breast was strong, silent satisfaction (it's in the book).

Emma Thompson (playing Elinor in *Sense and Sensibility*), 1995

8 July

Wake dizzy. Very mad. Kept still all day, hot & feeble. Dr read. Took nux. Rub & hot water at night. Slept well. Letters from A.[nna].

Louisa May Alcott, 1887

Made my bed and had breakfast 7.30 – scrambled egg and bacon, tea, bread, also cornflakes. Good! At 7.50 we had to muster on the parade ground and were taken in two lorries to R. N. Barracks, Chatham. Chatham is a cold windy place, as far as I could see, absolutely full of the Navy, of course. We stood in queues in various places for what seemed like a long time. We are, on the whole, a silly giggly lot and look rather dreary in our motley civilian clothes …

Barbara Pym, at Wren training camp, 1943

… Fyodor went off to pawn both our rings again, without mine having brought him the same luck as before. He lost, and we were once again without money. Our mid-day meal was still not paid for and we were thankful not to owe any more for our rent, and to have ordered in tea, coffee, and sugar. Next, Fyodor tried to sell my lace scarf at all sorts of places, but each time he was told they had no use for it, and passed on to another address. For three hours did he traipse the street without any success whatsoever …

Anna Dostoevsky, 1867

Last night, unpremeditatedly, I went to Laxworth, whom I think an unpleasant old man. I said, 'I think I'm pregnant and I want to stop it.' 'Huh, there's many a woman in your position,' he growled. 'Will the man stand by you?' 'Good Lord no,' I said. 'He's abroad with another woman.' 'That sort of rotter, eh?' he sniggered. I went to see him again this morning – revolting.

Loran Hurnscot, 1926

9 July

Pilgrimage to Littlehampton to see the children. John was supposed to be in a very naughty mood, but I really do see an improvement in him. His voice is much more normal and he answers more. His strange charm quite unimpaired. He has grown immense.

Cynthia Asquith, 1916

… I'd been to confession the day before … Liane de Pougy's confession has to be an awkward business, don't you think? She managed it in a few words! 'Father, except for killing and stealing I've done everything.'

Liane de Pougy, 1919

To Laxworth, where I spent the most ghastly hour of my whole life. Nothing terrifies me like physical pain, *nothing*. It is hideous, it drags everything down to one mindless level – you're just a tortured animal. No grief, no sorrow, no bitter suffering of the mind is as unnerving as physical agony – in it one's utterly degraded, beyond all philosophy, beyond all hope and thought.

Loran Hurnscot, 1926

10 July

Papa is much beloved in my family. Everybody likes him and says he's a very good man and a very good husband. I like hearing it but I'm always surprised at their just saying that papa's a good husband and never saying that mama's a good wife. Nevertheless, from the bottom of my heart I believe that only Our Lady could be better than mama …

When I see mama getting up at five in the morning, going out in the yard in all this cold, struggling with wet, green wood to start the kitchen fire to have our coffee and porridge ready by six, I feel so sorry I could die. She begins then and goes without stopping until evening, when we sit on the sofa in the parlor. I sit holding mama's arm on one side and Luizinha's on the other, to keep warm. Renato and Nhonhô sit on the floor beside the stove, and mama tells stories of bygone days … But this pleasant time never lasts very long. At half-past eight mama goes back to the kitchen to struggle with green firewood and get our porridge.

And yet nobody ever says mama's a good wife.

Helena Morley (aged 15), 1895

Now we haven't got a groschen. Fyodor was simply beside himself at the thought of having ruined me, and being once again without any means. He made another solemn resolution never to play roulette any more, as it is quite obvious Fate does not mean us to win …

Anna Dostoevsky, 1867

11 July

I went up to Mr Boyd, & fancied he was glad to see me. I really believe he was. When we had talked we read the seven chiefs, and when we had read we talked, and when we had talked I assisted him in learning some passages in the Prometheus. Happy day! – He said once, 'is it really your opinion that you will leave this house'? Yes: I answered – 'it is indeed'.

'And will you go away then next month – ?' I thought there was in his voice an expression of dejection. The tears came fast into my eyes! – I wish he may miss me …

… How tired I was, & unwell this evening. As, on our return I was sitting by myself in our bedroom, I heard what I used to hear in the summer of 1828 [when her mother died], & only *then* – the *deathwatch*. I grew sick & pale, & dizzy – & slept miserably all night – solely I believe from the strong unaccountable impression produced on me, by this circumstance. I have mentioned it to nobody, & don't much like mentioning it here. There never was a more foolishly weakly superstitious being than I am.

Elizabeth Barrett (Browning), 1831

Today I was woken by [her daughter] Emily saying, 'Granny's on the telephone.' I saw it was only 8.15, and said 'Oh God.' 'Granny sounds quite cheerful,' said Emily. For a second I thought egotistically that she might have got up early and liked the piece I'd written on Henley for the *Mail on Sunday*. But she just said that Daddy had just died. …

Feel bitterly ashamed of myself for not getting down to Haslemere to say goodbye to him.

Arrange to go straight down to Brighton to be with Mummy, but take the dogs for a quick cold walk first. Wish I could take them too to comfort me.

Notice, despite weedkiller, the heartsease is blooming again in the stricken Graveyard – but not for me. Two magpies for joy rise out of the blackthorn copse – the same as they did the day Fortnum died. Their credibility has really gone for ever now …

I am also bitterly ashamed that I feel a stab of disappointment at having to go to Brighton and missing my last Putney street party this evening. Is grief ever perfect?

Jilly Cooper, 1982

… I have never mentioned the absorbing subject – the subject which has filled our thoughts to the exclusion of Clive and Mary and literature and death and life – motor cars … We talk of nothing but cars. … yesterday we commissioned Fred to find us and bring instantly to our door a

Singer. We have decided on a Singer. And the reason I am distracted now is that Fred is going to ring me up and say if I am to have my first lesson this evening. This is a great opening up in our lives …

Virginia Woolf, 1927

12 July

I feel so terribly far away from the baby, in one of those numb periods the pendulum has swung into. I do not try to pull him back, I only feel the inevitable farawayness and do not try to fight it. Heavy, thick, unfeeling – I still feel dumbly and mutely sad. And yet it is not that poignant and comforting *missing him* that is, in its way, possession.

Anne says it will come back. She is comforting and I, who dread, in a way, this new baby, feeling it will stand between me and Charlie [her murdered son], feel comforted at her saying that the new thing will be a contrast to bring him back, that he will get closer. And then, at night, I dream, as though to justify her saying this, that I am looking at the new baby and, for the first time, I see next to it – Charlie's face.

Anne Morrow Lindbergh, 1932

I went to the slaughterhouse and got a few bones. I'm ill. I bought two sweet rolls for João and Vera. I found some tomatoes. I met an educated and well-speaking black who told me he lived in Jaçanã. I wanted to ask him his name but I was embarrassed. He gave two cruzeiros to João and I bought some kerosene. I went home, then went to Senhor Manuel to sell some scrap iron. The junkyard was closed. I went back home and laid down. I was cold and upset inside. The people of the favela know that I'm ill. But nobody shows up here to help me out. I didn't let João go out today and he spent the entire day reading. He talks to me and I tell him of the unfortunate things that exist in the world. My son now knows what the world is; between us the language of children has ended.

Carolina Maria de Jesus, 1958

I asked if he could point me toward Bloomsbury, I wanted to walk home.

'Go on up to O-burn Street and follow the bus.'

Looked for O-burn Street, looked for Auburn street and finally stumbled on the street he meant: High Holburn [sic]. And that's what they mean by a cockney accent.

Time to go crouch under that sadistic shower …

Helene Hanff, 1971

13 July

It was Wednesday, market day. All around us were huge, sweaty, red-faced men in work clothes finishing their meal, not very reassuring. They looked at us, but politely. My friends' charm got to work. Their voices became less loud. No one lit a pipe, or spat on the floor, or swore. We were like a charming little performance for them. The commonest of all kept winking at me. We ate like ogres. The pâté was really excellent, the chicken exquisite. As for the steak, we cried out with admiration … All these men seemed like our brothers!

Certainly the Ritz, where we went five or six times, is amusing, like a big liner packed with smart strangers; but the food there is horrible.

Liane de Pougy (at the Cochon d'Or, Paris), 1924

The anniversary of our wedding day. Celebrated it right joyfully by my first drive abroad with baby, Henry, nurse, and Tom, and our first dinner in the new dining-room. Hillard joined us. Charles provided a handsome bouquet and resurrected for the occasion some of our wedding-cake whose existence I knew not of. What a year this day completes! What a golden chain of months and days, and with this diamond clasp, born a month ago! I wonder if these old walls ever looked upon happier faces or through them down into happier hearts.

With this day my journal ends, for I have now a living one to keep faithfully, more faithfully than this.

Fanny Longfellow, 1844

Much better day, – in spite of the violent rain last night which agitated me teeth & all! – Arabel [her sister] & I got out of bed & ran to Minnie (little dears!) and I was in a thunder-&-lightning fright; & and my teeth did what my tongue does sometimes – *chattered*.

Elizabeth Barrett (Browning), 1831

14 July

The other day I asked for a late pass, Gowler said I was 'too old' to stay out late, I'd 'had my day' and I was 'burning the candle at both ends'.

I remember I used to say – when something exceptionally nice had happened to me – 'Tomorrow do thy worst, for I have lived today.' Is this my tomorrow? If so, what has been my day? Let me think. My mind dwells on past holidays. Mountain mostly. Clambering up them, standing on top of them, ski-ing down them. Seeing them in all their moods ...

Mountain memories always fill me with nostalgia.

Eva Williams, VAD, 1944

Here is a query, which I shall be able to answer decidedly at the end of this volume, most likely before. What is indicated by all these symptoms – this constant shortness of breath, this most harassing hard cough, this perpetual expectoration, now ringed with blood, this quick pulse, this painfully craving appetite, which a very little satisfies even to disgust, these restless, feverish nights, continual palpitations of the heart, and deep, circumscribed flushes? Is it a consumption really come at last, after so many threatenings? I am not taken by surprise, for I have had it steadily, almost daily, in view for two years, and have always known that my lungs were delicate. I feel no uneasiness on the subject, even if my ideas (I cannot call them fears) prove right. It must be my business to prepare for another world; may God give me grace to do so!

Emily Shore, 1838

I am amazed that life seems to get more and more interesting as one gets older – and also perhaps saner, serener, more tough. It is no doubt the Indian Summer before the hand of decrepitude strikes and health crumbles.

Frances Partridge, 1955

Opened the shutters & lighted the kitchen fire. Shook my sooty things in the dusthole & emptied the soot there. Swept & dusted the rooms & the hall. Laid the hearth & got breakfast up. Clean'd 2 pairs of boots. Made the bed & emptied the slops. Clean'd & wash'd the breakfast things up. Clean'd the plates; clean'd the knives & got dinner up. Clean'd away. Clean'd the kitchen up, unpack'd a hamper. Took two chickens to Mrs Brewer's & brought the message back. Made a tart & pick'd & gutted two ducks & roasted them. Clean'd the steps & flags on my knees. Blackleaded the scraper in front of the house; clean'd the street flags too on my knees. Wash'd up in the scullery. Clean'd the pantry on my knees & scour'd the tables. Scrubbed the flags around the house & clean'd the window sills. Got teas at 9 for the master & Mrs Warwick in my dirt, but Ann carried it up. Clean'd the privy & passage & scullery floor on my knees. Wash'd the dog & clean'd the sinks down. Put the supper ready for Ann to take up, for I was too dirty to go upstairs. Wash'd in a bath & to bed without feeling any the worse for yesterday [when she had climbed the chimney to sweep it].

Hannah Cullwick, 1860

15 July

Have finished 'Little Women', and sent it off, – 402 pages. May is designing some pictures for it. Hope it will go, for I shall probably get nothing for 'Morning Glories.'

Very tired, head full of pain from overwork, and heart heavy about Marmee, who is growing feeble.

Louisa May Alcott, 1868

[My mother] was herself only when alone. I used to watch her brace herself for people; even, occasionally, for me. And then watch her straight, narrow back relax, her shoulders drop a little, as she set out for a walk. A few steps away from the house and her feet would begin to skim.

This satisfaction with being solitary was a tremendous source of freedom for me. It implied a delight in self and affirmed my own obsessive sieving of experience. By taking her mind totally off me, she gave me my own autonomy. I knew from experience that she was careful and responsible. I realized that she would have watched me had she not been sure that I was all right. And, if she were sure, I could be sure. Very early in my life, I set out stoutly to look around at everything.

Anne Truitt, 1974

Anniversary of the day on which I got married and on which, with one direct stroke which took my breath away, I lost my virginity.

Liane de Pougy, 1935

16 July

Still no news of Roland [her fiancé]. If it were not for the nursing I don't know how I could bear this – but nursing takes all one's energy and occupies a great deal of the time that would otherwise have been spent on sad thought. In between my duties I can scarcely bear thinking about him. Something has happened I am sure. He would never willingly keep me so long without a word, as if one has no time for letters there are always Field Service postcards. I feel as if I couldn't go on much longer without news of some sort, & yet it is no good feeling like that because one *has* to go on, come what may ... I often wonder just how I should take it if I heard he was dead. Sometimes my heart feels very tumultuous, full of passion & fierce desire; at others it is possessed by a sort of blank & despairing resignation to what one feels must be inevitable. But enough of this; writing about it only makes it worse.

Vera Brittain, 1915

Tolstoy wrote: 'To love is to prefer another to oneself.' Perhaps I prefer Georges [her husband] to myself – sometimes; but if he preferred me to himself at the same time it would be like two polite people trying to get through a doorway and confounding themselves with courtesy, that dance of hesitation and withdrawal. I offer Georges the best part of the cake, he offers it to me, and all three, including the cake, get nowhere …

Liane de Pougy, 1923

This morning I stand face to face with twenty five years of life, that ere the day is gone will have passed by me forever … The first ten are so far away, in the distance as to make those beginnings indistinct; the next 5 are remembered as a kind of butterfly existence at school, and household duties at home; within the last ten I have suffered more, learned more, lost more than I ever expect to, again. In the last decade, I've only begun to live – to know life as a whole with its joys and sorrows. Today I write these lines with a heart overflowing with thankfulness to My Heavenly Father for His wonderful love & kindness; for his bountiful goodness to me, in that He has not caused me to want, & that I have always been provided with the means to make an honest livelihood …

Ida B. Wells, 1887

Rubbed Mrs Spence for the second time. Very sorry not to stay with Grandmama. I am such a creeping worm that if I have anything of the kind to do, I can do without marriage, or intellect, or social intercourse, or any of the things people sigh after … My mind is absorbed with the idea of the sufferings of man, it besets me behind and before. A very one-sided view, but I can hardly see anything else and all the poets sing of the glories of this world seem to be untrue. All the people I see are eaten up with care or poverty or disease. When I go into a cottage I long to stop there all day, to wash the children, relieve the mother, stay by the sick one.

Florence Nightingale, 1846

17 July

Alas, alas! My poor Journal! how dull unentertaining, uninteresting thou art! – oh what I would give for some Adventure worth reciting – for something which would surprise – astonish you!

Fanny Burney (aged 15), 1768

Visited several shops – Selfridges where we had lunch at an exciting new snack bar with high red leather and chromium plated stools. We ate huge toast sandwiches and drank iced coffee. We had tea at D. H. Evans. I bought some scarlet rouge and lipstick and some scent – also a brown spotted silk scarf.

Barbara Pym (aged 19), 1932

Still no news either of or from him [her fiancé] – though I watched for each post with a feverish impatience that was agony. Something really *must* have happened this time. If it is the worst, may God – if there is a God – help Mrs Leighton and me! If only it could mean that he is wounded! I, last of all people, want him to suffer, but suffering can change to health, while nothing can change Death to Life. And if he were to suffer physically, I should at any rate equal the agony mentally.

Vera Brittain, 1915

18 July

Traveled 22 miles. Crossed one small creek and have camped on one called Rock Creek. It is here the Indians are so troublesome. This creek is covered with small timber and thick underbrush, a great hiding place; and while in this part of the country the men have to guard the stock all night. One man traveling ahead of us had all his horses stolen and never found them as we know of. (I was very much frightened while at this camp. I lay awake all night. I expected every minute we would be killed. However, we all found our scalps on in the morning.)

Amelia Stewart Knight, 1853

This air makes one feel rather lightheaded and excited. The inhabitants look wretchedly thin, pale and cadaverous and are mere beasts of burden, born to carry *Messieurs et Mesdames les voyageurs* and their requirements to the 'Pleasant Alpine Resort'. Father says, and I agree, that the Swiss do not seem endowed with a high moral nature. The wretched landlord, a most thriving one, actually refused to count our humble afternoon tea with our *pension* …

As for the scenery it is simply glorious …

Beatrice Webb, Murren, 1882

I too would dearly love to see my own folk again, and yet I dread to think of going back to Russia. I am so afraid lest Fyodor [her husband] might stop loving me there. Am I really and truly not quite sure of it, I wonder? I keep on being seized with a dreadful fear lest anyone else should come along and usurp the place I now hold in his heart. Often I fancy him as a kind of man who has never been in love, but only imagined it for himself, and never yet found true love at all. I tell myself he is not capable of being in love, being far too preoccupied with other thoughts and ideas, to let these earthly things possess him …

Anna Dostoevsky, Baden-Baden, 1867

I am a bubble, without reason, without beauty of mind or person; I am a fool. I daily fall lower in my own estimation. What an infinite advantage it would be to me to occupy my time and thoughts well. I am now seventeen, and if some kind and great circumstance does not happen to me, I shall have my talents devoured by moth and rust. They will lose their brightness, lose my virtue, and one day they will prove a curse instead of a blessing. Dreaded day!

Elizabeth Fry (aged 17), 1797

19 July

There is no such thing as a helpless black woman (even M…, who plays the helpless creature, plays it to D's whiteness, plays it his white ideas about women …). There is no cultural conditioning, no unspoken expectation anywhere, that would allow me to believe I could afford to be helpless. The attitude of helplessness, of dependence, is foreign to me, based on assumptions that are alien to my upbringing. There was only one dominant theme in my childhood: holding on, no matter what … shifting and turning and choreographing and juggling and manipulating life to stay inside it! To live! And perhaps even grow … If a man came along … all right, so much the nicer … But the game goes on, the necessity to be a self goes on. I don't know how to be helpless. I don't know how not to make things work.

Kathleen Collins, no year

They break my heart and torture me, and now they call for the doctors – Nikitin and Rossolimo. Poor me! They do not know how to cure someone who has had wounds inflicted on her from all sides! The chance reading of a page from [Tolstoy's] old diary disturbed my soul and my tranquillity, opened my eyes to his present infatuation with Chertkov [Tolstoy's publisher] and irrevocably poisoned my heart … Nikitin was amazed to see how thin I had become. It is all because of my grief and my wounded loving heart – and all they can say is leave him! Which would be more painful than anything else.

I drove to the river for a swim, and felt even worse. The water is very low in the Voronka, like my life, and it would be hard to drown in it at present; I went there mainly to estimate how much deeper it might get.

Sophia Tolstoy, 1910

20 July

I'm mortified and holding my breath. J. D. [Jonathan Demme, director of *Beloved*] just calls and wants to come over and talk to me. On a Sunday! It's so serious he's coming to my hotel on his day off. Word has it it's about dailies, but it could be – of all mortifying things – weight …

Thank God it wasn't about weight. What a relief! But if this doesn't whip me into shape, nothing will. 'Cause God, God save me from the weight-disappointment talk. I remember the mortifying potato chip moment: when I opened the car door leaving J. D.'s house last May, there, right on the car seat, were bags of chips – that weren't mine! Mortifying. He was so alarmed he had to call me about it …

Oprah Winfrey, 1997

I had a short letter from Roland [her fiancé] at last this morning, written in a great hurry. He says he is at present leading 'too peripatetic an existence' for letter-writing.

Vera Brittain, 1915

An attack on Hitler's life, but unfortunately the bastard wasn't killed.

Joan Wyndham, 1944

We have now had two quiet peaceful days without Chertkov. The doctors left earlier on. I suppose they were asked here merely to testify that I am mad, just in case. Their visit was completely pointless.

Sophia Tolstoy, 1910

21 July

Now I am getting really hopeful, now things are going well at last. Yes, really, they're going well! Super news! An attempt has been made on Hitler's life and not even by Jewish communists or English capitalists this time, but by a proud German general, and what's more, he's a count, and still quite young …

… I can't help it; the prospect that I may be sitting on school benches next October, makes me feel far too cheerful to be logical! Oh dearie me, hadn't I just told you that I didn't want to be too hopeful? Forgive me, they haven't given me the name 'little bundle of contradictions' all for nothing!

Anne Frank, 1944

On 4 August, the Secret Annexe where the Frank family were hiding was betrayed to the German Security Police.

Using this hospital as a health-farm is ridiculous and mad. Thinking I'm on holiday, making friends with Kitty and her baby, with depressed Zena, wandering around the wards, 'little drinks' on the open air of Hampstead, dreaming about the houses I pass and eating scones for tea, while all the time I am seriously ill and lost and sick – it's further madness …

I've made so many attempts and then returned to drinking. Is this my 'bottom'? I'm in a psychiatric ward in London, my New York apartment rented because I can't emotionally live in it, paying the rent on another house I can't live in in Los Angeles and getting rent of a sort for the Pimlico house I can't live in, either … Again I fantasise about Rex's life [her ex-husband, Rex Harrison]. He'll be working hard at the moment in that horrible New Amsterdam Theater in New York, with the humidity of summer, in preparation for a long tour of America with *My Fair Lady*, eight shows a week, having to sing, memorise, energise in huge auditoriums. Could I do it? No. Would I want to? No.

Perhaps, though I don't know how, stopping drinking will lead me somewhere out of this nowhere I am now. I pray to God, let this be so.

Rachel Roberts, 1980

22 July

Two last night. M– [Maria Lawton] spoke in the very act. 'Ah,' said she, 'Can you ever love anyone else?' She knows how to heighten the pleasure of our intercourse. She often murmurs, 'Oh, how delicious,' just at the very moment. All her kisses are good ones …

Anne Lister, 1824

Lev Nik. [her husband] again lost his temper with me at dinner today, after I had voiced my chagrin and bewilderment at never being shown any copies of his latest works to read, since Chertkov [Tolstoy's publisher] immediately takes away all his manuscripts. I again burst into tears, left the table and went upstairs to my room. He thought better of it and came after me, but our conversation soon turned acrimonious again. Eventually, though, he invited me to take a stroll around the garden with him, which I always appreciate so much, and all our resentment seemed to pass.

Sophia Tolstoy, 1910

This was a memorable day – the most interesting, in my whole Life – It made me feel very strange – I was afraid to reflect or to think least I should lose the courage which every Woman stands in need of on such an occasion – I was obliged to dress in a hurry to attend my little Catholic Priest who received my Confession, when that was over I found Robert and Walter already arrived – My dear Bridegroom was even perhaps more agitated than his Bride – We were instantly married by the Catholic Priest and no Woman ever pronounced her vows with a happier heart – Robert pronounced his with a firmness and at the same time a feeling which greatly affected me – We had but just time to breakfast, and then I had to dress for the second marriage – my *bridal array* consisted of a white satin under dress and a patent net over it, with a long veil … My Sisters seemed to feel a great deal when I left them – But they knew I was happy –

Eugenia Wynne Campbell, 1806

23 July

Finally Fyodor [her husband] came back in a great state: he had lost five thalers, and made it out to be all my fault, as I had refused to go for a walk with him. That, he said, was why he had lost, and he now demanded another five thalers from me. He wanted to go again to the tables, and again lose, for of course that is what would happen. I regretted bitterly not having gone out with him, when this would never have happened. But how could I have foreseen he would have been so utterly unreasonable? Though of course I knew, really, that he would never have been able to keep away from the tables ... There is no doubt that Fyodor wants protecting, not only from others, but from himself, for of will power he has none at all. He promises, he gives his word of honour, and then promptly acts contrariwise.

Anna Dostoevsky, 1867

Read Theocritus *Idyll* 16. Meditated characters for *Middlemarch*. Mrs F. Malleson came.

George Eliot, 1869

Since making the last entry I have learnt enough to drive a car in the country alone. On the backs of paper I write down instructions for starting cars. We have a nice little shut up car in which we can travel thousands of miles. The world gave me this for writing *The Lighthouse*, I reflect, a book which has now sold 3,160 (perhaps) copies; will sell 3,500 before it dies, and thus far exceeds any other of mine. All images are now tinged with driving a motor. Here I think of letting my engine work, with my clutch out.

It has been, on the whole, a fresh well ordered summer. I am not so parched with talk as usual ...

Virginia Woolf, 1927

24 July

... I made a huge effort at work to stop doing non-essential things. As an MP you risk drowning under an ocean of froth camouflaged as 'absolutely essential meeting/engagements'. Some of it is critical. But much could be dealt with by a phone call or letter. And much is absolute nonsense. I even stopped working most weekends, which is unheard of for an MP, and especially for me. I did post and admin at home, but I wouldn't get suited and booted to do a local MP gig unless I knew it would really make a difference. I went to my [Parliamentary] Whips and said, 'My husband is leaving me unless you let me see him one evening a week. Just one night let me get home at eight p.m. instead of midnight' ...

... I got the hang of saying no. I perfected it when I was invited to meet President Clinton at the White House ... It's true, the US President is a very important man. But Tiberio [her husband] was the most important man in my life, so I had to blow out the President. The 'old' Oona would never have done so. The new 'I gotta get a life for me and my husband even if it kills me' Oona didn't take long to make the decision. I'd changed.

Tiberio didn't see it that way ...

Oona King, 2002

When I got up to go home at six he said, 'How would you like it if I robbed you of your virginity?'

I thought for a minute.

'I don't *think* I should mind very much, but then I hardly know you well enough to say.'

Joan Wyndham (aged 18), 1940

... They brought me a Yankee soldier's portfolio from the battlefield ... One might shed a few tears over some of the letters. Women – wives and mothers – are the same everywhere ...

Mary Boykin Chesnut, Confederate States, 1861

Feeling of terrible insecurity and cowardice in facing this ordeal of having a baby. This time (I wasn't before) I am afraid of death, afraid of going anywhere without C.[harles, her husband], afraid because death now seems so near. I feel as though there were no escape from that inevitable and dreadful moment when we must be separated. And it does not seem, as before, a hazy, unreal, distant moment banishable from the world of youth.

Anne Morrow Lindbergh, 1932

I had a little fever in the night which alarmed Robert [her husband] who flew for the Doctor and wanted to send for Sir Walter Farquhar – how much his agitation, and the affection he showed me, endeared him to me – every instant makes me more sensible if my happiness in being united to a Being, I so dearly love, and who has such a heart and so much feeling with which he amply repays my affection – after all the uneasiness, the fears, my Love for him has cost me it impossible for me to describe with what gratitude I look towards my God for having now placed me in a situation which sanctions all my tenderness and even makes it a duty … Robert would not leave me for an instant the whole day – He is the kindest and best Nurse –

Eugenia Wynne Campbell, 1806

25 July

I felt tired, but ironed my washing, as I'm going out to the Centre in the morning. My husband is very sulky about it. He said, 'When the war got over, I thought you would always be in at lunch-time.' I said, 'Well, you always have a good lunch left – much better than many men whose wives are always at home.' He said, 'Well, I like you there always.' No thought as to either my feelings or to any service I could be doing. I thought of the false sentiment my generation had been reared with, the possessiveness which stood as the hallmark of love, with no regard to differences in temperament, inclination or ideals – when the 'head of the house' was a head, a little dictator in his own right; when a person of limited vision, or just plain fear of life, could crib and confine more restless spirits ... I had a pang as I wondered what I would do when all my little war activities stopped, when he *could* say plaintively, '*Must* you go?' or 'I don't feel like ...' – and I wondered if my weak streak would crop up as strong as ever, and I'd give in for peace and to that unspoken, but *very* plain Victorian-Edwardian accusation, 'I feed and clothe you, don't I? I've a right to say what you do.' It's not 'love', as the sloppy Vic-Eds sang, it's sheer poverty of mind and fear of life. If you love a person in the real sense, you want them to be happy, not take them like butter and spread them thinly over your own bread, to make it more palatable for yourself.

Nella Last, 1945

I had the oddest dream last night that I ever dreamt; even the remembrance of it is very extraordinary. There was a very nice pretty young *lady*, who I (a girl) was going *to be married to!* (the very idea!) I loved her and even now love her very much. It was quite a settled thing and we were going to be married very soon.

Emily Pepys (aged 10), 1844

When will I learn not to look for in man what I demand of women!! And to be satisfied with what they are capable of giving. Then only shall I be able to marry.

Ivy Jacquier, 1917

I was exhausted by all the agitation, and the journey there and back, and barely managing to climb the stairs I straightaway lay down on my bed, for fear of meeting my husband and being the butt of his jibes. But in fact, to my great joy, it all turned out quite differently. He entered my room with tears in his eyes and thanked me tenderly for returning: 'I realised that I simply could not live without you,' he said weeping. 'I felt shattered, I went to pieces ... We are so close, we have grown so used to one another ... I am so grateful to you for coming back, darling, thank you ...'

And he embraced me and kissed me, clasping me to his thin chest, and I cried too and told him I loved him just as passionately and intensely as when I was a girl, and that it was a joy to cling to him and be one with him again; and I begged him to be more open and straightforward with me, and not to give me occasion to be suspicious and anxious … But the moment I broached the subject of his conspiracy with Chertkov [Tolstoy's publisher], he closed up and would not talk about it …

Sophia Tolstoy, 1910

26 July

Benjamin Bunny travelled in a covered basket in the wash-place; took him out of the basket near Dunbar, but proved scared and bit the family. Not such a philosophical traveller as poor Spot [her late dog]. It is the first time for ten years we have travelled without him, and coming back to the district where we had him first, I thought it rather pathetic.

He used to be very much in evidence – it would be unkind to say in the way, – just before starting, jumping about the carpetless floors with his heavy chain and getting between the men's legs until safely hoisted on to the top of the railway bus in front of the luggage, setting off. He smiled benignly between his curls, and usually captivated the driver. He had a passion for carriage exercise. I suppose it was the dignity of the thing which pleased him, for he looked profoundly miserable after the first half hour. The difficulty was to prevent his riding off in omnibuses, like any other gentleman.

Beatrix Potter, 1892

At Frank's boy's birthday party. I had a particularly bad time … realising that I've missed out entirely on that life, that I wanted to rear a child and see her grow up, give her all the things lacking in me. Though I played with the idea of adoption, I wish I'd taken it more seriously, or that Rex had.

Rachel Roberts, 1980

The plane lifted – and suddenly it was as if everything had vanished: Bloomsbury and Regent's Park and Russell Square and Rutland Gate. None of it had happened, none of it was real. Even the people weren't real. It was all imagined, they were all phantoms.

I sit here on the plane trying to see faces, trying to hold onto London, but the mind intrudes with thoughts of home: the mail piled up waiting for me, the people waiting, the work waiting.

Bits of Prospero run in my head:

Our revels now are ended. These our actors

... were all spirits and

Are melted into air, into thin air ...

Helene Hanff, 1971

27 July

Yesterday to Laxworth, who told me to come today instead, so I had a moment's respite.

Loran Hurnscot, 1926

A gray day, cool, gentle. The strangling noose of worry, of hysteria, paralysis, is miraculously gone. Doggedly, I have waited it out, and doggedly, been rewarded.

Sylvia Plath, 1958

Slept restlessly and ill. The past and the present floated in a turbid stream of thought, and the current glided so rapidly along, that I could not distinguish the objects it bore upon its surface. My impression was that of standing in the midst of a chafing, boiling current, against which I was vainly endeavouring to stand upright. The effect of this sort of waking dream was intensely painful. 'Tis such nights that unfit us for the days which are to follow.

Lady Charlotte Bury, 1810

This morning I went for a long walk with Stenilber and we talked about gestures. Each period, each fashion, brings its own ... There was that charming one of lifting the dress and showing just enough to make one guess the rest, and build desire. Now we all go décolletée. Is it cold? There's a pretty, shy way of spreading your fingers over a fur crossed at the throat. Skirts are short, no more need to lift them, one stretches an arm at eye-level to read the time from one's wrist-watch. There have been charming movements of the lips against the mesh of a veil; the lipstick gesture, so frequent that one no longer notices it, the powder puff, become so natural; the sharp little tap of the walking-stick, or when not using it, tucking it very high under one's arm-pit. Me, I like taking a cane when I go out. It gives my spirit a touch of virility!

Liane de Pougy, 1919

28 July

Went at lunch-time, full of dread, and there I met the kind kind Bee who had come to put me into a taxi if it was necessary. Laxworth gave me an injection, I waited for the horrors to begin, but except for a bearable discomfort, nothing happened. I came home feeling moderately well and very hungry. In the afternoon I slept ...

As for my own acquaintance with Laxworth, the mental process has been simple in the extreme. While something in me wanted it, yes I was pregnant, I might have a baby. But from the moment I finally decided against it, it ceased to be a potential child, it became a disease, a growth, that had to be removed. This is perhaps too simple: could only be so simple with a completely unmaternal woman.

Loran Hurnscot, 1926

Shirley [her daughter, the future politician Shirley Williams], after being put to bed, climbed right over the rails of her hired cot, which is an inch or two lower than the one at home, and fell with a terrific bump on the floor. I heard it in my room and dashed in to find her already at the door, roaring but apparently unhurt. She will now have to be strapped; where she gets all this adventurous rashness from I cannot imagine. As Gordon's mother is the only unknown element I suppose she must be responsible for S.'s terrifying traits.

Vera Brittain, 1932

I am eighteen today. How time does go. I feel as if I had been going on such a time.

Beatrix Potter, 1884

29 July

Spent the greatest part of the day in preparation for the arrival of Les Epoux. Decorated the rooms with Flowers and smartened little Swanbourne for this gay Occasion. They did not come till ten o'clock, the Bells rang all the Evening and half the night – Eugenia is not improved in her looks but appears a happy little creature – *et ils sont tres tendres*.

Betsey Wynne Fremantle, 1806

We had several people to breakfast with us – I made a Will, with infinite joy – then had so many things to do, that it was past two o'clock before we left Town – We departed as usual from Argyle House – soon after nine we reached Swanbourne in the midst of the ringing of bells and joyful shouts – I was most happy to see my Sisters altho' they *will* not treat me with *respect* …

Eugenia Wynne Campbell, 1806

Down to the cottage, housekeeperless, to a weekend of hard domestic work and cooking. No one has any idea of the problems of a woman Minister!

Barbara Castle, 1966

Last night from six o'clock I had a very feverish time, beginning with a sudden flooding, and going on with periodic violence till night. I had never been told how these things were conducted. So I went and had a bath, and as that which nature intended to be a child slowly dissolved from me, the last link with Barny [her lover] dissolved too. I met nice Mr Walsh punctually at ten o'clock and started work on the MSS [manuscripts] he wants copied.

Loran Hurnscot, 1926

30 July

A Paper to be opened
  when Anne is
  25 years old
  or my next birthday after
  if
  – all be well –

It is Friday evening – near 9 o'clock – wild rainy weather. I am seated in the dining room 'alone' – having just concluded tidying our desk-boxes – writing this document – Papa is in the parlour. Aunt up stairs in her room – she has been reading *Blackwoods* magazine to papa – Victoria and Adelaide are ensconced in the peat-house – Keeper is in the kitchen – Hero in his cage – We are all stout and hearty as I hope is the case with Charlotte, Branwell and Anne, of whom the first is at John White Esq., Upperwood House, Rawden; the second is at Luddenden foot and the third is I I [sic] at Scarborough – editing perhaps a paper corresponding to this – A scheme is at present in agitation for setting us up in a school of our own as yet nothing is determined but I hope and trust it may go on and prosper and answer our highest expectations. This day four years I wonder whether we shall still be dragging in in our present condition or established to our heart's content Time will show –

I guess that at the time appointed for the opening of this paper – we (i.e.) Charlotte, Anne and I – 'shall' be all merrily seated in our own sitting-room in some pleasant and flourishing seminary having just gathered in for the midsummer holydays our debts will be paid off and we shall have cash in hand to a considerable amount. papa Aunt and Branwell will either have been – or be coming – to visit us – it will be a fine warm summery evening, very different from this bleak lookout Anne and I will perchance slip out into the garden a minutes to peruse our papers. I hope either this or something better will be the case –

Emily Brontë, 'Diary Paper', 1841

I should here try to sum up the summer, since August ends a season, spiritual as well as temporal. Well, business has been brisk. I don't think I get many idle hours now, the idlest being, oddly enough, in the morning. When the dull sleep of afternoon is on me, I'm always in the shop, printing, dissing [sic], addressing; then it is tea, and Heaven knows we have had enough visitors. Sometimes I sit still and wonder how many people will tumble on me without my lifting a finger.

Virginia Woolf, 1925

He [her neighbour Mr Boyd] was very kind in his manner to me today; & spoke in an anxious manner of our unhappy business. He said 'Well! it is not certain', with respect to my going away; as if the un-certainty were a relief to him. Well: if it *is* certain, – if I *do* go away – nobody will be left behind who cares for him more than I care. *More!!!* …

Miss [Nelly] Bordman kissed me when I went away. Curtseying in the morning, & embracing in the evening! – But I never dislike such as a general principle. It is the principle of warm hearts & unsuspicious heads.

Elizabeth Barrett (Browning), 1831

I went to Teresina [a palmist]. She exclaimed when she touched me, and said she had never seen so 'shocked' and 'scorched' a hand, and that no one could have a blacker bit of life than I was now traversing. This was very satisfactory and rather comforting. She at once saw both my present pains: held out *no* hope about Basil [Lord Basil Blackwood, a friend, missing in action] – seeing just a blank – but implored me not to accept the medical opinion as to John [her son] and said she was positive it was only a *temporary* trouble and that it was very important for me to keep hopeful and not to 'turn against him'. She saw what a loss Basil would be and, what with that and Beb [Cynthia's husband] being away, said I had a time of great loneliness and emotional blank to go through …

Lady Cynthia Asquith, 1917

31 July

The danger of living with somebody, for me, is the danger of living without one's normal diet of passion. Things are so readily equalized, soothed, forgotten with a laugh, with perspective. I don't really want perspective, except my own …

Patricia Highsmith, 1956

Grilling hot again. As soon as I had had breakfast, I went along to see John doing his lessons. He did his drill quite nicely, and some writing and counting all right – only somehow it gives you the impression of a *tour de force* like a performing animal.

I boldly decided to bathe off the pier as the machines were all full. I shall never bathe anywhere else again! It was the most delicious thing I have ever done – down a ladder straight into the bottomless green water. Apparently there is no risk of drowning as there is a man in a boat, a raft, a life-buoy, etc. There was a strong current taking one inwards, so I rowed out and swam back. Luxurious dressing rooms, too. It is a great discovery.

Lady Cynthia Asquith, 1916

Yesterday was Emily's birthday and the time when we should have opened our 1845 paper but by mistake we opened it today instead … Charlotte has lately been to Hathersage in Derbyshire on a visit of three weeks to Ellen Nussy she is now sitting sewing in the Dining-Room. Emily is ironing upstairs. I am sitting in the Dining Room in the Rocking chair before the fire with my feet on the fender. Papa is in the parlour. Tabby and Martha are I think in the Kitchen. Keeper and Flossy are I do not know where. Little Dick is hopping in his cage – When the last paper was written we were thinking of setting up a school – the scheme 'Has been' dropt and long after taken up again and dropt again because we could not get pupils – Charlotte is thinking about getting another situation – she wishes to go to Paris – Will she go? She has let Flossy in by the bye and he is now lying on the sofa ... This afternoon I began to set about making my grey figured silk that was dyed at Keighley – What sort of a hand shall I make of it? E. and I have a great deal of work to do – when shall we sensibly diminish it? I want to get a habit of early rising. Shall I succeed? We have not yet finished our Gondal chronicles that we began three years and a half ago when will they be done? ... I wonder how we shall all be and where and how situated on the thirtieth of July 1848 when if we are all alive Emily will be just 30. I shall be in my 29th year, Charlotte in her 33rd and Branwell in his 32nd; and what changes shall we have seen and known and shall we be much changed ourselves? I hope not – for the worst at least – I for my part cannot well be *flatter* or older in mind than I am now – Hoping the best I conclude.

Anne Brontë, 1845

To Laxworth, yesterday, to pay him five pounds for not letting that child exist. He wisely warned me to take life more quietly and to rest a good deal. After doing some work I felt exhausted and ill, so I came home in a taxi, thinking that rushing off after that profuse night was the height of rashness. Don came to dinner. We had wine and told him we were celebrating, but what, we did not say.

Loran Hurnscot, 1926

Gathered vegetables, pulled apples. Went to the Dressing-room, frizzing, powdering. That operation over, read till two; ev[ening]. Mr and Mrs Mytton arrived ... Account of Buxton. Lady Derby there: limbs paraletic. Cannot walk without the assistance of two persons, not yet thirty. What a melancholy, what an awful lesson. She was sitting by the door of her lodging one day, the Duchess of Devonshire was driving by in her carriage and seeing Lady Derby in that forlorn situation she instantly alighted, went to her, embraced her and each burst into tears.

Lady Eleanor Butler, 1788

After lunch I took some Yeastvite tablets and continued to take them after tea and supper. A slightly unromantic way of curing lovesickness I admit, but certainly I feel a lot better now ... I think I shall try to develop a 'Whatever is, is right' attitude of mind – and quite honestly I suppose all this *is* rather good for me – and an affair with Lorenzo probably wouldn't be!

Barbara Pym (aged 18), 1933

August

'*Away from her I pine & pine, and can accurately call myself lovesick.*'

Alice Walker, 1993

1 August

—

… I herewith record my conviction that we are at the edge of the reign of knickerbockers, a very different matter to the bloomer mania which excited Mr Punch.

The weak point of that fad, and of the divided skirts, was the endeavour to assert that they 'didn't show', and ought to be worn universally and on all occasions. To wear knickerbockers with more or less overskirt, frankly as a gymnastic costume, for cycling or other more or less masculine amusement is a different matter, and whether desirable or not has a definite reason, and I shall be much surprised if, within a very few years, a lady cannot appear in them without exciting hostile comment.

Beatrix Potter, 1894

This evening I spent in Lover's Lane. How beautiful it was – green and alluring and beckoning! I had been tired and discouraged and sick at heart before I went to it – and it rested me and cheered me and stole away the heartsickness, giving peace and newness of life.

I owe much to that dear lane. And in return I have given it love – and fame. I painted it in my book [*Anne of Green Gables*] and as a result the name of this little remote woodland lane is known all over the world. Visitors to Cavendish ask for it and seek it out. Photographs of its scenery have appeared in the magazines. The old lane is famous.

L. M. Montgomery, 1909

When English persons set out from their own firesides, they must lay aside the cloak of prejudice, or they will be wretched the whole time they are absent. I find, in the first place, that one must learn to *do everything in public*. I do not know that I have been one moment alone since I left Calais. The women walk in and out of one's room, whether one is dressed or not …

Lady Charlotte Bury, Dijon, 1814

I suddenly thought tonight, 'I know why a lot of women have gone into pants – it's a sign that they are asserting themselves in some way.' I feel pants are more of a sign of the times than I realised. A growing contempt for man in general creeps over me. For a craftsman, whether a sweep or Prime Minister – 'hats off'. But why this 'Lords of Creation' attitude on men's part? I'm beginning to see I'm a really clever woman in my own line, and not the 'odd' or 'uneducated' woman that I've had dinned into me … I feel that, in the world of tomorrow, marriage will be – will *have* to be – more of a partnership, less of this '*I* have spoken' attitude. They will talk things over – talking *does* do good, if only to clear the air. I run my house like a business: I have had to, to get all done properly, everything fitted in. Why, then, should women not be looked on as partners, as 'business women'? I feel thoroughly out of time, I'm not as patient as I used to be, and when one gets to fifty-three, and after thirty-two years of married life, there are few illusions to cloud issues.

Nella Last, 1943

2 August

Yesterday in pain all day. We motored down to the caravan, Mark and Pernelle and I. It is charming to be with them – if I didn't feel so oddly ill.

Loran Hurnscot, 1926

A week ago, last Sunday morning, my right breast looked exactly the same as my left. I know that because I noticed nothing irregular when I had a bath first thing. By Sunday evening when undressing for bed, I did a double-take in the mirror. My chest had radically changed – the right didn't match the left any more. Grimly incongruous to think that a week ago I had cancer and didn't know it.

Victoria Derbyshire, 2015

This evening I went to my own room for my cloak, and, as usual, found Madame La Fite just waiting for me. She was all emotion – she seized my hand – 'Have you heard? *O, mon Dieu! – O, le bon Roi!* Oh, Miss Burney! – What an horreur!'

I was very much startled, but soon ceased to wonder at her perturbation; she had been in the room with the Princess Elizabeth, and there heard that an attempt had just been made upon the life of the King [George III]! ...

The Queen had the two eldest Princesses, the Duchess of Ancaster and Lady Charlotte Bertie with her when the King came in. He hastened up to her, with a countenance of striking vivacity, and said:

'Here I am! Safe and well – as you see! – but I have very narrowly escaped being stabbed.'

His own conscious safety, and the pleasure he felt in thus personally showing it to the Queen, made him not aware of the effect of so abrupt a communication. The Queen was seized with a consternation that at first almost stupefied her ...

Fanny Burney, 1786

3 August

Women growing old – many traces of age. The fact is, many middle-aged ladies who look twenty years younger than their age show it. A stranger – marveling at the clear, smooth skin, unlined throat – is shocked at the age revealed by her thinking. There are things, like a bald head, that can't be helped but can at least be hidden. The end of sex finds women resenting older men, who are invariably childish, demanding, selfish and catty. Men as they age seem to go home to Mama, after leaving her on her own for 30 years. Suddenly their men friends are unsatisfactory; they want Mama's cookies and warming pan. This is just the time Mama finds the company of her own sex most rewarding. Don't be sorry for elderly ladies on sprees – they're usually having the time of their life without having to do what the Man says.

Dawn Powell, 1951

Foolscap sheet from M– [Mariana Lawton] … She seems much interested in Lady Eleanor Butler and Miss Ponsonby and I am agreeably surprised (never dreaming of such a thing) at her observation … 'Tell me if you think their regard has always been platonic & if you believed pure friendship could be so exalted …' I could not help thinking that surely it was not platonic. Heaven forgive me, but I look within myself & doubt. I feel the infirmity of our nature & hesitate to pronounce such attachments uncemented by something more tender still than friendship.

Anne Lister, 1822

Lord Thanet was married to Miss Sackville. Beauty without art had in this case its reward; he had never spoken to her when he wrote to her Mother the following proposals: 800l [£800] a year Pin Money, 3000 Joynture & 50,000l for the younger Children … Nelly O'Brien (whom he had kept some Years) thought it hard that Ld Thanet should turn her out of his House before she was brought to Bed, &, as she says, he had so good a Precedent to follow, the Duke of Grafton permitting the Duchess to bed before he sent here away.

Elizabeth Percy, Duchess of Northumberland, 1767

4 August

Late as it is & almost too excited to write as I am, I must make some effort to chronicle the stupendous events of this remarkable day. The situation is absolutely unparalleled in the history of the world … It is estimated that when the war begins *14 millions* of men will be engaged in the conflict. Attack is possible by earth, water & air, & the destruction attainable by the modern war machines used by the armies is unthinkable & past imagination.

This morning at breakfast we learnt that war is formally declared between France and Germany …

Vera Brittain, 1914

As long as I've memory, the 4th of August 1914 will stay in my mind. The shock when war came seems to always remain. In fact, I think the years make it stand out more clearly. And mankind never learns, and women bear and rear children unthinking of what lies ahead. Life has to be lived with courage, and then we have to pass on, but it grows more complicated and puzzling. It's been a really wretched Bank holiday, dull and overcast, with heavy showers.

Nella Last, 1947

It seems a very long time since I['ve] written anything about my little darling, and I feel as if I had been negligent about it; only it is so difficult to know when to begin or when to stop when talking, thinking, or writing about her ...

How all a woman's life, at least so it seems to me now, ought to have reference to the period when she will be fulfilling one of her greatest and highest duties, those of a mother. I feel myself so unknowing, so doubtful about many things in her intellectual and moral treatment already, and what shall I be when she grows older, and asks those puzzling questions that children do? I hope I shall always preserve my present good intentions and sense of my holy trust, and then I must pray to be forgiven for my errors and led to a better course ...

Elizabeth Gaskell, 1835

5 August

Last night in the midst of talking of how much we miss each other T. said 'Maybe we should live together.' She was nervous and half-joking suggesting such a thing. But I am ready to try it. Away from her I pine & pine, and can accurately call myself lovesick. I haven't felt good since the last time I kissed her. We know we love each other. We know we can live in the same house, in harmony with her dogs. Other practical matters frighten us, though.

Alice Walker, 1993

… This morning I finished the first chapter of *Middlemarch*. I am reading Renouard's *History of Medicine*.

George Eliot, 1869

I feel awful on waking but a bit better now sitting in the sun writing this, also trying to finish off my novel. Shall I write more in this notebook?

Perhaps what one fears about dying won't be the actual moment – one hopes – but what you have to go through beforehand – in my case this uncomfortable swollen body and feeling sick and no interest in food or drink.

Barbara Pym, 1979

6 August

… Denny [her son] is being very gay and un-grown-up about his wedding, in fact he kept on giggling. The question is how to get the maximum number of wedding presents. I don't think either of them want a 'quiet wedding' – they want the maximum possible fun. They also seem to realise my point of view: that in order to keep going with what is, after all, the rather wearing job of family organisation, I have to have some pegs stuck into the future to climb along by; all the pegs I had at midsummer have been knocked out, leaving gaps, and they are providing me with one. After which no doubt I can start again on my own. (This is different from my life as a writer.) So Denny was discussing details with me and making it all sound great fun …

Naomi Mitchison, 1940

When the alarm goes off at 3.45 a.m., I leap out of bed. It feels so good being able to go to work and present the programme. Louisa's abroad on holiday, but I've already emailed her to let her know I'm planning on letting our team know today …

I begin in a relatively clear, understated voice. 'I just wanted to have a really quick chat with you to let you all know that [deep breath] … I have breast cancer. It looks like I'll be having a mastectomy in the next few weeks or months. It's going to be fine. It won't affect the programme, and I'll work as much as I can …'

Afterwards, many of the team hug me, and later, they all send me wonderful emails, which I will keep forever. Today is a good day.

Victoria Derbyshire, 2015

From Mother, I learned: 'I love you' means 'I don't love anyone else.' The horrid woman was always challenging my feelings, telling me I had made her unhappy, that I was 'cold'.

As if children owe their parents love + gratification! They don't. Though parents owe these things to their children – exactly like physical care.

Susan Sontag, 1964

A rainy morning. I ironed till dinner time – sewed till near dark – then pulled a basket of peas, and afterwards boiled and pickled gooseberries. William came home from Keswick at 11 o'clock. A very fine night.

Dorothy Wordsworth, 1800

… I noticed Flight Sergeant Kelly hurrying across the field. First she walked a bit, then she broke into a run and walked again. It seemed off because she wasn't late for the transport.

When she came up to us she said, 'There's a terrible bomb been dropped on Japan – the worst ever! It's to do with re-directing the energy from the sun, or something. Everybody thinks the Japs will surrender any minute!'

She probably expected a barrage of questions – or even cries of 'Good show!' – but there was nothing, only a shocked silence.

She went on to tell us that it was called an atomic bomb and the whole of Hiroshima had been wiped out and the Japs would certainly sue for peace within the next few days.

I think I was stunned, not so much because of the bomb as at the thought of the war ending. Later, when the meaning finally sank in, I felt the strangest mixture of elation and terror. It was as if my whole world had suddenly come to an end. Five years of security and happy comradeship, the feeling of being needed – and ahead a kind of uncharted wilderness, lonely and frightening.

At the same time there was a small but undeniable feeling of excitement, like the end of school term, the hols looming ahead. I was vividly aware of everything about me, the dusty golden ragwort, the blue sky, even the knots in the wooden gate under my hand.

Joan Wyndham, 1945

7 August

Oh my God, this atomic bomb. Mankind will exterminate itself and this earth if we don't soon exercise some restraint. Surely the Jap war is over today. They can't possibly go on now.

Edie Rutherford, 1945

It is a strange drama – One self acting as a permanent Chorus to the shifting scene – How altered is everything – How enthusiasm, love & hope have disappeared – One storm – one dark wave closed my destiny leaving me a weed on the strand – Since then, tossed by adversity – the sport of falsehood – the victim of ingratitude, what has been – what is my fate?

Mary Shelley, 1829

I shall not write about the most painful thing in the world which gnaws at my heart day and night – [her husband] Lev N.'s coldness and cruelty to me. He has not so much as said hello to me today – he doesn't say a word all day and is sullen and angry; he behaves as though I interfere with his life, as though I am a burden to him. And all because for my sake he has stopped seeing Chertkov [Tolstoy's publisher] …

We lived quite happily without Chertkov for several decades. And what now? We are the same people, but now sisters quarrel with their brothers, the father is ill-disposed towards his sons, the daughters towards their mother, the husband hates his wife, the wife hates Chertkov, and all because of that gross, stupid, corpulent figure who has insinuated himself into our family, ensnared the old man, and is now destroying my life and happiness …

I shall now pray again. The moment I think of prayer I become easier in my mind; it is such a joy to be able to kneel down here and enter into communion with God, for He will comfort me, calm my fears, heal my sorrowing soul and soften my husband's stony heart.

Sophia Tolstoy, 1910

8 August

And that is exactly what happened: God answered my prayer astonishingly quickly. Today my [her husband] Lyovochka's heart melted and he was kind and affectionate to me – even tender. I thank Thee, Lord! I can endure endless physical suffering, just so long as that lifelong emotional bond with Lyovochka endures, and there is no more of that coldness which destroys me.

Sophia Tolstoy, 1910

Sorted old letters & burned many. Not wise to keep for curious eyes to read, & gossip-lovers to print by & by. Lived in the past for days, & felt very old recalling all I have been through. Experiences go deep with me, & I begin to think it might be well to keep some record of my life if it will help others to read it when I am gone. People seem to think our lives interesting & peculiar.

Life rather a burden.

Louisa May Alcott, 1885

If I could choose, I'd like to be a man when I 'come again'. Men *do* seem to get the best out of life, all the responsibility and effort, all the colour and romance. I've an old school-friend who is rather plain and so thoroughly nice that she is dull. We were once talking of 'what we would like to be next time', and I said I'd like to be a man; she rather surprised me when she said, 'I'd like to be a courtesan.'

Nella Last, 1940

9 August

I thought today, looking forward to the pain of this labor, that I would and have suffered more pain than he did that night – at least I hope that is true. And that helps me. I'm glad I can feel what he felt and much more. I'm glad he felt no more.

Anne Morrow Lindbergh, 1932

... I brought up the subject of the new bomb at work yesterday. Horror of its power is definitely the chief reaction ...

All at work commented on the cost of this atomic bomb research and remembered the howl that always goes up if 2/6d. weekly is suggested for adding to old age pensions. We live in a mad world.

Edie Rutherford, 1945

On Monday, Miss Newcomb, Jane, & I took up our residence at Boronggoop. We found Armstrong & Owens digging the garden, which is fenced. This is Thursday night, & every thing is now nearly arranged in the house; we have also got a number of garden & flower seeds put in the ground.

Miss Newcomb, who is my partner, I hope for life, is the best & most clever person I have ever met with; there seems to be magic in her touch, every thing she does is done so well & so quickly. Our arrangement for the day is as follows: rise at 7 o'clock, break fast at 8 (previously to which we have prayers, at which Miss N. presides, & prays extempore very beautifully), dinner at 2 (excellent dinners we have, as Vere, Armstrong's wife, turns out to be a good cook), at ½ past 6 tea, prayers at 8, and to bed at 10.

Anne Drysdale, Australia, 1841

10 August

The TV phenomenon of the summer is *Big Brother,* and its theme tune is, 'It's only a game show, it's only a game show.' I start singing to myself all the time,

'It's only a miscarriage, it's only a miscarriage.'

Three weeks later and I feel fine. The thing that upset me most at the time ('no baby') now makes me feel much better. I didn't lose anything. At any rate, that's the spin I'm putting on it. Otherwise I might mope around and become a baby snatcher. And hey, it's only a miscarriage.

Oona King, 2000

Mother:–

My acute anxiety + dread of her growing old, looking old – at one time I even wished to die first because I wouldn't be able to bear seeing that – It would be something like 'obscene' …

I'm afraid of my mother – afraid of her harshness, her coldness (cold anger – the rattling coffee cup (ultimately, of course, afraid she'll just collapse, fade out on me, never get out of that bed. Any parent, any affection (though I've assented to a fraudulent contract to get it) is better than none …

But if I'm afraid of my mother, she is also afraid of me. On a more specific level, afraid of my judgement. Afraid I will find her stupid, uncultivated (hiding *Redbook* under the bedcovers when I came in to kiss her goodnight), glamorous, morally deficient …

I didn't feel, deep down, that my mother ever liked me. How could she? She didn't 'see' me. She believed what I showed her of myself (that carefully doctored version). I felt she needed me, that's all …

The old puzzle: I 'see' someone. But then how can that person 'see' me?

Susan Sontag, 1967

All the time one keeps on thinking of this bomb, and what it may make the future look like. A perpetual menace over everything but may be as salutary as hell fire was in its time ... Probably the world is in for a period of communism. It will be unpleasant in some ways but it won't destroy other values nearly as badly as Nazi-ism. I intend that my children shall survive.

Naomi Mitchison, 1945

When I went into [her neighbour] Mr Boyd's room, I cd. not help being grave & silent ... At last I said – I cd. not help it – 'I am sorry that you wd. not let me come up stairs before' – And then came the assurance that he had never intended me to stay away; & an observation coldly enough made, that I was 'fanciful'. Tears again. They *would* come.

We talked, & talked cheerfully – but I went away sadly. My spirits are broken, by strokes of pain from every side; & I am become morbidly & foolishly sensitive ...

Elizabeth Barrett (Browning), 1831

11 August

What a weight there is on my heart today. It is like lead, only colder. I wish I had not gone yesterday, where I did ... I wish I had commanded myself sufficiently to avoid making that foolish observation! I wish I had never gone to Malvern! Vain wishes, all of them! –

Elizabeth Barrett (Browning), 1831

Frost this morning. Three of our hands got discontented and left this morning, to pack through. I am pleased, as we shall get along just as well without them and I shall have three less to wait on ...

Amelia Stewart Knight, 1853

Hugh [her husband] was obliged to go to Nice for three days, and he was unhappy because I couldn't go. I sent him away just loaded down with tenderness and love and thoughtfulness. My love for him is my religion ... I love him with my senses. I love him with re-creations of our life together, of past love. I love him with my mind, admire him. I love him gratefully for his wide understanding, his love of me. I *want* to love him, because he *ought* to be loved. I hate myself for whatever I make him suffer for.

Anaïs Nin, 1929

It is very sweet this warm and close companionship in work. The danger is that I shall lean on him [Sidney Webb, her husband] too much and get into a chronic state of watching him at work and thinking that I am working too. But our happiness in each other takes naught from the world ... and it should exalt our effort, strengthen our capacity to make this happiness possible to other men and women.

Beatrice Webb, 1891

12 August

More beautiful by far than a morning in spring or summer. The mist – the trees standing in it – not a leaf moves – not a breath stirs. There is a faint smell of burning. The sun comes slowly – slowly the room grows lighter. Suddenly, on the carpet, there is a square of pale, red light. The bird in the garden goes 'snip – snip – snip' – a little wheezy, like the sound of a knife-grinder. The nasturtiums blaze in the garden: their leaves are pale. On the lawn, his paws tucked under him, sits the black and white cat ...

Katherine Mansfield, 1920

I haven't one friend of my own age and generation. I wish I had. I don't know if it's my own fault. I haven't a single thing in common with them. They're all snarled up in grandchildren or W. A. or church teas or bridge or society. None of them like painting and they particularly dislike my kind of painting. It's awkward, this oil and water mixing. I have lots more in common with the young generation, but there you are. Twenty can't be expected to tolerate sixty in all things, and sixty gets bored stiff with twenty's eternal love affairs. Oh God, why did you make me a pelican and sit me down in a wilderness? These old maids of fifty to sixty, how dull they are, so self-centred, and the married women are absorbed in their husbands and families. Oh Lord, I thank Thee for the dogs and the monkey and the rat. I loafed all day. Next week I must step on the gas.

Emily Carr, 1934

… the girls and I and Joan discussing this business of babies. It really is doing in both Joan and to a lesser extent Ruth. And the same thing has happened to me. I can no longer concentrate myself, feel I ought to be doing something else, at any rate I ought to be in half an hour.

One is listening for the telephone or for a child. Even if I want to join in a conversation I feel myself impelled to distract myself, not to give full concentration, to read a book at the same time. I can't now think in a pointed way about anything. I can rather more easily concentrate when writing. But it is rare to have an hour undistracted. Because of this I know I can never be first class at anything. The mornings are slightly better, but are more occupied by other things. By the evening I am too tired to do anything. I cannot even read a serious book now … What we might do is lost except in so far as we can pass it on to our children in our chromosomes. The fact that our children are voluntarily begotten makes it all the more difficult. We cannot just say they are something that has happened to us, an act of God or however it should be expressed. We deliberately took on this burden. Yet we didn't know beforehand how crippling it would be.

Naomi Mitchison, 1945

After prayers I wrought, and heard Mr Ardington read: after, I prayed, and dined, and then I went about busy till almost night, when I went to private prayer.

Lady Margaret Hoby, 1601

13 August

So tired and hot and hurt at having to wait so long for this baby, so sick of the discomfort and pains that mean nothing, and going to bed each night thinking, 'Perhaps tonight,' and waking up, 'Perhaps today,' and looking ahead and thinking, 'This is the last music lesson' or 'the last doctor's appointment' or 'the last Sunday' and finding it isn't.

Anne Morrow Lindbergh, 1932

Busy with domesticities. The days are more serene, but last night was sleepless and troubled in the old way. The whole frightful story – [her husband] Hu's death, the wild unhappy months in Italy, the bitter renewal with Barny [her lover], our break and my attempt at suicide and then conception and stopping it – showed up as a long dreadful nightmare.

Loran Hurnscot, 1926

How depressed I felt yesterday evening. How I hung upon the past, as if my life as well as happiness were in it! How I thought of those words [of her dead mother's] 'You will never find another person who will love you as I love you' – And how I felt that to hear again the sound of those beloved, those ever ever beloved lips, I wd. barter all other sounds & sights – that I wd. in joy & gratitude lay down before her my tastes & feelings each & all, in sacrifice for the love, the exceeding love which I never, in truth, can find again.

Elizabeth Barrett (Browning), 1831

14 August

Yesterday morning, as I was enjoying my hot bath, there opened a roar of aeroplanes overhead, then machine guns and rapid explosions, shaking the walls and the roof. 'I must not be found naked,' I thought, and hurriedly put on my underclothing.

Beatrice Webb, 1940

Yesterday took place the 1st private execution within the prison yard, only officials and reporters being present. A thing to return thanks for, the doing away of the horrible mob-scenes.

Lucy (Lady Frederick) Cavendish, 1868

I have spent just on five years with this wretched Georges Ghika, irresponsible and debauched, rejecting actions but brimming over with evil words ... He had lost his virility – the desire to recover it tormented him. So at night he would direct all his evil ardour on to me, would try, begin again, fruitlessly. To him that, and only that, is what love means ... He would soon fall asleep and snore while I, despairing, would pray ...

Liane de Pougy, 1931

The best way for a homosexual relationship to work is on an affair basis, preferably with separation more than togetherness. Love is an idea, a dream. Those are cherished, made more beautiful by dreaming and by imagination. They are kept free of strife, embarrassment, guilt, and that merging of personalities which can only go so far before it becomes oversaturated and crystallizes into something else. There is not enough difference between people of the same sex for them to maintain that healthful tension and misunderstanding that a man and a woman do.

Patricia Highsmith, 1958

15 August

Martha Ingham came here to pay her church-pew rent ... mentioned a famous kind of man at Manchester who cures most inveterate rheumatisms, etc., by literally sweating people in a sort of stove. He watches them while they are in it, & knows when they have been long [enough] by a particular vein in the head.

Anne Lister, 1821

After private prayer I wrought, and talked with my Cousin Robert Dakins: and after dinner I went about, and walked abroad, and heard Mr Ardington read: after, I Came home and went to private prayer, I praise God, having obtained to overcome in some measure disordered affection.

Lady Margaret Hoby, 1601

16 August

Labor pains start at about 12 Monday night. About 3.45 into town, slowing up for each pain. I felt so strange (in the grip of something inevitable and tremendous, an iron hand) passing through the everyday streets of New York, past milk wagons and trucks, newsstands and advertisements, and I going to the biggest thing in life except death, and the nearest thing to that ...

The pain was just as terrible, so terrible that you are not yourself any more – you are pain – everything in the world is pain. Sometimes more particular than that: you are impaled by it, unable to escape. Racing with pain, trying to escape into the gas while the tongues of pain lick at your heels, like the tide overtaking you.

But the labor was so much shorter this time (only four hours in the apartment) that I was not tired out and much more conscious in between pains and much more rebellious: no restraint of courage or endurance ...

Finally waking up very sore but with the weight free from my abdomen, and that same unmistakable shrill bleat – uncertain hesitating bleat, across all other sounds, as though it were the only sound – of the baby …

Then later all day (with a wheeling head and the recurring afterpains) I was blissfully happy, relieved, saying and thinking over and over, 'The baby is all right, all right, he is here, he's all right,' until C.[harles] said, 'He has a wart on his left toe,' and began teasing me. But I could not get over it. Out of last fall, out of this winter, a perfect baby. It was a miracle.

And I felt years removed from the night before and the months before that night. I felt I had given birth to more than a baby: to new life in myself, in C., in Mother. C., a teasing boy again; Mother, gently, softly gay as she used to be with Charlie [her son who was killed]. And I felt as if a great burden had fallen off me. I could not imagine the baby would do this for me, but I felt life given back to me – a door to life opened. I *wanted* to live, I felt power to live. I was not afraid of death or life: a spell had been broken, the spell over us that made me dread everything and feel that nothing would go right after this. The spell was broken by this real, tangible, perfect baby, coming into an imperfect world and coming out of the teeth of sorrow – a miracle, My faith had been reborn.

Anne Morrow Lindbergh, 1932

I had a long haircombing with her [the recently widowed Katharine Asquith] … She admitted that, had she been offered the choice of whether she would buy her ten years happiness at the price of the suffering now involved, she would do so, but she said she would have tried to teach herself to live a little more on herself and not so exclusively on another human being. I think what she says is true, that you can roughly divide human beings into two classes, one of which *live on themselves* (however much they may love), and the other who live on some other person. I suppose I really belong to the first category – persons are luxuries to me. She regards the remainder of her life as a bad debt to be discharged.

Lady Cynthia Asquith, 1917

Many air raids ... They came very close. We lay down under the tree. The sound was like someone sawing in the air just above us. We lay flat on our faces, hands behind head. Don't close your teeth, said L.[eonard].

Virginia Woolf, 1940

... Mrs Cunningham came in, and said in speaking of my size, that if she were I, she would not go out any more, Mother said that I went against her wishes – leading to the inference that she thought it improper for me to go, – and was then foolish enough to tell me of the conversation – I felt it a good deal – it made me rather unhappy – I could have forgiven it in a young person who did not know the importance of exercise, the tediousness of the last few weeks of pregnancy, and the effort necessary to a walk – in the healthiest person under such circumstances – but here were persons who had had large families – candidly admitting that they thought it my duty to let my health & that of my child suffer, rather than offend against common prejudice ...

Caroline Healey Dall, 1845

17 August

My beloved and I went the Home Circuit. Walked to the Gate. Met the Vicar. Invited him to coffee. The good man more stupid than ever, incredible and impossible as that appeared to us the last time we saw him.

Lady Eleanor Butler, 1790

– My twentieth birthday – Very, very fast the years are passing away – and I – Ah! how little am I improving them ... Twenty years! I have lived. I shall *not* live twenty years more – I feel it. I believe I have but a few years to live. – Them I *must*, I *will* improve. – I will pray for strength to keep *this* resolution; – I have broken so many. *This* I *must* keep ...

Charlotte Forten, 1857

Rex [Harrison] just called from America, in control of himself, looking forward to watching *Face the Nation* on television, shaved and bathed, active and interested in things. It's very sweet of him to call me. But no one gets through any more. I'm submerged by it all, not wanting to do anything, see anybody … convinced it's just over for me. Simply find the way out. No tears today. My great faults have won over the nice little virtues. I just seek obliteration.

Rachel Roberts, 1980

… Shall I then describe how I fainted again? That is the galloping hooves got wild in my head last Thursday night as I sat on the terrace with L.[eonard]. How cool it is after the heat! I said. We were watching the downs draw back into fine darkness after they had burnt like solid emerald all day. Now that was being softly finely veiled. And the white owl was crossing to fetch mice from the marsh. Then my heart leapt: and stopped: and leapt again: and I tasted that queer bitterness at the back of my throat; and the pulse leapt into my head and beat and beat, more savagely, more quickly. I am going to faint, I said, and slipped off my chair and lay on the grass … The pain, as of childbirth; and then that too slowly faded; and I lay presiding, like a flickering light, like a most solicitous mother, over the shattered splintered fragments of my body. A very acute and unpleasant experience.

Virginia Woolf, 1932

18 August

I'm amazed that I'm on the cover of *Life* magazine with a title that says I'm the most powerful person. How'd that happen? Feels like someone else.

Oprah Winfrey, 1997

Nothing to record; only an intolerable fit of the fidgets to write away. Here I am chained to my rock; forced to do nothing; doomed to let every worry, spite, irritation and obsession scratch and claw and come again. This is a day that I may not walk and must not work ... I hear poor L.[eonard] driving the lawn mower up and down, for a wife like I am should have a latch to her cage. She bites!

Virginia Woolf, 1921

After I was ready I prayed privately, and, because I was weak and had pain in my head, I wrought little but wound yarn and walked till dinner time: after which I went about the house, and did walk abroad, working little all that day because of my weakness, less I should be disabled to keep the Lord's day as I desired and am bound: before supper, I prayed and examined myself, not so particularly as I ought to have done, which I beseech the Lord to pardon for his Christ's sake, and give me grace here after to be more careful ...

Lady Margaret Hoby, 1599

19 August

I love to watch my little rabbit, stretching his mouth, wriggling, and his nostrils quivering with a yawn. And as I look at his inarticulate efforts (and we watch and say something trivial) I think: Perhaps you are perfectly conscious but unable to say so, as I was (half under gas) and waking up to this world. You are still half in the other world and look down on our mundane talk with contempt and bewilderment.

Anne Morrow Lindbergh, 1932

1 a.m. Face it kid, you've had a hell of a lot of good breaks. No Elizabeth Taylor, maybe. No child Hemingway, but god, you are growing up. In other words, you've come a long way from the ugly introvert You were only five years ago. Pats on the back in order? O.K., tan, tall, blondish, not half bad. And brains, 'intuitiveness' in one direction at least. You

get along with a great many different kinds of people. Under the same roof, close living, even. You have no real worries about snobbishness, pride, or a swelled head. You are willing to work. Hard, too. You have willpower and are getting to be practical about living – and also you are getting published. So you got a good right to write all you want. Four acceptances in three months – $500 *Mlle*, $25, $10 *Seventeen*, $4.50 *Christian Science Monitor* (from caviar to peanuts, I like it all the way).

Sylvia Plath, 1952

Back to reality. I am fragile today. The holiday's over, the next bit of life begins and I feel vulnerable …

I know I want to be open about cancer, so now is as good a time as any. Around 7.25 p.m., I post this:

> Hi, have been diagnosed with breast cancer & am
> having a mastectomy in a few weeks. Family, friends,
> work & NHS staff are being brilliant 1/2
> Will be doing the programmes as much as possible
> during treatment in the months ahead 2/2

The very act of sending this message makes me think 'Shit, it really is real', as though somehow it wasn't before. A piece of information I'd shared only with close family and work colleagues is now echoing around social media and there's no going back.

Within milliseconds messages begin to pour in …

Victoria Derbyshire, 2015

20 August

Soon began on the erotics last night. Her warmth encouraging … [I said] 'This is adultery to all intents & purposes.' 'No, no,' said she. 'Oh, yes, M– [Mariana Lawton]. No casuistry can disguise it.' 'Not this then, but the other.' 'Well,' said I, choosing to let the thing turn her own way. 'I always considered your marriage legal prostitution. We were both wrong. You to do it, I to consent to it. And, when I think of blaming others, I always remember nothing can at all excuse us but our prior connection.' I did not pursue the subject, nor did M– seem to think much of it. The fear of discovery is strong. It rather increases, I think, but her conscience seems seared so long as concealment is secure …

Anne Lister, 1823

… After breakfast taking Mr Benjamin Bunny to pasture at the edge of the cabbage bed with his leather dog-lead, I heard a rustling, and out came a little wild rabbit to talk to him, it crept half across the cabbage bed and then sat up on its hind legs, apparently grunting. I replied, but the stupid Benjamin did nothing but stuff cabbage. The little animal, evidently a female, and of a shabby appearance, nibbling, advanced … face twitching with excitement and admiration for the beautiful Benjamin, who at length caught sight of it round a cabbage, and immediately bolted. He probably took it for Miss Hutton's cat.

Beatrix Potter, 1892

I have married eight years yesterday: various trials of faith and patience have been permitted me; my course has been very different to what I had expected; instead of being, as I had hoped, a useful instrument in the Church Militant, here I am a care-worn wife and mother, outwardly, nearly devoted to the things of this life: though at times this difference in my destination has been trying to me; yet, I believe those trials (which have certainly been very pinching), that I have had to go through, have been very useful, and brought me to a feeling sense of what I am …

Elizabeth Fry, 1808

I do not think I shall ever have a sensation which is not mixed with ambition. I despise people who are nobodies.

Marie Bashkirtseff (aged 18), 1879

21 August

Went into the garden immediately after breakfast, but saw nothing of the wild rabbit except its tracks. Benjamin's mind has at last comprehended gooseberries, he stands up and picks them off the bush, but has such a comical little mouth, it is a sort of bob cherry business.

Beatrix Potter, 1892

John [her son] rather trying all day; when I mentioned the possibility of a smack he merely replied: 'Smack! Smack! If you want to smack anybody, smack yourself!'

Vera Brittain, 1932

What wonderful things there are in the world, only one must look for them.

Ivy Jacquier, 1923

[Her friend] Alice came over. She is very depressed and looks awful. Times are pretty bad. Jews are not allowed to keep more than a thousand guilders of their income. Apparently that's a pretty low blow. And other measures too. But I don't care. As long as Jules isn't picked up and sent away, as long as we can stay here in our cosy house, I can stand anything, and I hope I'll be able to help others. Poor Alice, I don't think she's got much guts. She gets downhearted so quickly. Oh well, I guess most people are depressed these days. But I want to be strong! I want to come out of this war tough and unbeaten. And if we're not allowed to go to school any more, well then I'll just keep on working, and learning things, and getting wiser!

Edith Velmans, 1941

22 August

The whole of the day was spent viewing this town [Liverpool] which is truly fine, and the docks which are reckoned famous – We went on board some Guinea-men [i.e. slave ships] and my heart revolted at the relation of the cruelties practised upon the wretched Negroes during their passage – The manner in which the Ship is arranged for their accommodation is sufficient to make one commiserate their sufferings, were not additional barbarities executed towards these unhappy wretches – Who has giv'n us the right thus to treat our fellow creatures? – God alone will show it on the great day when we are to account for our deeds –

Eugenia Wynne Campbell, 1806

… Even were there the excuse, though a bad one, of supposing *her heart interested* in any one person, I could forgive – nay, feel sympathy with her Royal Highness [Caroline of Brunswick, estranged wife of the Prince Regent]: but taking pleasure merely in the *admiration* of low persons, is beneath her dignity as a woman, not to mention her rank and station. I am sometimes tempted to wish Lord H. F[itzgeral]d had continued to love her; for I am sure, poor soul, had anyone been steadfast to her, she would have been so to them; and though, as a married woman, nothing could justify her in being attached to any man, yet it is a hard and cruel fate, to spend the chief part of one's existence unloving and unloved …

… While opprobrium was heaped on the Princess of Wales, and the smallest offence against etiquette or priority which she had committed, was magnified into *crime*, the Prince ran a career of lawless pleasure unrebuked, nay, even applauded! How true is the proverb –: 'One man may steal a horse, and another may not look over a hedge.' I am not one of those who think that crime in *the one* sex alters its nature and becomes a virtue in the other.

Lady Charlotte Bury, 1813

Wore my black-and-white gown. It was much dewdropped [commented on]. Letty [her sister-in-law] and I had an exquisite vision of Adele [American heiress Adele Grant] in hat and stays. Really her legs are poems, and if I had such knees and feet, I feel I should be safe from all the 'slings and arrows of outrageous fortune'. They would be an unfailing source of consolation.

Lady Cynthia Asquith, 1915

An event of no small consequence to our little family must here be recorded in the 'Thraliana'. After having long intended to go to Italy for pleasure, we are now settling to go thither for convenience. The establishment of expense here at Streatham is more than my income will answer; my lawsuit with Lady Salisbury turns out worse in the event and infinitely more costly than I could have dreamed on …

The persecution I endure from men too who want to marry me – in good time – is another reason for my desiring to be gone. I wish to marry none of them, and Sir Philip's teasing me completed my mortification; to see that one can rely on *nobody*! The expenses of this house, however, which are quite past my power to check, is the true and rational cause of our departure. In Italy we shall live with twice the respect and at half the expense we do here …

Hester Lynch Thrale Piozzi, 1782

23 August

Day follows day, beautiful, happy, golden outside and in. Our friends are lovely, gay, well-behaved, delicious and pleased with everything. … At night … Things hot up. The Duchess came to stretch out on my bed, with Natalie [American heiress Natalie Clifford Barney] in between us. We embraced, gentle caresses. It was charming – perhaps a little nerve-wracking. Camille kept her head turned away so that she should see nothing. Georges [her husband] read poetry aloud. Natalie remembered something Marguerite Moreno said when she was staying with friends in the country, on a rainy day. Someone asked 'What shall we do?' In her melodious, well-trained voice Marguerite dropped the one word: 'Fornicate'.

I love my friends. No, my Lord, it can't be a great sin? It is you who sent them to me, with open hearts, you who made them so sweetly fond and sensual, it's You who make them lean over me with such tenderness – surely it is?

… The sin would be if there were lies in it, dishonesty, trickery, if there were an ulterior motive – snobbery or gross sensuality – or if decisive gestures had been made, but the blossoming of these tentative caresses, like inhaling the perfume of a flower?

Liane de Pougy, 1922

I am spending much of today trying to reply to or favourite all the messages I continue to receive from people on Facebook and Twitter. It's important to me that I acknowledge as many people as I can, because I want each one to know how much their sensible, sympathetic words mean to me.

Victoria Derbyshire, 2015

Burgo [her son] has been accepted by the Newbury Grammar School, and today we took him to see his future headmaster, packing into the car with a lot of baskets of fruit and vegetables. We liked Mr Starr and were cheered up by the interview; for one thing it was clear Burgo had passed easily and on his merits. Lunched at the Chequers Inn, and were aware that the news was just starting in the Lounge. Then we heard the Marseillaise. 'Paris must have been retaken!' I said. And so it had. Here is a piece of news that brings nothing but pleasure. An old dog of a Lesbian, dressed as a man, with a stock and cropped grey hair, sat down beside us: 'Glorious news, isn't it,' she said, and especially that the Free French did it themselves.'

Frances Partridge, 1944

24 August

R. [her husband Ralph] and I lay in bed last night thinking and talking of nothing but the fall of Paris, and the probability of peace soon. I woke feeling 'I must get up – things are happening.' Janetta said she had been far too excited to sleep; and when I took some eggs to Mrs Mills, the baker's wife, she said, 'I couldn't sleep for thinking peace might come soon.' So we all sit, like people in the waiting-room of a hospital while a life or death operation goes on ...

Frances Partridge, 1944

Shall I draw my physical portrait? Tall, and looking even more so: 1.66 metres, 56 kilos in my clothes. I run to length – long neck, face a full oval, but elongated, fairly perfect; long arms, long legs. Even complexion, fine-skinned, mat. I use just a touch of rouge, it suits me. Rather small mouth, well-shaped, superb teeth. My nose? They say it's the marvel of marvels. Small ears like pretty shells, almost no eyebrows – hence a little pencil-line whenever I want it. Eyes hazel green, prettily shaped, not very large, but my gaze is wide. Hair thick, very fine, incredibly fine, a pretty shiny chestnut brown. Hardly any grey hairs. One or two, to prove that I don't dye.

Liane de Pougy, 1919

... When I said that I was homely, [her cousin] Ester exclaimed, 'You homely? Just let me fix you up and you'll see.' I agreed, and she got the scissors and cut my bangs and combed my hair, then she put rice-powder on my face and when I looked in the mirror I saw that I wasn't homely at all. They laughed when I told them that what we do here is to grease our hair with chicken fat to keep it plastered down ... Ester thought it was funny when I told her that Mama Tina used to say, 'The pretty lives, the homely lives.' She said, 'It's true, but the pretty ones live better.' How happy I am today to be pretty at last!

Helena Morley (aged 12), 1893

Are we at war? At one I'm going to listen in … Museums shut. Searchlights on Rodmell Hill. Chamberlain says danger imminent. The Russian pact a disagreeable and unforeseen surprise. Rather like a herd of sheep we are. No enthusiasm. Patient bewilderment. I suspect some desire 'to get on with it'. Order double supplies and some coal. Unreal. Whiffs of despair.

Virginia Woolf, 1939

25 August

Does Mama [her stepmother] have a sixth sense which has alerted her to my moments of joy during the past weeks and is she trying to make me pay for them? One would swear to it!

There isn't a colder, pricklier, harder-to-please person in the whole wide world; I am utterly weary of it. Honestly, I find my life at the moment a complete fiasco and myself a thoroughly miserable girl. Yet I'm not all that demanding: a little sunshine, a little affection – all I ask is to enjoy these things in peace. *Peace*, what a heavenly word: no raised voices, no arguments, no commotion, no angry frowns. Just pleasant, gentle harmony.

Henriette Dessaulles (aged 16), 1877

I went to look for water and made coffee. I didn't buy bread. I didn't have money. I was going to take the children out when I saw a girl on her way to school and I asked her if there were going to be classes. She said yes. I dressed José Carlos and João went the way he was. I promised to bring them some lunch. I went out with [her daughter] Vera. There was no paper in the streets because another man had picked it all up. I did find some scrap metal.

Carolina Maria de Jesus, 1958

26 August

Proof of whole book [*Little Women*] came. It reads better than I expected. Not a bit sensational, but simple and true, for we really lived most of it, and if it succeeds that will be the reason of it. Mr N.[iles, her publisher] likes it better now, and says some girls who have read the manuscript say it is 'splendid!' As it is for them, they are the best critics, so I should be satisfied.

Louisa May Alcott, 1868

I was looking in Mama's trunk for something the other day and the first thing I saw was, at the top of a great many Journal books or something of that sort a piece of paper on which was written 'If I die, let these be burnt', and something else which I did not see! I am sure I should like to see them very much, and I do not see why they should be burnt.

Emily Pepys (aged 11), 1844

Let me consider the circumstances, while I am calm, in a degree. I may have to leave this place where I have walked & talked & dreamt in much joy; & where I have heard most beloved voices which I can no more hear, & clasped beloved hands which I can no more clasp: where I have smiled with the living & wept above the dead & where I have read immortal books, & written pleasant thoughts, & known at least one very dear friend – I may have to do this; & it will be sorrow to me! – But let me think of it calmly. I can take with me the dear members of my own family – & my recollections which, in some cases, were all that was left to me here: I can take with me my books & my studious tastes, – and above all, the knowledge that '*all things*' whether sorrowful or joyous, 'work together for good to those who love God' … There is *one* person, whom it will indeed pain me to leave. But he may follow us, – & in the meantime he will write to me & not forget me. Oh! I hope not!

Elizabeth Barrett (Browning), 1831

27 August

I think if I do not see Teddy soon I shall give him up, as there is no use loving a boy one is never to see. It would seem by this as if I did not love him much, but really I think if I was going to see him much my love would all return, as it is not near gone yet. In fact I still like him very much indeed, and if he comes to the school here I shall love him as much as ever again, if he still cares for me; he has not written to me for a long time.

Emily Pepys, 1844

… Francis [Ford Coppola] is feeling the pressure of being at the financial limit, having all the chips on the table … Perhaps there is a part of me that wants him to fail. Be back in some simple life-style and all that. At one point in the past, it was really strong, as if returning to a 'simple' life would take me out of where I was and I would be happier. At least I know now that it doesn't change things that much. You can be rich and unhappy, or poor and unhappy. I guess women have a hard time as the man grows more successful, powerful, and wish for a time when the balance was more equal. It comes from the fact that the relationship changes. The successful man is usually good at what he does, and likes it, and spends a lot of time doing it – and less and less time with his wife and family? When I stopped feeling like a victim, I started having a lot of fun with Francis. We have odd moments of really interesting time together, rather than more usual amounts of time half tuned out.

Eleanor Coppola, during the making of Apocalypse Now, 1976

A woman gives much when she consents to become mother and wife. I put the mother first because it is the relationship that absorbs her life, for which she suffers and should be loved. Poor little Mother. Looking back I see how bitterly she must have felt our want of affection and sympathy and for that I feel remorse.

… It is strange, how I now feel the presence of her influence and think of her as an absent friend who does sympathise with my new life, but cannot tell it me. I never asked for her sympathy while she lived, but now she, through the medium of my memory, gives it me. When I work, with many odds against me, for a far distant and perhaps unattainable end, I think of her and her intellectual strivings, which we were too ready to call useless, and yet will be the originating impulse of all my ambition, urging onward towards something better in action or thought. When I feel discouraged and hopeless, when I feel that my feeble efforts to acquire are like blind groping in space for the stars, the vision of her will arise persistent always in action and in desire. Persevere.

Beatrice Webb, 1882

28 August

We are in the Belleville Hotel ... sleeping in bunks. Every morning at crack of dawn we have to hit the parade ground and all day long there are lectures in the Nissen huts on how to be an administration officer.

Here is a typical day's programme – parade (and at least four things found wrong with my appearance – 'Ropy do, Wyndham, your collar is filthy!'). Then a lecture on VD and scabies, followed by compulsory hockey in a thunderstorm – then another lecture on pregnant WAAFs. As if this wasn't enough we have a compulsory cello concert after dinner – can you imagine, after all that a *cello* concert?

Joan Wyndham, 1941

When she had gone out, my husband said, 'You know, you amaze me really, when I think of the wretched health you had just before the war, and how long it took you to recover from that nervous breakdown.' I said, 'Well, I'm in rhythm now, instead of always fighting against things' – but stopped when I saw the hurt, surprised look on his face. He never realises – and never could – that the years when I had to sit quiet and always do everything he liked, and *never* the things he did not, were slavery years of mind and body.

Nella Last, 1942

29 August

Felt in a terrible breadwinning bustle merely because I had to be at Barrie's by eleven! [She had taken a post as secretary to J. M. Barrie, author of *Peter Pan*.] Breakfasted downstairs punctually at nine and then tried to get letters and diary done before starting …

It takes me twenty minutes from door to door to get to Barrie by Underground. I found his favourite ward Michael with him – a delightful Eton boy. The work I did was easy enough – it is only socially rather difficult, because undefined. I don't quite know when to go, when to talk, when silently to work.

Lady Cynthia Asquith, 1918

I love friends. They are to me the most delightful and the most precious of gifts that existence offers. So delightful to me is the breaking through of barriers – of which I have and had a few more than most people, I am sure.

Patricia Highsmith, 1958

Poor baby drooping today, and at night very feverish with symptoms of dysentery. Dr Hoffendahl wrapped her in wet bandages about the abdomen, also one on her head. I watched her all night and the fever yielded to these good measures.

Fanny Longfellow, 1848

I was for several days much alarmed by a change that I saw in the shape of the Princess's figure [Caroline, Princess of Wales], and I could not help imparting the terrible fear I felt to Lady –. She had also noticed it; but I was much relieved by her telling me she knew for certain it was only caused by the Princess having left off stays, – a custom which she is very fond of. She ought to be warned not to indulge in this practice; for it might give rise to reports exceedingly injurious to her character.

Lady Charlotte Bury, 1813

30 August

I felt extremely uncomfortable all day but walked out and dined at table. Mr Tookey was sent for in the evening and towards twelve o'clock I was happily delivered of another boy.

Betsey Wynne Fremantle, 1807

The canvas is placed on the easel; all is ready, it is only I who am missing.

If I were to tell everything! The horrible fears …

And here's September, the bad weather is near.

The least chill I now take may force me to keep my bed for two months, and then there'll be the convalescence …

And my picture!! I shall have sacrificed everything and …

The moment has come to believe in God and to pray …

Yes, it is the fear of being taken ill; in the state I am in, an attack of pleurisy may carry me off in six weeks.

This is the way I shall end, no doubt …

Such aspirations, such disease, such plans, such … and all to die at twenty-four years of age, on the threshold of everything.

Marie Bashkirtseff, 1884

Very hot. Darling baby very feeble though without fever. She is as quiet and patient as possible, uttering no complaint. Very restless and wakeful all night.

Fanny Longfellow, 1848

I did not feel very well all day, but took a drive in the afternoon with all the Children – towards ten o'clock I sent for Dr Tookey, and was happily and safely brought to Bed a few minutes after twelve, of another Boy – the largest Child born of the whole lot, according to Tookey's report.

Betsey Wynne Fremantle, 1810

31 August

I was woken at about 4 a.m. by the telephone. It was Torje in Toronto. He had just returned from dinner and turned on CNN. 'I thought you'd want to know; there's been a car crash in Paris. They're saying that Dodi Al Fayed is dead, and Princess Diana is injured ...'

About five hours later the phone woke me again ... She's dead. Like the rest of the nation, I can't quite take it in. It's not just the loss, both to her family and to the country; although that goes without saying. There's something more, something deeper, something harder to define. We always think that those things 'won't happen to us'. Yet if they can happen to a member of the Royal Family, a family which should be cocooned in the cotton wool of invincibility, safe and untouchable, it most certainly can happen to any one of us. Her life hasn't been quite the fairytale she was promised – it's been closer to a movie script, with its outrageous extremes of tragedy, melodrama and glamour. Until now, I've never seen her as real, just a face on the news-stands. But in her horrific and pointless death, she's at last become vulnerable and real to me, and to everyone else. How sadly ironic that it's only when she's robbed of her life that I can finally think of her as human.

Deborah Bull, 1997

A poet friend quoted another writer – who? – that we write to prolong the time between our two deaths: the physical death of our being when we cease to exist, and the death of us when no one remembers us, which can be weeks, months, years ...

I write to prolong my memory of life now, to see that I have had thought, emotions, ideas, encounters, and experiences. If I cannot remember, it is as if I had not lived those days, and that my life was the barest of details I do remember. By writing it down, it is engrained, and my thoughts continue, are part of some stream and not just discrete bits from the day's menu, the same offerings, and my eating the same things I liked last time.

Amy Tan, 'August 2008'

September

'War is on us this morning … I don't know why I write this,
or what I feel, or shall feel. All is hovering over us.'

Virginia Woolf, 1939

1 September

War is on us this morning. Hitler has taken Danzig: has attacked – or is attacking – Poland. This after a day in London, submerged doubts and hopes. Now at 1 I go in to listen I suppose to the declaration of war. A dull hot day. I don't know why I write this, or what I feel, or shall feel. All is hovering over us.

Virginia Woolf, 1939

The nine o'clock news. Dick [her husband] looks desperately unhappy. The boys quiet and horrified. Joan cries at her husband's feet; I go over to her. The girls seem all right. Tony hopes Bill won't try to come back from America; she has only one moment of looking like tears. Chamberlain's speech. Horribly like Asquith in '14 … We take notes of a few regulations; I write some cards. It seems impossible. The gladiolus on the shelf shine and ramp at us …

Naomi Mitchison, 1939

Haunted. Can't shake Diana's death. Trying to figure out what it means to me and the rest of the world. What did she come to show us? What are we supposed to get from this untimely death? Take nothing for granted. Even a Princess living in a castle can hit the wall. I pray to have no fear to move forward and do what needs to be done. To do it for the greater Glory and Honor of my creator. So, I'm starting this week to 'take myself down': physically, emotionally, spiritually. To go to the place one needs to go to create the last scene of *Beloved*. The '30 women' scene is coming up. Wrestling with my fears of dying, and not being prepared. I need to take the time to redo my will. Get my house in order. Diana's death has shown me it is irresponsible to live otherwise. As the Bible says, 'Be ye also ready.' I feel changed by this death of a Princess. I feel there is no time to waste. And, I need to turn up the throttle … *and live more intensely.*

Oprah Winfrey, 1997

I dreamt last night that I was married, just married, & in an agony to procure a dissolution of the engagement. Scarcely ever considered my single state with more satisfaction than when I awoke! – I never *will* marry: but if I ever were to do such a foolish thing, I hope I may not feel as I did last night!

Elizabeth Barrett (Browning), 1831

At Grundlsee, the day before yesterday, I pulled out one of my molars. First I loosened it with a finger, then I pressed it inwards with a nail-file, causing the gum to turn blue. Finally I took a piece of thick twine and pulled at it until it fell into my hand. I should add that it took frequent pauses, during which I considered calling the whole thing off. Only the fear of a swollen jaw and even greater pain persuaded me to keep at it. It hurt like mad and blood flowed profusely. But it gave me the inner satisfaction of prevailing over myself. It's not easy to pull out one of your own teeth, especially if it's scarcely loose. Every yank signified a fresh battle with my own nerves. But I'm glad to be rid of the brute.

Alma Schindler (Mahler-Werfel), 1899

2 September

Awful news: they are planning to close the theatres! I rushed straight off to the New to see John and Edith Evans for the last time doing *The Importance* [*of Being Earnest*]. Sat in the gallery. People in the street seemed really quite cheerful, and all the people in the gallery queue were talking to each other, which is unusual for the English!

When I got home Mummy and Sid [sculptor Sidonie Houselander] were absolutely furious with me for going to the theatre. They seemed to think it was a dreadfully frivolous thing to do at such a time.

Joan Wyndham (aged 17), 1939

I am making the drawing for the *Figaro*, with rests of an hour between, as I am dreadfully feverish. I can't go on. I have never been so ill; but as I don't say anything about it, I go out and I paint. Why mention it? I am ill, that's enough. Will talking about it do any good? But to go out.

The illness is of a kind which allows it when you are feeling better.

Marie Bashkirtseff, 1884

3 September

———

Bedtime

Well, we know the worst. Whether it was a kind of incredulous stubbornness or a faith in my old astrological friend who was right in the last crisis when he said 'No war', I never thought it would come. Looking back I think it was akin to a belief in a fairy's wand which was going to be waved.

I'm a self-reliant kind of person, but today I've longed for a close woman friend – for the first time in my life. When I heard Mr Chamberlain's voice, so slow and solemn, I seemed to see Southsea Prom the July before the last crisis. The Fleet came into Portsmouth from Weymouth and there were hundreds of extra ratings walking up and down. There was a sameness about them that was not due to their clothes alone, and it puzzled me. It was the look on their faces – a slightly brooding, faraway look. They all had it – even the jolly-looking boys – and I felt I wanted to rush up and ask them what they could see that I could not. And now I know.

Nella Last, 1939

This morning war was declared by the Prime Minister over the radio.

Five minutes after the National Anthem, while we were still sitting around feeling rather sick, the air-raid warning went. For a moment we didn't believe our ears – we hadn't had time to realise we were at war – then we went down to our gas room and began damping the blankets with pails of water.

When the room was ready we went and sat on the front doorstep waiting for the first gun. The balloon barrage looked too lovely in the sun against the blue sky, like iridescent silver fish swimming in blue water. After a bit the all-clear sounded. We heard afterwards that it had all been a mistake.

Joan Wyndham, 1939

Five years. Had we known that Sunday morning five years ago – of all the blood, toil, sweat and tears, air raids, flying bombs, and collapse of France – could we ever have faced it? Now France is liberated, our troops are in Belgium, and victory certain. It said in yesterday's Times, 'The work stretches into the unknown years, there will be no pause after battle, and for this generation no discharge.' With these thoughts in mind I went to evensong in Ganges' chapel.

Eve Williams, VAD, 1944

Discharged Betsy Haynes the kitchen maid for Idleness, dirt, and *Such a Tongue*!

Lady Eleanor Butler, 1789

There was a marvellous breeze, a pretty waitress at the restaurant, music, and of course drink. Drink which drowned the terror I'm feeling at the chaos my life is in. The apprehension I have about the expensive nursing homes for the really sick – for that's what I'll come to. Next stop after Ibiza: Peter Coyle and stopping the denial of my grave alcoholism. The great fear is that it isn't that: that it's insanity without an outlet. I long for a man to turn to in bed, as I saw Marco turn to Jackie. Yes, I want to be told and reassured that my skin is soft, my hands and feet pretty – I also want to be told what to do and how to do it.

Rachel Roberts, 1980

4 September

The weary journey last night, the mooing of the cattle for water, their exhausted condition, with the cry of 'Another ox down,' the stopping of train to unyoke the poor dying brute, to let him follow at will or stop by the wayside and die, and the weary, weary tramp of men and beasts, worn out with heat and famished for water, will never be erased from my memory. Just at dawn, in the distance, we had a glimpse of Truckee River, and with it the feeling: Saved at last! Poor cattle; they kept on mooing, even when they stood knee deep in water. The long dreaded desert has been crossed and we are all safe and well. Here we rested Thursday and Friday – grass green and beautiful, and the cattle are up to their eyes in it.

Sallie Hester (aged 14), 1849

Violet [her sister-in law] and I had a very nice tête-a-tête … During our hair-combing I was horrified to see a nightmare monster of, I suppose, some sort of spider creeping on my wall. I was astonished at my display of femininity and became quite hysterical. It was so huge – I could scarcely believe I was in England. To sleep in such company was out of the question – what were we to do? Violet made heroic efforts to catch it in a shroud, but its eight legs were terribly swift and it always evaded her. Finally, feeling like 1st and 2nd murderer, we had to collaborate with fire irons and at last the deed was done. But, never, never have I felt so convinced in the survival of personality after death. I *know* that creature was not finished by my shovel.

Lady Cynthia Asquith, 1917

There was a time when I despised all notions of adhering to any regular course of existence; I did not believe that such was requisite, or contributed as much as it does to health and peace. I liked sometimes to be out all day, and return at night to my meals. Sometimes, I would sit up late and rise early, at others lie in bed for days. I did not believe that such irregularity could injure my health, much less affect my mind. But

I am convinced now, that nothing tends so much to enervate or excite (according to the nature of the person) as leading this sort of unsettled life. It is the dull round of hours for meals, and sleep, and exercise, which is most likely to preserve health, and that calm of spirit which, though it precludes vivid sensations of pleasure, spares those who lead such lives many a severe pang.

Lady Charlotte Bury, 1813

5 September

I wake and feel relieved. It is gone – that weight of horror. it is not there in the morning. I feel fresh and strong and able to conquer it.

Outside by the pool with Charles [her husband].

Anne Morrow Lindbergh, 1932

… I have suffered much today, – my friends Mrs P.[uttnam] and her daughters were refused admission to the Museum, after having tickets given them, solely on account of their complexion. Insulting language was used to them – Of course they felt and exhibited deep, bitter indignation; but of what avail was it? none, but to excite the ridicule of those contemptible creatures, miserable doughfaces who do not deserve the name of men. I will not attempt to write more. – No words can express my feelings. But these cruel wrongs cannot be much longer endured. A day of retribution must come. God grant that it may come very soon!

Charlotte Forten, 1854

Passed a sleepless night last night as a good many of the Indians camped around us were drunk and noisy and kept up a continual racket, which made all hands uneasy and kept our poor dog on the watch all night. I say poor dog, because he is nearly worn out with traveling through the day and should rest at night, but he hates an Indian and will not let one come near the wagons if he can help it, and doubtless they would have done some mischief but for him. Ascended a long steep hill this morning, which was very hard on the cattle, and also on myself, as I thought I should never get to the top, although I rested two or three times ...

Amelia Stewart Knight, 1853

I am frightfully contented these last few days, by the way. I don't quite understand it. Perhaps reason has something to do with it. Charleston and Tilton knocked me off my perch for a moment. [Her sister] Nessa and her children; Maynard [Keynes] and his carpets. My own gifts and shares seemed so moderate in comparison; my own fault too – a little more self control on my part, and we might have had a boy of twelve, a girl of ten. This always makes me wretched in the early hours. So I said, I am spoiling what I have. And thereupon settled to exploit my own possessions to the full; I can make money and buy carpets; I can increase the pleasure of life enormously by living it carefully. No doubt, this is a rationalisation of a state which is not really of that nature. Probably I am very lucky. Then, I am extremely happy walking on the downs. I like to have space to spread my mind out in. Whatever I think, I can rap out, suddenly, to L.[eonard]. We are somehow very detached, free, harmonious. Hence I come to my moral, which is simply to enjoy what one does enjoy, without teasing oneself oh but Nessa has children, Maynard carpets.

Virginia Woolf, 1926

6 September

Our first air raid warning at 8.30 this morning. A warbling that gradually insinuates itself as I lay in bed. So dressed and walked on the terrace with L. Sky clear. All cottages shut. Breakfast. All clear.

All meaning has run out of everything. Scarcely worth reading papers. The BBC gives any news the day before. Emptiness. Inefficiency. I may as well record these things. My plan is to force my brain to work on *Roger*.

But Lord this is the worst of all my life's experiences ... Am I a coward? Physically I expect I am. Going tomorrow to London I expect frightens me. At a pinch enough adrenalin is secreted to keep one calm. But my brain stops. I took up my watch this morning and then put it down. Lost. That kind of thing annoys me. No doubt one can conquer this. But my mind seems to curl up and become undecided. To cure this one had better read a solid book like Tawney. An exercise of the muscles ... Shall I walk? Yes. It's the gnats and flies that settle on non-combatants. This war has begun in cold blood. One merely feels that the killing machine has to be set in action.

Virginia Woolf, 1939

I have been unwell all the morning. *Nota bene*, never eat *new* honey. Lay in bed nearly all day, in consequence of that *nota bene* not having been noted yesterday.

Elizabeth Barrett (Browning), 1831

The morning of Diana's funeral, and my friend David and I joined several thousand people in Hyde Park to watch her cortege pass by. It has been the most extraordinary occasion, the most comprehensive and controlled display of public grief I am ever likely to witness. It was a bright and sparkling day, and the simplicity of the horse-drawn gun carriage contrasted sharply with the glamour of Diana's life. But I am sensing a mood here in the country which I find unsettling, a mood which verges on anarchy. I hope 'the people' have thought about where this will take them; the funeral demonstrated the need for formality and tradition to hold us together in times of tragedy, and yet I'm strongly aware of a potentially destructive element in the emotions on display.

Deborah Bull, 1997

7 September

Mr Delanos came for dinner, but Betsey was not able to sit it out, and afterwards her Misery began. We sent for [Dr] Tookey who spent three hours with Mr Delanos, and about nine I called him upstairs he was not there long, for Betsey was soon delivered of a nice little girl. I was quite happy when it was over. She really had an uncommon good time. I slept with Emma in the little room and had an uncommon good night. I *do* not think much of a Lying in.

Harriet Wynne, 1805

Love in a cottage is sentimental, but the parties must be very pleasing to each other to make it tolerable … If this is what beauty leads to, I am well content to have a red nose and a shorn head, I may be lonely, but better that than an unhappy marriage.

Beatrix Potter (aged 19), 1885

Midnight. Well here I sit in the air raid shelter with screaming bombs falling right and left, and Sir John Squire, roaring tight, sitting opposite me next to his Scotch Presbyterian cook. Squire's breath fills the shelter and the cook looks as if she's going to be sick. Sid is reading Maxim Gorky and I'm trying to write this diary, though I can't see very well as there is only a storm lantern. Squire keeps on saying he wants to read Wodehouse's *Uncle Fred in the Springtime* once more before he dies.

The bombs are lovely, I think it's all thrilling. Nevertheless, as the opposite of death is life, I think I shall get seduced by Rupert [Darrow] tomorrow. Rowena has promised to go to a chemist's with me and ask for Volpar Gels, just in case the French thingummy isn't foolproof.

Joan Wyndham (aged 18), 1940

Doctor thinks baby decidedly better today. The bad symptoms in her head have gone away, but she is very, very weak, so that she can hardly bear being moved and does not seem to know me, which is very hard to bear.

Fanny Longfellow, 1848

I lunched with Grannie Cooper who told me that this morning she put her name down for war work and described herself as 'Eighty but active'. We talked of Poland. Afterwards I walked to the gun shop in Pall Mall and brought a small .25 Colt revolver. The shopkeeper said I may not take possession of it until I get a licence …

Countess of Ranfurly, 1939

8 September

Sister & Mamma have gone up the Rhigi & I am left to chaperone myself until seven this evening. – How I hate travelling in Europe, & above all travelling in Switzerland. I began hating it when I had reached the advanced age of six, & now that I am seventeen I continue in the same frame of mind. – I believe I am fated like the 'wandering Jew' to be on a perpetual journey, & I do wish it would come to an end. – If we settle down in a place as we did at Baden & at Nice, I like it well enough, & enjoy myself extremely, but such intervals like oasis in the desert are extremely rare, & there are months & months, composed of dreary days, spent in nasty cars, or shut up in rooms at a hotel. – If I were perfectly well, & could walk, go sight-seeing, ride horseback, & sketch as much as I want to, it might be endurable, but as it is now, I can't bear it …

So I went from Wednesday until Saturday, three days without being worse, Sunday not so well, & Monday in bed where I have been until now, exhausted with heat & absolutely miserable. And so it is all the time, besides my original illness which has now lasted two years, I have these small intermittent diseases, which a well person would consider annoying enough. To go way back when we went to Florida, I was laid up a week in Richmond with that horrid nettle rash, & the same in

New York. – And that fearful sun-stroke in Nice that put me back three months; & then at Rome I was so sick, & we had such a fearful week at the hotel in Florence, & then two weeks in Lucca, which I shudder every time I think of, & then in Baden I had a cold, & a swelled face, & then all my dreadful faint turns … And all these, except the faints, seem to have been so unnecessary & entirely unconnected with my illness I don't believe in people who try to remember everything horrid that happens to them; I try to forget, & succeed admirably …

Julia Newberry (aged 17), 1871

I'm thinking about last night – he kissed me. What would Monsieur Prince say? He'd explode! But I wonder why. I let Maurice do it because he asked me, because he was sad, I wouldn't have wanted to make him even sadder, especially not by refusing him such a tiny thing.

As far as I am concerned, well, between him kissing me and him telling me tenderly that he loves me, I'd rather hear him say he loves me. Besides, letting yourself be kissed by a man isn't done, so I won't allow Maurice to do it often. I'm preoccupied with all of this now, but yesterday it was much simpler. He asked me and I said yes, because I would have hated to disappoint him. That's all. And that the Good Lord and all His angels may have seen us doesn't bother me one bit. I couldn't feel less guilty.

Henriette Dessaulles (aged 15), 1875

In the office 3.55 p.m. Even at this moment some dreadful thing may be happening – a husband deciding to leave his wife, a love affair being broken, someone dying, languishing with hopeless love or quarrelling about the Church of South India in the Edgware Road as I nearly did with Bob on Sunday. And I sit typing, revising, and 'translating' Harold Gunn's MS, waiting for tea.

Barbara Pym, 1955

9 September

Barbara [one of her dogs] particularly naughty at dinner. Leaps onto the table and nicks everyone's chop bones. After the children go to bed I say, 'Ought she to go, because I can't manage her?' Leo [her husband] says: 'Yes,' very forcibly. Take dogs out on Common and cry and cry. Feel utterly suicidal. The dogs ignore me.

Jilly Cooper, 1980

Barbara stayed with the family and moved with them to the country in 1982 to become one of Jilly's favourite dogs of all time.

Good press on the Severn Bridge – and my hat. It is almost incredible how much the spotlight is put on one's appearance by TV. Millions of people just talking about the HAT – and about the fact that I bowed instead of curtseying to the Queen. The Sun had a nice photo of me facing the Queen but smiling past her. I was in fact smiling at one of Philip's cracks. When he saw my name as Minister of Transport on the commemorative plaque he said, 'That's pretty cool. It was practically finished before you came along.' 'Not a bit of it,' I replied, 'It is entirely due to me that it was finished five months ahead of schedule. Anyway I intend to be in on the act.'

Barbara Castle, 1966

Baby showed some pain today, which went all through my nerves. Pretty good day on the whole. She looks to me like mother, her sharpened features giving her a much older look.

Fanny Longfellow, 1848

10 September

It would be useless for me with my pencil to describe the awful road we have just passed over. Let fancy picture a train of wagons and cattle passing through a crooked chimney and we have Big Laurel Hill … The men and boys all had their hands full and I was obliged to take care of myself and little ones as best I could, there being no path or road except the one where the teams traveled. We kept as near the road as we could, winding around the fallen timber and brush, climbing over logs creeping under fallen timber, sometimes lifting and carrying Chat [her seventh child]. To keep from smelling the carrion, I, as others, holding my nose … I was sick all night and not able to get out of the wagon in the morning.

Amelia Stewart Knight, 1853

I wonder if it's true that all women are born actors. I wonder what I'm *really* like. I know I'm often tired, beaten and afraid, yet someone at the canteen said I radiated confidence … What would I *really* be like if all my nonsense and pretence was taken from me? I have a sneaking feeling I'd be a very scared, ageing woman, with pitifully little. It's an odd thing to reflect: *no* one knows *any*one else, we don't even know ourselves very well.

Nella Last, 1942

After private prayers I went about the house, and then ate my breakfast: then I walked to the church with Mr Hoby: after that I wrought a little, and neglected my custom of prayer, for which, as for many other sins, it pleased the Lord to punish me with an Inward assault. But I know the Lord hath pardoned it because he is true of his promise, and if I had not taken this Course of examination, I think I had forgotten it. After dinner I walked with Mr Hoby and, after he was gone, I went to get tithe apples: after I Came home, I prayed with Mr Rhodes, and, after that, privately by my self, and took examination of my self; and so, after I had walked for a while, I went to supper, after that to the Lector, and so to bed.

Lady Margaret Hoby, 1599

11 September

Sinking, sinking away from us. Felt a terrible desire to seize her in my arms and warm her to life again at my breast. Oh for one look of love, one word or smile! Mary was with us all day. Painlessly, in a deep trance, she breathed. Held her hand and heard the breathing shorten, then cease, without a flutter. A most holy and beautiful thing she lay and at night of look angelic and so happy.

Fanny Longfellow, 1848

I do not feel very confident that I can make anything satisfactory of *Middlemarch*. I have need to remember that other things which were accomplished by me, were begun under the same cloud. G. [her partner George Henry Lewes] has been reading *Romola* again, and expresses profound admiration. This is encouraging.

George Eliot, 1869

I hope I may never live through such a moment again. I turned faint and sick and my head buzzed. There was the green door with the three bells, and after that two flights of stairs leading up to doors that opened on to nowhere. Below the stairs I could make out the splintered remnants of broken-down floors, Prudey's gum tree wedged upside down with its leaves moving in the breeze, and the bed I was seduced on hanging out over the street with three foot of solid mortar where Rupert [Darrow]'s head should have been. Leonard's studio was completely gone.

I rushed up to a warden and said, 'Where are all the people from that house?'

'Couldn't say miss, no bodies though, at least none that I've seen ... ' Choking back my sobs I ran down the street to my studio to see if Rupert might have gone there after the bomb. When I arrived I found I'd locked the door and hadn't got the key, but outside on the landing was deposited one guitar in a dented and dusty case, one un-neutered male ginger cat in a basket, very cross, and one gas mask inscribed 'RUPERT CHARLES

AUSTIN DARROW, STILL LIVING BY THE GRACE OF HIS OWN INGENUITY'. Arcana came out in her nightdress and said, 'Your friend came round with these in the middle of the night. He'd just been blown up, it was most extraordinary, he seemed to treat the whole thing as a joke. I couldn't believe him at first, he looked so cheerful.' Thank you God, I thought, thank you for saving Rupert.

Joan Wyndham (aged 18), 1940

12 September

... I wonder that every colored person is not a misanthrope. Surely we have everything to make us hate mankind. I have met girls in the schoolroom they have been thoroughly kind and cordial to me, – perhaps the next day met them in the street – they feared to recognize me; these I can but regard now with scorn and contempt, – once I liked them, believing them incapable of such meanness. Others give the most distant recognitions possible. – I, of course, acknowledge no such recognitions and they soon cease entirely, to make us hate mankind. These are but trifles, certainly, to the great, public wrongs which we as a people are obliged to endure. But to those who experience them, these apparent rifles are most wearing and discouraging; even to the child's mind they reveal volumes of deceit and heartlessness, and early teach a lesson of suspicion and distrust. Oh! it is hard to go through life meeting contempt with contempt, hatred with hatred, fearing, with too good reason, to love and trust hardly anyone whose skin is white, – however lovable, attractive and congenial in seeming.

Charlotte Forten, 1855

When I got home there was a parcel from Cliff [her son], and when I opened it I laughed till the tears came. It was my birthday gift, but he said he was sending it now in case I needed it. It's a 'syren suit'!! It's navy stockinette, with a zip front to the 'blouse' and to make ankles snug; 'roomy enough and easy-fitting enough to slip on or wear anything extra underneath'. It's the maddest, most amusing thing a sedate matron of fifty-one ever possessed! I often wonder what I look like in that one's eyes, and I've a great thankfulness he has not a lot of money to spend, for his taste in hats, etc. is not mine, and I know he would buy me some queer and unsuitable ones.

Nella Last, 1940

I have hardly had time or strength as yet to describe the events I have lately passed through. I did not experience the joy some women describe when my husband first brought me my little babe, little darling! I hardly knew what I felt for it, but my body and spirits were so extremely weak, I could only just bear to look at those I loved, and I felt dear baby at first a quiet source of pleasure, but she early became a subject for my weakness and low spirits to dwell upon, so that I almost wept when she cried; but I hope, as strength of body recovered, strength of mind will come with it.

Elizabeth Fry, 1801

13 September

Started to take 3 o'clock train for country, bought ticket, got on train, felt violent impulse to get off and did, just as train started. When I came home I was puzzled to receive a phone call from Carol, asking me to go to Hollywood, via Stratoliner, next day, at $500 a week, dialoguing 'Du Barry Was a Lady.' Actually wanted to go – just to get out of general mess, but [George] Hale would not let me off show.

Dawn Powell, 1941

Ascended three steep, muddy hills this morning. Drove over some muddy, miry ground and through mud holes and have just halted at the first farm to noon and rest awhile and buy feed for the stock. Paid 1.50 per hundred for hay. Price of fresh beef 16 and 18cts. per pound, butter ditto 1 dollar, eggs, 1 dollar a dozen, onion 4 and 5 dollars per bushel, all too dear for poor folks, so we have treated ourselves to some small turnips at the rate of 25 cents per dozen. Got rested and are now ready to travel again … there we are in Oregon and making our camp in an ugly bottom, with no home, except our wagons and tent. It is drizzling and the weather looks dark and gloomy …

Amelia Stewart Knight, 1853

14 September

A cold, dark day in sympathy with our gloom … She is everywhere. In the garden I see only her merry steps and little hands grasping the flowers with glee and shouting 'Pretty,' and then I see her with them in her cold hands. But she is playing with the flowers in Paradise, I fondly trust.

Fanny Longfellow, 1848

Two weeks here have inexplicably withered away. Yesterday we both bogged in a black depression – the late nights, listening sporadically to Beethoven piano sonatas – ruining our mornings, the afternoon sun too bright and accusing for tired eyes, meals running all off-schedule – and me with my old panic fear sitting firm on my back – who am I? What shall I do? The difficult time between twenty-five years of school routine and the fear of dilatory, dilettante days. The city calls – experience and people call, and must be shut out by a rule from within. Tomorrow, Monday, the schedule must begin – regular meals, shoppings, launderings – writing prose and poems in the morning, studying German and French in the afternoon, reading aloud an hour, reading in the evenings. Drawing and walking excursions … I must be happy first in my own work and struggle to that end, so my life does not hang on Ted's [Hughes, her husband] … Who else in the world could I live with and love? Nobody.

Sylvia Plath, 1958

Should I have found such pleasure for a common working man? I might if I had found a working man as could love as purely & be as Massa is (I mean in everything but his learning) & honour him as much, but that's a difficulty I doubt, the finding such a one. And so when I was young & did meet with Massa (whose face I'd seen in the fire) I made my mind up that it best & safest to be slave to a gentleman, not wife & equal to any vulgar man, still with the wish & determination to be independent by working in service and without the slightest hope o' being rais'd in rank either in place or by being married. And so at last after all these nearly twenty years by God's help & Massa's true heart & fervent love to me (more than ever I could dare to hope for from anyone but him, & I always trusted Massa). I am as I am. A servant still, & a very low one, in the eyes o' the world. I can work at ease. I can go out & come in when I please, & I can look as degraded as ever I like without caring how much I am despised in the Temple, or in Fetter Lane or in the streets.

Hannah Cullwick, 1873

… My beautiful boy, who grows bigger & bigger, – & perfectly astonishes me by his appetite – I have named William Cranch – for my dear, old, friend the Judge. He is not four weeks old until next Thursday – and I am so – well! though rather weak. Certainly I have had most skilful attendance. The day after my confinement Miss Alexander – enquired whether I felt any lameness – or strain in performing – my natural function – and when I answered – no – she said, 'well – I must give you credit for being an extremely well made woman – and myself some little, for not hurrying you – with so large a child – there was every danger of a rupture.' Much as I liked her, I cannot help feeling that the wiser course, would have been to have left nature to herself, after the birth of my child. If the placenta had not been torn away – I believe my pains would have returned and expelled it as soon as I was strong enough to bear the flooding that must ensue …

Caroline Healey Dall, 1845

15 September

No invasion yet. Rumours that it was attempted, but barges sank with great loss. Raids over Brighton this afternoon. Mabel goes tomorrow; so pray God the Church Bells don't ring tonight. Now we go to our last Cook-cooked dinner for I don't know how long. Could it be the end of resident servants forever? This I pray this lovely fitful evening, as well as the usual Damn Hitler prayer.

Virginia Woolf, 1940

… Who would have thought it, we said constantly to one another, when we two as schoolgirls stood on the moorland near Bournemouth, watching the sunset and the trees against it, discussed our religious difficulties and gave vent to all our world-sorrow, and ended by prophesying we should in ten years be talking of cooks and baby linen, boys going to their first school and other matronly subjects, who would have thought of our real future? She, struggling for her livelihood with queer experiences of a working woman's life; of another with her cook and big establishment but also absorbed in work outside home duty; both passed through the misery of strong and useless feeling … Who would have thought it! Will another ten years bring as great a change or have we settled down in the groove we are destined to run in?

Beatrice Webb, 1885

I had a tooth out the other day, curious and interesting like a little lifetime – first, the long drawn drag, then the twist of the hand and the crack of doom! The dentist seized my face in his two hands and exclaimed, 'Bravo, Miss James!' and Katharine and Nurse shaking of knee and pale of cheek went on about my 'heroism' whilst I, serenely wadded in that sensational paralysis which attends all the simple, rudimentary sensations and experiences common to man, whether tearing of the flesh or the affections, laughed and laughed at 'em.

Alice James, 1890

16 September

How dear is 'every plot of ground Paced by those blessed feet around.' The little white bonnet is at my side out of doors and at night. I fancy a cry in the nursery and listen thinking she must be there. But I thank God all tears are wiped from her eyes and that she can never know such grief as mine.

Fanny Longfellow, 1848

And then I am forty-seven: yes: and my infirmities will of course increase. To begin with my eyes. Last year, I think, I could read without spectacles; would pick up a paper and read it in a tube; gradually I found I needed spectacles in bed; and now I can't read a line without them. What other infirmities? I can hear, I think, perfectly: I think I could walk as well as ever. But then will there not be the change of life? And may that not be a difficult and even dangerous time? Obviously one can get over it by facing it with common sense – that it is a natural process; that one can lie out here and read; that one's faculties will be the same afterwards; that one has nothing to worry about in one sense – I've written some interesting books, can make money, can afford a holiday. Oh no; one has nothing to bother about; and these curious intervals in life – I've had many – are the most fruitful artistically – one becomes fertilised – think of my madness at Hogarth – and all the little illnesses – that before I wrote *To the Lighthouse*, for instance. Six weeks in bed now would make a masterpiece of *Moths* ...

Virginia Woolf, 1929

A physical set-back let me fall into the depth of misery. If only I were a little more backed-up by my health, I *know* I could bear my sorrows well enough. As it was, I felt overwhelmed all through the day and *terribly* detached – miles off the earth – what Johnson calls 'a gloomy gazer' on life and human beings.

Lady Cynthia Asquith, 1917

... Still very biliously inclined, but writing my journal has amused & done me good. I seem to have opened my heart to an old friend. I can tell my journal what I can tell no one else. I am satisfied with M– [Mariana Lawton] yet unhappy here [Scarborough]. I seem to have no proper dress. The people stare at me. My figure is striking. I am tired of being here. Even if I looked like other people I should soon be weary of sauntering on the sands. I dawdle away my time and have no pleasure in it ... M– came up to me for a few minutes before dinner ... We touched on the subject of my figure. The people staring so on Sunday had made her then feel quite low ... She had just before observed that I was getting mustaches [sic] & that when she first saw this it made her sick. If I had a dark complexion it would be quite shocking. I took no further notice than to say I would do anything I could that she wished ...

Anne Lister, 1823

17 September

In camp yet. Still raining. Noon – It has cleared off and we are all ready for a start again, for some place we don't know where ...

A few days later my eighth child was born. After this we picked up and ferried across the Columbia River, utilizing skiff, canes and flatboat to get across, taking three days to complete. Here husband traded two yoke of oxen for a half section of land with one-half acre planted to potatoes and a small log cabin and lean-to with no windows. This is the journey's end.

Amelia Stewart Knight, 1853

After dinner met two journalists; interviewed by one (all of us) for a National Press Association article. The other told me I was on a list, published a few days ago in the News Chronicle, of the first people whom the Gestapo intended to arrest when the Nazis invaded England.

Vera Brittain, 1945

Talked a little after we got into bed. Told M— I would not be with her again in strange places till I had an establishment of my own & that degree of importance which would carry me thro', for that she, & she owned it, had not consequence enough to, as it were, pass me off. If she were a Lady Mary it would be very different, but I knew her feelings & excused them … She said I did not know her feeling; the objection, the horror she had to anything unnatural. I shewed her I understood her & then observed upon my conduct & feelings being surely natural to me inasmuch as they were not taught, not fictitious, but instinctive. Said from my heart, I could make any sacrifice for her, tho' she could not for me. I could have braved anything. Yes, I have often felt I could have rushed on ruin. She said it was lucky for us both her feelings were cooler. They tempered mine. I said this was not necessary. I had met with those who could feel in unison with me … My feelings now began to overpower me. I thought of the devotion with which I had loved her, & of all I had suffered. I contrasted these with all the little deceits she has put upon me & with those cooler feelings with which she thought it so lucky to have tempered mine. I thought of these things & my heart was almost agonized to bursting …

Anne Lister, 1823

18 September

… I got a good deal of amusement & also annoyance out of Dudley Campbell who is madder than ever about his blessed vegetarianism. He now eats all his nasty little messes *cold*, & *drinks nothing*. It makes me shudder to see him breakfasting off slices of brown bread and raw apples. He has now given up butter, cream & milk, tea, coffee & cocoa. I am glad my daily bread is not under his command.

Mary, Lady Monkswell, 1889

I was all misery; the day was wretched. We had a fire in the drawing-room by which I sat all day without stirring. We had a good dinner of venison and a fig. We were all cross, Betsey on account of receiving a stupid letter from the husband, Justine unwell and I all thinking. I was delighted when it was bed time. I read Mde de Sevigny until I was quite tired. Rubbed mercury.

Harriet Wynne, 1804

'We have need of all our courage' are the words that come to the surface this morning; on hearing that all our windows are broken, ceilings down, and most of our china smashed at Mecklenburgh Square. The bomb exploded. Why did we ever leave Tavistock [Square]? – what's the good of thinking that? The Press – what remains – is to be moved to Letchworth. A grim morning. But I did forge ahead with *Pointz Hall* all the same.

Virginia Woolf, 1940

19 September

Oh, what a wretch I am! If I haven't forgotten to put in the grand news!! SEBASTOPOL HAS FALLEN! Yes, thank God, at last He has sent his much-prayed-for blessing.

Lucy (Lady Frederick) Cavendish, 1885

… Sunday is a dreadful day; no possibility of getting news, but one has to wait and work all the same. It is extraordinary that one can go about one's business with apparent cheerfulness, knowing that all that counts in life may be gone *in aeternum*. I should lie awake at night thinking of it too, if it weren't that I get so tired that I sleep in spite of myself. But now – only to end each day of waiting, to bring the next with some possibility of definite news – is all that matters.

Vera Brittain, 1915

Yesterday, 19th, we bought a little ring snake fourteen inches long, it was so pretty. It hissed like fun and tied itself into knots in the road when it found it could not escape, but did not attempt to bite as the blind worms do. Smelt strong but not unpleasant: Blind worms smell like very salt shrimps gone bad.

Beatrix Potter (aged 17), 1883

... I hate these Country Accoucheurs – these Demi Savan[t]s: They are so forward to produce their Instruments. A London Hospital would have saved the Child! I doubt not, tho' the birth was laborious, I find there was no wrong Presentation, only a Lentor [slowness] in the pains perhaps – With Opium & Encouragement, & not putting her too soon upon Labour, I verily do think that a skilful Practitioner might have brought the Baby forward with the Forceps at worst – but they are so plaguy hasty. – Either Doctor Denman or an old Woman would have waited – but since the horrid death-doing Crochet [hook] has been found out, & its use permitted – Oh! many & many a Life has been flung away.

Hester Lynch Thrale Piozzi, 1797

20 September

To make Lodinum [laudanum]. The Lady Powells Receipt sent me by my d[ea]r sister Austen In my distress, of which she has Taken of It near Two years her selfe: – Sep: 20: sent 1712: For the Colic – &c.

Take Two ounces of the Best opium; And one ounce of fine saffron; Cut the opium very thin and small; and pull the saffron Into small pieces; then infuse them In A quart of the best sack [fortified wine] In A Deep Earthen Pot Covered with a Bladder pricked full of Pin Holes: And – then Set It In A kettle, or skillet of Boiling Water, Till the Quantity In the Pot be half Wasted ...

Elizabeth Freke, 1712

At the end of our rehearsal, came home. The weather is sunny, sultry, scorching, suffocating.

By the by, Essex [Black servant of ship's captain] called this morning to fetch away the Captain's claret jug: he asked my father for an order, adding, with some hesitation, 'It must be for the gallery, if you please, sir, for people of colour are not allowed to go into the pit, or any other part of the house.' I believe I turned black myself, I was so indignant.

Fanny Kemble, New York, 1832

I went to the store and took 44 cruzeiros with me. I bought a kilo of sugar, one of beans, and two eggs. I had two cruzeiros left over. A woman who was shopping spent 43 cruzeiros. And Senhor Eduardo said; 'As far as spending money goes, you two are equal.'

I said:

'She's white. She's allowed to spend more.'

And she said: 'Color is not important.'

Then we started to talk about prejudice. She told me that in the United States they don't want Negroes in the schools.

I kept thinking: North Americans are considered the most civilized. And they have not yet realized that discriminating against the blacks is like trying to discriminate against the sun. Man cannot fight against the products of Nature. God made all the races at the same time. If he had created Negroes after the whites, the whites should have done something about it then.

Carolina Maria de Jesus, 1958

I'd been invited to aioli. There were two sorts, one with lemon, the other without. With it: a big dish of cod, several dozen hard-boiled eggs in a bowl, octopus in wine, a multitude of snails, bowls of fat winkles, a mountain of potatoes and carrots, beetroots, chick-peas, green beans, etc. More than a dozen dishes of aioli! A vast green melon as sweet as honey, an ice from *Philippe*, the best cake-shop, and champagne to follow the ... wine and complete my tipsiness. The last beautiful grapes from the bare vines, blue figs – their skins split as though wounded, peaches, pears, delicious coffee. 'A liqueur?' suggested Mayol. 'I have a little Marc which is not to be sniffed at.' – 'Stop!' I cried. 'I'm done, I couldn't touch another thing!'

Liane de Pougy, 1931

21 September

We've just bottled our honey. Very still and warm today. So invasion becomes possible. The river high; all soft blue and milky; autumn quiet – twelve planes in perfect order, back from the fight, pass overheard.

Virginia Woolf, 1940

We talked a lot – or rather Rupert [Gleadow] did and I listened – about his father and Trinity [College] and lots of things. Before we went out he had made the suggestion that we should go to bed – we had much fun and a fight over that.

Barbara Pym (aged 17), 1932

We drank a bottle of champagne tonight (forbidden, because of D.'s [Lloyd George] excess of sugar) but much enjoyed. D. said: 'There is a great advantage in virtue – it enables you to enjoy sin so much more.'

Frances Stevenson, 1934

The anger that I felt for my right breast last year has faded, and I'm glad because I have had this extra year. My breasts have always been so very precious to me since I accepted having them it would have been a shame not to have enjoyed the last year of one of them. And I think I am prepared to lose it now in a way I was not quite ready to last November, because now I really see it as a choice between my breast and my life, and in that view there cannot be any question.

Somehow I always knew this would be the final outcome, for it never did seem like a finished business for me. This year between was like a hiatus, an interregnum in a battle within which I could so easily be a casualty, since I certainly was a warrior. And in that brief time the sun shone and the birds sang and I wrote important words and have loved richly and been loved in return. And if a lifetime of furies is the cause of this death in my right breast, there is still nothing I've never been able to accept before that I would accept now in order to keep my breast. It was a 12 month reprieve in which I could come to accept the emotional fact/truths I came to see first in those emotional weeks last year before the biopsy. If I do what I need to do because I want to do it, it will matter least when death comes, because it will have been an ally that spurred me on.

Audre Lorde, 1978

I am definitely experiencing pre-op nerves, or something. While I'm in the office trying to prepare for today's programme by reading various briefs, doubts force their way into my head about whether I should have an implant at all. Why would I want something foreign inside me? What if that goes wrong? I can't work out if I really mean it, or if it's just fear of what's to come forcing me to distance myself from reality and pretend it's not happening.

If I don't have an implant I could simply be flat on one side, with no nipple and a smile-shaped scar. I could live with that.

Victoria Derbyshire, 2015

22 September

Diana [Lady Diana Manners] announced herself bilious and stayed in bed till after luncheon. She was in a wonderful green chiffon confection and held a levée. Even Cyril Scott was at her bedside – why admit a stranger? I deprecate the bedroom habit. She was in great difficulty as to the composition of a telegram to her bereaved aunt Lady Robert Manners.

Lady Cynthia Asquith, 1917

I helped Rupert to pack – he went in a hat and looked about 17! I would have loved to go to the Lakes with him and Miles. It was seriously rather awful parting from him, we'd had such a heavenly week together. I never imagined it would be so good. I actually wept a bit!

Barbara Pym (aged 19), 1932

I'm peeved with Louise: she's deluded me – robbed me of my best illusion. I've often watched dogs copulating – and was always revolted by the pivoting motions of the male. Well, I said to myself, that's just doggy behaviour. But now Louise tells me that humans do it in exactly the same way. I'd imagined something calm and dignified . . . And that's what Klimt called 'physical union", this jiggling about. It's revolting, disgusting. No, there's nobody I could imagine doing it without feeling revulsion...Do humans pull the same daft faces as dogs? Ughhhhhhh. When a man introduces himself, I now imagine him rocking up and down on top of me – and can scarcely bring myself to shake his hand.

Alma Schindler (Mahler-Werfel), 1900

Catch a train to Blackburn, leaving Ted [her husband] to bring up Janet and packing cases by car. I read up my background briefing on the way and do two meetings on my arrival. Am on the top of my form. This pleases me immensely, because I am determined to make this my last election if the results will let me – I want to go out on the peak, not in the trough, of my ability. I hate people who hang on, keeping the young ones out.

Barbara Castle, 1974

A fine day

We came home from school this afternoon after the end of classes. After dinner Mother asked us to go to the buckwheat fields to bring back the bales that had already been cut. I couldn't really walk any further, but Mother forced us to go. She had already harvested so much of the grain herself, how could I refuse her, especially since Father is still away working in Inner Mongolia.

It's in order to feed and clothe us that Mother works so hard. If it weren't for us, she wouldn't have to harvest buckwheat. It's right that she asks us and equally right that we help. Otherwise how would we be worth all the trouble she takes over us? She wears herself out so that we can have a different future from hers. She exhausts herself to provide food for us when there's nothing left, and then she exhausts herself all over again, without getting anything out of life for herself. She doesn't want us to live the way she does. That's why we have to study. We'll be happy. Unlike her.

Ma Yan, 2000

23 September

Things come in and out of focus so quickly it's as if a flash goes by; the days are so beautiful now so golden brown and blue; I wanted to be out in it, I wanted to be glad I was alive, I wanted to be glad about all the things I've got to be glad about. But now it hurts. Now it hurts. Things chase themselves around inside my eyes and there are tears I cannot shed and words like cancer, pain, and dying.

Later, I don't want this to be a record only of tears. I want it to be something I can use now or later, something that I can remember, something that I can pass on, something that I can know came out of the kind of strength I have that nothing nothing else can shake for very long or equal.

My work is to inhabit the silences with which I have lived and fill them with myself until they have the sounds of brightest day and the loudest thunder. And then there will be no room left inside of me for what has been except as a memory of sweetness enhancing what can and is to be.

Audre Lorde, 1978

Just as I was looking round on my preparations [for her move to a country cottage] Dorothy came in like a ghost, and bowed herself on my shoulders and began to cry. Bridget [Dorothy's baby] was ill: spots, which her doctor could not diagnose. Neither of us realised that the sherry I poured out was cherry brandy. This rather clouded the start ... We went by Guildford and beyond Alton lunched in a nut copse, talking about great aunts. A delicious lunch: cold chicken, beer, pears and madeira [sic]. And midges. And ash trees. Their green fronds so flatly distinct on a grey sky that they looked like transfer patterns on china ...

Sylvia Townsend Warner, 1930

Today is the day on which I have reigned longer, by a day, than any English sovereign, and the people wished to make all sorts of demonstrations, which I asked them not to do until I had completed the sixty years next June. But notwithstanding that this was made public in the papers, people of all kinds and ranks, from every part of the kingdom, sent congratulatory telegrams, and they kept coming in all day.

Queen Victoria, 1896

On Fourth day, my lovely boy was born, a willing mind to suffer was hard to get at; I longed to have the cup removed from me. I had to acknowledge present help in trouble, so that I could only give thanks; indeed I have renewed cause for thankfulness and praise, which my poor unworthy mind has felt little able to render since, being weak at times, tempted and tried; but I desire to abide near, and cling to that power, that can pardon and deliver.

Elizabeth Fry, 1809

I don't stop today. Who knew there was so much to get organised before a mastectomy? ...

Before sleeping, I write a letter each to my boys. I want them to know how much I love them. I tell Mark these will be in my bedside drawer, and he's to give them to [her sons] Oliver and Joe should anything happen to me. He tells me nothing is going to happen, but still manages to humour me because he knows it is something I need to do ...

Victoria Derbyshire, 2015

24 September

I realize that a diary should be written up daily even if the day is without particular events and there seems little of note worth recording. No day is really without interest, being filled with thought, memories, plans, moments of particular hope and occasional moments of depression. Every day is lived in the present, but also vicariously in the past and one can write a novel of 100,000 words covering just one hour of a human life. But it seems too egotistical to spend the last hours of every day contemplating the minutiae of unrecoverable moments. I say my prayers and am grateful for the comfort of bed.

P. D. James, 1997

Read Madame de Sévigné. My Love drawing. From seven till nine in sweet converse with the delight of my heart, over the Fire. Paper'd our Hair.

Lady Eleanor Butler, 1785

Walked in the stubble fields near the Mill. The Country heavenly, and peopled with happy busy industrious beings, every hand employed about their Harvest. This delicious day is worth a million.

Lady Eleanor Butler, 1789

I wish I had a good fat stolid temperament, I believe such people have the easiest time. They sit through life with folded hands, and don't bother about anything. – I don't believe that I shall ever be in love! ... I believe that true love is founded on mutual esteem, confidence, similarity of tastes & strong sympathies. It is certainly the only kind that can last! I believe that if a girl can feel all this for an honorable upright, God-fearing man, she should marry him, & that whether the rest of her life be happy or unhappy, she will never have to wish herself unmarried. But I think it is better for any one to scrub floors, than to marry for any other motive.

Julia Newberry (aged 17), 1871

At about eight-ish, I start thinking about filming something and recording a few thoughts about how I'm feeling. It's the first step to trying to do what I considered doing weeks ago – demystifying this, if that's possible. Before today, I had little idea of what a mastectomy actually involves – now I can share some of my experience. I want to be factual, honest and open, and most importantly, acknowledge that this is my own personal experience. Everyone is different and depending on their diagnosis, will approach it in a variety of ways.

I'd come prepared to do this, and I begin by writing two signs in black felt tip on some drawing paper that [her partner] Mark got me from the Tesco opposite the hospital. The first one reads, 'This morning I had breast cancer'. The second one reads. 'This evening I don't'. I film myself holding them up to the three-by-three-inch Go Pro camera. Then I think about the words I am going to say. I'll feel really stupid if a nurse walks in right now and sees me talking to myself, so I get on with it.

7.55 p.m.: 'I'm in hospital, as you can see. I'm in a hospital room, and today I had a mastectomy, and … I feel … all right. I can't believe it …

'The word "cancer" has such a chilling effect on people, me included, but I've learned over the last few weeks that this illness does not have to be elevated to some uber-powerful status. It's simply an illness, which the NHS treats with expertise and care.'

Victoria Derbyshire, 2015

25 September

A nourishing, opulent day: to be cherished. For months Beatrice and her old friend have intended a bush picnic to give me a whiff of the spring flowers …

A sudden post-noon clearance in the downpour and off we went to French's Forest and found a creek swollen to Jounama [Pondage] proportions, and many spring flowers including a waratah or two, surviving like a flame amid the dark greenery. It took me back to childhood and poignant nostalgia for things and relatives long gone, and at the same time so fleeting, so ephemeral that now I sit in the silence they have left, with the Australian way of life they strove so laboriously and unrewardedly to establish, now ready for swamping by fecund hordes, who will leave as little remaining record of us as we left of the Aborigines.

Miles Franklin, near Sydney, Australia, 1949

Our first fire; the evenings grow damp; the sun is like a watered ribbon, grey blue mauve pink silver. The trees have not turned yet. Sally is good and begins lessons. We blackberry.

Ivy Jacquier, 1926

Their Majesties visit Sheffield today. Hope our Mayor won't leave all his aitches behind him. I'm told he has improved a lot since he took office. Good. There was plenty of room for it.

Edie Rutherford, 1945

After that we quit being funny and made love very seriously and I was filled with peace and delight. You can't write about sensuality mingled with tenderness and pity, it just becomes maudlin or goes bad on you in some way – so call it love and leave it at that, one of the few transcendent and satisfying things left in this bloody awful life.

Joan Wyndham (aged 18), 1940

26 September

I found two letters on my plate this morning – one from the Red Cross, the other a tiny thin envelope from Roland [her fiancé] … I opened the one from Roland – without apprehension, though the thunder clouds have so long been gathering over the West that I might have known … It was a very tiny note, but God knows it said enough.

'I know nothing definite yet, but they say all posts will be stopped very soon. *Hinc illae lacrimae* ['Hence these tears']. Till life and all …'

This, I somehow knew, was It …

To him I sent a little note written straight from my heart. Ordinarily I would never have admitted so much, but Death is an excuse for anything, everything.

'If this word,' I said, 'should turn out to be a *Te moriturum saluto* [I salute thee who are about to die], perhaps it will brighten the dark moments a little to think how you have meant to Someone more than anything ever has or ever will. What you have striven for will not end in nothing, all that you have done & been will not be wasted, for it will be a part of me as long as I live, and I shall remember, always. Yes, "till life & all" … Au Revoir.' He may never get that & read it. But it has been a satisfaction to me to send it all the same. – Oh! it is terrible to love someone like this. I try to be brave & calm, but I can't. It hurts me so … and he in danger, my darling –

Vera Brittain, 1915

Beautiful day but one of wretchedness to me. Went to town and saw [her stepmother] Harriot and the dentist. The glare and noise bruised all my wounded nerves.

Fanny Longfellow, 1848

Everyone talking today about how the King's face was obviously made up with tan make-up. Oh well, they are on stage in a sense.

Edie Rutherford, 1945

27 September

I felt last night bitterly and passionately that I have lived too much in the last few years, had lived too intensely, been too sad and too happy. That I had felt too much. That life was too precious – much too precious. I want to be delivered from that feeling. Make life humdrum, ordinary. I want routine and dull rounds – I want monotony like Chrysis' fable: 'for our hearts are not strong enough to love every moment.'

It isn't for the moment you are struck that you need courage but for the long uphill climb back to sanity and faith and security.

Anne Morrow Lindbergh, 1932

Yes, it has come. The storm which has so long been threatening has burst at last over the Western Front ...

Later news reports the Germans still hard pressed by the Allies, & furious fighting proceeding more or less along the line – hand to hand battles with the bayonet. I wonder if he ever used the dagger he bought.

It has been a dreadful day – waiting and waiting & able to settle to nothing. Ah! a year of war has taught me what these victories mean, though we certainly haven't had much experience of victory. At first it is all splendour & glory & advance & captures & wonderful achievements. And then gradually come admissions of hardly-earned triumphs being won back by the enemy, stories of horror which the papers dare not print on their principal pages, & long, long casualty lists in which each name means a home rendered desolate.

Vera Brittain, 1915

A visit to Alix and James, such as we made today, gives us a glimpse of our own futures. They are just so much older and crazier than Ralph and me; like hens that have been chivvied a little closer to the execution shed, and are cackling louder and losing more feathers though they aren't yet inside ...

One of the few consolations of age, I agreed with Bunny the other day, is its irresponsibility. This world is no longer of my making, or much to do with me. Take it away and do what you like with it. I don't even greatly care if you drop it and break it. I'm interested in a detached way by your antics, that's all. No, I'm afraid that won't do. Nobody wants to end up as a selfish old person insisting on having the railway carriage window up (or down, as the case maybe), besides which it's physically impossible to be so disengaged.

Frances Partridge, 1958

28 September

... I was on the look-out for telegrams and telephone messages all day, but nothing came. I tried to make time pass by walking & walking & then cycling over the hills, for I could not rest. In the town this evening I met Miss Sharp & Dorothy Adie, who both congratulated me on my engagement. I could not even pretend to be pleased or that I had anything to be congratulated for; it was such irony to receive congratulations on the possession of a fiancé when I did not even know whether he was alive or dead.

There was no peace of mind to be gained from all this walking & wondering. News of further British victories in the evening papers did not seem to make matters any better. In those dreadful hours I cursed Providence because I was not a man and in it all. A woman – especially now – has nothing to make up to her for such anxiety and suspense as this ...

Vera Brittain, 1915

... at times a working life is weary for a woman. The brain is worn and the heart unsatisfied, and in those intervals of exhaustion the old craving for love and devotion, given and taken, returns and an idealised life of love and sympathy passes before one's eyes.

Beatrice Webb, 1886

I am an ornery character, often hard to get along with. The things I cannot stand, that make me flare up like a cat making a fat tail, are pretentiousness, smugness, the coarse grain that often shows itself in a turn of phrase. I hate vulgarity, coarseness of soul. I hate small talk with a passionate hatred. Why? I suppose because any meeting with another human being is collision for me now. It is always expensive, and I will *not* waste my time. It is never a waste of time to be outdoors, and never a waste of time to lie down and rest even for a couple of hours. It is then that images float up and then that I plan my work. But it is a waste of time to see people who have only a social surface to show. I will make every effort to find out the real person, but if I can't, then I am upset and cross. Time wasted is poison.

May Sarton, 1970

Intense depression: I have to confess that this has overcome me several times since September 6th (or thereabouts). It does not come from something definite, but from nothing. ... I saw myself, my brilliancy, charm, beauty (&c., &c. – the attendants who float me through so many years) diminish & disappear. One is in truth rather an elderly dowdy fussy ugly incompetent woman vain, chattering & futile. Then he [Leonard] said our relations had not been so good lately …

But it is always a question whether I wish to avoid these glooms. In part they are the result of getting away by oneself. These nine weeks give one a plunge into deep waters; which is a little alarming, but full of interest. One goes down into the well and nothing protects one from the assault of the truth.

Virginia Woolf, 1926

29 September

Our dear Victoria was this day engaged to Prince Frederick William of Prussia, who had been on a visit to us since the 14th. He had already spoken to us, on the 20th, of his wishes; but we were uncertain, on account of her extreme youth, whether he should speak to her himself, or wait till he came back again. However, we felt it was better he should do so; and during our ride up Craig-na-Ban this afternoon, he picked a piece of white heather, (the emblem of 'good luck') which he gave to her; and this enabled him to make an allusion to his hopes and wishes, as they rode down Glen Girnoch, which led to this happy conclusion.

Queen Victoria, 1855

This afternoon I sorted out & went through various old papers & bits of rubbish precious for what they recall, & put them tidy, in readiness for leaving them for some months. They took me away from the present & back to the days before the War, even back to the St Monica's days, which after all were not so long ago though they seemed like centuries. I was back once more in the dreams of those days – ardent, impersonal dreams and ideals, in which no man ever had a part. The average girl may think of little else but love & marriage & a home, but I never did. Love came to me quite unbidden – unwanted almost, with all the grief & pain it has brought me. But – if I could give all else up to keep him, I would give it gladly.

Vera Brittain, 1915

One day when I was walking with Mother, she said, 'When you marry.' 'But perhaps I shall not marry,' I suggested shyly. 'That may be,' answered Mother calmly. It seemed to me as if something had been torn asunder in my heart, and it felt very bitter. Would the day come when I should have to kill all my aspirations towards love and limit my interests to books and public service? Oh, not that! Not that! …

Nelly Ptashkina (aged 15), 1918

Firearm Certificate No.2802 has arrived from the Leicestershire Police. A note was enclosed: 'We had a good laugh over your application – 'For use against parachutists'. 'Now I can collect my revolver and ten rounds of ammunition.

Countess of Ranfurly, 1939

30 September

Do always, or almost always unless it interferes with a specific desire to work, do always what you want to do.

Patricia Highsmith, 1947

It seems they will not give a child Christian burial at Hatfield unless it has been baptised. I believe it is still a common superstition that a child goes to the wrong place unless baptised. How can anyone believe that the power above us – call it Jehovah, Allah, Trinity, what they will – is a just and merciful father, seeing the end from the beginning, and will yet create a child, a little rosebud, the short lived pain and joy of its mother's heart, only to consign it after a few days of innocence to eternal torment?

All outward forms of religion are almost useless, and are the cause of endless strife. What do Creeds matter ... Believe there is a great power silently working all things for good, behave yourself and never mind the rest.

Beatrix Potter (aged 18), 1884

Talked to Lord M.[elbourne] of my growing disinclination to business: 'You must conquer that,' he said, 'it isn't unnatural when the first novelty is over, but you mustn't let that feeling get the better, you must fight against it.' I had said it was unnatural for a young woman to like business.

Queen Victoria, 1839

... The last day of September – *immensely* cold, a kind of solid cold outside the windows. My fire has played traitor nearly all day, and I have been, in the good, old-fashioned way, feeling my skin *curl*.

Katherine Mansfield, 1918

October

---

*'Rabbits are creatures of warm volatile temperament
but shallow and absurdly transparent.'*

Beatrix Potter, 1892

1 October

We took two sisters from the village to visit their other sister 'terminally' ill in the Churchill. Driving in the car, the smell of poverty. They are still that old-fashioned category 'the poor', harking back to the old days when they were in service at a North Oxford vicarage and things were so much better. Not for them the glories and advantages of the welfare state. Looking at one of them with her hairy chin and general air of greyness one couldn't help thinking that this was as much a woman as a glamorous perfumed model.

Barbara Pym, 1977

… The question of women's fate interests me tremendously. This interest lives in me somehow fundamentally; it is called forth neither by writing nor conversation, but has taken root in me of its own accord …

Does the education of woman prepare her for the serious tasks of life. The evil of this education is rooted far back in the centuries. Give women scope and opportunity, and they will be no worse than men.

Nelly Ptashkina (aged 15), 1918

There is no mercy for me in this island. I am more and more disposed to try the continent. One day the paper rings with my marriage to Johnson, one day to Crutchley, one day to Seward. I give no reason for such impertinence, but cannot deliver myself from it. Whitbread, the rich brewer, is in love with me too; oh, I would rather, as Ann Page says, be set breast deep in the earth and bowled to death with turnips …

Hester Lynch Thrale Piozzi, 1782

My present feelings for the babe are so acute as to render me at times unhappy, from an over anxiety about her, such a one, as I never felt before for any one. Now it appears to me, this over anxiety arises from extreme love, weak spirits and state of health, and not being under the influence of principle, that would lead me to overcome these natural feelings, so far as they tend to my misery. For if I were under the influence of principle, I might trust that my dear infant was indeed under the care and protection of an infinitely wise and just Providence, that permits her little sufferings for some good end ...

Elizabeth Fry, 1802

2 October

Wet, very *weet*. Much concerned with the toothache and swollen face of Benjamin Bouncer, whose mouth is so small I cannot see in, but as far as I can feel there is no breakage. This comes of peppermints and comfits.

I have been quite indignant with papa and McDougall, though to be sure he is a fascinating little beggar, but unfortunately has not the sense to suck the *minties* when obtained.

Beatrix Potter, 1892

I am installed housekeeper; mamma has given the whole of the household accounts into my keeping. I am glad of it; it will greatly assist mamma, and will be of much service to me. I am highly pleased by the idea of making myself useful in some way, now that I cannot do it by teaching my brothers and sisters.

Emily Shore (aged 17), 1837

On the Eighth of July I finished my journal [8 July 1822 saw the drowning of her husband, the poet Percy Bysshe Shelley]. This is a curious coincidence – The date still remains, the fatal 8th – a monument to shew that all ended then. And I begin again? – oh, never! But several motives induce me, when the day has gone down, and all is silent around me, steeped in sleep, to pen, as occasion wills, my reflexions and feelings. First; I have now no friend. For eight years I communicated with unlimited freedom with one whose genius, far transcending mine, awakened & guided my thoughts; I conversed with him; rectified my errors of judgement, obtained new lights from him, & my mind was satisfied. Now I am alone! Oh, how alone! The stars may behold my tears, & the winds drink my sighs – but my thoughts are a sealed treasure which I can confide to none. White paper – wilt thou be my confident? I will trust thee fully, for none shall see what I write …

Mary Shelley, 1822

I received the Holy Communion for the first time in my new home, and felt drawn closer to it. Had happy Sunday reading and talking together; showed my Fred [her new husband Lord Frederick Cavendish] a beautiful prayer by Jeremy Taylor for married people to say for each other. A day of much happiness indeed – blessings both of earth and heaven are outpoured upon me.

Lucy (Lady Frederick) Cavendish, 1864

There'll come a time, when you have to say hell with you to everybody on earth. When you have tried your best, and destroyed yourself, to live with somebody, simply because that is what the rest of the world does, then say goodbye.

Patricia Highsmith, 1957

3 October

I have thought of M. today. We are no longer together. Am I in the right way, though? No, not yet. Only looking on – telling others. I am not in body and soul. I feel a bit of a sham … And so I am. One of the K. M.'s is so sorry. But of course she is. She has to die. *Don't* feed her.

Katherine Mansfield, 1922

On Saturday a long call from B. He thinks he can come East even sooner than he'd originally planned. I am thrilled. But calmly. It is always momentous whenever I see him, but now I see it is possible to live without him – though I do not choose that option. I love him, finally, with open hands.

I've made up my mind, apparently, to fight my depressions and so, a week before my period I was careful to eat well, rest, get in some pleasant activities – movies, walks, friends – and to take my vitamins religiously, and to take Pamprin – 2 pills a day for seven days. Result: no (knock on wood!) depression so far, & my period started today! I feel happy. All day I've walked about gazing at clouds. Loving them. Saying quiet prayers to the Spirit of the Universe, and loving Brooklyn. I may well stay here forever. And today I feel that's okay.

Alice Walker, 1977

At twelve went down to below the terrace, near the ballroom, and we were all photographed by Downey by the new cinematograph process, which makes moving pictures by winding off a reel of film. We were walking up and down.

Queen Victoria, 1896

4 October

William told me the other day that I was not of a jealous disposition; I do not think he knows me. In general, Marianne [Gaskell's year-old daughter] prefers being with me, I hope and think; yet at times she shows a marked preference for Betsy, who has always been, as far as I can judge, a kind, judicious and tender nurse … There will come a time when she will know how a mother's love exceeds all others; & meanwhile, I will try never to put myself in rivalry with another for my child's affections but to encourage very good & grateful feeling on her part towards every one; and particularly towards a faithful & affectionate servant.

I have been much gratified these few days past by the beginning of self-restraint in the little creature; she has sometimes been washed in water either too hot, or too cold, and taken a dislike to it. This week past I have in general got up to wash her myself, or see by the thermometer that the water was the right heat (from 85 to 90) and Betsy and I have tried to distract her attention & prevent her crying; this last two days she has tried hard to prevent herself from crying, giving gulps & strains to keep it down. Oh may this indeed be the beginning of self-government!

Elizabeth Gaskell, 1835

On Monday, 4th October 1802, my brother William was married to Mary Hutchinson. I slept a good deal of the night, and rose fresh and well in the morning. At a little after 8 o'clock I saw them go down the avenue towards the church. William had parted from me upstairs. When they were absent my dear little Sara prepared the breakfast. I kept myself as quiet as I could, but when I saw the two men running up the walk, coming to tell us it was over, I could stand it no longer, and threw myself on the bed, where I lay in stillness, neither hearing or seeing anything till Sara came upstairs to me, and said, 'They are coming.' This forced me from the bed where I lay, and I moved, I know not how, straight forward, faster than my strength could carry me, till I met my beloved William, and fell upon his bosom. He and John Hutchinson led me to the house, and there I stayed to welcome my dear Mary. As soon as we had breakfasted, we departed. It rained when we set off. Poor Mary was much agitated, when she parted from her brothers and sisters, and her home. Nothing particular occurred till we reached Kirby. We had sunshine and showers, pleasant talk, love and chearfulness.

Dorothy Wordsworth, 1802

My gray hair is very noticeable now. Sometimes I think it's glorious. Sometimes I'm not sure. Mostly I console myself it is natural & therefore honest and that I love both naturalness & honesty. In fact, practicing both is my religion.

Alice Walker, 1996

... About this time we lost many of our comforts, our white Biscuits, Cheese, Porter, and desert were all finished, and the Coals were very low that we could have nothing but boiled Meat. Some of the passengers appeared very much discontented, but as Mr D. was well, and Mary very fat I did not mind.

Sarah Docker, sailing to Australia, 1828

5 October

... we had in our Gardens a second summer, for artichokes bore twice, white Roses, red Roses: and we, having set a musk Rose the winter before, it bore flowers now. I think the Like has seldom been seen: it is a great fruit year all over.

Lady Margaret Hoby, 1603

... The Journal – I have absolutely given up. I dare not keep a journal. I should always be trying to tell the truth. As a matter of fact I dare not tell the truth. I feel I *must* not. The only way to exist is to go on and try and lose oneself – to get as far as possible away from *this* moment. Once I can do that, all will be well.

Katherine Mansfield, 1920

If I said this all [her experience of mastectomy] didn't matter I would be lying. I see this as a serious break in my work/living, but also as a serious chance to learn something I can share for use. And I mourn the women who limit their loss to the physical loss alone, who do not move into the whole terrible meaning of mortality as both weapon and power. After all, what could we possibly be afraid of after having admitted to ourselves that we had dealt face to face with death and not embraced it? For once we accept the actual existence of our dying, who can ever have power over us again?

Now I am anxious for more living to sample and partake of the sweetness of each moment and each wonder who walks with me through my days. And now I feel again the large sweetness of the women who stayed open to me when I needed that openness like rain, who made themselves available.

Audre Lorde, 1978

6 October

Afterwards, I happened to be alone with this charming Princess and her sister Elizabeth, in the Queen's dressing-room. She then came up to me, and said,

'Now will you excuse me, Miss Burney, if I ask you the truth of something I have heard about you?'

'Certainly, ma'am.'

'It's such an odd thing, I don't know how to mention it,; but I have wished to ask you about it this great while. Pray is it really true that, in your illness last year, you coughed so violently that you broke the whalebone of your stays in two?'

'As nearly true as possible, ma'am; it actually split with the force of the almost convulsive motion of a cough that seemed loud and powerful enough for a giant. I could hardly myself believe that it was little I that made so formidable a noise.'

'Well, I could not have given credit to it if I had not heard it from yourself! I wanted so much to know the truth, that I determined, at last, to take courage to ask you.'

Fanny Burney, 1786

Yesterday afternoon, when he and I were sitting in the garden, I asked Sidney: 'Do you wish to go on living?' He sat silent, surprised at the question, then slowly said '*No.*' He is physically comfortable, he is always reading and not actually bored, he loves and is loved, he is mildly interested in other people and keen to hear the news. But he resents not being able to think and express his thoughts, and thus help the world he lives in.

Beatrice Webb, 1941

We came to Hardwick, in the same regal style as last year: special train, swarms of horses, dogs, carriages, and servants, and barouche and four to meet us at Chesterfield.

Lucy (Lady Frederick) Cavendish, 1865

7 October

Two wonderful letters from Caroline [her lover]. 'My dear, my dear, you are a miracle. I have lost my heart and everything else to you already.' [Her husband], alas, is spiteful – C.'s word – so all is a bit perilous. But the good news is that she'll be able to come over to Paris November 12 and will not have to stay with S. until the 15th – How wonderful that will be – 'we can therefore be alone at least for these few days without anyone knowing.'

Patricia Highsmith, 1962

The War is like a snowball which gathers volume as it goes on rolling. Every day seems to take us further from the end. Every month introduces some new & complicated element which further involves all the elements already there. It is too gigantic for the mind to grasp. And through everything, involving things still more, runs everyone's personal interests & loves & despairs, most terrible of all.

Vera Brittain, 1915

I am beginning to rub my eyes at the prospect of peace. I think it will require more courage than anything that has gone before. It isn't until one leaves off spinning round that one realises how giddy one is. One will have to look at long vistas again, instead of short ones, and one will at last fully recognise that the dead are not only dead for the duration of the war.

Lady Cynthia Asquith, 1918

8 October

My diary again. It's sad to be going back to the old habits I gave up since I got married. I used to write when I felt depressed – now I suppose it is for the same reason.

Relations with my husband have been so simple these past two weeks, and I felt so happy with him; he was my diary and I had nothing to hide from him.

But ever since yesterday, when he told me he didn't trust my love, I have been feeling truly terrible …

… What is he doing to me? Little by little I shall withdraw completely from him and poison his life. Yet I feel so sorry for him at those times when he doesn't trust me; his eyes fill with tears and his face is so gentle and sad. I could smother him with love at those moments and yet the thought haunts me: 'He doesn't *trust* me, he doesn't *trust* me.' Today I began to feel we were drifting further and further apart …

Sophia Tolstoy (aged 18, and only recently married), 1862

Marmee's birthday, sixty-eight. After breakfast she found her gifts on a table in the study. Father escorted her to the big red chair, the boys prancing before blowing their trumpets, while we 'girls' marched behind, glad to see the dear old Mother better and able to enjoy our little fête. The boys proudly handed her the little parcels, and she laughed and cried over our gifts and verses.

I feel as if the decline had begun for her, and each year will add to the change which is going on, as time alters the energetic, enthusiastic home-mother into a gentle, feeble old woman, to be cherished and helped tenderly down the long hill she has climbed so bravely with her many burdens.

Louisa May Alcott, 1868

I had thought that the making of *Apocalypse Now* was over. I was comfortable being home, starting a Zazen [meditation] class, meeting once a week with friends to analyze dreams, making fig jam. I could see

Francis was in some deep conflict. We had long conversations about the theme of the film …

Two weeks ago, Francis was as miserable as I have ever seen him. I asked him to tell me about his conflicts, really tell me. He began to cry. He said he was in love with another woman. He said he loved her and he loved me, that we each represented part of himself and he couldn't give up either. I listened to the person I love, in complete anguish and pain. Suddenly I could see the conflict for him was not about peace and violence. The conflict for him would be about romantic ideals and practical reality. A man who loves romance, loves illusion. He's a filmmaker, in the very business of creating illusion. And he loves his wife, he loves his children and fifteen years of that reality. I could see it so clearly. Then, the emotion rose up from my feet like a tide. It hit me in the chest and knocked me backward. I saw myself pick up the vase of flowers and throw it. I heard the words pour out of my mouth. I saw myself go downstairs, and the fragments of white dishes hit the red kitchen walls. I was blind with rage. I was raging at my blindness.

Eleanor Coppola, 1977

9 October

We had a horrid shock. L.[eonard] came in so unreasonably cheerful that I guessed a disaster. He has been called up. It was piteous to see him shivering, physically shivering, so that we lit the gas fire, and only by degrees became more or less where we were in spirits; and still, if one could wake to find it untrue, it would be a mercy.

We had a short walk by the river. As it is a fine, fairly still evening, perhaps I shall have a raid to describe tomorrow. We have a liver and bacon Clumber [spaniel] in view, the property of a man taken for the army.

Virginia Woolf, 1917

Should I throw these Nembutals away and try to live? Rex [Harrison] didn't call, which threw me into another emotional burst ... and I wept and wept, listened to by two avid young girls who are patients here, one a hard little Mod, the other a complainer. I was putting off leaving for Los Angeles, based on the prospect of our meeting in San Francisco. When Jeffrey Lane called and, later, Arnold Weissberger, I plunged back into comparisons between other people's lives and my own ... I, too, want to be able to get up and bathe and walk to work, to work, to be with people, to lunch and drink and return to the office and then to the East Side [of Manhattan] for more conviviality. No time for morbid thoughts ... Then I thought of Joan Collins who, busy though she is, writes her sex manual and receives a lot of money for it, writes another book on beauty, will soon open in a West End play – never having known the depths I have, or been in a clinic for alcoholism ... Instead of thinking on the positive side, I plunged into hell again.

Rachel Roberts, 1980

You see, I do nothing. I have a fever all the time. My doctors are two precious idiots. I have sent for Potain, and again placed myself in his paws. He cured me once. He is kind, attentive, honest. It seems that my emaciation has nothing to do with my lungs; it is a thing I caught accidentally, and of which I didn't speak, always hoping that it would pass of itself, and preoccupied by my lungs, which are not worse than before.

I need not bore you with my illnesses. But the fact is I can do nothing!!! Nothing!

Yesterday I had begun dressing to go to the Bois [de Boulogne], and felt so weak that I was on the point of giving it up twice.

But I got there all the same.

Marie Bashkirtseff, 1884

10 October

Today finished my fourth novel, about anthropologists (no title as yet). [It became *Less than Angels*.] Typed from 10.30 a.m. to 3.30 p.m. sustained by, in the following order, a cup of milky Nescafé, a gin and French, cold beef, baked potato, tomato and grated cheese, rice pudding and plums.

In a love affair it comes as something of a shock to a woman to realize that the man does not of necessity feel that everything about her is delightful (the long Victorian earrings with the old raincoat).

Barbara Pym, 1954

I have neither a husband like Rex, nor acting, to be my support system. Life must be something else, not just taking clothes to the cleaners or giving 'dinner parties' to suspicious friends. Must change. Tried. Failed. So try again. Have to contribute and *NOT DRINK*.

Rachel Roberts, 1980

The Western Isles are inhabited by Portuguese who are fond of buying black clothes whenever Ships call there, which they frequently do to take in water & which we should have done, had not the lateness of the Season in which we quitted England made it necessary not to lose an hour on the passage as we are doubtful of reaching Quebec before the St Lawrence is filled with Ice.

I should have liked to have gone on Shore here, as the Climate is said to be delightful & the Islands abounding in grapes, Oranges, Melons, Chestnuts, etc. No boats came to us with fruits & they rarely fish beyond their harbour on account of the heavy squalls to which the Coast is subject which endangers their being blown out to sea. From the description of the Islands I would like to make a voyage here instead of going to Tunbridge or other watering Places, where people frequently ennuyer [bore] themselves. The scheme would be more enlarged & I believe much more amusing.

Elizabeth Simcoe, 1791

11 October

Got up at ½ p. 9 and breakfasted at 10. Wrote to Lord Melbourne. Signed. My dear Cousins came to my room ... They remained some little time in my room and really are charming young men. Albert really is quite charming, and so excessively handsome, such beautiful blue eyes, an exquisite nose, and such a pretty mouth with delicate moustachios and slight but very slight whiskers; a beautiful figure, broad in the shoulders and a fine waist. At about ½ p. 10 dancing began. I danced 5 quadrilles; 1. with Ernest; 2. with dearest Albert ...

Queen Victoria, 1839

My love of solitude is growing with my growth. I am inclined to shun the acquaintance of those whom I do not like & love; on account of the *ennui*; & the acquaintances of those whom I might like & love – on account of the *pain*! – Oh the pain attendant on liking & loving, may seem a little cloud – but it blots from us all the light of the sun!! –

Elizabeth Barrett (Browning), 1831

At eighteen years old I had a husband and a child. At that age I ran away from it all, driven by a fatal destiny.

Until I was eighteen: family, principles, routine and gentleness. From eighteen to thirty-six (another eighteen years) I lived in the fray and among passions – all of them – either experienced or endured. I learnt to know the world, a sad distinction. At thirty-six I met Georges. And now, after another eighteen years, my life is renewed. Now I am alone and free [Georges had left her], purified by that long period of duty, tenderness and trust. Alone and free: proud words, you will be my rule and my creed. Alone, I will draw nearer to You, my God! There is my desire and my will.

And yet ... close to me, under my roof, just opposite the door of my room, sleeps the most beautiful of women, the most ardent, the most seductive. Is it yet another test? Is it consolation?

Liane de Pougy, 1926

12 October

The cistern is cleaned, the roof is checked. The garden has been tidied. All the rites governing life are going smoothly, both within me and around me. More smoothly than before, actually, more easily, more gracefully and naturally than when he was here. Georges is a hostile being, blundering and ill-natured. Stupid and without principles. One has to face it, he was a brute! I knew it, but I believed he was mine, bound and attached to me with all his wicked strength.

The day after he left – and may it be a compensation from Heaven – all my rheumatism suddenly vanished; every pain in my body disappeared. Nervous shock, said the astonished doctors. I felt refreshed and rejuvenated and everyone said as much, all around: 'You are looking so young and beautiful' – I, who thought to die!

Liane de Pougy, 1926

My last day and our first. It was a bridal of earth and sky, and we spent the morning lying in the hollowed rump of the Five Maries, listening to the wind blowing over our happiness, and talking about torpedoes, and starting up at footsteps. It is natural to be hunted, and intuitive. Feeling safe and respectable was much more of a strain …

Sylvia Townsend Warner, 1930

And as I sat with mist outside and exhaustion inside, dully writing cheques, I suddenly knew that our 12th October 1930 was real and abiding: far beyond any reality of today. It is still there. We are still lying on the Maries in sun and wind.

Sylvia Townsend Warner, 1970

Sunday. I spent the day resting. Worked out 20 minutes finally around 12.30 p.m. Napped all afternoon. Dreaming Sethe dreams [the character she had just finished playing in *Beloved*]. Releasing her. Read an astonishing article today about a group of slaves living in Africa who know no rebellion. 'God created me to be a slave just like he created a camel to be a camel.' Will and desire are concepts of the free, the author says. So are making plans. 'She had no plans.' No concept of future. She and her children spend their days numbed by freedom.

Oprah Winfrey, 1997

13 October

I am perfectly bewildered by the rush of events, I don't know what to write or what to think. Half of Chicago is in ashes, it is too awful to believe, to [sic] dreadful to think about. And the suspense is so fearful, the reports so vague & no one can get direct information. Mr McCagg & seven or eight other Chicago men are here, the fire began Sunday night, here it is Friday & we know nothing. I haven't a doubt the stores on Kinzie street are gone, but I cant & wont imagine our house is burnt. But oh the misery of the people, & the destitution of the poor, the sick people & the little babies. And all the people who are just comfortably off, & have lost their all. The immediate destitution is bad enough but the wearing, saving, pinching years that will come to so many are worse. We may lose a very great deal, but Papa once said that if the entire city were to burn down, we should still have enough to live on. I am so thankful that he was saved the knowledge of this awful fire, & the destruction of the city he was so proud of, it would have embittered all the last days of his life. This state of suspense is perfectly dreadful; & I have begun to run down again, as fast as possible. My head is as heavy as lead, & I am so nervous & wretched that I don't know what to do.

Julia Newberry (aged 17), Paris, 1871

Thoughts of suicide are growing again, with greater strength than before. But now I nurture them in silence. Today I read in the newspaper about a little girl of fifteen who took an overdose of opium and died quite easily – she just fell asleep. I looked at my big phial – but still lacked the courage.

Life is becoming unbearable. It has been like living under bombardment from Mr Chertkov [Tolstoy's publisher] ever since Lev Nik. visited him in June and completely succumbed to his influence …

Lev Nik. has been infected by Chertkov's vile suggestion that my main motivation was self-interest. What 'self-interest' could there possibly be in a sick old woman of 66, who has both a house, and land, and forest, and capital – not to mention my 'Notes', my diaries and my letters, all of which I can publish?

I am hurt by Chertkov's evil influence, hurt by all their endless secrets, hurt that Lev Nik.'s 'will' is going to give rise to a lot of anger, arguments, judgements and newspaper gossip over the grave of an old man who enjoyed life to the full while he was alive, but deprived his numerous direct descendants of everything after his death.

Sophia Tolstoy, 1910

We dined at Queen's Restaurant, Sloane Square. Just as we had finished and were emerging, there was a bustle and we heard the magic word 'Zeppelin'. We rushed out and found people in dramatic groups, gazing skywards. Some men there said they saw the Zeppelin. Alas, I didn't! But our guns were popping away and shells bursting in the air. I felt excited pleasurably, but not the faintest tremor and I longed and longed for more to happen. Bibs [her sister] was the only member of the family who had sufficient imagination to be frightened and [her sister-in-law] Letty's fun was spoilt by the thought of the children. My only words were: 'Something for my diary!'

Last Cynthia Asquith, 1915

My eldest Son Samuel is gone this day towards Cambridge to be a Scholar at St John's College, God of his mercy grant that he may do worthily there, and bring great honour to his Holy Name, and comfort to his Parents. And keep him in all ways from sin, and danger and the infection of evil company. Make him an example of sobriety and godliness to all his Companions, and let thy grace be present and follow him all his days.

Mary Woodforde, 1687

Decided I'd better go to Confession – after all Rupert [Darrow] hadn't poked me for nearly two weeks, and I thought maybe he never would again, which is as near as I'll ever get to a firm purpose of amendment, so I'd better go while the going's good.

I was petrified and started straight off with the bit about making love to get it over with – my first mortal sin! I could almost hear Father Corato's hair rising on his scalp. He could hardly wait for me to finish before launching his attack.

'And er – how many times have you – ah – have you –'

I thought, oh God the record's stuck, but just then he got a brainwave and called it 'committed this sin'.

'Oh,' I said cheerfully, 'only twice, and we used birth control once, and he's not married!'

After that I was given a long talk on preserving my chastity in future to which I replied rather unconvincingly that I'd do my best. I have an awful feeling he *can* recognise my voice! He jolly well should do, he's been to supper enough times. Finally I got *fifty* (!) Hail Marys right off, and staggered out feeling distinctly chastened.

Joan Wyndham (aged 19), 1940

14 October

After a little pause I said to Lord M.[elbourne], that I had made up my mind (about marrying dearest Albert). – 'You have?' he said … 'I think it is a very good thing, and you'll be much more comfortable; for a woman cannot stand alone for long, in whatever situation she is.' … Then I asked, if I hadn't better tell Albert of my decision soon, in which Lord M. agreed. How? I asked, for that in general such things were done the other way, – which made Lord M. laugh …

Queen Victoria, 1839

Very weary and wretched, I seem to have lost interest in the future and can enjoy my children only from hour to hour. I feel as if my lost darling were drawing me to her – as I controlled her before birth so does she me now.

Fanny Longfellow, 1848

… I shall arrange it, so as not to depend on love, let alone wait for it as so many girls do. I shall live. If love comes I shall take it; and if not I shall regret it, wildly regret it, but I *shall* live all the same.

I see in my imagination a small flat, furnished with exquisite comfort … Beauty everywhere, softness, cosiness. And I am the mistress of it – a woman and a personality at the same time. I live an interesting life: writers, artists, painters forgather at my house, a really interesting circle, a close, friendly community. I know no picture more attractive than this. I am free, independent. In these surroundings, in which there is even no place for it, I shall not regret love. Life is full without it. It is only the dawn of love which I should miss … those moments, the memory of which beautifies all the life of man.

Nelly Ptashkina (aged 15), 1918

Clean'd 3 pair o' boots & lit the fires. Swept the steps & shook the mats. Got our breakfast & wash'd up after. Clean'd the knives & made the fire up & got dinner. Clean'd away after & got ready to go to Massa. Reach's him 'fore 5 & we had a nice evening together … Massa told me to black my face like it was that night I clean'd after the coleman [sic]. So I did, & got the dinner & clean'd the boots & wash'd up the things & Massa's feet with it black, & M. seem'd pleas'd wi' it so but said my hands wasn't looking so thick & red as they did Sunday when he read them verses to me. They was rhymes in the country talk & some o' the words I know'd how to speak better than Massa even. While I made the cigars I sat 'tween his knees and heard Massa read some verses he'd made up for me … When the cigars was done I put coals on & had a little petting, for I'd washed the black of my face in the water I wash'd the feet in, & at ½ past 9 Massa walk'd wi' me up the lane & saw me get in an omnibus. I got home by ½ past ten & to bed.

Hannah Cullwick, 1863

15 October

At about ½ p. 12 I sent for Albert; he came to the Closet where I was alone, and after a few minutes I said to him, that I thought he must be aware of why I wished [him] to come here, and that it would make me too happy if he would consent to what I wished (to marry me); we embraced each other over and over again, and he was so kind, so affectionate. Oh! to feel I was, and am, loved by such an Angel as Albert was too great delight to describe! he is perfection; perfection in every way – in beauty – in everything! I told him I was quite unworthy of him and kissed his dear hand – he said he would be very happy and was so kind and seemed so happy, that I really felt it was the happiest brightest moment in my life, which made up for all I had suffered and endured. Oh! how I adore and love him, I cannot say!! how I will strive to make him feel as little as possible the great sacrifice he has made; I told him it was a great sacrifice, – which he wouldn't allow … I feel the happiest of human beings.

Queen Victoria, 1839

Today I must always remember I suppose. I went to tea with Rupert [Gleadow] (and ate a pretty colossal one) – and he with all his charm, eloquence and masculine wiles persuaded … [Several pages of the diary torn out.]

Barbara Pym (aged 19), 1932

My prison concerns truly flourishing: surely in that a blessing in a remarkable manner appears to attend me; more apparently, than in some of my house duties. Business pressed very hard upon me: the large family at Mildred's Court, so many to please there, and attend to – the various accounts – the dear children and their education – my husband poorly – the church – the poor – my poor infirm aunt whom I have undertaken to care for – my public business, and my numerous friends and correspondents … I have felt helped, even He whom my soul loves has been near; but I have also had some perplexity and discouragement, thinking that some of those very dear, as well as others, are almost jealous over me, and ready to mistrust my various callings …

Elizabeth Fry, 1818

… I had a letter from Page today for my photo and a personal sketch of how 'Anne' came to be written to give 'inquisitive' editors. It seems that *Anne* is a big success. It is a 'best seller' and is in its fifth edition – I cannot realize this. My strongest feeling seems to be incredulity. I *can't* believe that such a simple little tale, written in and of a simple P. E. I. [Prince Edward Island] farming settlement, with a juvenile audience in view, can really have scored out in the busy world …

One of the reviews says 'the book radiates happiness and optimism.' When I think of the conditions of worry and gloom and care under which it was written I wonder at this. Thank God, I can keep the shadows of my life out of my work. I would not wish to darken any other life – I want instead to be a messenger of optimism and sunshine.

Pleasant? Yes, of course it is pleasant. It is a joy to feel that my long years of struggle and unaided effort have been crowned with success. But that success has also evoked much petty malice, spite and jealousy. It does not hurt me, because none of my *real* friends have been guilty of it. But at times it has given me a sort of nausea with human nature.

L. M. Montgomery, 1908

16 October

The pain was so intense yesterday that despite Antabuse, I took a Scotch and ginger ale, then another. Dragged Jeffrey Lane to the Connaught to have Champagne, then went to the club and had some wine. The beauty of the birds lifted my spirits somewhat. Next it was to Jeffrey's flat to have some sherry …

I don't want to swallow these pills and die. I don't want to be a suicide. All and everyone would not be surprised one bit. The alternative is to try and live again – and not through, of all people, Darren [Ramirez] … I like Jeffrey Lane's attitude – go out and get it for yourself. There is no god, as I understand him. When we die, we die. Supposing I could get Rex [Harrison] back, then what? Would I have the courage to take the back seat?

Rachel Roberts, 1980

I have a terrible amount of fever, which exhausts me. I spend all my time in the *salon*, changing from the easy-chair to the sofa.

Dina reads novels to me. [Dr] Potain came yesterday, he will come again to-morrow. This man no longer needs money, and if he comes, it is because he takes some little interest in me.

I can no longer go out at all, but poor Bastien-Lepage comes to me; he is carried here, put in an easy-chair, and stretched out on cushions – I am in another chair drawn up close by, and so we sit until six o'clock.

I was dressed in a cloud of white lace and plush, all different shades of white; the eyes of Bastien-Lepage dilated with delight.

'Oh, if I could only paint!' said he.

And I –

Finis. And so ends the picture of the year.

Marie Bashkirtseff, Paris, 1884

Sometimes I've a cold fear on me when I look at my husband. He never had a very firm hold on realities. Now he has an interest in nothing. At one time I grew frettish if I was not 'bright and amusing'. Often now he never speaks for the whole evening unless it's a grunt or 'Yes' or 'Oh'. I think of his parents and shudder. Beyond breathing and eating, they have not been alive for years, say quite frankly that they 'don't want bothering' when their sons or daughters call. No memory, no interest in themselves or the outside world. I'm heart thankful the boys are not like that. I'd rather never have their company than that they should grow so afraid and indifferent to life. All my wild rebellion seems over. Strong people don't dominate like weak ones. In a strong person there is something to fight, a chink in their armour somewhere. Everyone has something. I count my blessings and find I've a good many, and most of us walk alone …

Nella Last, 1946

17 October

Yes the whole North Side [of Chicago] is in ashes, literally in ashes, & every memory connected with my home is gone, every association, every link; never never to be again, irreparably & irrevocably gone. – No one ever loved their home more than I did mine; I loved every angle in the house, every carpet, every table, every picture on the walls, every book in the library, the stairs, the basement, the garret. When the house was rebuilt Papa's room was left untouched, & it was so exactly as it has always been, that his presence seemed to be there; it was sacred, & that is gone! And then my studio, my beautiful studio, & the private staircase, & my room that I have looked forward to furnishing myself in pink & grey.

Julia Newberry (aged 17), 1871

By putting rouge on my cheeks and listening when they tell me I am beautiful and rejuvenated, will I wind up forgetting what life has laid on my heart?

Liane de Pougy, 1926

I awakened without a kiss, had breakfast alone, dressed without talk: I had nobody to brush, to kiss good-bye; I am having lunch with Mother, and tonight I will sleep alone again. Am I glad to be alone? Was there anything I wanted to do while Hugh [her husband] is away that I cannot do when he is here? No. I miss him deeply, I have no desires, no joy at my independence; and I feel as if I were half alive. This wonderful life I praise so often seems blank and stupid today. I could do without my mirror, without lovely clothes, without sunshine – none of these things are necessary when I am alone. I did a few things to take advantage of my solitude, sleeping on the left side of the bed, which I prefer to the right, and wearing gloves with cold cream. And then, of course, I was glad to have the bathroom to myself. Usually I have to scratch at the door and 'miaow' desperately to be allowed in, and even then I often get a shoe or a clothes brush on the head. Also, I slept fifteen minutes longer than usual.

Anaïs Nin, 1927

After private prayers I walked abroad, then I was busy with my Maids: after, I prayed and dined, and then went about the house: and at night paid the servants their wages, and workmens' bills.

Lady Margaret Hoby, 1601

18 October

My diary has become a rather cumbersome friend whom I still love but no longer need; it is to Maurice [her fiancé] now that I write page after page to keep him informed of all my pleasures – these are making my head spin, but I'm not really enjoying them all that much. I'm too honest to state that I'm bored in society. I miss Maurice, he has been here only one Sunday. He says he's awfully busy at his office and it's essential that he not neglect his new practice. But I'm definitely not bored either at the balls or at the innumerable receptions and parties. I'm being fussed over, admired, and … loved, I'm afraid! …

How I wish I could go home! What's the use of all this gallivanting; what good can it possibly do me to see so many people and lead such a frivolous life! I feel homesick this evening for my own quiet little world – my tower, my big room, Maurice, Papa's strong tender arms around me … Oh, I miss everything that I have to do without here, where I'm supposedly having such a good time!

Henriette Dessaulles (aged 19), 1880

I do not know why I have not written this for ages. Since Vittel in July it has been good, quiet, married and friendly here … [I] could work well, only Sally [her daughter] is difficult. She is self-important and self-conscious, demonstrative and full of little ways, but at her worst with me … Later. I was tired out even in my legs by Sally … Then she got charming and played alone, mothering her doll. Then nurse came in and took her, and eating alone suddenly I saw the roses in the cream basket vase were lovely and I read Chekhov's 'Seagull'.

Ivy Jacquier, 1925

Charles went to Boston to have a tooth filled. I was left alone with my baby, yesterday morning. I felt stronger through the morning than I expected but went to bed with a most shocking headache – and feeling as if I could not endure the care for another day. The baby cried for nearly two hours with colic, and my head throbbed for every cry …

Caroline Healey Dall, 1849

I gave a birthday dinner party. Of the four guests one was a vegetarian, one a diabetic, one treating for biliousness, and the remaining one a straightforward eater. I cooked all afternoon to pacify the vagaries of each and it was a good supper but I hated food-stuffs as I dished up the messes. We three old sisters make much of our birthdays, meeting at one or the other of our houses, exchanging visits and gifts and sitting round fires to talk.

Emily Carr, 1933

19 October

My dearest Albert came to me at 10 m to 12 and stayed with me till 20 m p.1. Such a pleasant happy time. He looked over my shoulder and watched me writing to the Duchess of Northumberland, and to the Duchess of Sutherland; and he scraped out some mistakes I had made. I told him I felt so grateful to him and would do everything to make him happy. I gave him a ring with the date of the ever dear to me 15th engraved on it. I also gave him a little seal I used to wear. I asked if he would let me have a little of his dear hair.

Queen Victoria, 1839

I shall go crazy if I write any more about the fire [of Chicago], – I have felt so bad that I have been in bed for several days, & yesterday afternoon when Mamma and Sister came in, I was lying on the sofa, & feeling as bad as I have ever done since I was first taken sick. – My head felt as if it were filled with molten lead, & it seemed to me as if there was nothing left in the world to live for. I was so wretched that I could not determine how much of my wretchedness was caused by physical weakness, & how much by mental worry & distress. – There was to be a little dance at Annie Zborowska's in the evening to which I had been invited some time previously; we all know by experience how much good a little excitement has done me, & so I decided to make a tremendous effort & go, as no matter what happened I could not feel much worse than I did already. – When 'Auguste' had dressed my hair, & I was arrayed in a 'Worth' gown, I could not help feeling more comfortable, & so away I went …

Julia Newberry (aged 17), 1871

20 October

I love to stand at the edge of an abyss, at the very edge, so that a single movement, and … today, stepping close to the brink of a precipice, although not so deep as I should have wished, the thought came into my mind that some day I should die thus, crashing headlong into the chasm.

My walk today has evoked this premonition … But I feel it more now, after the walk, than during it …

Nelly Ptashkina (aged 15), 1918

Less than two years later she did indeed die falling from a precipice, near Chamonix.

And Rex [Harrison] … ? Why do my legs go to jelly when I think of San Francisco and our planned visit? Is it because he really is the last resort? That if I feel there is no hope for me with him, then my number really is up? …

… I don't have the face for film stardom. I'm not Lucille Ball. I can't stop the clock. You don't usually have love affairs at fifty-three. You marry a man who is difficult to please. You don't have children. You get divorced in a blaze of publicity. You go into shock. You retaliate or escape into affairs and try to keep up the old life-style. You find a friend who is *tender*. You try to build him into what he isn't, thereby losing what he is.

Acting never was to you, perhaps, quite what it was to Joan Plowright and Maggie Smith. It was perhaps more of a means to an end. You want the ease and the luxury you once tasted. All that is true. It does not enable me to rise above it, however.

Rachel Roberts, 1980

… To Tavistock Square [where the Woolfs' former house had been destroyed by a bomb] … Three houses, I should say, gone. Basement all rubble. Only relics an old basket chair (bought in Fitzroy Square days) and Penman's board To Let. Otherwise bricks and wood splinters. One glass door in the next house hanging. I could just see a piece of my studio wall standing; otherwise rubble where I wrote so many books. Open air where we sat so many nights, gave so many parties. The hotel not touched. So to Meck [Mecklenburgh Square, where their subsequent home had also been damaged]. All again litter, glass, black soft dust, plaster powder. Books all over dining room floor. Only the drawing room with windows almost whole. A wind blowing through. I began to hunt out diaries. What could we salvage in this little car? Darwin and the silver, and some glass and china.

Virginia Woolf, 1940

21 October

Bought Herrings and Oysters. Loud and violent altercation between [her servant] Mary and the Fisherman. Mary Triumphant.

Lady Eleanor Butler, 1785

I remember Charles Buller saying of the Duchess de Praslin's murder, 'What could a poor fellow do with a wife who kept a journal but murder her?' There was a certain truth hidden in this light remark. Your journal all about feelings aggravates whatever is factitious and morbid in you; that I have experience of. And now the only sort of journal I would keep should have to do with what Mr Carlyle calls 'the fact of things'. It is very bleak and barren, this fact of things, as I now see it – very; and what good is to result from writing of it in a paper book is more than I can tell. But I have taken a notion to, and perhaps I shall blacken more paper this time, when I begin quite promiscuously without any moral end in view; but just as the Scotch professor drank whisky, because I like it, and because it's cheap.

Jane Carlyle, 1855

... I do not feel that I could say ought to support the [progressive] cause efficiently – besides that on some topics (especially with regard to my own sex) I am far from making up my mind. I believe that we are sent here to educate ourselves & that self denial & disappointment & self control are a part of our education – that it is not by taking away all restraining law that our improvement is to be achieved – & though many things need great amendment – I can by no means go so far as my friends would have me. When I feel that I can say what will benefit my fellow creatures, I will speak – not before.

Mary Shelley, 1838

Sometimes, there is a series of exalted sentiment in what [Princess Caroline] says and does, that quite astonishes me, and makes me rub my eyes and open my ears, to know if it is the *same* person who condescends to talk low nonsense, and sometimes even gross ribaldry. One day, I think her all perfection – another, I know not what to think. The tissue of her character is certainly more uneven than that of any other person I was ever acquainted with. One day, there is tinsel and tawdry – another, worsted – another, silk and satin – another, gold and jewels – another *de la boue, de la crasse* [the mud, the dirt] ...

Lady Charlotte Bury, 1811

22 October

… Waking at three I decided I would spend the weekend at Paris. Got so far as looking up train, consulting Nessa about hotel. Then L.[eonard] said he would rather not. Then I was overcome with happiness. Then we walked round the square love making – after twenty-five years can't bear to separate. Then I walked round the lake in Regent's Park. Then … you see it is an enormous pleasure, being wanted: a wife. And our marriage is so complete.

Virginia Woolf, 1937

… Felt much happier today, i.e. more tranquil and resigned. To be patient is the hardest of all lessons, I find, in either physical or mental pain.

Henry has so much more than I!

Fanny Longfellow, 1848

… should I for once say what I really believe, that love is far the most important thing in life, a stronger, potentially more permanent and all-pervading force than the wildest of girlhood dreams suggests. People talk, out of a sort of prudery, as if it vanished entirely after five or six years of marriage, and only an affable, humdrum relation was left, enabling couples to jog along pretty well if they allowed each other plenty of freedom. But it needn't be like that at all. It's a hopeless failure if it is. After twenty years together one can be in a sense just as deeply in love as ever one was. Love doesn't simply fade away like 'old soldiers'; it changes its character, naturally, and matures, but its depth and richness can be as great as ever.

Frances Partridge, 1945

23 October

A wet day and all its luxuries.

Caroline Fox, 1848

I thank Heaven that at present, though I am damnable, I am in love with nobody, except *myself*.

Katherine Mansfield, 1907

A stormy day within doors, so I walked out early, and walked, walked, walked. If peace and quietness be not in one's own power, one can always give oneself at least bodily fatigue – no such bad succedaneum [substitute] after all. Life gets to look for me like a sort of kaleidoscope – a few things of different colours – black predominating, which fate shakes into new and ever new combinations, but always the same things over again. To-day has been so like a day I still remember out of ten years ago; the same still dreamy October weather, the same tumult of mind contrasting with the outer stillness; the same causes for that tumult. Then, as now, I had walked, walked, walked with no aim but to tire myself.

Jane Carlyle, 1855

To the oculist. Small child sat opposite me, with enormous glasses on, lenses magnified many times. She looked with these large pensive eyes – unnaturally large, like cow's eyes – all over the room, and *me* (feeling very uncomfortable). I felt as if the cow had licked me all over with her large tongue.

Anne Morrow Lindbergh, 1927

24 October

A fine day and all its luxuries.

Caroline Fox, 1848

Woke up to terrible morning misery. The dreary detail of the John [her son] tragedy blackens life. One can never dismiss it from one. It is a past, present, and future nightmare. I loved my idea of that baby more than I have ever loved anything – and it was just something that never existed!

Lunched with Whibley …

Lady Cynthia Asquith, 1917

This has been a bad day for me because my work overtook me instead of my keeping ahead of it, which always makes me feel depressed & unequal to being the exceptional & brilliant person I am determined to be. As a rule when I hear brilliant people like Miss Barton & Miss Rowe spoken of, I feel determined even to out-do them in glory, but on depressing days I feel I can never get to anything like their standard. But I can!

Vera Brittain, 1914

I have a horrid cold but the weather being fine I walked to Mursley to see an old Man who is a Hundred years old, his name is Peek, he married a few years ago a woman beyond seventy, who now takes care of him and her own Mother who is past a Hundred, manages a small Dairy and does everything, the two Centurions have lived too long and are almost returned to Childhood.

Betsey Wynne Fremantle, 1806

25 October

... My heart is very sore to-night, but I have promised myself not to make this journal a 'miserere', so I will take a dose of morphia and do the impossible to sleep.

Jane Carlyle, 1855

... Marriage is slavery, it prevents one from surrendering herself to that supreme happiness which the initiated call love – and so I think it is. Human personality must develop quite freely. Marriage impedes this development; even more than that, it often drives one to 'moral crimes', not only because forbidden fruit is sweet, but because the new one, which could be perfectly legitimate, becomes a crime. Would man and woman be less happy if they lived together without being married, simply as 'lovers'? – possibly not even in the same house, but meeting every day; in short, leading the life of a regularly married couple. If they love one another, what can hinder them from settling down together?

Nelly Ptashkina (aged 15), 1918

Mimi [Franchetti]'s love is ardent, impassioned, total, jealous. Italian love! It sings, it screams, it shouts out in keeping with her beauty, her gestures, the fire of her glance. Mimi is all about excess.

We stay in bed late in the morning; we have breakfast; we tease each other; we laugh; we embrace. We open our post. She gives me an Italian lesson: verbs, vocabulary, dictation translation. We have a very good time. She sings me the blues, which I adore, or else Italian songs, in her deep, vibrant voice. We separate, then meet again on the little rock-beach. Mimi hunts for pebbles ... Time passes quickly. Everyone is astonished by my bright face, suddenly rejuvenated. Everywhere people say to me: 'Your expression has changed. Monsieur le Prince [Georges] never laughed, you looked as though you were bored.' It was true, yet I thought I possessed a marvellous treasure!

Liane de Pougy, 1926

26 October

William [her brother, the psychologist William James] uses an excellent expression when he says in his paper on the 'hidden self' that the nervous victim 'abandons' certain portions of his consciousness ... I have passed thro' an infinite succession of conscious abandonments and in looking back now I see how it began in my childhood, altho' I wasn't conscious of the necessity until '67 or '68 when I broke down first, acutely, and had violent turns of hysteria. As I lay prostrate after the storm with my mind luminous and active and susceptible of the clearest, strongest impressions, I saw so distinctly that it was a fight between my body and my will, a battle in which the former was to be triumphant to the end ... When all one's moral and natural stock in trade is a temperament forbidding the abandonment of an inch or the relaxation of a muscle, 'tis a never-ending fight ...

Alice James, 1890

Poor J. B. in a distressing delirium, having taken in ten hours the morphia intended for forty-eight. He was tearing off his clothes, crying out, 'I'm a glorified spirit! I'm a glorified spirit! Take away these filthy rags! What should a glorified spirit do with these filthy rags?' On this E.– said coaxingly, 'Why, my dear, you wouldn't go to heaven stark naked!' on which the attendants who were holding him were mightily set off.

Caroline Fox, 1839

Time rolls on! Time! And what does it bring? I live in a desert – its barren sands feed my hour-glass and they come out fruitless as they went in. I write without hope – I study without the repayment of a happy thought – I live unloved.

What can I do? how change my destiny? Months change their names – years their cyphers – my brow is sadly trenched – the blossom of youth faded – my mind gathers wrinkles – What will become of me?

Fortune! I must upbraid you – Why is the companion of Shelley companionless – the centre of a loved circle deserted by all? Why cannot

I tame the spirit of youth and be content with my books my fireside my boy? Why is not all different from what it is? ...

I was loved once! still let me cling to the memory – but to live for one's self alone – to read & to communicate your reflections to none – to write & be cheered by none – to weep, and in no bosom, no more on thy bosom, my Shelley to spend my tears – this is misery!

Mary Shelley, 1824

27 October

I have been home from the hospital a week, with the new baby – Anne! With so many thoughts – life rushing by and no time to catch up. Life goes in the baby's routine – the delicious newness of it. The absorption of it, physically. Nursing, resting, lying in the sun, eating, drinking (for the milk!), nursing, and resting. Life itself is perilously precious – sitting in the sun watching golden wasps, a few left, and leaves falling one by one, and the sky, very blue against the last reds of the trees. I can only sit and praise life and collect my thoughts that wander – still unattached to earth and life. The day is terribly cut up, no big chunk of it to spend on anything, except at night from 8–10, when I am so sleepy.

Anne Morrow Lindbergh, 1940

... Thank God my long toil at the women's lecture is this moment ended. I am back from speaking at Girton, in floods of rain. Starved but valiant young women – that's my impression. Intelligent, eager, poor; and destined to become schoolmistresses in shoals. I blandly told them to drink wine and have a room of their own ... I get such a sense of tingling and vitality from an evening's talk like that; one's angularities and obscurities are smoothed and lit. How little one counts, I think: how little anyone counts; how fast and furious and masterly life is; and how all these thousands are swimming for dear life. I felt elderly and mature. And nobody respected me.

Virginia Woolf, 1928

28 October

Lev Nik. [her husband] has left! My God! He left a letter telling me not to look for him as he had gone for good, to live out his old age in peace. The moment I read those words I rushed outside in a frenzy of despair and jumped into the middle pond, where I swallowed a lot of water; Sasha and Bulgakov dragged me out with the help of Vanya Shraev. Utter despair. Why did they save me?

Sophia Tolstoy, 1910

… [Marianne] began with one word a day, in 'Mama's lessons', but as it was of course one new word, she now sometimes reads nearly a line. She seems to like it and takes pains. Sometimes in her sewing lessons (of six stitches in seaming), I fear I am not patient enough. Oh God, in whose hands are all hearts make me more even-tempered. With her I do try a great deal, but Oh my Father help me to regulate my impatient temper better!

She is a most sympathetic little thing …

Elizabeth Gaskell, 1838

I've started doing bloody IVF again. It's the best thing in the world, obviously, the chance to have a baby, but this much stress … In fact IVF doesn't have to be stressful, I shouldn't put people off, it's just tricky trying to do it when you're an MP, with George Galloway on your back …

Oona King, 2004

… Please God, don't let the visit to Rex [Harrison] be more pain. Don't let my fear interfere with it. Please God, give us another chance, and give me the strength to love him properly and him love me. Let us energise each other. Let him need me, God, but let me be able to meet his needs. If I can't live for myself, let me be able to make him happy. Give us a miraculous chance, I beg of you.

Rachel Roberts, 1980

29 October

The dear little Angel expired at nine o'clock, on Monday morning the 29th Octr. She knew not Cole, on Saturday, and her agonies were great from that day to the moment of her death. My affliction almost overpowers me, at the loss of such a darling and lovely Child, but on account of my Baby I am obliged to exert myself in this severe trial.

Betsey Wynne Fremantle, 1810

A misty, misty evening. I want to write down the fact that not only am I not afraid of death – I welcome the idea of death. I believe in immortality because he [her brother, dead in the trenches] is not here and I long to join him. First, my darling, I've got things to do for both of us, and then I will come as quickly as I can. Dearest heart, I know you are there, and I live with you, and I will write for you. Other people are near, but they are not close to me … You have me. You're in my flesh as well as in my soul. I give others my 'surplus' love, but to you I hold and to you I give my deepest love.

Katherine Mansfield, 1915

The election is beginning to roar in the newspapers. L. [Leonard – standing as a candidate] has a chance of getting in. We have bitten off a large piece of life – but why not?

Virginia Woolf, 1922

30 October

I cry day and night and suffer dreadfully. It is more painful and terrible than anything I could have imagined. Lev Nik. [Her husband] did visit his sister in Shamordino, then travelled on beyond Gorbachevo – who knows where. What unspeakable cruelty!

Sophia Tolstoy, 1910

... When I was walking out Benjamin [Bounce, her pet rabbit] I saw Miss Hutton's black cat jumping on something up in the wood. I thought it was too far off to interfere, but as it seemed leisurely I went up in time to rescue a poor little rabbit, fast in a snare.

The cat had not hurt it, but I had great difficulty in slackening the noose around its neck. I warmed it at the fire, relieved it from a number of fleas, and it came round. It was such a little poor creature compared to mine. They are regular vermin, but one cannot stand by to see a thing mauled about from one's friendship for the race ... I just had enough sense not to show the stranger to Benjamin Bounce, but the smell of its fur on my dress was quite enough to upset the ill-regulated passions of that excitable buck rabbit.

Whether he thought I had a rival in my pocket, or like a Princess in a Fairy Tale was myself metamorphosed into a white rabbit I cannot say, but I had to lock him up.

Rabbits are creatures of warm volatile temperament but shallow and absurdly transparent. It is this naturalness, one touch of nature, that I find so delightful in Mr Benjamin Bunny, though I frankly admit his vulgarity. At one moment amiably sentimental to the verge of silliness, at the next, the upsetting of a jug or tea-cup which he immediately takes upon himself, will convert him into a demon, throwing himself on his back, scratching and spluttering. If I can lay hold of him without being bitten, within half a minute he is licking my hands as though nothing has happened.

Beatrix Potter, 1892

Saw Mr N.[iles] of Robert Brothers, and he gave me good news of the book [*Little Women*]. An order from London for an edition came in. First editions gone and more called for. Expects to sell three or four thousand before the New Year.

Mr N. wants a second volume for spring. Pleasant notices and letters arrive, and much interest in my little women, who seem to find friends by their truth to life, as I hoped.

Louisa May Alcott, 1868

... I am getting awfully tired of this diary. I never seem to write about what is really happening in my mind, and the various jealousies and resentments and fear that seem to get into me and the idiotic worries in the night, and thinking I've paid the tink[er]s too much and wondering if I'm making a hell of a muddle of the farm or if everyone is really laughing at me and if my various boyfriends are really double crossing me. Or for that matter this plain god-awful feeling that one is getting old, that the only pleasures of the flesh left to one are eating and drinking – which I have never taken very seriously, that one regrets all lost opportunities, and oh god being fed-up with Carradale. Often in my dreams I get a horror of age, in the dream I am young and think no, it's all right and then I wake up and age and work and weariness on me ...

Naomi Mitchison, 1944

31 October

Mummy is suspicious, because I haven't had the curse for two months.

'You're either anaemic or pregnant,' she said, 'and I mean to find out which.' So she's taking me to a doctor. She keeps on asking me if I'm still a virgin or whether there's any cause to believe I'm going to have a baby. She's really put the fear of God into me – it's not so much the thought of having a baby, it's the ghastly maternal fuss that would attend such an occurrence.

Joan Wyndham (aged 19), 1940

Since I last wrote I have been called to another death-bed scene; our old and valued Roman Catholic friends, the Pitchfords, have lost their eldest son, a sweet good boy. I felt drawn in love, I trust, I may say, Christian love, to be much with them during their trial; I felt it right to leave my family, and spent First-day [Sunday] evening with them, when all hope of their child's life was given up ... My mouth was remarkably opened in prayer and praises, indeed all day, at their house, something of the holy influence appeared to be over us. A fresh living proof that what God had cleansed, we are not to call or to feel common or unclean. It surely matters not by what name we call ourselves, or what outwards means we may think right to use, if our hearts are but influenced by the love of Christ, and cleansed by His baptism, and strengthened by His Spirit, to prove our faith by love and good works. With ceremonies or without ceremonies, if there be but an establishment upon the Rock of Ages, all will be well.

Elizabeth Fry, 1829

Indira Gandhi has been assassinated.

'They got her and missed Maggie,' said F.

'Only just.'

'She'd finished cleaning her teeth only a few moments before.'

'It's because those idiots mess around with bombs,' I said. 'Guns are more accurate.'

As if we were professionals, or had considered such actions ourselves.

Helen Garner, 1984

… I can see no hope, even if L. N. [her husband] does at some point return. Things will never be as they were, after all he has made me suffer. We can never be straightforward with one another again, we can never love one another, we shall always fear one another now. And I fear for his health and strength too.

Sophia Tolstoy, 1910

November

'A good cry yesterday morning washed away some of the shadows from my soul …'

Helen Keller, 1936

1 November

Began the second part of 'Little Women.' [Sometimes known as *Good Wives*.] I can do a chapter a day, and in a month I mean to be done. A little success is so inspiring that I now find my 'Marches' sober, nice people, and as I can launch into the future, my fancy has more play. Girls write to ask who the little women marry, as if that was the only aim and end of a woman's life. I *won't* marry Jo to Laurie to please any one.

Louisa May Alcott, 1868

At 7 p.m. came my most beloved Albert and stayed with me till 10 p.m. … He was so affectionate, so kind, so dear, we kissed each other again and again … Oh! What too sweet delightful moments are these!! Oh! How blessed, how happy I am to think he is *really* mine; I can scarcely believe myself so blessed. I kissed his dear hand, and do feel so grateful to him; he is such an angel, such a very great angel! – We sit so nicely side by side on that little blue sofa; no two Lovers could ever be happier than we are! … He took my hands in his, and said my hands were so little he could hardly believe they were hands, as he had hitherto only been accustomed to handle hands like Ernest's [his brother's].

Queen Victoria, 1839

… Yesterday I had tea in Mary's room & saw the red lighted tugs go past & heard the swish of the river: Mary in black with lotus leaves round her neck. If one could be friendly with women, what a pleasure – the relationship so secret & private compared with relations with men. Why not write about it? truthfully?

Virginia Woolf, 1924

I see before me clearly the ideal life for work … Love and cheerfulness in my home life; faithful friendship with a few … and lastly charity and sympathy towards women of my own class who need it, whether they be struggling young girls, hard-pressed married women or disappointed spinsters. Every woman has a mission to other women – more especially to the women of her own class and circumstances. It is difficult to be much help to men (except as an example in the way of persistent effort and endurance in spite of womanly weakness); do what one will, sentiment creeps in, in return for sympathy. Perhaps as one loses one's attractiveness this will wear off – *certainly* it will. At present it is only with working men one feels free to sympathise without fear of unpleasant consequences …

Beatrice Webb, 1887

I am growing weak; I have eaten nothing for five days now, and have just drunk a little water. Today I feel slightly better, and am not such a prey to my passionate love for L. N. [her husband] which has so tormented my heart, and is now so poisoned. I received the eucharist, talked with the priest and decided to take a little food, for fear of not being able to go to Lev Nik. should he fall ill. My son Misha arrived. I did a little work.

Sophia Tolstoy, 1910

2 November

I received a telegram from the *Russian Word* first thing this morning: 'Lev Nik. ill in Astapovo. Temperature 40.' Tanya, Andryusha, the nurse, and I all left Tula for Astapovo on a special train.

Sophia Tolstoy, 1910

Couldn't eat breakfast. Was Sid [sculptor Sidonie Houselander] looking at me strangely? Funnily enough I hadn't given much thought to this pregnancy thing till now, but all at once I began to feel more and more certain that I was in for it, that it was true, that nothing could stop it. I was buggered and bitched.

I broke out in a cold sweat and tore back to the studio. There I found a bottle of quinine pills left behind by Prudey, and I remembered how she told me the girls in Redcliffe Road used to take them when their curse was late. It said 'Take one or more as directed'. So I took six, swallowing them with water.

Sitting now at the switchboard I feel queer, giddy and remote. If I hold out my hand it shakes and I can't feel my fingers much, they're all cotton-woolly. Oh dear God, get me out of this, never no more, I promise! It's not the baby, it's the home fuss that worries me. Sid *must know* by now – I couldn't face her, that would be too much. Wish my fingers didn't miss the holes when I dial. Wonder how soon it will show. I tried looking it up in books where girls have babies, but they never give accurate dates. Why did this have to happen to me?

Joan Wyndham (aged 19), 1940

The pain and self-defeat even more unbearable. I can't go on. I prayed that Rex [Harrison] would be the answer. I've never ever got over my halcyon days with him and however much I try, I can't. I'm utterly immobilised. No longer does he energise me as I hoped he would. Acting doesn't either, even though I've been asked to be in *Hamlet*.

Memo: Buy Acme juice machine. Celery juice or tomato, three times daily. Soups: Lemon, tomato, cucumber, bell pepper (red or green), romaine lettuce (long leaves), celery. Vitamins: B12 and Folic acid, B6 and B3. Swami Muktananda on La Cienega, for 8.30 p.m.

Rachel Roberts, 1980

My birthday. I strike 30. In 1849 I was just half an hour old. The doctor had said 'take it away' (meaning me) & good old Tudney [the nurse] did take it away, wrapped it in cotton wool, poured brandy down its throat & it lived to marry one of the nicest young men in London, & to have two splendid boys. If it were not for that good old nurse (she wore an entire cage of false teeth, had a light brown front & a strip of black velvet over her head) I should not at this moment be sitting in this romantic spot – my bedroom at Woodtown – looking forward with extreme joy to seeing my precious Bino & Gerard next Friday, looking forward to a pretty ball at Lady Rosslyn's on 10 Dec., and looking still more forward to Bob getting into Parliament, & a long & pleasant life at 7 Chelsea Embankment.

Mary, Lady Monkswell, 1879

3 November

When I went over in the morning Rupert [Gleadow] was sitting at the table writing to his ma and listening to Beethoven on the wireless …

I took a deep breath and pulled my shabby old coat around me. 'Yes I suppose I do – Mummy thinks I'm pregnant.'

I watched Rupert's face change from cheerful cynical amazement to blank horror.

'What?' he shouted, as the realisation hit him.

'Yes,' I said calmly. 'I haven't had the curse for two months.'

'Haven't had the curse for two months! Then you *are* pregnant! Oh my God, I feel sick and ill!'

Prudey prowled around shaking with laughter. 'Oh, how exciting, I *am* glad I called on you this morning! Have a cigarette, darling. Now do be careful, won't you, and don't let Rupert throw you down the stairs.'

Joan Wyndham, 1940

This small funk or pique I'm in: that the bloom is off the rose with Deborah [her friend], Rhyan [Deborah's daughter], the cat and real estate … It's a strange thing this longing I have for solitude, for privacy. I really don't like to see anyone in the morning before I'm ready. It really is odd trying to live with other people's scents and habits. D. & R. eat differently. They wash their clothes constantly.

But do I really resent the fact that I'm half a million in debt? It's not exactly debt; it's a mortgage. The interest is tax deductible. It's manageable. What I resent somewhat is D.'s inability to help with it – after I insisted she take her equity money & put Rhyan in a better school.

I think this funk is solely about not being able to go to Mendocino – everything else is manageable; everything else is even interesting.

I'm sad that I can't live with anyone, though. Apparently. But at least I'm observing myself: I'm so rigid. I notice stuff I wish was beneath notice. I'm critical. I'm a pain in the butt, really. Goddess, how did I get so tight? And I like to think of myself as generous. Not.

What smarts though is that I am generous to Deborah & I feel it is, has become, one-sided. I know her resources, financially, are less than mine. But she could offer a walk through an interesting spot she knows, or a movie on tv. Something. Or dinner.

But this is just muttering. It isn't important.

I shall try to let my mood elevate itself. Keep knowing that it is the country I need. Amazing what the beauty & solitude there do for me.

Alice Walker, 1996

Friday Night, November 3rd, I were sitting in my Chamber All A Lone Reading some part of my Will, When on A sudden my head Catcht all A Fire, and In three minutes time burnt all my head Cloths Close to my haire: And I being all A Lone Could not get them off, or any body to me, that It was God's great Mercy I was not Burnt to death, & I do humbly thank him for It.

Elizabeth Freke, 1710

4 November

I scalded my foot with coffee after having been in bed in the afternoon – I was near fainting and then bad in my bowels. Mary [her sister-in-law] waited upon me until 2 o'clock, then we went to bed, and with applications of vinegar I was lulled to sleep about 4.

Dorothy Wordsworth, 1802

Lev Nik. is worse. I wait in agony outside the little house where he is lying. We are sleeping in the train.

Sophia Tolstoy, 1910

Monday morning

Still a terrible pain in my stomach. Could the quinine be working? It feels like – yes it must be!

Later

I could feel the blood coming out. I dashed into the bathroom, fell on my knees, thanking God again and again. I nearly wrecked the bathroom in my jubilant frenzy. The nightmare veil lifted and I suddenly saw the room with sane eyes again.

After Mass I ran to the telephone and phoned Rupert. 'Darling,' I said, 'I've got the curse!'

Rupert's voice was completely unemotional. 'Oh have you? Well that's a relief. You working this morning? OK I'll be round in half an hour.'

I suppose my nature must be very uncontrolled, for I would like to have fallen on his neck and cried with relief, but with Rupert it's not possible …

I didn't tell him about the quinine because I felt rather guilty about it already. Had I been pregnant? Had the quinine worked, and if so, is it as big a sin as an abortion? I suppose I will never know. In any case both Rupert and I dropped the subject and he'll probably never mention it again.

Joan Wyndham, 1940

How great a Change has been wrought in Female Manners within these few Years in England! I was reading the Letter in the 3rd Vol. of the *Spectator* 217, where the Man complains of his indelicate Mistress: I read it aloud to my little daughters of 11 & 12 Years old, & even the Maid who was dressing my Hair, burst out o' laughing at the Idea of a *Lady* saying her Stomach ach'd, or that something stuck between her Teeth. Sure if our Morals are as much mended as our Manners, we are grown a most virtuous Nation!

Hester Lynch Thrale Piozzi, 1782

5 November

───

… There is evidently little hope. I am tormented by remorse, the painful anticipation of his end, and the impossibility of seeing my beloved husband.

Sophia Tolstoy, 1910

The greatest part of this summer has been passed in rather an unsettled way, what with visits to Knutsford, Warrington and to the sea-side, and I fear this is the only excuse I have for so long neglecting to enter anything in my journal. A great progress has naturally been made by the dear little subject [her daughter] since writing last …

… We have not begun yet to teach her anything feeling in no hurry to urge her little capacity forward, and in this we have been in many ways confirmed. We heard the opinion of a medical man lately, who said that till the age of three years or thereabouts, the brain of an infant appeared constantly to be verging on inflammation, which any little excess of excitement might produce. If we give her habits of observation, attention & perseverance, in *whatever* objects her little mind may be occupied with, I shall think we are laying a good foundation, and four years old will be time enough to begin with lessons, &c., & even then it shall be in compliance with her own wish to learn, which I wish to excite. So much for *intellect*. Now for morals …

Elizabeth Gaskell, 1836

Was the day as we hear the Prince of Orange landed at a place in the West. Ever since we have the sound of wars and desolation in our Land, and Soldiers continually passing up and down which keeps us in continual expectation of a Battle. But good God of all Battles do thou bring good out of all our distractions and preserve our King, and establish the Church on a firm foundation. And put an end to all wars and differences between us and give peace in our days O Lord …

Mary Woodforde, 1688

6 November

Dreadful atmosphere of anticipation. I can't remember anything very clearly.

Sophia Tolstoy, 1910

Going up in the elevator to see Richard Rosenthal, for one marvellous moment I felt like Rachel Roberts again. After resting up and deciding to do *Hamlet*, I held my head high in the elevator. I looked out at my fellow human beings who were a poor lot. I came back to myself for a few blessed minutes, the fear inside abated a bit and I wanted to live and act again. Now it's returned again, so it's difficult to write because I'm shaking with the familiar terror.

Rachel Roberts, 1980

Mended Mr C.'s dressing-gown. Much movement under the free sky is needful for me to keep my heart from throbbing up into my head and maddening it. They must be comfortable people who have leisure to think about going to Heaven! My most constant and pressing anxiety is to keep out of Bedlam! that's all … Ach! If there were no feelings 'what steady sailing craft we should be,' as the nautical gentleman of some novel says.

Jane Carlyle, 1855

… This is the first November which I have spent without terrible despondency, gloom overtaking the greyness of my life throughout the year. And now I am no longer on the bank watching with cold but intense curiosity the surface currents. I am swimming in mid-water with another by my side and a host to the fore and the rear of me …

Beatrice Webb, 1890

About 4 this morning the Mate informed us the land was very near. The morning was very fine, and we were all soon on deck. Nothing could exceed the beauty of the scenery, we passed on the left, Wilson's promontory, and the Coast of New Holland, about 4 miles distant ...

Sarah Docker, emigrant to Australia, 1828

7 November

My forty-fourth birthday (and La Stupenda's [Joan Sutherland's] sixtieth, I heard on the radio on the way to the pool). M. won't come out with me for breakfast. The law student, embarrassed perhaps, offers himself as company.

Helen Garner, 1986

At 6 o'clock in the morning Lev Nikol. died. I was allowed in only as he drew his last breath. They would not even let me take leave of my husband. Cruel people.

Sophia Tolstoy, 1910

CHATSWORTH. I am worried by my new maid turning out dreadfully huffy with the Duke's household, and unmanageable when I tell her to show my gowns to other people. She is going. It perplexes me sadly how all I say and do, though it is not without prayer, seems to fail utterly with one maid after another. This is the 4th I have had that has behaved ill in her rapports with some fellow-servant or other, and they have not a notion that they can be in the least to blame, though by their own showing (certainly in this one's case) all grows out of the pettiest jealousy and pride ... I wonder how they understand our blessed Lord's words about the peace-makers, the poor in spirit, the meek and the lowly. It makes one fear that one may be doing something like it, according to one's different temptations, with the same self-complacency; but then one does learn a little to mistrust oneself.

Lucy (Lady Frederick) Cavendish, 1866

A remark of the woman in the next cubbyhole at [the] hairdresser's yesterday: 'My husband says he doesn't know what I do with my money. I tell him I'd like him to have the spending of it.' I wonder if there is any marriage where such a situation isn't all the time arising. I have often offered my Husband the wifely job, but he shies away instantly. He may be mystified about what I do with his allowances to me, but he apparently would rather go on being mystified than take over the job. Dear knows there are times, often, when I'd be glad to have no money to handle. Like royalty …

Edie Rutherford, 1945

The Vicar's large Dog went mad last night and was shot this morning. There must be some mysterious cause of all these large dogs in the country going mad. I suspect it originate from Potions administered to them by the numerous Vagabonds with which the roads and Villages Swarm, under the appearance of maim'd Sailors, servants out of place, Pedlars, etc., who meditate an attack upon the house and thus remove the incorruptible guardians from them.

Lady Eleanor Butler, 1788

8 November

We are leaving with the body. They have lent us the carriage in which we were staying.

Sophia Tolstoy, 1910

My beloved made me take an emetic, and by that kindness, anxiety, and tenderness which constitutes the happiness of my Life, she softened the Pain I endured.

Lady Eleanor Butler, 1789

Without the bloody panic, I'd be performing well in a good play and going home to my neat apartment every night and, if I was lonely, I could have two little cats on the bed as Rosie once was, tea and toast and the *New York Times* in the morning, a massage, somewhere like the Women's Health Club in the afternoon, a bath and a taxi to the theatre. That's what *should* have happened and be happening. Why is it, then, that not only did I prevent it happening, but that when I describe it, I feel a sort of revulsion and a knowledge that it isn't right for me. Is it too ordinary? Too repetitious? Why do my thoughts instantly turn to wine when I think of the theatre as I've just described it? Do I want heightened reality still? I've done only three Broadway shows in my time, and they were done in conjunction with sex and violence and drink.

Rachel Roberts, 1980

A fine day

It's market day. In the English class I'm sitting next to the window. Suddenly I see a shadow from the corner of my eyes. I lift my head. I see Mother behind the window. I'm staggered. It's been so long since I've seen her. Even through the window I can see that her face is all black and swollen …

She takes us to the market. She buys us vegetable soup for fifty fen and we also get bread to dunk in the bowl.

After we've eaten, we go off to buy winter clothes. With good padded clothes, we won't be cold. We each get a jacket and shoes and socks. In no time at all we've spent over a hundred yuan. What a pity! I feel both happy and sad. Money is so hard to earn and so easy to spend. You don't even notice it going.

I don't know how Mother and Father have earned these hundred yuan, how many days it took, how many tens of hours, hundreds of minutes, thousands and thousands of seconds. And I spent all this hard-earned wealth as if it were nothing at all.

When I grow up, what won't I do for my parents!

Ma Yan, 2001

9 November

Back in Yasnaya. Crowds of people at Zaseka. We lowered the coffin on to the station and they came to pay their last respects. Masses of young people and delegations. They all followed the coffin from Zaseka to Yasnaya Polyana. We buried Lev Nikolaevich.

Sophia Tolstoy, 1910

We had this morning got to the north of Jervis's Bay. We could plainly see the smoke from numbers of fires along the Coast. You can form but little idea of the joy we felt at being so only a few hours sail distant from Sydney. Yesterday we expected to be at Sydney today and even talked of going to Church. But today the wind being quite contrary we were obliged to tack about, and made very little progress.

Sarah Docker, emigrant to Australia, 1828

A nice day

Tomorrow we go home, and I'm so happy.

Tonight during the study hour there was a blackout. All the comrades were thrilled. They were happy not to have electricity to see by: a whole hour in which to have fun.

But I'm happy just to go home, to sit down with my mother and talk things over.

Several weeks have passed since we were all together at home. This time when we get there, I'm going to ask my parents how they spent every single day, and especially how Mother's health is. I think her pains started again when she was up in the mountains.

Ma Yan, 2001

10 November

Mr Charles Stewart's Lady was delivered of a Son. God make it his servant.

Mary Woodforde, 1685

I have made my first probation in writing & it has done me great good, & I get more calm. The stream begins to take me in a new channel in as much as to make me fear change. But people must know little of me who think that abstractedly I am content with my present mode of life …

I am allowed to have some talent. That is sufficient methinks to cause my irreparable misery – for if one has genius what a delight it is to associate with a superior – Mine own Shelley – the sun knows of none to be likened to you – brave, wise, gentle – noblehearted – full of learning, tolerance & love. – Love. What a word for me to write. Yet, my miserable heart, permit me yet to love. To see him in beauty – to feel him in beauty – To be interpenetrated by the sense of his excellence – & thus to love, singly, eternally, ardently – & not fruitlessly, for I am still his – still the chosen one of that blessed spirit – still vowed to him for ever & ever.

Mary Shelley, 1822

A few days ago I got a vision of a house that I would feel at home in. It was made of eucalyptus, glass and adobe. A contemporary structure in a natural setting. I would have to build it. I walked up by the old water tank today, looking for a site.

Through the years, Francis and I have argued over and over again about our house. He has said all he ever really wanted from me was to make him a home. Once, in a crazy argument in the Philippines, he told me that he would spend a million dollars, if necessary, to find a woman who wanted to make a home, cook and have lots of babies. I could never tell the truth, even to myself, because I thought it would be the end of my marriage. I am not a homemaker. I have always wanted to be a working person. But the kind of work I have done over the years hasn't earned any money, so it looks like I am playing and lazy.

Right now I am feeling a giant relief. I am off the hook. The other woman in Francis's life is not the ultimate homemaker either; she is not dying to step in and take over the mansion.

Eleanor Coppola, 1977

11 November

———

Oh why was I born for this time? Before one is thirty to know more dead than living people? Stanway, Clouds, Gosford [her family homes] – all the settings of one's life – given up to ghosts. Really, one hardly knows who is alive and who is dead. One thing is that now at least people will no longer bury their dead as they used. Now they are so many one *must* talk of them naturally and humanly, not banish them by only alluding to them as if it were almost indelicate.

Lady Cynthia Asquith, 1915

Peace!

London today is a pandemonium of noise and revelry, soldiers and flappers being most in evidence. Multitudes are making all the row they can, and in spite of depressing fog and steady rain, discords of sound and struggling, rushing beings and vehicles fill the streets. Paris, I imagine, will be more spontaneous and magnificent in its rejoicing. Berlin, also is reported to be elated, having got rid, not only of the war, but also of its oppressors. The people are everywhere rejoicing. Thrones are everywhere crashing and the men of property are everywhere secretly trembling. 'A biting wind is blowing for the cause of property,' writes an Austrian journalist. How soon will the tide of revolution catch up the tide of victory? Will it be six months or a year?

Beatrice Webb, 1918

I feel the multitudinous conceivings of my brain clamoring, from time to time, like molecules of steam under a pot lid. They make a steady din. I do not hope for one so big as to blow the lid off. I must do that myself. I wish I knew the engineering.

Patricia Highsmith, 1942

I received today a charming letter from Mrs Gaskell, in which she says, 'Since I heard, from authority, that you were the author of 'Scenes of Clerical Life' and 'Adam Bede', I have read them again: and I must, once more tell you how earnestly, fully, and humbly I admire them. I never read anything so complete and beautiful in fiction, in my life before'. Very sweet and noble of her! – I have been very poorly almost all this week, and sticking terribly in the mud so far as my writing is concerned.

George Eliot, 1859

12 November

From Waterloo Station we took a taxi which, to my amazement, could carry our twelve pieces of baggage! I shall never forget the two trunks and three big cases of Braille notes I brought for literary work on the top of the taxi and the other seven stowed inside. I wondered if we should reach the Park Lane Hotel alive – I thought the trunks might fall through the roof, but soon I was convinced of our perfect safety. We drove through the usual London mist pierced by innumerable electric lights. With ripples of excitement in her fingers Polly enumerated the places we passed:

'Helen! The Houses of Parliament – you remember our dining there with Sir Ian Fraser when Teacher [Anne Sullivan] was here.'

'Westminster! …'

'The Mall! …'

'Now we have come to Piccadilly …'

A heartbreaking sense of emptiness swept over us because Teacher was not beside us to repeat those names in a voice full of happy memories and anticipation of another visit to the Park Lane where everything pleased and rested her.

Almost in tears I arrived at the hotel. Everyone there, even the clerks at the desk, the head porter and the doorman, welcomed with such a friendly warmth, it made me feel that I had come home, and I was less lonely. At the Park Lane we do always experience a deep sense of true English hospitality.

Helen Keller, visiting London, 1936

The war seems more terrible every day, the bombing of England that has gone on for months, the pictures of smoking Coventry, boarded-up London, the stories of hospitals, amputations, children's terror. One wants to suffer oneself and feels it would be easier than this watching and not knowing what to do.

Anne Morrow Lindbergh, 1940

Our unfortunate mother's sufferings were put an end to this morning, she expired at seven o'clock. Eugenia was called to her but she could not speak one word and died in her arms. We left the house almost immediately and removed to a lodging only three doors from it. It is a great comfort to us all that we came to town. Though it is shocking to be present at this scene of distress, still I feel much less the shock having been near her than if I had been away, as I should always have feared that she might have wished to see me in her last moments.

Betsey Wynne Fremantle, 1799

Princess Di wowed [Washington] DC, she really did. I got multiple reports of the magic of it all. Her whirl across the dance floor in the East Room of the White House in the arms of John Travolta in the midnight-blue velvet Victor Edelstein dress – epic … Once again the Reagans know how to create the iconic pictures. Those ten minutes on the dance floor were instant history, glamour for the ages.

Tina Brown, 1985

13 November

A good cry yesterday morning washed away some of the shadows from my soul, so that I am able to see more of life's brightness and to chat with a few people …

I was glad Polly's eyes were so full of charming sights. With my own senses I perceived the odours of fresh bread, wine-shops and passing motor buses. A whiff of enchanting English violets made my heart give a little jump, and we went into the florist's to buy some.

I knew when we entered Green Park by the smell of grass and burning leaves. It was a blessed corner to commune with nature away from the street traffic – men, women and children walking just for the pleasure of it, dogs gambolling without leash or muzzle, pigeons and gulls. I touched the noble plane-trees and oaks, and enjoyed the softness of the grass. The sparrows were very cocky and so fearless we almost stepped on them …

Helen Keller, 1936

It is time I started a new journal. Come, my unseen, my unknown, let us talk together. Yes, for the last two weeks I have written scarcely anything. I have been idle; I have *failed*. Why? Many reasons. There has been a kind of confusion in my consciousness. It has seemed as though there was not time to write. The mornings, if they are sunny, are taken up with sun-treatment; the post eats away the afternoon. And at night I am tired …

I must make another effort – at once. I must begin all over again. I must try and write simply, fully, freely, from my heart. *Quietly*, caring nothing for success or failure, but just going on.

I must keep this book so that I have a record of what I do each week. (Here a word. As I re-read *At the Bay* in proof, it seemed to me flat, dull, and not a success at all. I was very much ashamed of it. I am.) But now to resolve! And especially to keep in touch with Life – with the sky and this moon, these stars, these cold, candid peaks.

Katherine Mansfield, 1921

14 November

May came full of expectation and joy to visit good Aunt B. and study drawing. We walked about and had a good home talk, then my girl went off to Auntie's to begin what I hope will be a pleasant and profitable winter. She needs help to develop her talent, and I can't give it to her.

Went to see Forrest as Othello. It is funny how attentive all the once cool gentlemen are to Miss Alcott now she has a pass to the new theatre.

Louisa May Alcott, 1856

Who do I think I'm kidding? I'm in a fucking awful mess. I'm being looked after by Carol and about to go to an intensive bit of Indian meditation with Swami Muktananda because it's preferable to being alone all day in Hutton Drive [Los Angeles].

I read about Reagan's friends, Betsy Bloomingdale, the Jurgensens, Mrs William French Smith: how they are disciplined! Getting up at 5.30 a.m., exercising, breakfast at 6.30 a.m., working all day, entertaining, dressing well, with children and grandchildren ... and I wonder that I'm depressed? ...

... Why can't I just be me? I could correct the scruffiness. Buy some simple clothes. Get some Calvin Klein expensive ones. Some shoes. Some proper face cream. Have my hair done. Write to my friends, to my friends. Read *Hamlet*. Contact Frank Dunlop. But I *can't* do any of these things. I've been like a lost soul for eighteen months. I'm in this painful depression because inevitability has caught up with me. I made no preparation for my fifties and no one made preparation for me. You don't marry a man twenty years your senior [Rex Harrison], a temperamental man without a home, much as you loved him – and love him: that's the fact of the matter – and expect serenity. (I wasn't looking for serenity, either.) You don't fail to have children of your own, or by adoption, and expect the joy of them in middle age. You don't divorce when you're forty-two and live first with a gentle, penniless young man and expect stability and emotional satisfaction or with a sexy, emotionally unrestrained young man nearly twenty years your junior and expect to be settled like George and Margaret whom I acquired after the health farm. Hardly preparation for the wives of the Reagan Set!

I *dread* being alone so much. 'You'll be left alone,' Mum said. Just read in the *Los Angeles Times* about the severely retarded women who 'were all dressed appropriately, and obviously felt some pride in their own appearance'. It's about time I started taking pride in mine, too.

Rachel Roberts, 1980

We kissed each other so often, and I leant on that dear soft cheek, fresh and pink like a rose ... It was ten o'clock and it was time for his going ... I gave Albert a last kiss, and saw him get into the carriage and – drive off. I cried much, felt wretched, yet happy to think that we should meet again so soon! Oh! how I love him, how intensely, how devotedly, how ardently! I cried and felt so sad. Wrote my journal. Walked. Cried.

Queen Victoria, 1839

I'm afraid there is no rest on earth for me, because I shall forever avoid it. The rope I am given everywhere lies slack around my feet and tangles me up.

Patricia Highsmith, 1950

15 November

CHATSWORTH. Rained nearly all day. Womankind staid at home, and some of us had three furious games of tennis-battledore in the banqueting room. Gentlemen drove to the shooting place and then – drove back again.

Lucy (Lady Frederick) Cavendish, 1866

Fearful hurricane. Reading, drawing. Loud rap at the Door. Lady Templetown's Servant, soon followed by that charming woman herself, and her sweet Daughter. Such mutual joy at meeting, on our part so unexpected. Got tea and coffee instantly. Cake, brown and white bread

and butter, toast and butter, an excellent bright fire. Shutters closed.
Curtain let down. She exclaimed, with surprise and admiration of the
beauty and comfort of our little abode. The latter greatly enhanced by the
fearful Storm which raged and howled about the Mountains.

Lady Eleanor Butler, 1789

Roses and Lilies secured from frost by Muck.

Lady Eleanor Butler, 1790

16 November

Talked of Mama and the necessity of speaking to her about … leaving
the house [when Victoria married]; Lord M.[elbourne] said he feared
I should have a great deal of difficulty in getting her out of the house.
'There must be no harshness,' said Lord M., 'yet firm.'

Queen Victoria, 1839

Wrote the last word of *Adam Bede* and sent it to Mr Langford.
Jubilate.

George Eliot, 1858

For him [Piozzi] I have been contented to reverse the laws of nature, and
request of my child that concurrence which, at my age and a widow, I am
not required either by divine or human institution to ask even of a parent.
The life I gave her she may now more than repay, only by agreeing to what
she will with difficulty prevent; and which, if she does prevent, will give
her lasting remorse; for those who stab *me* shall hear the groan …

Hester Lynch Thrale Piozzi, 1782

To the Club for a change, as I have written like a steam engine since the 1st. [John] Weiss read a fine paper on 'Woman Suffrage.' Good talk afterward …

Louisa May Alcott, 1868

Somewhere [Indian diplomat] Ap[p]a Pant has remarked that air-travellers arrive in two instalments and for me this is Disembodied Day, that dreamlike interval before the mind has caught up with the body; and because a natural parsimony compels me to eat all the meals served *en route* the body in question feels so overfed I wish it could have been left behind, too.

Oddly enough Rachel [her 5-year-old daughter] seems immune to jet-lag, despite having had less than three hours' sleep. I chose to stay in this hostel [the YWCA, Mumbai] for her sake, thinking it would serve as a not too unfamiliar half-way house between Europe and Asia. But such solicitude was soon proved needless and I last saw her disappearing up the street with two new-found Indian friends. It seems she has gone to lunch with someone; I feel too exhausted to find out exactly with whom or where.

Of course even I was buoyed up, for the first few hours after our landing at 7.00 a.m., by the simple fact of being back in India. Emerging from the cool plane into warm, dense air (72°F, according to official information) I was instantly overwhelmed by that celebrated odour of India which I had last smelt many hundreds of miles away, in Delhi. It seemed to symbolise the profound – if not always apparent – unity of this country. And it is not inappropriate that one's first response to India should involve that sensual experience least amenable to analysis or description.

Dervla Murphy, 1973

17 November

Our cold baths have driven away the last sign of our colds. They are really marvellous if you can bear them. As the hour approaches we begin to paw the ground, nothing could rein us in, not the icy house, the pleading of our friends, our aches and pains – we disregard it all. Undress very quickly, in and out! You emerge merry and brisk, refreshed and ready for anything, rather proud of your heroism …

Liane de Pougy, 1919

For just a few minutes, there, in the delivery room, the doctor and I came face-to-face with each other. All our strengths and weaknesses hanging in the balance, suspended between this new life that stubbornly resisted an easy birthing. I, howling like a bull, feared I had come to the limit of my strength before I could suck this creature out into the open. The doctor, cursing my weakness, refused to listen to my pain, a pain that is like none other on the face of the earth. I swear it: it is as if your whole body were being ripped inside out hour after agonizing hour. And then it was all obliterated in a second, as I leaned forward to see the head and the shoulders and the bowled-up legs come out of me. From somewhere, somehow, beyond me came one last push, lasting and lasting until my child had cleared the light of day.

Kathleen Collins, 1972

I think one of my pleasantest memories of Esthwaite is sitting on Oatmeal Crag on a Sunday afternoon, where there is a sort of table of rock with a dip, with the lane and fields and oak copse like in a trough below my feet, and all the little tiny fungus people singing and bobbing and dancing in the grass and under the leaves all down below, like the whistling that some people cannot hear of stray mice and bats, and I sitting up above and knowing something about them.

I cannot tell what possesses me with the fancy that they laugh and clap their hands, especially the little ones that grow in troops and rings amongst dead leaves in the woods. I suppose it is the fairy rings, the myriads of fairy fungi that starts into life in autumn woods.

I remember I used to half believe and wholly play with fairies when I was a child. What heaven can be more real than to retain the spirit-world of childhood, tempered and balanced by knowledge and common-sense, to fear no longer the terror that flieth by night, yet to feel truly and understand a little, a very little, of the story of life.

Beatrix Potter, 1896

Finished my thirteenth chapter. I am so full of my work, I can't stop to eat or sleep, or for anything but a daily run.

Louisa May Alcott, 1868

18 November

—

Went to Buckingham, to see Doctor Williams, who found me better, and ordered me to wear flannel waistcoats. We walked out and it was so dirty that I went in to Mrs East who lent me one of her daughter's pairs of stockings which I put on rather unwillingly – we were very merry.

Harriet Wynne, 1803

I have a charming idea – in my next year's journal I will note down the flowers over which I spend so many happy hours arranging them in the drawingroom [sic], & in the big vases on the stairs. They are more worthy to be remembered than most people.

Mary, Lady Monkswell, 1890

Two little embryos were put into my womb today. I have to enjoy it because, as I've said before, this is probably the closest I'll come to parenthood: looking at those little screwed-up images on screen. For the first time, one of the embryos was at the blastocyst stage. No, it had gone past the blastocyst stage, it had started hatching. And the other one had just turned into a blastocyst. And there was a third little one that didn't quite make the grade, so that's been popped in the freezer.

Anyway I don't think I could be more stressed if I tried. Work is hell on wheels. Tiberio [her husband] is at Cranfield, so he wasn't with me today. His MBA workload remains insane …

So, back to the stress. Have I mentioned that it's getting to me? Mind you, I think that injecting myself full of drugs doesn't help. On the other hand I've done four IVF cycles so far, and catastrophic failure hasn't left me too depressed, just with that general sense of desperation that any infertile person has – you know, that run-of-the-mill exquisite torture, wanting-to-kill-yourself-because-you-can't-have-children kind of thing. Apart from that, I'm fine.

There's a good quote in Alan Clark's book. It's him saying how pleased he is when he gets on the train, because he has some peace and quiet. 'For an hour and a half I'm isolated, trundling along, and no one can get at me with a, 'Will you, can we, did you, have you, are you, if you, but you, three-bags-full query.' And then one sentence later he says, 'I must be very near a nervous breakdown.' Alan mate, I'm with you.

Oona King, 2004

19 November

Spent yesterday in Paris. Went on the metro for the first time. It's comfortable, diverting, economical, but you're stuck up against each other, breathing in each other's faces, travelling underground.

Liane de Pougy, 1920

Heavens! a new Distress! my Child, my Sophia will not die: arrested by the Hand of God – apparently so: She will die without a Disease – Fits, sudden, unaccountable, unprovoked; Apoplectic, lethargic like her Father. Woodward and Dobson are called: they say her Disorder should be termed Attonitus: 'tis an instant Cessation of all Natures Pow'rs at once. I saved her in the first Attack, by a Dram of fine Old Usquebough [whisky] given at the proper Moment – it reviv'd her, but She only lives I see to expire with fresh Struggles.

Oh spare my Sophia, my Darling, oh spare her gracious heaven – & take in Exchange the life of her wretched Mother!

She lives, I have been permitted to save her again; I rubbed her while just expiring, so as to keep the heart in Motion: She knew me instantly, & said you warm *me* but you are killing *yourself* – I actually was in a burning Fever from exertion, & fainted as soon as I had saved my Child.

Hester has behaved inimitably too, *all* our Tenderness was called out on this Occasion: dear Creatures! they see I love them, that I would willingly *die* for them; that I *am* actually dying to gratifie their Humour at the Expense of my own Happiness: they can *but* have my Life – let them take it! ...

Hester Lynch Thrale Piozzi, 1783

20 November

Mrs and the three Miss Thrales and myself all arose at six o'clock in the morning, and 'by the pale blink of the moon' we went to the sea-side, where we had bespoke the bathing-women to be ready for us, and into the ocean we plunged. It was cold, but pleasant. I have bathed so often as to lose my dread of the operation, which now gives me nothing but animation and vigour. We then returned home, and dressed by candle-light ...

Fanny Burney, Brighton, 1782

Growing old is certainly far easier for people like me who have no job from which to retire at a given age. I can't stop doing what I have always done, trying to sort out and shape experience. The journal is a good way to do this at a less intense level than by creating a work of art as highly organised as a poem, for instance, or the sustained effort a novel requires. I find it wonderful to have a receptacle into which to pour vivid momentary insights, and a way of ordering day-to-day experience ...

May Sarton, 1974

I have been fretting inwardly all this day at the prospect of having to go and appeal before the Tax Commissioners at Kensington tomorrow morning. Still, it must be done. If Mr C. should go himself he would run his head against some post in his impatience; and besides, for me, when it is over it will be over, whereas he would not get the better of it for twelve months – if ever at all.

Jane Carlyle, 1855

I must not forget Naomi's [Royde-Smith's] proposed evidence (called but not chosen) in the *Well of Loneliness* case [concerning the obscenity trial of Radclyffe Hall's openly homosexual novel]. Do you consider this a suitable book for general reading?

I do. I consider it most valuable. I was for many years mistress in a girl's school, and if this book had then been available I should have given it to read to any girl inclined to sexual perversion. I should have said to her, 'Let this be a warning to you, first, as to what sort of treatment the world will mete out to you if you go on like this; second (Naomi wriggled and bridled) as to what sort of book you may end by writing.'

Sylvia Townsend Warner, 1928

21 November

It's [her friend] Paul's fortieth birthday party. Back in the summer, after I was diagnosed, making sure I was at this event was one of my priorities. My aim was to have treatment done and dusted by today. How naïve I was in the early days of cancer. But at least I'm here, along with all of Paul's close friends and family, in a Surrey hotel preparing to celebrate.

As I wash my hair over the bath, several long, wet strands suddenly begin to collect in the plughole. Not loads, but enough for me to know that this is down to the chemo.

It's a surprise, but I'm unruffled, and as I see some of the hair detaching itself from my head, I say out loud, 'Oh, wow' …

Victoria Derbyshire, 2015

O me miseram! not one wink of sleep the whole night through! so great the 'rale [sic] mental agony in my own inside' at the thought of that horrid appealing. It was with feeling like the ghost of a dead dog, that I rose and dressed and drank my coffee, and then started for Kensington. Mr C. said 'the voice of honour seemed to call on him to go himself.' But either it did not call loud enough, or he would not listen to that charmer ...

Jane Carlyle, 1855

The royal wedding seems to go off without a hitch. I think the young man will hold his own in that marriage. I think people who slept on London pavements in the cold and wet are crazy, and likely some cases of pneumonia will develop this weekend.

Husband is now reading *Economics for the Exasperated* and each page gets him more exasperated.

Edie Rutherford, 1947

And spent the morning tidying a ruined garden. Cleared all the michaelmas daisies, etc., V. lopped apple-trees. Glazed polyanthus look very pretty, even yellow privet is tolerable with an ermine edging. It was a most beautiful morning, everything bloomed with silver, falling rime sparkling, Tom and Toad [cat and Pekinese] kissing each other. We lunched off cold pork and then as bargained, I went to bed.

Sylvia Townsend Warner, 1937

22 November

It all began so beautifully. After a drizzle in the morning, the sun came out bright and clear. We were driving into Dallas. In the lead car were President and Mrs Kennedy, John and Nellie Connally, a Secret Service car full of men, and then our car with Lyndon and me and Senator Ralph Yarborough ...

Then, almost at the edge of town, on our way to the Trade Mart for the Presidential luncheon, we were rounding a curve, going down a hill, and suddenly there was a sharp, loud report. It sounded like a shot. The sound seemed to me to come from a building on the right above my shoulder. A moment passed, and then two more shots rang out in rapid succession. There had been such a gala air about the day that I thought the noise must have come from firecrackers – part of the celebration. Then the Secret Service men were suddenly down in the lead car. Over the car radio system, I heard 'Let's get out of here!' and our Secret Service man, Rufus Youngblood, vaulted over the front seat on top of Lyndon, threw him to the floor, and said, 'Get down.'

Senator Yarborough and I ducked our heads. The car accelerated terrifically – faster and faster. Then, suddenly, the brakes were put on so hard that I wondered if we were going to make it as we wheeled left and went around the corner. We pulled up to a building. I looked up and saw a sign, 'HOSPITAL'. Only then did I believe that this might be what it was. Senator Yarborough kept saying in an excited voice, 'Have they shot the President? Have they shot the President?' I said something like, 'No, it can't be.'

As we ground to a halt – we were still the third car – Secret Service men began to pull, lead, guide, and hustle us out. I cast one last look over my shoulder and saw in the President's car a bundle of pink, just like a drift of blossoms, lying on the back seat. It was Mrs Kennedy lying over the President's body …

It was decided that we would go immediately to the airport. Hurried plans were made about how we should get to the cars and who was to ride in which car. Our departure from the hospital and walk to the cars was one of the swiftest walks I have ever made.

We got in. Lyndon told the agents to stop the sirens. We drove along as fast as we could. I looked up at a building and there, already, was a flag at half-mast. I think that was when the enormity of what had happened first struck me …

We all sat around the plane. The casket was in the corridor. I went in the small private room to see Mrs Kennedy, and though it was a very hard thing to do, she made it as easy as possible. She said things like, 'Oh, Lady Bird, we've liked you two so much … Oh, what if I had not been there. I'm so glad I was there.'

I looked at her. Mrs Kennedy's dress was stained with blood. One leg was almost entirely covered with it and her right glove was caked, it was caked with blood – her husband's blood. Somehow that was one of the most poignant sights – that immaculate woman exquisitely dressed, and caked in blood.

I asked her if I couldn't get someone in to help her change and she said, 'Oh, no. Perhaps later I'll ask Mary Gallagher but not right now.' And then with almost an element of fierceness – if a person that gentle, that dignified, can be said to have such a quality – she said, 'I want them to see what they have done to Jack.'

Lady Bird Johnson, 1963

Been to Sally's [her daughter's] dancing lesson. What it is to have someone always merry and gay to be counted on in the house, like Sally. Really, whatever comes she is a daily pleasure now and the self-indulgence of hugging her ought to compensate if she turns into a difficult daughter. *Tiens! Je suis heureuse!* But unproductive – and when that happens I feel extravagant and wish for possessions. In town I bought an old Derby biscuit group – I fear it is not intrinsically beautiful. Now I want a glass pen, a patchbox I have seen, and lots of flowers, not chrysanthemums!

Ivy Jacquier, 1926

23 November

The room was full, but I hardly knew who was there. Lord M.[elbourne] I saw looking at me with tears in his eyes, but he was not near me. I then read my short Declaration [of her engagement]. I felt my hands shook but I did not make one mistake. I felt more happy and thankful when it was over.

Queen Victoria, 1839

Then sent him to the Village for the man with the Bear. The man bought it. A tame huge animal, female I suppose by the Master calling it Nancy. We fed it with Bread and Mutton. It drank Small Beer.

Lady Eleanor Butler, 1790

Yesterday I went to town and bought this book to enter scraps in, not a diary of statistics and dates and decency of spelling and happenings but just to jot me down in, unvarnished me, old me at fifty-eight – old, old, old, in most ways and in others just a baby with so much to learn and not much time left here but maybe somewhere else. It seems to me it helps to write things and thoughts down. It makes the unworthy ones look more shamefaced and helps to place the better ones for sure in our minds. It sorts out jumbled up thoughts and helps to clarify them, and I want my thoughts clear and straight for my work.

I used to write diaries when I was young but if I put anything down that was under the skin I was in terror that someone would read it and ridicule me, so I always burnt them up before long …

Emily Carr, 1930

24 November

———

This was the day that President Kennedy lay in state at the Capitol. It was a day I will never forget – nor will the people of America …

To me, one of the saddest things in the whole tragedy was that Mrs Kennedy achieved on this desperate day something she had never quite achieved in the years she'd been in the White House – a state of love, a state of rapport between herself and the people of this country. Her behavior from the moment of the shot until I last saw her was, to me, one of the most memorable things of all. Maybe it was a combination of great breeding, great discipline, great character. I only know it was great. Her composure is one of the things that keeps coming back to me. Another is the contrast with the death of FDR [Franklin D. Roosevelt], because this time there's something much worse about it. There is a shame for the violence and hatred that has gripped our land. But there is also a determination to help wipe it out!

Lady Bird Johnson, 1963

I never expected this total despair. Even as I look back on it, I remember days of vitality and happiness and hope. And now faced with hopelessness, I can't believe what is happening to me, to Ray, to Rachel Roberts ...

I never really wanted a real husband. I wanted to act. But I knew I was bad at looking after myself, so I chased after Alan because he was so steady and good. Rex [Harrison] upset my life, not just because he was so self-centred, not only because he'd lived and loved so much more than I had, but because of something in me that didn't want just to be a man's wife. The loss of my play, *A Lesson from Aloes*, and its subsequent triumph in New York – and the realisation that it was the chance of a lifetime in comparison with what I get offered, and could have been something that could have led somewhere *had I been well and different*, it had its predictable traumatic effect on me ...

Rachel Roberts, 1980

... Oh, why – oh, why isn't anything unlimited? Why am I troubled every single day by the nearness of death and its inevitability? I am really diseased on that point. And I can't speak of it. If I tell J. [her husband, John Middleton Murry] it makes him unhappy. If I don't tell him, it leaves me to fight it. I am tired of the battle. No-one knows how tired.

Katherine Mansfield, 1921

I fed Rainbow, Diamond Snowflake Jasper pheasant this morning Branwell went down to Mr Driver's and brought news that Sir Robert Peel was going to be invited to stand for Leeds Anne and I had been peeling apples for Charlotte to make us an apple pudding and for Aunt nuts and apples Charlotte said she made puddings perfectly and she was of a quick but limited intellect ... The Gondals are discovering the interior of Gaaldine. Sally Mosley is washing in the back kitchen.

It is past Twelve o'clock Anne and I have not tidied ourselves, done our bedwork or done our lessons and we want to go out to play we are going to have for Dinner Boiled Beef, Turnips, potatoes and apple pudding. The Kitchin [sic] is in a very untidy state Anne and I have not done our music exercise which consists of b major Tabby said on my putting a pen in her face Ya pitter pottering there instead of pilling a potate [sic] I answered O Dear, O Dear, O dear I will directly with that I get up, take knife and begin pilling …

Emily and Anne Brontë, 1834

25 November

The horrible Christmas turmoil draws near. How I hate it. It is not Christian: it is barbarous. Am I mean or is it consequent on seeing people give so lavishly when unable to do so that has set up revolt inside me? I do not know. I am always making up my mind to give my paintings away freely, and then I don't much. So often doubt of people really wanting them stops me …

Emily Carr, 1936

I can't control it any more and I've been trying with all my failing strength. I'm paralysed. I can't do anything and there seems to be no help anywhere. What has happened to me? Is it that my dependence over the years on alcohol has so severely debilitated me that now, without it, I just cannot function at all? Or is it that my nervous system from birth has always been so very frail that life for me is too much to cope with? That I was the hopelessly dependent little girl who found everything too hard to handle, so that my intelligence and talent have been overcome now that I'm in my fifties and I can't withstand it? Day after day and night after night, I'm in this shaking fear. What am I so terribly frightened of?

Life itself, I think.

Rachel Roberts, 1980

On the following day, Rachel Roberts' body was discovered in the Los Angeles house where she was staying. The coroner decided she had taken her own life.

What a blessing I can write in this little book without fearing that anyone will ever read and ridicule the nonsense and half-sense I scribble. This has been the attraction of a 'diary-book' to me – one can talk one's little things out to a highly appreciative audience, dumb but not deaf. And sometimes this is a necessary safety-valve to save one from that most painful operation, watching one's most cherished chicks hatched by unwearied perseverance coolly trodden underfoot. Now my honest desire is to appear commonplace and sensible, so that none of my dear kind family will think it necessary to remark to themselves or to me that I am otherwise than ordinary; to be on the right side of ordinary is the perfection of prudence in a young woman ...

Beatrice Webb, 1882

26 November

Strange, this is the date of my birthday. It was tolerably fine this morning & I started at 11. The sun broke out in Hatton garden & I took that for good luck & come along with a better heart, carrying my bundle, & a bag with all my working things in. And I thought, 'O *come*, this sun looks *better*, & I *do* hope this is my last move, for I am tired o' going to fresh places.' So about 20 minutes past 11 this morning I enter'd Massa's service, as his own real servant & maid of all work, & come to live in his kitchen, after eighteen years o' loving him and serving him in other folk's kitchens ...

Hannah Cullwick, 1871

When I get married I wonder if I'll love my husband as much as mama loves my father? God willing. Mama lives only for him and thinks of nothing else. When he's at home the two spend the whole day in endless conversation. When papa's in Boa Vista during the week, mama gets up singing wistful love songs and we can see she misses him, and she passes the time going over his clothes, collecting the eggs, and fattening the chickens for dinner on Saturday and Sunday. We eat best on those days.

Helena Morley (aged 13), 1893

I do Christmas lists in the morning. I hate Christmas. It was not meant to be like this but simple and unmaterialistic. And I have not the guts to cut it out. I do less and less each year, but still I do not break the habit completely.

Anne Morrow Lindbergh, 1943

27 November

Had a marvellous morning hunting for holly with D. [Lloyd George] in the woods behind Old Barn [her house in Surrey]. It was a divinely beautiful day, the little mauve clouds in a sunny blue sky reminding one of early spring rather than late November. But the woods were autumnal, the larches dropping gold from their boughs, the birches looking more ethereal than ever in their slender bareness, the hollies almost vulgar in their wealth of red berries. D. knew exactly where to seek for the holly treasure: he seemed to have marked down at some time or other every holly tree on the estate, & made for them unerringly … I think these rambles through the woods for a definite treasure take him back to his childhood: in fact, he is the boy D. again, with all the eagerness and enjoyment of boyhood.

Frances Stevenson, 1934

Universal deep snow. Such weather never remembered by the oldest person.

Lady Eleanor Butler, 1807

… I am sorry I have not seen Mrs Besant [activist Annie Besant] again. We met and [I] felt interested in that powerful woman, with her blighted wifehood and motherhood and her thirst for power and defiance of the world. I heard her speak, the only woman I have ever known who is a real orator, who has the gift of public persuasion. But to see her speaking made me shudder. It is not womanly to thrust yourself before the world. A woman, in all the relations of life, should be sought. It is only on great occasions, when religious feeling or morality demand it, that a woman has a right to lift up her voice and call aloud to her fellow-mortals ...

Beatrice Webb, 1887

I have given my Piozzi some hopes – dear, generous, prudent, noble-minded creature; he will hardly permit himself to believe it ever can be ... For rectitude of mind and native dignity of soul I never saw his fellow.

Hester Lynch Thrale Piozzi, 1782

Lunched at the Golden Egg. Oh, the horror – the cold stuffiness, claustrophobic placing of tables, garish lights and mass produced food in steel dishes. And the egg-shaped menu! But perhaps one could get something out of it. The setting for a breaking-off, or some terrible news or an unwanted declaration of love.

Barbara Pym, 1964

28 November

Thanksgiving Day and much to be thankful for ...

Today was one of those glorious golden days when just to be alive is enough. There are green velvet patches of oats here and there, and the Spanish oak outside the picture window of the dining room is a blaze of red. On the hillsides the oaks are turning from red to russet – the sumac here and there more brilliant, but some of its leaves have fallen, for fall is advancing.

In the evening about twenty of us set to on Mary's delicious Thanksgiving dinner. And indeed, every one of us at the table, I am sure, was thinking of how much he had to be thankful for ...

There are just fifty-two days left until our time in this job is over. It seems like an eternity, and yet, only yesterday when it began.

Lady Bird Johnson, LBJ Ranch, 1968

Father's birthday. He would have been 96, 96 yes, today; and could have been 96, like other people one has known: but mercifully was not. His life would have entirely ended mine. What would have happened? No writing, no books; – inconceivable. I used to think of him and mother daily, but writing *The Lighthouse* laid them in my mind.

Virginia Woolf, 1928

Since I last wrote in this Journal, I have suffered much from physical weakness, accompanied with mental depression. The loss of the country has seemed very bitter to me, and my want of health and strength has prevented me from working much – still worse, has made me despair of ever working well again. I am getting better now by the help of tonics, and shall be better still if I could gather more bravery, resignation, and simplicity of striving. In the meantime my cup is full of blessings: my home is bright and warm with love and tenderness, and in more material vulgar matters we are very fortunate.

George Eliot, 1860

Last night before dinner I missed Ralph [her husband] for a while. For the thousandth time I wondered, 'Is he all right? Could he perhaps be feeling ill?' Usually after the first panic and wild wobbling on my base, my equilibrium has been restored. This time, however, I felt it was odd that he should be in the library at this cold evening hour. I ran upstairs and found him lying down. No, he was not all right. Going through the kitchen to look at the stove he had suddenly felt a constriction in the chest, like two bars. He took a pill and then another, but remained limp and drowsy, wanting no food and unable to face the company. I am in a spurious way so armoured against these set-backs that a dreadful unearthly calm settled down on me, partly to make me able to face his dread of my 'fussing'. But along with this grey *tristesse* was the awareness of a huge crater opening, black and menacing. Paralysed in mind and hardly able to talk, I went downstairs and cooked dinner and somehow sketched a part in the conversation until the meal was over, when I was able to go up and lie beside Ralph.

This morning he swears he is better, but is in no great hurry to get up. We must 'greet the unknown' with all possible common-sense, but I am full of doubts which I cannot voice to him.

Frances Partridge, 1960

29 November

Nancy Astor elected the first woman MP. I am beginning to understand why she has so few friends. I used to think it was jealousy, but I know now that it was true when they told me she was treacherous & not to be trusted. In spite of her repeated protestations of friendship & goodwill to me, I find that she takes every opportunity of saying spiteful things about D. [Lloyd George] & myself. It is almost incredible, but it is true. Anyhow, she will get her reward in the House of Commons! I do not think any wise woman would choose to sit in the House!

Frances Stevenson, 1919

It is long since I recorded aught in these pages, which were intended to have been devoted to the spiritual state of my mind; to mark from time to time the progress I made in holiness; and to be a warning to me lest I, like Lot's wife, should look back again …

Oh never, never let me rest, my God, when my heart wanders from Thee. Draw me perpetually as hitherto. Warn me, counsel me, afflict me, so Thou but secure me! And if ever I am again mistress of a family, let nothing hinder my taking many opportunities each day to pray with them, to read to them in the Bible, and to teach them of Heaven as God shall give me utterance. Let not the dread of being scoffed at by my husband for pretending to sanctity, any more have influence with me.

Ellen Weeton, 1818

I wish sometimes I was a religious woman and could find comfort and faith in bombarding God with requests and demands … My next-door neighbour has every religious service on at all hours, and finds comfort in it. I wish I could do so – I would only find irritation at the loud noise. She says she prays to God to strike Hitler dead. Cannot help thinking if God wanted to do that he would not have waited till Mrs Helm asked him to do so.

Nella Last, 1939

My birthday, thirty-six. Spent alone, writing hard. No presents but Father's 'Tablets'.

I never seem to have many presents, as some do, though I give a good many. That is best perhaps, and makes a gift very precious when it does come.

Louisa May Alcott, 1868

30 November

Sophia will live and do well; I have saved my Daughter sure enough, perhaps obtained a Friend: they are weary of seeing me suffer so, and the eldest beg'd me Yesterday not to sacrifice my Life to her Convenience; She now saw my Love of Piozzi was incurable. She says, Absence had no Effect on it, and my Health was going so fast She found, that I should soon be useless either to her or to him. – It was the hand of God & irresistible She added, & begged me not to endure any longer such unnecessary Misery. –

So now we may be happy if we will, and now I trust some other cross Accident will [not] start up to torment us; I wrote my Lover word that he might come & fetch me, but the Alps are covered with Snow, & if his Prudence is not greater than his Affection – *my* Life will yet be lost, for it depends on his Safety: Should he come at my Call, & meet with any Misfortune of the Road – Death with accumulated agonies would end me – May Heaven avert such insupportable Distress!

Hester Lynch Thrale Piozzi, 1783

Went out with Mr Peachman a coursing with our Dogs and brought home a fine young Hare. No Person has call'd on us since the 13th and nothing has happen'd worth mentioning since the 16th. I have spent the latter end of this Month in walking, reading the History of England and making Shirts for Uncle.

Nancy Woodforde, 1792

... last night was much worse than my fears. I dropped into exhausted sleep, but soon awoke and listened to [her husband] Ralph's struggling breathing for four hours, while the clock snailed round its course. But why describe such agony? We are both alive this morning – that's all I can say ...

Ralph does seem a little better this evening and with more appetite for his supper. He has even read more. I went downstairs while he was eating, and listened to Berlioz's *Symphonie Fantastique* on the wireless without much pleasure. I left Ralph a walking-stick to bang on the floor if he wanted me – but I never expected to hear, nor shall I ever forget that dreadful 'thump, thump, thump' ...

Frances Partridge, 1960

I realize over and over again that my journal writing is like a witness to the moments I've lived. When I read what I've noted, thought about, the words come as a surprise, something I would have forgotten, and often don't even remember thinking. So to read them I recapture them. Being present is the necessity of recording consciousness. I think of each moment as gone, and they are like little deaths, millions of little deaths before physical death. Writing is the witness to myself about myself. Whatever others say of me or how they interpret me is a simulacrum of their own devising.

Amy Tan, 2008

December

---

1 December

———

Now I am *absolutely alone and for ever.*

Frances Partridge, 1960

Roland's [her fiancé's] letters put me into the seventh heaven at once. For the later one, written on the 27th, said that he pretty definitely expected to get leave on Dec. 31st. 30 days! – if he doesn't 'get hit by something in the meanwhile' – O merciful God! And I *may* get leave too – but even if I don't I shall see something of him, & even to see him for an hour – They were such sweet letters, too. He wants to see me in the blue & white pyjamas I told him I was sitting by the fire in, and recalls a day in the drawing room at Buxton, the first time he came, when I had been washing my hair, and afterwards played Edward's accompaniment in my dressing-gown, with my hair hanging down my back.

Vera Brittain, 1915

That is exactly it: marriage is to me another word for suicide. I cannot bring myself to face an act of *felo de se* for a speculation in personal happiness. I am not prepared to make the minutest sacrifice of efficiency for the simple reason that though I am susceptible to the charm of being loved I am not capable of loving. Personal passion has burnt itself out, and what little personal feeling still exists haunts the memory of that other man ...

In the meantime poor Sidney Webb writes me despairing letters from his sick-room, letters which pain me deeply with their strong emotions. I am surrounded by men, am constantly meeting others to whom I am more or less attractive, partly no doubt because I am the first cultivated woman with whom they have been frankly intimate. I have that fatal gift of intimacy and as yet in spite of middle age (!) it is united to personal attraction. All this is egotistical, but what of that, it is true, and becoming moreover an uncommonly awkward factor in my life. It is hateful to feel the ground rotten beneath you, to be ignorant of the *real nature* of your influence. 'Some women mistake the power of beauty for the result of capacity,' said Mr Haldane significantly. Are all women 'nailed to their sex'?

Beatrice Webb, 1890

Tomorrow Mama will be 69. Or is it 70? I've sent flowers. I used to fear she'd die before me, and I thought I couldn't bear it. Now I realize I can bear her passing because, dying, she would still be part of the soul within me. There is also a feeling I would be freed in some way. To be more myself. But what I try to remember is that the struggle to be free must mean becoming free among others, not *over* others: the dead, the weak, the forgotten.

Alice Walker, 1981

Sang through the Mahler songs all morning. I'm beginning to like some of them. It's pretty dour stuff ...

Alma Schindler (Mahler-Werfel), 1901

2 December

This afternoon: Mahler.

He told me he loved me – we kissed each other. He played me his pieces – my lips are sealed ... His caresses are tender and agreeable. If only I knew! He or – the other.

I must gradually get Alex [composer Alexander von Zemlinsky] off my mind. I'm terribly sorry. If it weren't for all that, I would have got engaged today. But I couldn't respond to his caresses. Someone was standing between us ... I told him so – without mentioning names. I had to tell him ... If only he had come three years earlier! An unsullied mouth!

Alma Schindler (Mahler-Werfel), 1901

Tiredness and dejection give way if one day off is taken instantly. I went in and did my cushion. In the evening my pain in my head calmed. Ideas came back this is a hint to be remembered. Always turn the pillow.

Virginia Woolf, 1939

We called at Pearce's Hotel on the Begum of Oude, who is leaving England (where her husband is ambassador), on a pilgrimage to Mecca. Her bright little Hindustani maid told us she was 'gone down cappin's'; so to Captain Clavel's we followed her and spent a most amusing half-hour in her society. She was seated in great state in the midst of the family circle, talking English with great self-possession despite her charming blunders. Her dress was an immense pair of trousers of striped Indian silk, a Cashmere shawl laid over her head, over a close covering of blue and yellow silk, two pairs of remarkable slippers, numbers of anklets and leglets, a great deal of jewellery, and a large blue cloak over all. She was very conversable, wrote her name and title in English and Arabic in my book, and offered to make an egg curry.

Caroline Fox, Falmouth, 1836

My dearest Albert did not dress, but lay on his sofa ... Sir James [Clark, the doctor] came over and found him in much the same state ... sometimes lying on his sofa in his dressing gown, and then sitting in an armchair in his sitting room ... he kept saying, it was very well he had no fever, as he should not recover! – which we all told him was foolish and he must never speak of it. He took some soup with brown bread in it which unfortunately disagreed with him.

Queen Victoria, 1861

3 December

Doctor Williams called and made me undergo a *blushing* operation. He finds me much about the same and I had to rub my side with Mercury which was very nasty work. I took an immense dose of Calomal.

Harriet Wynne, 1803

I dined with the Sangers last night, & enjoyed society. I wore my new black dress, & looked, I daresay, rather nice. That's a feeling I very seldom have; & I rather intend to enjoy it oftener. I like clothes, if I can design them.

Virginia Woolf, 1921

At Kew station there was a young woman, freckled and damp curls, whom I asked if there was a lady's waiting room. She called me dear, and came a step after me to add I would not have to pay anything. It is a great shame of railways to charge, but it made me wonder if I was wanting new clothes …

Beatrix Potter, 1896

… At the age of seven & twenty in the busy metropolis of native England I find myself alone – deserted by the few I knew – disdained – insulted … Wherefore should it be so? Ever ready – too ready – to undervalue myself, I might attribute this to the defects of my character – did not other circumstances disclose the truth – it is because I am a woman – a poor & unprotected – did there exist in men's breasts a spark of that chivalrous spirit which in our youth we are taught to believe is not utterly extinct – methinks many circumstances should awaken interest – It is not so – with masculine insensibility they are willing to wound the wounded & disdain one fallen on evil days – Most women I believe wish that they had been me – so do not I – change my sex & I do not think my talents would be greater – & I should be like one of these …

Mary Shelley, 1824

I'm on the horns of a *terrible* dilemma. I keep repeating the words 'my beloved' and follow them with 'Alex'. *Can* I really love Mahler as he deserves and as I really am able? Shall I ever understand his art, & he mine? With Alex the sympathy is mutual. He loves every *note* of me. Mahler just said:

This is really serious. This I didn't expect!

How shall I break it to Alex? – I'm on first-name terms with Mahler now. He told me how much he loved me and I could give him no reply.

Do I really love him? – I have no idea. Sometimes I actually think not. So much irritates me:

his smell,

the way he sings,

the way he speaks [can't roll his rrrr's] …

One question *plagues* me: whether Mahler will inspire me to compose – whether he will support my artistic striving – whether he will love me like Alex: because *he* loves me utterly.

Alma Schindler (Mahler-Werfel), 1901

4 December

All day a storm has been raging as bad as any we had during that dreadful winter two years ago. We are drifted completely up. It is bitterly cold, too. Of course there was no mail and I am lonely. Oh, are we going to have another awful winter? My soul cringes at the thought. Altogether I'm disgruntled. The only thing I had to pass the time away today – for I couldn't write amid so many discomforts and worries – was fancy work. What a solace that is to a woman!!!!

L. M. Montgomery, PEI, 1906

Rowena rings to say, in a dead sort of voice, 'The worst has happened, Billy Bolitho says I'm definitely pregnant. Can you lend me fifteen quid till Saturday?' I said I could give her six, which was all I had, because I know just how she feels, and if she doesn't have the abortion before

Saturday it will be too late. I met her in Dean Street and we wandered down to Durand's in the icy cold for a *delicious* lunch. Christ, their pastries are good! Poor Rowena couldn't eat anything.

She says that her only other chance is to put lots of ether soap up her bottom for ten days. Billy Bolitho says it's tough but infallible, but R. says, 'How will I keep it from my Mum if I go around smelling like an operating theatre?'

Joan Wyndham (aged 19), 1940

I hardly ever begin to write here that I am not tempted to break out into Jobisms about my bad nights. How I keep on my legs and in my senses with such little snatches of sleep is a wonder to myself. Or, to cure anyone of a terror of annihilation, just put him on my allowance of sleep, and see if he don't get to long for sleep, sleep, unfathomable and everlasting sleep as the only conceivable heaven.

Jane Carlyle, 1855

5 December

Today the Begum [of Oude] began almost at once on theology, asking mamma if 'she was a religieuse,' and then began to expound her own creed. She took the Koran and read some passages, then an English psalm containing similar sentiments, then she chanted a Mahometan collect beautifully in Arabic and Hindustani. She made mamma write all our names that she might send us a letter ... She was coming to visit us today, but had to embark instead, after expressing her hopes that we should meet again in Oude!

Caroline Fox, 1836,

God has something for me to do for Him – or He would have let me die some time ago ... Oh for some great thing to sweep this loathsome life into the past.

Florence Nightingale, 1845

My thoughts are ever more frequently of him [Mahler]. His dear *sweet* smile. – This is the man I kissed. Or rather – he kissed me. Now I believe that I really love him. Alex weighs on me like lead. I long for him really badly now, have to think constantly of him, of his dear, sweet eyes. – If only I'd already broken it to him. It will be *dreadful*.

Alma Schindler (Mahler-Werfel), 1901

By two o'clock we had collected our kit from the hotel and were on the way to meet Kay. Then suddenly Rachel [her daughter] said, 'Stop! I hear a band!' (She has become passionately addicted to every form of Indian music.) Obeying, I too could hear gay, martial airs and then, in the near distance, we saw half a dozen drummers and pipers crossing the road at an intersection. They were following a palanquin clumsily decorated with plantain leaves, coconuts, papayas, bunches of bananas and branches of bougainvillaea, and behind them trailed a procession of a hundred or so shabbily dressed men and women. The palanquin was preceded by a boy of about twelve, carrying a smouldering length of sandalwood, so I knew that despite the gay music a corpse was on its way to the burning ghats. When I had explained the situation Rachel exclaimed, 'Let's follow and see what happens!' Which we did – this being a traveller's attitude of which I thoroughly approve – though the procession led us away from the hospital.

Rachel seemed a little disappointed by her first corpse. 'He doesn't *look* very dead,' she observed. Nor did he, poor chap, as he sat cross-legged amidst the bougainvillaea, wearing a grey woollen turban, red *lunghi* and brown sports jacket …

Dervla Murphy, 1973

6 December

This morning it's beautiful out. Beginning the day's fast for Ramadan, the girls in the dorm tell each other funny stories. We've lit the incense we all bought together and we watch it burn. We tell each other we can soon go home and ask our mothers to make us noodles and rolls, so that we don't go around starving all the time.

When I hear a comrade say this, I feel really bad. It reminds me that I didn't come in first in class. How will I be able to face going home and eating the meals Mother prepares?

But I have confidence in myself. At the end-of-term exams, if I don't come in first, I must at least come in second.

Ma Yan, 2000

... Within moments the Appayyas had made us feel like dear friends instead of total strangers, and before sitting down to a superbly cooked lunch I had my first bath for a week and massacred the numerous fleas which had been my constant companions since that night we spent in Kushalnagar's Hilton. So this afternoon all is right with my world.

Dervla Murphy (South Coorg), 1973

... Miss Juliet was a specimen of a Southern lady. She could not travel alone; she was pale and looked dissipated ... She was a horrid animal. She told me her mother was married at thirteen and her sister at fifteen and says it is the custom in the Slave States. So Mrs P. said; she herself was married at fifteen and her husband's first wife was fifteen. Miss Juliet could not walk a mile, says few South state American women can; so say all the ladies here in the boat. Slavery makes all labour dishonourable and walking gets to be thought a labour, an exertion.

Barbara Leigh Smith Bodichon (on a Mississippi steamer), 1857

He [Mahler] loves me no more – I'm unhappy. Today I shall go to him and won't find him in. I'd like to weep on his breast …

Alma Schindler (Mahler-Werfel), 1901

7 December

Gustav [Mahler] was here. –

We kissed each other over and over again. In his embrace I feel so warm. If only he still loved me as much – but I consider him fickle, dreadfully fickle. He tried to convert me, in many senses.

I shan't be seeing him for nineteen days. On Monday he's going to Berlin. I don't know what else to write, but my feelings are *for him* and *against* Alex]. Never before have I watched the clock as avidly as today. I couldn't work for sheer longing …

More than ever, a huge question mark hangs over my future. Everything is up to him. Today he confessed everything to me, all his sins – I even confessed some of mine.

He guessed Alex's name & was *appalled – couldn't* understand it.

Enough now – for both of us – and no concern for the mysteries of 'tomorrow'. Today *is real* at least, and is *beautiful,* yes – beautiful.

Alma Schindler (Mahler-Werfel), 1901

Now, we are – without a King? With a Queen? What? The Simpson affair is on the surface. It was on Wednesday 2 December that the Bishop commented on the King's lack of religion. On Thursday all the papers, *The Times* and *Daily Telegraph* very discreetly mentioned some domestic difficulties; others Mrs Simpson. All London was gay and garrulous – not exactly gay, but excited. We can't have a woman Simpson for Queen that was the sense of it. She's no more royal than you or me, was what the grocer's young woman said. But today we have developed a strong sense of human sympathy: we are saying Hang it all – the age of Victoria is over. Let him marry whom he likes. Harold [Nicolson] is glum as an undertaker, and so are the other nobs. They say Royalty is in Peril.

The Empire is divided. In fact never has there been such a crisis. Spain, Germany, Russia – all are elbowed out. Parties are forming. The different interests are queuing up behind Baldwin or Churchill. Mosley is taking advantage of the crisis for his ends. In fact we are all talking nineteen to the dozen; and it looks as if this one insignificant little man had moved a pebble which dislodges an avalanche. Things – empires, hierarchies, moralities – will never be the same again.

Virginia Woolf, 1936

Deep unbearable despair all day. I didn't sleep all night and wept all morning. My daughter-in-law Sonya came, Ilya [her son] arrived for dinner, and things became slightly more cheerful …

Sophia Tolstoy, 1910

8 December

G. [George Henry Lewes] had a bad headache, so we walked out in the morning sunshine. I told him my conception of my story [*Romola*], and he expressed great delight. Shall I ever be able to carry out my ideas? Flashes of hope are succeeded by long intervals of dim distrust …

George Eliot, 1861

… It's truly amazing how friendly I'm becoming with Mama [her stepmother] Was I bewitched before, I wonder? Did her attitude towards Maurice [her fiancé] divide us as much as all that? I keep asking myself how it's possible that there was so little mutual understanding, so little harmony between us. Even her temper outbursts don't affect me any more; I know they are short-lived and I know she is genuinely fond of me; therefore nothing she says hurts me.

She must be as pleased as I am about this improvement in our relationship. Without wishing to boast, I suspect she is quite bowled over by my cheerfulness, my good humour, and that whole side of my nature she knew nothing about; she is discovering that we have a great deal in common. I'm a revelation to her – I see in her eyes, in her whole attitude. And she is beginning to like Maurice; she enjoys chatting with him, thinks he is such a serious, well-informed young man, and so witty too!

In short, it's heaven!

Henriette Dessaulles (aged 19), 1880

He [Prince Albert] wanders for moments a little, seldom smiles and is still very impatient ... so impatient because I tried to help in explaining something to Dr Jenner and quite slapped my hand, poor dear darling ... Went in again to see my dearest Albert. He was so pleased to see me – stroked my face and smiled and called me his *Frauchen* ... He was so dear and kind. Precious love!

Queen Victoria, 1861

9 December

He [Prince Albert] wanders frequently and they say it is of no consequence tho' very distressing, for it is unlike my own Angel. He was so kind calling me *gutes Weibchen* ('excellent little wife'), and liking me to hold his dear hand. Oh! It is an anxious, anxious, time but God will help us thro' it.

Queen Victoria, 1861

Lately Hugh [her husband] and I have had three differences between us. Oh, they are little enough in themselves, but I don't understand why there should be *any*. I am struggling to discover if it is my fault ... If we are to be happy, or at least if he is to be happy, I must never *go against* Hugh, I must not *contradict* him, I must never *argue* with him.

Anaïs Nin, 1925

I simply can't work – walk around the room, go over to his [Mahler's] picture, reread his last letter – I love him!

At midday he sent me a big box of pralines and this dear, sweet letter. I believe I shall become a better person, he purifies me. My *desire* for him is unbroken.

This afternoon: Muhr [yet another suitor]. We made a lot of music together. Finally he again asked how things stood with me. I had no choice but to tell him the truth, no matter how hard it was. He stood before me, pale and trembling:

Fraulein, if you turn me down, I shall kill myself.

I felt so sorry for him. I do like him very much – as a friend – and am convinced that I wouldn't be doing badly if I accepted him. But some things lie beyond our power …

Alma Schindler (Mahler-Werfel), 1901

10 December

G. B. S. [George Bernard Shaw] and Charlotte staying here … As I watched the handsome 'Ancient' talking and laughing … I realised that I should miss him more than anyone else in our intimate circle: he is the most closely associated with our long married life, most continuously our friend. And Charlotte is a fit mate. Enthroned in the world's esteem and enrobed in wealth, they smile at each other and gaze with an amused good nature on the rest of the world. It is a pleasant sight to look on! 'We never think or talk of old age, we try to forget we are old,' said Charlotte; and G. B. S. acquiesced.

Beatrice Webb, 1929

We had a party of Jack, Maran, Hilda & Bob Maxwell & Fanny Moysey, Leo Scarlett & Gennadius the Greek *chargé d'affaires*, & all went to a great ball given by the Rosslyns in honour of Miss Maynard's coming out. The most interesting part of it to me is this – that after a period of 3 years & 6 months I once more enjoyed a time which obliged me to talk, to dance, to sit up late, & to exert myself. Another interesting fact I have laid to heart is that it is possible to have a daughter of 18 & yet to look very nice (see Lady Rosslyn), though I fear this is only to be done by a *Countess* with *fair hair*.

Mary, Lady Monkswell, 1879

… Great avalanches of snow. Windsor is, or was, yesterday immobilized: we were snowed in for much of the day. Now it's a blue wild snow-glaring world, with mist rising from the river, really quite beautiful. How lovely this world is, really: one simply has to look.

Joyce Carol Oates, 1977

11 December

Edward VIII has just abdicated. He gave up his crown for love of a woman. He didn't give in: that is royal. He's left everything for the one he loves; a marvellous and courageous lover. This story is like my own writ large. I was younger than Mrs Simpson on my marriage to Georges Ghika who was many years younger than I, but who was very serious, fundamentally very serious and didn't often laugh.

Liane de Pougy, 1936

Oh dear! I wish this Grange business were well over. It occupies me (the mere preparation for it) to the exclusion of all quiet thought and placid occupation. To have to care more for my dress at this time of day more than I ever did when young and pretty and happy (God bless me, to think that I was once all that!) on penalty of being regarded as a blot on the Grange gold and azure, is really too bad. Ach Gott! if we had been left in the sphere of life we belong to, how much better it would have been for us in many ways!

Jane Carlyle, 1855

... Ilya Vasilevich [the valet] and I tidied up [her husband] Lev Nikolaevich's things to save them from moths and depredation. It was terribly painful – life in general is torture. I wrote to Tanya and E. Fyod. Yunge. I went to sleep in the afternoon to the sounds of a terrible gale. Loneliness, remorse, despair!

Sophia Tolstoy, 1910

The difficulty about all this dying is that you can't tell a fellow anything about it, so where does the fun come in?

Alice James, 1891

12 December

———

... I have almost ever since I have been a little under the influence of religion, thought marriage at this time was not a good thing for me, as it might lead my interests and affections from that Source in which they should be centred, and also, if I have any active duties to perform in the church, if I really follow, so far as I am able, the voice of Truth in my heart, are they not rather incompatible with the duties of a wife and a mother? And is it not safest to wait and see what is the probable course I shall take in this life, before I enter into any engagement that affects my future career? So I think, and so I have thought. But to look on the other side. If truth appears to tell me I may marry, I should leave the rest, and hope whatever my duties are, I shall be able to perform them ...

Elizabeth Fry (aged 19), 1799

Emily Carr, born Dec.13, 1871, at Victoria B.C., 4 a.m., in a deep snow storm, tomorrow will be sixty-two. It is not all bad, this getting old, ripening. After the fruit has got its growth it should juice up and mellow. God forbid I should live long enough to ferment and rot and fall to the ground in a squash ...

Emily Carr, 1933

Mr Clerkson the Chaplin was here by Nine o'Clock and celebrated the Catholick Marriage Ceremony before breakfast in the School room, the Miss Pouletts came in time for it. Harriet looked modest for the first time in her Life, in a long french lace Veil and behaved very well ...

Betsey Wynne Fremantle, 1807

Today is my family Christmas day. Decided to have it early, when everyone can make it. The deal is that Miri [her aunt] pays for it, I put it on, and the rest of the family turn up ...

The family Christmas day is fab, a really nice atmosphere, everyone having a good time. As [her friends] John and Quin are leaving, they say, 'You've got a great family, lots of interesting people, there's never anyone you don't want to speak to.'

It makes me realise something for the first time: I've got a great family. A *fantastic* family. The only person missing is Dad. I spoke to him yesterday. Better warn him he's started a new life in Australia [in a newspaper report]. This reminds me, returning briefly to the fiction factory, that a journalist rang me to say they've got hold of the old rumour in circulation that I had an affair with Jack Straw ...

... I've got to stick to the important stuff and remember that today's newspapers are tomorrow's chip paper.

Oona King, 2004

13 December

I do not mourn at old age. Life has been good and I have got a lot out of it, lots to remember and relive. I have liked life, perhaps the end more than the beginning. I was a happy-natured little girl but with a tragic streak, very vulnerable to hurt. I developed very late. Looking back is interesting. I can remember the exact spot and the exact time that so many things dawned on me. Particularly is this so in regard to my work ...

Emily Carr, 1940

Found him [Prince Albert] very quiet and comfortably warm, and so dear and kind, called me *gutes Frauchen* and kissed me so affectionately and so completely like himself, and I held his dear hands between mine … They gave him brandy every half-hour.

Queen Victoria, 1861

Then we had the Broadcast. 'Prince Edward speaking from Windsor Castle' as the emotional butler announced. Upon which, with slight stammer at first, in a steely strained voice, [he] began: 'At long last … I can speak to you … The woman I love … I who have none of these blessings …' Well, one came in touch with human flesh I suppose. Also with a set pigheaded steely mind … a very ordinary young man: but the thing had never been done on that scale …

Virginia Woolf, 1936

14 December

This evening we had a Bill from poor Sam's [their son's] Tutor in which he tells us he has a dangerous cut in one of his Fingers which makes them fear a Gangrene, which God of his mercy prevent. He is at a great distance from us and all his relations, but Oh, my dear Lord, do thou supply all our love and care in taking him into thy special protection … I give him up into thy hands, do with him as thou seest best, and give us all patience to bear whatever thou layest on us.

Mary Woodforde, 1688

Went over at 7 as I usually did. It was a bright morning; the sun just rising and shining brightly … Never can I forget how beautiful my darling looked lying there with his face lit up by the rising sun, his eyes unusually bright gazing as it were on unseen objects and not taking notice of me … Sir James was very hopeful, so was Dr Jenner, and said it was a 'decided rally', but that they were all 'very, very, anxious' … I asked if I might go out for a breath of fresh air. The doctors answered 'Yes, just close by, for half an hour!' ... I went out on the Terrace with Alice. The military band was playing at a distance and I burst out crying and came home again ... Sir James was very hopeful; he had seen much worse cases. But the breathing was the alarming thing – so rapid, I think 60 respirations in a minute ... I bent over him and said to him *Es ist Kleines Frauchen* ('it is your little wife') and he bowed his head; I asked if he would give me *ein Kuss* ('a kiss') and he did so. He seemed half dozing, quite quiet ... I left the room for a moment and sat down on the floor in utter despair. Attempts at consolation from others only made me worse ... Alice told me to come in ... and I took his dear hand which was already cold, though the breathing was quite gentle and I knelt down by him ... Alice was on the other side, Bertie and Lenchen ... kneeling at the foot of the bed ... Two or three long but perfectly gentle breaths were drawn, the hand clasping mine and ... all, all, was over ... I stood up, kissed his dear heavenly forehead and called out in a bitter and agonising cry, 'Oh! My dear Darling!'

Queen Victoria, 1861

Lovely and very mild. This day 2 years ago the Prince Consort died. A *Times* leading article takes the opportunity to give the poor Queen another of its numerous lectures about coming out again, as if two years of the most piteous and terrible of all widowhoods was too much to allow for mourning! At the same time it is only fair to say that the tone was loyal and loving, and full of respect for the Prince's memory.

I feel in something of a dream.

Lucy (Lady Frederick) Cavendish, 1863

15 December

Well, it is of no use to go on always struggling with weakness and incapability of exertion, I cannot hold out forever; and now I begin to feel thoroughly ill. I am afraid I must relax.

Emily Shore (aged 17), 1837

When I had gone to bed I realised what it was that had caused me to 'give way'. It was the effort of being up, with a heart that won't work. Not my lungs at all. My despair simply disappeared – yes, simply. The weather was lovely. Every morning the sun came in and drew more squares of golden light on the wall, I looked round my bed on to a sky like silk. The day opened slowly, slowly like a flower, and it held the sun long, long before it slowly folded. Then my homesickness went. I not only didn't want to be in England, I began to love Italy, and the thought of it – the sun – even when it was too hot – always the sun – and a kind of *wholeness* which was good to bask in.

All these two years I have been obsessed by the fear of death. This grew and grew and grew gigantic, and this it was that made me cling so, I think. Ten days ago it went, I care no more. It leaves me perfectly cold ... Life either stays or goes ...

... It might comfort others to know that one gives up caring; but they'd not believe any more than I did until it happened. And, oh, how strong was its hold upon me! How I *adored* life and *dreaded* death!

I'd like to write my books and spend some happy time with J. [her husband John Middleton Murry] (not very much faith withal) and see L. in a sunny place and pick violets – all kinds of flowers. I'd like to do heaps of things, really. But I don't mind if I do not do them ... Honesty (why?) is the only thing one seems to prize beyond life, love, death, everything. It alone remaineth. O ye who come after me, will you believe it? At the end *truth* is the only thing *worth having*: it's more thrilling than love, more joyful and more passionate. It simply can*not* fail. All else fails. I, at any rate, give the remainder of my life to it and it alone.

Katherine Mansfield, 1919

The Christmas silly season is on. Off to ITV to record a snippet on the 'twelve Lords a-leaping' of the famous seasonal song. My task was to show Peter Hayes [political correspondent] about the difficulties that would be involved in teaching twelve members of the Upper House to 'leap'. I'm not sure if he actually intends to try this ... I suggested that the simplest way to make them all leap was to publish a white paper on the abolition of the Upper House. That would start them jumping.

Deborah Bull, 1997

I receive a Christmas card, sent to the office, from David and Samantha Cameron. This has never happened before, so conclude it must be because I have cancer. In reality it simply means I've somehow got onto a Downing Street press officer's list somewhere, yet I can't help but feel touched.

Victoria Derbyshire, 2015

16 December

Haemorrhage returned, showing the operation was not wholly successful …

Man, it seems to me, has no case against death; if he has been thwarted in the past and is suffering pain in the present, death comes to him as a deliverer from all his woes. If he is among the fortunate ones as we have been, then he must accept the last phase, which need not be distressful if he wills to end it …

Beatrice Webb, 1933

This morning: first to the dentist, then lessons at Frau Radnitzky's. I am learning the 'Emperor' Concerto now. When I play Beethoven, I always feel as if my soul were at the dry cleaners, and that the ugly black stains caused by the impurities and nervous traumas of Wagner were being removed.

Alma Schindler (Mahler-Werfel), 1899

I am now on the eve of doing something which will materially affect my future situation. In the morning, I set off for Leigh, for I must either bestir myself, or starve. I have waited 3 full weeks for a remittance; my brother has kindly lent me £5, but I must not live on credit. If great exertions are necessary, I have great exertions in contemplation.

Oh, my Father, let me go forth in Thy strength. Work for me by what means soever Thou seest best. Desert me not in this hour of great trial. Be my Guide and my Counsellor. Give me the wisdom of the dove; and oh, have pity on me, and more particularly for the 3 ensuing days, in which I have much to do. Deal gently with Thy servant; let not the anguish of mind which I must expect to endure, 'Oh! Let it not quite overwhelm me. Give me much strength.

Ellen Weeton, 1818

17 December

These people are very kind and pleasant, if only they wd. not (some of them) talk of the blacks with the true old slaveholder sort of contempt: whether justified or not by facts, it comes with the worst sort of grace from any English people, whose forefathers have most of the evils to answer for, having held the poor creatures enslaved, and forbidden their education.

Lucy (Lady Frederick) Cavendish, Jamaica, 1871

At p. 22 only. I am extremely spiritless, dead, and hopeless about my writing. The long state of headaches has left me in depression and incapacity. The constantly heavy-clouded, and often wet, weather tends to increase the depression. I am inwardly irritable, and unvisited by good thoughts. Reading the *Purgatorio* again, and the *Compendium Revelationum* of Savonarola. After this record, I read aloud what I had written of Part IX to George [Henry Lewes], and he, to my surprise, entirely approved of it.

George Eliot, 1862

I cannot write about these last seventeen days [since the death of her husband Ralph] – not *now*, anyway. Nor can I see that I shall ever want to remember them. It's been all I could do to live them.

What has surprised me is that just because the blow has been so mortal, as if roughly, savagely cutting me in half and leaving me with one leg and one arm only, I am with what seems to me total illogicality under this menace struggling frantically to survive. Kitty West wrote to me that Ralph had once said that if I died 'he would not go on' and I know that's true. How much more rational and logical that seems. What earthly sense in this pitiful frantic struggle? The life-instinct must be much stronger than I knew.

My instant awareness of loss was total, final and complete. He was gone, and nothing that remained had any significance for me. Yet I feel it's impossible I can be really aware of what lies ahead and still want to live. Ergo, I'm not really aware of it; I have buried and suffocated some part of it, and one day I shall wake and find I've been falsely bearing the unbearable, and either kill myself or go mad.

Another discovery I have made: compared to the torture of being on the rack, the deadly fear of losing everything – *having* lost it, utter desolation is a state of calm. I have nothing to lose, I care about nothing. I may be stumbling on, blindly pushed by some extraordinary incomprehensible instinct, but I *don't care* at all. *There's nothing now that matters.*

Frances Partridge, 1960

18 December

A day of delicious retirement. In the evening my beloved and I wrote and signed a Paper. Sealed it with Three Black Seals and deposited it in the upper flat Drawer of the Desk. There to remain till after our Decease when we trust the request contained in it will be accorded.

Lady Eleanor Butler, 1790

Begin with [former student] A. L. in Beacon Street … I seem to be an institution and a success since I can start the boy, teach one girl, and take care of the little invalid. It is hard work, but I can do it, and am glad to sit in a large, fine room part of each day, after my sky-parlor, which has nothing pretty in it, and only the gray tower and blue sky outside as I sit in the window writing. I love luxury, but freedom and independence better.

Louisa May Alcott, 1856

Mary and I talked a lot about John [her son] in the evening, and she was most darling. I gathered someone had been critical of me, and had said she couldn't imagine not concentrating on him if he were her child. I said if I believed him to be really curable, I would never leave him, but I had long really inwardly realised the hopelessness of the case and determined to keep the cruel sorrow within certain limits – not to allow it to blacken all of life for me, but to keep myself sane for Michael [her younger son] and the best way to do that was to fix one's thoughts as much as possible on the latter.

Lady Cynthia Asquith, 1917

We had a letter from Mr Brown which gives us great hopes my poor Sam's finger is in a good way of curing, which God of his mercy grant.

We heard also that the King was very well received at his return to the City, as was also the Prince of Orange [the deposed James II and William of Orange appeared briefly to be in accord]. O God send a happy end of all our fears, to his glory and our comfort.

Mary Woodforde, 1688

19 December

I should like this to be accepted as my confession.

There is no limit to human suffering. When one thinks: 'Now I have touched the bottom of the sea – now I can go no deeper,' one goes deeper. And so it is for ever …

I do not want to die without leaving a record of my belief that suffering can be overcome. For I do believe it. What must one do? There is no question of what is called 'passing beyond it.' That is false.

One must *submit*. Do not resist. Take it. Be overwhelmed. Accept it fully. Make it *part of life* …

Life is a mystery. The fearful pain will fade. I must turn to work. I must put my agony into something, change it. 'Sorrow shall be changed into joy.'

It is to lose oneself more utterly, to love more deeply, to feel oneself part of life, – not separate.

Oh Life! accept me – make me worthy – teach me.

I write that. I look up. The leaves move in the garden, the sky is pale, and I catch myself weeping. It is hard – it is hard to make a good death ...

Katherine Mansfield, 1920

The house was very full: the play was *The Wonder*. My dress was not finished till the very last moment – and then, oh horror! was so small that I could not get into it. It had to be pinned upon me; and thus bebundled, with the dread of cracking my bodice from top to bottom every time I moved, and the utter impossibility of drawing my breath, from the narrow dimensions into which it squeezed me, I went on to play a new part. The consequence was, that I acted infamously, and for the first time in my life was horribly imperfect – out myself, and putting everybody else out. Between every scene my unlucky gown had to be pinned together; and in the laughing scene, it took the hint from my admirable performance, and facetiously grinned in an ecstasy of amusement till it was fairly open behind, displaying, I suppose, the lacing of my stays, like so many teeth, to the admiring gaze of the audience ...

Fanny Kemble, 1832

After school the comrades go out to get their meal. I stay behind in class all alone and write. There are only a few days left until Ramadan is over, and I want to hold out until the end.

When I go back to the dorm, the comrades are busy eating. They discuss things while they chew. I sit down beside them and listen.

Ma Yan, 2000

20 December

Frost and snow. Ted [her husband] and I nearly lost our fingers pulling snow-frozen ivy off the trees to decorate our cottage. The car broke down, we had great difficulty collecting the Christmas trees from Jackson's farm and Ted got into quite a suicidal mood. But I said that it is always a good sign when things go wrong before the night.

Barbara Castle, 1969

As we walked back to the bazaar, in quest of more tea, Rachel [her daughter] noticed that the young temple elephant was having his make-up put on. Blue and gold circles were being painted on his ears and trunk, and white stripes on his forehead, and then (big thrill!) he was caparisoned in red, blue and gold tasselled brocade – his Sunday Best, as it were. Next a thick silken rope with heavy brass bells on both ends was thrown over his back, he was given a small piece of wood to hold in his trunk and off he went towards the main temple entrance. 'Let's follow him!' said Rachel, almost stuttering with excitement – though quarter of an hour earlier she had been complaining of acute dehydration. So we did.

… On arriving at the main temple entrance, where he was directly opposite the image of Sri Subrahmanya in its central sanctum, he slowly knelt – giving an uncanny impression of reverence – then raised his trunk and solemnly trumpeted three times in greeting to the god. Being a sacred elephant his touch is greatly valued and Laksmi-alone-knows what he earned in the next hour as he stood by the main entrance with his attendant squatting beside him. Many people presented him with food, which he delightedly popped into his mouth, but he had been trained to give his blessing only for cash. I handed him 10 paise, to find out what an elephantine blessing feels like, and it is quite a pleasant sensation to have that sensitive tip of trunk laid gently on one's head.

Dervla Murphy, 1973

... As I read over Mr Dall's Journal, I feel that I ought not to regret so bitterly his continued absence. I am amazed to see how little his family life satisfied him, & how the care he was obliged to take of the house & children in our days of poverty & suffering, wore on his health & spirits. ...

One remark amused me – *& pained*, pained because it showed how little he ever understood me.

One day, when I had been cooking all day in a hot kitchen to provide for a large meeting of the Association, he writes – 'I am amused to see how determined Carrie is, not to be excelled as a housekeeper by any one she knows.'

No such determination ever entered my head. I did my cooking, as from a child I had always done everything, – as well as I possibly could, and I positively did not know or care how others did theirs, unless the failure was outrageous.

Caroline Healey Dall, 1861

21 December

Mother cantankerous, Lena babbling, taps dripping.

Miles Franklin, 1933

This is the shortest day of the terrestrial year, but in my soul's calendar it has been the longest ...

It seems years instead of two months since Teacher [Anne Sullivan] left, and I have experienced a sense of dying daily.

Every hour I long for the thousand bright signals from her vital, beautiful hand. That was life! The hand that with a little word touched the darkness of my mind, and I awoke to happiness and love; a hand swift to answer every need, to disentangle skeins of dark silence for a fairer pattern; a hand radiant with the light it retrieved that I might see, sweet with the music it transmitted to my inner ear. After fifty years I continue to feel her dear, communicative hand's warmth and urge in mine as, I am told, one maimed feels the life in a lost limb. Look as I will, it is not there;

and this heavy day has ground over me, as a glacier over a field once joyously green. More life has vanished in the Christmases which centred about Teacher, the festivities she graced lighting all beauty's candles, the rare sparkle of her personality seeking out new ways to create delight …

Helen Keller, 1936

Monday 21st, being the shortest day. Mary walked to Ambleside for letters. It was a wearisome walk, for the snow lay deep upon the roads and it was beginning to thaw. I stayed at home and clapped the small linen. Wm. [her brother] sate beside me, and read *The Pedlar*. He was in good spirits, and full of hope of what he should do with it. He went to meet Mary [William's future wife], and they brought 4 letters – 2 from Coleridge, one from Sara, and one from France. Coleridge's were melancholy letters, he had been very ill in his bowels. We were made very unhappy. Wm. wrote to him, and directed the letter into Somersetshire. I finished it after tea. In the afternoon Mary and I ironed, afterwards she packed her clothes up, and I mended Wm.'s stockings while he was reading *The Pedlar*.

Dorothy Wordsworth, 1801

It is finished: except for Cabinet. Harold [Wilson] has had to go to Australia for a funeral, so George [Brown] is in charge and he has kept chopping and changing the time until I've nearly gone mad. Finally he fixed 3 p.m. with six items on the list, only two of them really urgent. I was furious: how was I to get ready for fifty guests as our party tomorrow night? Spent the morning on frantic Christmas food shopping and having my hair done; then sat chafing in Cabinet while they all talked and talked. Finally I slipped out and sloped off to Hells Corner Farm, leaving them to it. Men have no sense of priorities.

Barbara Castle, 1967

22 December

If Santa Claus were to descend the chimney, reindeer, pack and all, there could not be more running to and fro here this morning. Round me are flowing two streams of Christmas cablegrams, letters and packages, one out to the post office, the other in at the holly-wreathed front door.

Six of us have been stirring the plum pudding, and now it is boiling, bubbling, sending a jolly odor through the house ...

Helen Keller, 1936

Windy Day. Walked two Miles in the Garden. No Letters from our friends, which I much wonder at, I wish they would think of us oftener than they do.

Nancy Woodforde, 1792

23 December

I want flowers today more than anything because it is cold and they are expensive. I want a deep pile carpet so that when I breakfast in bed I feel like a lady out of *Vogue*, and hardly hear Mabel come in; and I want a chest-of-drawers for [her husband] A. 'I think probably my 'Double Méprise' illustrations are going to be published in France privately, thanks to Doris. A fir tree, even untrimmed, in a room, is like a presence. We have [her daughter] Sally's first party. I look at the year which is almost ended. Resolve: to avoid casual drawing. Resolve: to let A. be as he is. Resolve: to exercise self-control. Compared with 1925 I suppose I have looked on Worcester as my settled home. I adore Sally.

Ivy Jacquier, 1926

This morning I awoke positively sure I had seen Teacher [Anne Sullivan], and I have been happier all day. I dreamed she was driving with Polly and me ...

A caress – and she was gone; yet I was not troubled. Somehow I knew her presence had been a blessed presence, and I awoke with peace that had not nested in my heart for long months ...

It is a real pleasure to walk through the streets of Glasgow to-day while doing our Christmas shopping. The crowds were dense, but good-humoured. Almost everyone was carrying parcels and holly, and I felt that the Christmas Spirit truly reigned in the city as well as out in the quiet countryside. The assistants, too, though working early and late in packed shops, found time to be pleasant and full of good wishes for 'a Merry Christmas.' Happily I anticipate tomorrow, with the children free from desk work and the heartache it often brings.

Helen Keller, 1936

At last we are on our way. With fourteen adults and six children to cater for over Christmas there is a hectic time ahead and I have a bilious reaction from the strain of the past weeks. But I have a hunch that this is going to be a great Christmas.

Barbara Castle, 1969

24 December

We have just had our present-giving at [her sister] Alice's, just we three old girls. Alice's house was full of the smell of new bread. The loaves were piled on the kitchen table; the dining room table was piled with parcels, things changing hands. This is our system and works well: we agree on a stated amount – it is small because our big giving is birthdays. Each of us buys something for ourselves to our own liking, goods amounting to the stated sum. We bring them along and Christmas Eve, with kissings and thankings, accept them from each other – homely, practical little wants, torch batteries, hearth brooms, coffee strainers, iron handles, etc.

It's lots of fun. We lit four red candles in the window and drank ginger ale and ate Christmas cake and new bread and joked and discussed today and tomorrow and yesterday and compared tiredness and rheumatics and rejoiced that Christmas came only once per year. We love each other, we three; with all our differences we are very close.

Emily Carr, 1935

It does not feel at all like Christmas Eve on which I am writing this, although Mrs Leggatt & I spent nearly all night filling the soldiers' red bags, which we made, with crackers, sweets and nuts. But if I have not the Christmas feeling, there is at least joy in my heart; I can think of nothing else but the probability of seeing him in two days' time. For I cannot, dare not, call it certainty yet, – dare not even allow myself to feel thrilled …

Vera Brittain, 1915

A very orthodox Christmas Eve so far as appearances went. Real Christmas card snow, but with what maimed rites it came to us. It was dreadful. The whole place seemed to ache [due to the death of her brother]. The children perforce dragged us through all the old paraphernalia, and poor darling Letty [her sister-in-law] kept up most valiantly until the evening …

The Allens came to dinner – oysters and woodcock – and we talked of food all the time. Afterwards, with very aching hearts, we went through the old stocking ritual – bending over the children's cots like the best. Letty was valiantly persevering for the children with set teeth. I hung up her stocking. This touched her very much – she thought it would be her first Christmas without one – and led to a complete breakdown, poor darling! She sobbed and sobbed, and it was heartbreaking …

Lady Cynthia Asquith, 1916

We got our Christmas fowl: 12/- plus 1/- for pulling insides out and well worth it as the thought of it puts me off the bird entirely. Husband scrubbed kitchen floor for me while I was out shopping this morning. I was staggered when I got in and discovered what he'd done. He had gone out for his pre-lunch walk and ale when I returned so I haven't seen him to thank him yet. I call that a really grand Christmas present. Never before has he done such a thing though he has done the bathroom floor (smaller) for some months now, not often mind, but at intervals. On Sunday mornings.

Edie Rutherford, 1945

Christmas Eve 1967! Certainly there will never in my life be another Christmas Eve like this. I had asked the operator to wake me about 4.15 a.m. I phoned to see if Lyndon was on schedule. He was due about 4.45.

I slipped downstairs at 4.30. Lynda [her older daughter] was already there. She had let Chuck [her son-in-law] sleep because he had a cold. We had been told when the plane touched down at Andrews and about 5 the helicopters settled to the ground on the White House lawn. The fastest, longest, hardest trip any President of the United States had ever taken was at an end …

About 6 o'clock [in the evening] we were gathered – the family and Marie Fehmer, solicitously watching over Lyndon's pile of gifts with her pad and pencil, to make notes on proper 'thank-you's.' Lyndon always appoints himself Santa Claus, but he likes to see the work go fast so he called on Patrick to help him …

There was an envelope of Savings Bonds from Lyndon, but, alas, the many good things that we get to eat year after year from old friends – the pecans, dates, candy and smoked turkey and grapefruit – some friends have been doing this for twenty years – we no longer receive. We just get the notice that edibles have been received and we write a nice thank-you letter. The Secret Service, in pursuit of duty, destroys the food. I cannot blame them. I can only bewail the waste. Occasionally something is sent to Ashton Gonella [LBJ's secretary] and she brings it in her own hands to the kitchen and we do get to eat it.

We unwrapped presents, and exclaimed, and showed, and thanked and kissed and sank knee deep in tissue paper and bright colored wrappings and ribbons. It was after 8 o'clock when everybody was finished, though I still had a bench piled high with gifts. We went in to dinner, all the family including Sam Houston and Marie. Luci [her younger daughter] gave a full and beautiful blessing and our Christmas reached its peak.

Lady Bird Johnson, 1967

25 December

Yesterday I dropped a clamouring crowd of tasks so that the children and I might make merry together. They were decorating the house, and kept stopping to show me a bit of mistletoe, declaring I should surely be caught, or a particularly bright sprig of holly berries. If I could not reach the festoons stretched across the hall, they would put a step ladder in a convenient place and tell me to climb up for a look. Every time a package arrived, we would bring it in and debate where to find space for it in the fast filling drawing-room. I laughed at the plump, beribboned, besprigged parcels that sat on this table exchanging compliments of the season with my Braille manuscripts and typewriter ...

Back by the drawing-room fire all eight of us undid boxes and bundles until the room literally felt like a snowdrift of tinsel, ribbons, straw and delicate bits of wool. Surrounded by such gaiety and everybody's pleasure in his own and others' gifts, I found carols softly chiming in my loneliness. It is true, contentment cannot be with me, but it means much that the peace of remembrance and love are mine.

Helen Keller, 1936

Woke to carols on the wireless, and an orgy of present-opening. I got Damon Runyon, Wodehouse and Thurber, a book on Surrealism, a record by Scarlatti, some new green trousers, milk chocolate and cigarettes, a book on chess problems, cold cream and stockings.

Mummy had to go on duty, so Yurka [her boyfriend] took me to the Brasserie for lunch. We had turkey and plum pudding, and I wore my new pink shirt and grey beret and was looking particularly glamorous and old …

Walking back to the post for night duty the pubs were all full of happy, drunken people singing 'Tipperary' and the latest Army song which goes 'Cheer up my lads, fuck 'em all'. I spent a dreary night in an unheated room, sleeping in my clothes on a hard bed. Talk about Christmas night in the workhouse!

Joan Wyndham (aged 19), 1940

Christmas Day. George [Henry Lewes] and I spent this lovely day together – lovely as a clear Spring day. We could see Hampstead from the park so distinctly that it seemed to have suddenly come nearer to us. We ate our turkey together in happy 'solitude à deux'.

George Eliot, 1857

Christmas! All the shoes left in my big granite fireplace were taken this morning by their owners. It was lovely to see all these curious, greedy, cheerful, delighted, surprised people jostling round my bed.

The truffle was eaten yesterday. Exquisite! I'd bought a little brown casserole with a close-fitting lid. As soon as I lifted the lid we were intoxicated by a heady, dizzying aroma. It smelt of richness, warmth, festivity, elegance, and the triumph of gluttony! I'd stewed this precious thing from Orangini for two hours, tightly sealed, over a low heat, with slices of ham, fillet of beef, good white wine, vegetable stock and rashers of bacon. My Georges ate it slowly, gravely, silently – and went on thanking me for it all day! There's nothing more sincere than the acknowledgement of a satisfied palate!

Liane de Pougy, 1924

Christmas is always a time much to be dreaded in this country by the sober and well-inclined. Drunken husbands distress their peaceably disposed wives: and well disposed men have to lament the riotous disposition of their mates who cannot resist temptation which these holidays hold forth to jollity and intoxication.

Christiana Brooks, Australia, 1825

It being very bad walking could not go to Church. Uncle had six poor old Men to Dinner in the Kitchen, gave them for Dinner Roast Beef and Plumb Pudding, small Beer and Strong and to each a Shilling a Piece to carry home to their Wives. Walked a Mile in the Garden.

Nancy Woodforde, 1792

26 December

A good Christmas. Because, Ted [Hughes, her husband] says, I was merry, I played, teased, welcomed Mother. I may hate her, but that's not all. I … love her too. After all, as the story goes, she's my mother.

Sylvia Plath, 1958

Great adventure! I did a day's nursing at the Winchcomb Hospital from eight to eight. I went in some trepidation, but I hadn't realised the tremendous psychological effect of a uniform. Directly I stepped into the ward I felt an entirely new being – efficient, untiring, and quite squeamish – ready to cut off a leg, though generally the mere sight of a hospital makes me feel faint. It's wonderful how right it puts one with the men, too. I feel so shy as a laywoman, but was absolutely at my ease as 'Nurse Asquith'. I loved hearing myself called 'nurse' and would certainly go on with it if I were free. I felt all the disciplined's fear of the Sister and the experienced VAD, and most terribly anxious to acquit myself well …

There really wasn't enough to do. Most of the cases were trench feet – quite raw, a horrible sight. I assisted at the dressing of them, feverishly obeying curt orders. The men were delightful. Made lots of beds after tea, tidied up lockers, etc., etc. Only got tired in the last hour. Got home at 8.30 feeling excited, and wound up, and very well. Far less tired than after an ordinary London day.

Lady Cynthia Asquith, 1916

At 8 I went to the communion service in our little chapel. I had not been to such a service for ages nor had any faith in all it is supposed to imply, but I went to-day because Christmas at a hospital is an entirely new & unusual experience for me, and I felt too that I must thank whatever God there be for Roland [her fiancé] and for all my love and joy ...

Directly after breakfast I went down to Brighton, sent on my way with many good wishes from the others. I walked along the promenade, and looked at the grey sea tossing rough with white surf-crested waves, and felt a little anxiety at the kind of crossing he had had. But at any rate he should be safely in England by this time, though he probably has not been able to send me any message to-day owing to the difficulties of telephones and telegrams of Sunday & Christmas Day combined, & the inaccessibility of Hassocks. So I only have to wait for the morrow with such patience as I can manage. Being a little tired with the energies of the night, I spent a good deal of the rest of the day in sleeping, thinking of the sweet anticipation of the morning and of the face and voice dearest of all to me on earth.

Vera Brittain, 1915

27 December

———

Well, I have had the nicest Christmas for years, and all because I was in the company of people I love and who love me.

I did a bit of dashing round to kiddies in various flats with oddments, found excitement each time of course. Then to help friends with whom we were having midday dinner. Goose was perfect and we had a lovely lunch, wash up, rest, tea, and played solo whist till 1 a.m. with a short break for a snack. Yesterday, Boxing Day, we reversed it – they came here to share our fowl, which I'm glad to say I had steamed for an hour before roasting as it turned out to be a chicken's grandmother.

Edie Rutherford, 1945

'Oh dear,' she said, 'I do wish I hadn't married. I wish I'd been an explorer.' And then she said dreamily, 'The Rivers of China, for instance.'

'But what do you know about the rivers of China, darling,' I said. For Mother knew no geography whatever; she knew less than a child of ten.

'Nothing,' she agreed. 'But I can *feel* the kind of hat I should wear.' She was silent a moment. Then she said, 'If Father hadn't died I should have travelled and then ten to one I shouldn't have married.' And she looked at me dreamily – looked through me, rather.

Katherine Mansfield, 1920

I had just finished dressing when a message came to say that there was a telephone message for me. I sprang up joyfully, thinking to hear in a moment the dear dreamed-of tones of the beloved voice.

But the telephone message was not from Roland but from Clare; it was not to say that Roland had arrived, but that instead had come this telegram, sent on to the Leightons by Mr Burgin, to whom for some time all correspondence sent to Lowestoft had been readdressed:

T 223. Regret to inform you that Lieut. R. A. Leighton 7th Worcesters died of Wounds December 23rd. Lord Kitchener sends his sympathy.
Colonel of Territorial Forces, Records, Warwick.

Vera Brittain, 1915

28 December

William, Mary and I set off on foot to Keswick. We carried some cold mutton in our pockets, and dine at John Stanley's where they were making Christmas pies.

The sun shone but it was coldish. We parted from William and later he joined us opposite Sara's rock. He was busy in composition and sat down upon the wall.

At John Stanley's we roasted apples in the oven.

Dorothy Wordsworth, 1801

The year is nearly over. Snow has fallen, and everything is white. It is very cold. I have changed the position of my desk into a corner. Perhaps I shall be able to write far more easily here. Yes, this is a good place for the desk, because I cannot see out of the stupid window I am quite private. The lamp stands on one corner and *in* the corner. Its rays fall on the yellow and green Indian curtain and on the strip of red embroidery. The forlorn wind scarcely breathes. I love to close my eyes a moment and think of the land outside, white under the mingled snow and moonlight – snow in the furrows. *Mon Dieu!* How quiet and how patient! If he were to come I could not even hear his footsteps.

Katherine Mansfield, 1914

Do you know the exquisite, self-respecting, firm feel of a mended garter and taut stockings [from those] that have slopped down your calves from a broken one? Well, that's the same feel you get from a good honest day's painting after a period of impossibility.

Emily Carr, 1933

Mama presented me this morning with an emerald ring. And Sister gave me a hundred dollars in gold. I slept till 11 this morning, & when I awoke I could not believe I was really seventeen years old. Seventeen rather eventful years take them all together. I have been twice to Florida, & three times to Europe. I have been to two boarding-schools, & gained a great many friends in different ways. Have been run-away with twice, & had my portrait painted. I have learnt how to faint, & have inherited a fortune. Have been through a long illness & had a terrible sorrow! And I might have been married if I had choosen [sic].

On the other hand I have never had on a long dress, or been into society as a young-lady; nor in the conventual form have I been to my first ball. – I have never given my photograph to a young man, or any other souvenir either, nor have I made my hair uneven by distributing locks among my friends. I have never waved my handkerchief to a male biped on the other side of the street, or appointed a rendezvous on my way to school. – I have never sworn eternal friendship to anyone, nor written poetry since I was eleven years old, I have never fancied myself in love, even in extreme youth, with either a little boy in knickerbockers, or a *man* with side-whiskers. –

Nor can I say I have been much in want of attention from the opposite sex. I can not remember when I *first* ran away from them, & their gallantries. I have a great many nice *friends*, & what I am chiefly proud of, *'old gentlemen' friends*, whom I can look up to with respect.

Besides, there are a number who are particularly fond of me, & whom I particularly hate.

Julia Newberry, 1870

29 December

Lots of excitement. The post had issued me with a tin hat so I could go out in the shrapnel, which is just as well as things turned out.

I'd been having lunch in [her boyfriend] Yurka's room when the first guns began. He said I must wait till there was a lull – only there wasn't one, for as the papers said next day, 'At half past six the full blast of the Nazi fury hit the capital.' I'll say it did! This was the night they set the city on fire, including six churches. St Bride's and St Laurence's were gutted, the Guildhall burnt out, and St Paul's only just escaped. The aeroplanes never stopped and the sound of their engines dive-bombing was deafening.

We stood on the steps of number 21 watching. The sky was already red as blood – it looked as if half London was on fire. Flares lit up the street like daylight and the stars were all put out.

Yurka stood behind me and pulling back my head he kissed me till I thought my lips would break. A bomb began coming down making a noise like an express train.

'For God's sake, get in!' he said, pushing me into his room, and shutting the door. 'You can't go home in this.'

He pressed me up against the bedroom wall, and began making love to me while I stood rigid, staring straight ahead. The room was dark except for the fire. I'm sorry to say I was a bit nervous, thinking that each bomb was for us, but Yurka didn't seem to notice. He was in ecstasy. I thought, at all costs I must keep quite still or he'd see how nervous I was, and tried to control the trembling muscles in my legs …

Joan Wyndham (aged 19), 1940

A thorough, thorough thaw with the usual effect on the spirits. I am reading the diary of Marie Bashkirtseff for the first time. It makes this one seen sadly insipid and impersonal. No doubt writing it in the form of a journal prevents it being at all an emotional review of one's life, but I'm sure if I exercised discrimination and only described peaks in my life I should never have the energy to write at all. To write about every day automatically is really far less effort.

Lady Cynthia Asquith, 1916

Out of my window are acres of vineyards, thick patches of yellow mustard blossoms among the rows of bare vines, blue-purple hills, slate sky, flocks of birds that rise in occasional clouds. The big fig tree looks old and small without its leaves. I am in this Victorian house, like a queen alone in her castle. The children are skiing. Francis is in New York receiving an honorary doctorate.

I was thinking about Jackie Kennedy in the White House. How she had to smile and shake hands, go where the Secret Service directed her, be a proper First Lady, Then, after she became a widow, she became visible, the center of international attention. She came into her own, in a way, only after her husband's death. There is a part of me that has been waiting for Francis to leave me, or die, so that I can get my life the way I want it. I wonder if I have the guts to get it the way I want with him in it.

Eleanor Coppola, 1977

My mood is … brilliant. I feel well, and for the first time in months, totally relaxed. I haven't felt like this since the last time I was on leave and didn't know I had cancer, although now realise the mutating cells were there then, lurking sinisterly inside me. That was June.

Video diary:

'It's the end of the year, and like you, no doubt, I'm looking forward to the year ahead. I cannot WAIT for 2016 to get cracking, I really can't, particularly the last few days of February when chemotherapy will end. Hurray. Then I'll have a little bit of radiotherapy, but everybody who's had radiotherapy says that compared to chemo, it's an absolute breeze …'

'… roll on 2016 I hope you have a brilliant year ahead, and thank you, thank you, thank you for your thoughtful and kind and inspiring messages – they have meant such a lot to me.'

Victoria Derbyshire, 2015

30 December

Cooking & cleaning – curse it. If Nor & Jack [her brother and nephew] were worth it or kind to me I should not mind so much, but they are a useless self-indulgent pair.

Miles Franklin, 1939

Reluctantly back to work. Why does one always feel so muzzy after a holiday.

Barbara Castle, 1968

Today we all but joined in wedlock. He let me feel his masculinity – his vigour – & it was a pure, holy sensation, such as I would never have expected. He must be suffering dreadfully. I can gauge his frustration by mine. Nobody knows how I long for him. And yet – I cannot imagine giving myself to him before the appointed time. A sense of injustice & shame would degrade the whole, holy mystery. My lover – in God.

When I'm on my own, I feel the emptiness – the missing other half.

We could scarcely bring ourselves to part. Why these dreadful conventions? Why can't I simply move in with him? Without a church wedding. We're consumed with longing, are dissipating our strongest desires …

When shall I be his! Another ninety nights!

Alma Schindler (Mahler-Werfel), 1901

After private prayers I kept all this day with Mr Hoby, who was very far out of temper with a looseness [of his bowels], fearing ague …

Lady Margaret Hoby, 1600

There in front of me lie the proofs – the galleys – to go off today … a sort of stinging nettle that I cover over. Nor do I wish even to write about it here. A diving relief has possessed me these last days – at being quit of it – good or bad. Now for action and pleasure again and going about.

Virginia Woolf, 1936

31 December

The old year is fled, never to come back again through all Eternity. All its opportunities for love and service gone, past recall. What a terrible thought ...

Caroline Fox, 1859

New Year's Eve, 11.55

This time last year He [her fiancé] was seeing me off on Charing Cross Station after David Copperfield – and I had just begun to realise I loved Him. To-day He is lying in the military cemetery at Louvencourt – because a week ago He was wounded in action, and had just 24 hours of consciousness more and then went 'to sleep in France'. And I, who in impatience felt a fortnight ago that I could not wait another minute to see Him, must wait till all Eternity. All has been given me, and all taken away again – in one year.

So I wonder where we shall be – what we shall all be doing – if we all still *shall* be – this time next year.

Vera Brittain, 1915

'Tis twelve! Farewell, old year! And welcome, welcome in the New! One year ago to-night I was in dear old Salem, and little did I imagine that the next New Year would find me here. But so it is! How little do we know. How little *can* we dream of what the future has in store for us. – But I must retire, and spend the first few hours of the New Year in the land of dreams.

Charlotte Forten, 1858

My whole life, I thought I'd be at a wild party at the end of the millennium. Instead, I was queuing outside Stratford tube station. It was the only way to get to the Dome ...

Finally, after what seemed like centuries, we arrived at the Dome. It looked spectacular. My heart leaped, and I thought, 'OK, let's just forget the wait. Celebrate. It's the new millennium. Have a drink.' There was nothing to drink. Tiberio [her husband] and I were getting really irritated because New Year's Eve is also our anniversary. Not our wedding anniversary, but the anniversary of when we started going out together. We decided to be cheerful and go on one of the Dome's rides that we'd heard so much about. We walked up the gangway to the Body Zone.

'Sorry,' said the woman at the top, 'we've just closed it.'

'What do you mean you've just closed it?' I was indignant. 'You let someone in a minute ago. And anyway, have a heart, it's New Year's Eve. This is meant to be a party, not a funeral.'

'That was the Prime Minister,' said the woman with her nose in the air, 'no one else is coming in. It's closed.'

At this point I was thinking, ' Well *fuck* the Prime Minister.' We decided we really needed a drink. It's sad and bad to associate celebration with alcohol, but once every thousand years … Then we rejoiced because we saw a long bar with hundreds of glasses of champagne. It was eleven p.m., and we were about to get out first drop to drink. We went running up and tried to mask overt desperation as we stood behind a row four-deep of people trying to grab champagne. About half of them got a glass, and then suddenly the bartenders said 'Sorry, that's it.' There were hundreds of glasses full of bubbly behind them, and at least 200 bottles of champagne on display. People started to shout.

'Sorry,' said the bartenders, who were wearing headsets and earpieces, 'we've just received instructions. No more champagne is to be handed out.'

A woman about ten yards away started screaming. 'What do you mean? We've been waiting three fucking hours in a fucking train station for the fucking millennium and you're telling us you won't give us one of those fucking glasses of fucking champagne behind you? What do you fucking mean?'

I couldn't have phrased a parliamentary question better myself …

Oona King, 1999

New Year's Eve alone in my apartment. The office closed at one. Harry [her husband Harold Evans] back in DC, so I wandered home. Got into my old sweatpants and wound down into morose self-communion about what I want from the year ahead. My fascination with New York success is beginning to pall. I look out of my Venetian blinds at the lighted irregular egg cartons of the apartment blocks across the street. I think with affection and a certain maternal protectiveness of my *Vanity Fair* staff alone in their own small apartments before whatever festivities they have in mind, or possibly, as with me, none ... There will always be something magical to me in creative collaboration and the bonds it forges. I silently wish them all Happy New Year.

Tina Brown, 1985

The last night of 1857. The dear old year is gone with all its *Weben* and *Steben*. Yet not gone either: for what I have suffered and enjoyed in it remains to me an everlasting possession while my soul's life remains ... My life has deepened unspeakably during the last year: I feel a greater capacity for moral and intellectual enjoyment; a more acute sense of my deficiencies in the past; a more solemn desire to be faithful to coming duties than I remember at any former period of my life. And my happiness has deepened too: the blessedness of a perfect love and union grows daily. I have had some severe suffering this year from anxiety about my sister, and what will probably be a final separation from her – there has been no other real trouble. Few women, I fear, have had such reason as I have to think the long sad years of youth were worth it for the sake of middle age ...

So good-by, dear 1857! May I be able to look back on 1858 with an equal consciousness of advancement in work and heart.

George Eliot, 1857

Diarists

Alcott, Louisa May, 1832–88

Author, famously, of *Little Women* (with its sequels *Good Wives*, *Little Men*, and *Jo's Boys*), Alcott's tight-knit family, her work as seamstress, governess and journalist often prefigures the lives of her famous heroines. A feminist and an active abolitionist, she never married. She was plagued by ill-health, possibly as a result of the mercury treatment prescribed during an illness in her youth.

Asquith, Lady Cynthia, 1887–1960

English socialite, writer and anthologist; daughter of the Earl of Wemyss; friend to D. H. Lawrence and secretary to *Peter Pan* creator J. M. Barrie. Married to Herbert Asquith, son of the Liberal Prime Minister, her diaries chronicle among other things her relationship with their eldest son John, who might today be diagnosed as autistic – and, notably, the tragedies of the First World War.

Ashton-Warner, Sylvia, 1908–84

New Zealand novelist, poet, pianist and teacher. The child-based or organic approach to education she developed, inspired by her work with Māori children, is still in use today.

Bashkirtseff, Marie, 1858–84

Born to a landowning family in Ukraine, growing up largely in France, from her earliest days Marie Bashkirtseff made no bones about her lust for fame. In life she sought success as a painter, but after her death from tuberculosis aged just 25, it was the hundred and more volumes of journals she left behind that brought her international (if not uncontroversial) recognition.

Blackjack, Ada 1898–1983

A missionary-raised Inuit (Iñupiak) woman from Alaska who, after divorce from her abusive husband, was recruited as cook and seamstress to the disastrous 1921 Arctic expedition to Wrangel Island. She was the only survivor: rescued after eight months alone, during which she'd had to teach herself traditional survival skills.

Bodichon, Barbara Leigh Smith, 1827–91

British freethinker, artist, educationalist and women's activist, benefactor of Girton College, Cambridge, and promoter of the Married Women's Property Act. Her diary records her journey to America on the occasion of her marriage to the French physician Eugène Bodichon.

Brittain, Vera, 1893–1970

Writer, feminist, socialist and, during the First World War, Voluntary Aid Detachment nurse. She is famous especially for her indictment of that conflict, which took the lives of her fiancé, Roland Leighton, friends and brother. Later diaries would explore her friendships with the novelists Phyllis Bentley and Winifred Holtby. She was the mother of the politician Shirley Williams.

Brontë, Emily, 1818–48 and Anne, 1820–49

The Brontë sisters are, of course, best known for their novels; most notably Emily's *Wuthering Heights* and Charlotte's *Jane Eyre*. The imaginative life they created together in their Yorkshire home, however (a life that saw their invention of the fictional realm of Gondal) saw Emily and Anne write occasional 'diary papers' together or singly; notably on their birthdays.

Browning, Elizabeth Barrett, 1806–61

Elizabeth Barrett's secluded youth has become a symbol of female repression. An illness in her teens (and subsequent addiction to pain-killing drugs) saw her often confined upstairs in the family home in Wimpole Street. In 1846 – by then one of the most popular writers of the day – she secretly married her fellow poet Robert Browning, and spent the rest of her life in Italy, alienated from her family. Her early diary, however, describes her relationship with – one is tempted to call it her crush on – the blind classical scholar Hugh Stuart Boyd, a neighbour in their country home.

Bull, Deborah, 1963–

From 1992 a principal dancer with the Royal Ballet, in 2002 Bull became a creative director at the Royal Opera House and, increasingly, a prominent figure in the arts world. In 2018 she was created Baroness Bull.

Brown, Tina, 1953–

High-flying British journalist, editor, and author; founder of Women in the World. Brown was only 25 when she recreated the ailing *Tatler* magazine; 30 when she moved to New York to do the same for *Vanity Fair*. The *Vanity Fair Diaries* reflect both the glittering, brittle society of the Eighties, and the professional pressures facing successful women.

Burney, Fanny, 1752–1840

English writer – briefly Keeper of the Robes to George III's wife Queen Charlotte – who in 1793 married the French exile General Alexandre d'Arblay. Her groundbreaking novel *Evelina* was published anonymously in 1778. Her equally famous diary, begun in 1768, extended across more than 70 years (and includes the unforgettable description of an unanaesthetized mastectomy). For most of her adult life, however, it took the form of journal-letters to family and friends.

Bury, Lady Charlotte, 1775–1861

Daughter of the Duke of Argyll, a one-time society beauty and lady of letters, Lady Charlotte in widowhood became lady-in-waiting to Caroline of Brunswick, estranged wife of the Prince Regent. Her diary chronicling life at court was published anonymously, and Lady Charlotte's authorship has sometimes been disputed.

Butler, Lady Eleanor, 1739–1829

One of the famous 'Ladies of Llangollen', two upper-class Irish women who ran away to Wales, to avoid pressure to make a conventional marriage, and enjoy 50 years of close and loving companionship, in what contemporaries like Anne Lister had little hesitation in seeing as a lesbian relationship.

Carlyle, Jane, 1801–66

Daughter of a Scottish surgeon, her marriage to the eminent philosopher and historian Thomas Carlyle was beset by personal and financial difficulties which exacerbated her already poor health. She destroyed most of her diaries; the preservation of one particularly gloomy year may or may not have been accidental.

Carr, Emily, 1871–1945

Canadian artist and writer. Though for much of her life she struggled to find recognition, she is now sometimes described as a 'Canadian icon'; one of the first significant artists to emerge from the West Coast and noted for her work on Indigenous peoples.

Castle, Barbara, 1910–2002

British Labour politician and high-profile Cabinet minister.

Cavendish, Lucy (Lady Frederick), 1841–1925

Born Lucy Lyttleton, the life of Lucy Cavendish was that of a Victorian society lady until, in 1882, her husband Lord Frederick Cavendish was assassinated in Dublin by Irish Republicans. Her subsequent work in the field of women's education bore fruit in the Cambridge college that today bears her name.

Chesnut, Mary Boykin, 1823–86

American would-be author, born in South Carolina, whose diaries chronicle the Civil War from the perspective of Southern plantation-owning society. Her husband served as aide to Confederate President Jefferson Davis, but she regarded herself as no friend to slavery.

Clifford, Lady Anne, 1590–1676

Aristocrat, heiress, patron and sometime chatelaine of Knole Park in Kent. Many difficulties in her first marriage to Richard Sackville, Earl of Dorset, arose from her steadfast refusal to trade away her family lands in Westmorland. Her second marriage to the Earl of Pembroke was likewise fraught, but her later years saw her as a powerhouse in the north, where she moved between her various castles.

Collins, Kathleen, 1942–1988

Groundbreaking artist, filmmaker and writer, known for the posthumously published *Whatever Happened to Interracial Love?* and *Notes From a Black Woman's Diary*.

Cooper, Jilly, 1937–

British journalist and novelist, whose published diary comically chronicles the life of a South London community.

Coppola, Eleanor, 1936–

Artist, writer, documentary-maker – and wife to the filmmaker Francis Ford Coppola, whose *Apocalypse Now* was chronicled in Eleanor's first published diary.

Cullwick, Hannah, 1833–1909

The diaries of Victorian maid-of-all-work Hannah Cullwick were kept at the urging of the man she called Massa – barrister and philanthropist

Arthur Munby, who was studying the conditions of working women. Their bizarre relationship saw her proclaim herself his slave – and hold him on her lap like a baby – yet she was reluctant to compromise her independence by secretly marrying him in 1873. Whatever the couple's dynamics, however, the diaries provide a rare 'downstairs' glimpse of Victorian society.

Curie, Marie, 1867–1934

Maria *Salomea* Sklodowska-Curie, Polish/French physicist, who famously conducted ground-breaking research on radioactivity – the first woman to win a Nobel prize. She turned briefly to diary-writing in grief at the 1906 death, in a road accident, of her husband and collaborator Pierre Curie. Her own death at the age of 66 is thought to be a result of her long-term exposure to radiation; but she is remembered as one of the most famous scientists of all time.

Dall, Caroline Healey, 1822–1912

American feminist, lecturer, Abolitionist and reformer; living around Boston and moving in the same circles as the Alcott family (see above). She wrote with unusual frankness about the difficulties of her marriage, and of motherhood.

Davis, Emilie, 1839–89

A young free Black woman living in Philadelphia during the Civil War, Emilie Davis worked as a seamstress, and took an active part in the life of her community.

de Beauvoir, Simone, 1908–86

French philosopher and noted feminist, author of *The Second Sex*. The diary quoted describes a visit to post-War America.

de Jesus, Carolina Maria, 1914–77

Carolina's aspirations to be a writer were seemingly at odds with her life as the Black single mother of three children, living in the slums of São Paolo, sharing a single tap with several hundred people and scavenging for scrap she could sell to buy food. After a journalist encountered her and got her diary published, it became a literary sensation, and she herself a powerful voice against Brazil's social inequality.

de Pougy, Liane, 1869–1950

One of the most famous Parisian courtesans, Liane's affairs with both men and women, her subsequent marriage to Prince Georges Ghika (and later retirement into religious life), gave her material for her fictional writing.

Derbyshire, Victoria, 1968–

British journalist and broadcaster (and lifelong diarist) whose frank chronicle of her experience through breast cancer touched many hearts.

Dessaulles, Henriette, 1860–1946

Canadian writer from Quebec whose teenage diary (ending, as do so many, on her marriage) attracted considerable attention.

Dostoevsky, Anna, 1846–1918

Stenographer, and then second wife, to the author Fyodor Dostoevsky, who was 25 years older than she. Her diary chronicles their life together, forced to flee abroad by the debts consequent on Dostoevsky's gambling addiction.

Eliot, George, 1819–80

Pseudonym of Mary Anne (or Marian) Evans; author of *Middlemarch* and one of the most revered novelists of the English language. Her intermittently kept diary began in 1849 (ten years before she published her first novel, *Adam Bede*, and five years before the beginning of her quasi-marital relationship with the already married George Henry Lewes), and continued until three years before her death.

Forten, Charlotte, 1838–1914

A teacher and activist living in Philadelphia before the Civil War, Charlotte Forten's diaries actively explore the wrongs she experienced as a Black woman.

Fountaine, Margaret, 1862–1940

Lepidopterist, traveller and lifelong diarist; one of the first women to win acceptance in the scientific field.

Fox, Caroline, 1819–71

Daughter of a wealthy Quaker family (her mother was cousin to Elizabeth Fry, see below). The self-awareness implicit in diary writing was encouraged by the Dissenting tradition: Fox's father offered his daughters a guinea if they would keep one regularly.

Frank, Anne, 1929–45

Perhaps the most famous of female diarists, whose explorations of her own teenage psyche, and sexuality, would have been infinitely worth reading even without the added weight given by her fate. The Jewish Frank family first fled from Germany to Holland where, from 1942 when Anne was 13 years old, they were forced to hide from the Nazis in the 'Secret Annexe'. They were betrayed in 1944, and Anne died in Bergen-Belsen concentration camp; her diary first published only two years after the end of the Second World War.

Franklin, Miles, 1879–1954

Australian writer and feminist, best known for her youthful novel *My Brilliant Career*, and its later film adaptation. The diaries quoted here date from her later life when, after a long absence, she returned to Australia.

Freke, Elizabeth, 1641–1714

English memoirist, poet and writer of recipes, born in Wiltshire to a wealthy Royalist family. Her diaries chronicle, extensively, not only her religious concerns but her fractious relations with her family.

Fry, Elizabeth, 1780–1845

Quaker and prison reformer; campaigning particularly for the protection of women (in Newgate and elsewhere), and against the death penalty and the slave trade. Her diaries reflect both her own spiritual and emotional life and her role in the development of many of our modern scruples.

Garner, Helen, 1942–

One of Australia's most acclaimed writers, whose fictional work draws extensively on the personal experience described in her diaries.

Gaskell, Elizabeth, 1810–65

The novelist Mrs Gaskell (*Cranford, North and South*) used an occasional journal to explore her relationship with her young daughters – one of the first, perhaps, to whom this would have seemed a fit subject of study.

Gladstone, Mary, 1847–1927

Daughter of the Prime Minister W. E. Gladstone. Before marrying in middle age, she gained considerable influence as one of her father's Downing Street secretaries.

Hanff, Helene, 1916–97

Writer, New Yorker and personality, Hanff is best-known for *84, Charing Cross Road*. The book, and subsequent film, chronicle her long-distance friendship with a London bookseller, and long-delayed visit to the city of which she'd always dreamt.

Hardy, Mary 1733–1809

Yeoman's daughter, wife to a Norfolk farmer and brewer, Mary Hardy kept an almost daily, brief record of her life for some 35 years.

Hester, Sallie, 1835–1911

Sallie Hester was 14 when, in 1849, her family took the trail to California. Her diary continues past the end of the 2,000-mile journey, but, like so many, ends on her eventual marriage (to an assayer from Eureka, Nevada): 'now, Dear Journal, I give thee up. No more jottings down of gay and festive scenes – the past is gone and the future is before me … '

Hillesum, Etty 1914–43

Like Anne Frank, Hillesum was a Jew living in Holland. Hillesum was older, and her diaries were self-exploratory in a different way – her lover was a leading psychoanalyst, and she later chronicled her own spiritual development. She nonetheless met a similar fate, dying in Auschwitz.

Highsmith, Patricia 1921–95

The noted (and, in her lifetime, notoriously secretive) crime novelist Patricia Highsmith – inventor of Mr Ripley, author of *Strangers on a Train* – left some 8,000 pages of notebooks and diaries, chronicling not only her working life but her turbulent personal relationships with (occasionally) men and (predominantly) women.

Hoby, Lady Margaret, 1571–1633

An Elizabethan gentlewoman reared in the strict Protestant tradition, Hoby is the first woman known to have written a diary in the English language. Concentrating heavily on her spiritual observance, it nonetheless gives an insight into her daily routine.

Hodgson, Winifred Vere, 1901–79

Teacher, charity worker and lifelong diarist who recorded daily life in London during the Second World War.

Hurnscot, Loran, 1896–1970

Pseudonym of the sometime writer and publisher Gay Stuart Taylor. Her tubercular husband 'Hu' first urged on her, and then resented, the sexual experimentations fashionable in advanced 1920s circles – notably with 'Barny', the writer A. E. Coppard. Her diaries were published under the telling title *A Prison, a Paradise*.

Jacquier, Ivy (Skinner) 1890–?

Born into an Anglo-French family, growing up largely outside Lyons and training as an artist across the Continent and then living in England with her Scottish husband, 'A.', an army officer, Jacquier wrote her diary in the inward-looking tradition of the French *journal intime*.

James, Alice, 1848–92

Sister to both the novelist Henry and the psychologist William James, Alice's life was one of chronic invalidism (sometimes diagnosed as 'hysteria'). Born in New England, she moved to Britain for a change of scene. Constrained by the conventions of upper middle-class society, ill-health was in Henry's opinion 'the only solution for her of the practical problem of life.'

James, P. D., 1920–2014

Britain's 'Queen of Crime' was also a high-ranking civil servant and an active life peer, widely honoured for her public service as well as her publications. She kept a diary, as an experiment, for the year preceding her 78th birthday.

Johnson, Lady Bird, 1912–2007

First Lady of the United States from 1963–69, whose diary details her time in the White House. Her husband Lyndon B. Johnson was thrust into the Presidency following the assassination of John F. Kennedy.

Keller, Helen, 1880–1968

Losing both her sight and her hearing after an illness when she was 19 months old, Helen was taught to read and write by her beloved companion and 'Teacher' Anne Sullivan. Her subsequent fame, her writing, speaking and campaigning career, did much to alter the perception of people with disabilities.

Kemble, Fanny, 1809–93

English actress and author from a famous theatrical family. Her extensive writings chronicle both the tour of America she undertook with her father – and her experience as abolitionist wife to a slave-owning Georgian planter.

King, Oona, 1967–

Former Labour politician, media personality, noted as only the second Black woman to be elected a Member of Parliament, King describes herself as 'multi-ethnic'. In 2011 she was created Baroness King of Bow.

Knight, Amelia Stewart, 1817–96

Pioneer who in 1853 took the Oregon Trail with her husband and seven children. It says something about the fortitude – and the resilience – of the pioneer women that she was pregnant throughout the journey her diary describes.

Langton, Anne, 1804–93

Anne Langton was 33 (and a skilled painter) when, in 1837, she left England for her brother's farm in Ontario, recording the daily life of, as the title of her journal has it, *A Gentlewoman in Upper Canada*.

Last, Nella, 1889–1968

Barrow-in-Furness housewife Nella Last – 'Housewife, 49' – was one of many contributors to the Mass Observation Archive. She was unusual, however, in continuing to write after the end of the Second World War – a diary that would eventually run to some 12 million words. When published, it struck a chord with many women, and was subsequently adapted for TV.

Lindbergh, Anne Morrow, 1906–2001

Anne – herself a noted aviator and writer – was best known as the wife of famous pioneer aviator Charles Lindbergh – and for the tragedy that befell them. In 1932 their toddler son was kidnapped from their home and later found dead; the kidnapper's trial became the subject of a media frenzy (even inspiring the crime behind Agatha Christie's *Murder on the Orient Express*). The Lindberghs lost public sympathy over their conviction that America should stay out of the Second World War, but in later life went on receive numerous honours.

Lister, Anne, 1791–1840

Anne Lister – 'Gentleman Jack' to disapproving contemporaries, as well as in the TV series based on her life – has been called 'the first modern lesbian'. The only surviving child of a Yorkshire landowner, highly educated and financially astute, she was notably masculine in appearance, breaking the conventions of her day – considering herself unofficially married to her most enduring female lover. Her diaries, encompassing some five million words and written partly in cipher, were first decoded by a descendent, but fully explored only in the late 20th century.

Longfellow, Fanny, 1819–61

Born Frances Appleton, Fanny was second wife to the *Hiawatha* poet Henry Wadsworth Longfellow and mother of their six children. She was one of many women whose diary ended at what she perceived to be a new stage of her life: in her case, not marriage, but motherhood. 'With this day my journal ends, for I have now a living one to keep faithfully, more faithfully than this.' In fact, she would begin another journal to chronicle the progress of the children.

Lorde, Audre, 1934–92

Self-described 'black, lesbian, feminist, socialist, mother, warrior, poet', Lorde was widely honoured for her work against racism, sexism and homophobia. *The Cancer Journals* of 1980 explore her experience of mastectomy.

Lowndes, Marie Belloc, 1868–1947

Novelist, and sister of the writer Hilaire Belloc.

Mahler-Werfel, Alma, 1879–1964

Vienna-born Alma Schindler's diaries – discovered and deciphered only years after her death – begin on a youthful relationship with Gustav Klimt, and end shortly before her marriage to Gustav Mahler. Herself a composer – and a controversial figure whose own writings on Mahler have been much disputed – she went on to marry the architect Walter Gropius before marrying the writer Franz Werfel.

Mansfield, Katherine, 1888–1923

Innovative and influential New Zealand-born writer. Her adult life in Europe, and on the fringes of the Bloomsbury Group, included an on/off relationship with the editor John Middleton Murry and a friendship with the adoring Ida Baker, who supported her travels in search of health after a diagnosis of the tuberculosis which eventually killed her.

Ma Yan, 1979–

The Ma family, Chinese Muslims, were living in a remote corner, thousands of miles north-west of Beijing, when in 2001 Frenchman Pierre Haski travelled there to film a documentary. As the team were leaving, a village woman approached, and thrust on them a letter and three notebooks. These represented the diary of her 14-year-old daughter, distraught because she'd been warned that (after five consecutive years of drought) the family could no longer afford her education. After Haski's publication of the diaries, they were translated into 17 languages; a foundation was set up to help girls in a similar position and Yan went on to study at the Sorbonne.

Mitchison, Naomi, 1897–1999

Scottish writer, farmer, socialist and feminist; wife to a Labour politician and friends with many of the great literary figures of her day.

Monkswell, Mary, Lady, 1849–1930

Society hostess and wife of Liberal politician Robert Collier, 2nd Baron Monkswell.

Montgomery, L. M. (Lucy Maud), 1874–1942

Canadian author best known for *Anne of Green Gables* and its sequels. Her diary describes her lonely youth and spells of depression, and a writing career set against many of the backdrops familiar to her eponymous heroine.

Morley, Helena, 1880–1970

Pseudonym of Alice Dayrell Caldeira Brant, a half-Brazilian, half-English girl living in the mining town of Diamantina and recording her dreams and daily adventures as a teenager in the 1890s.

Murphy, Dervla, 1931–2022

Irish cyclist and well-known travel writer, chronicling her adventures over some 50 years. The extracts quoted are from *On a Shoestring to Coorg*, describing the Indian journey she made with her five-year-old daughter Rachel.

Newberry, Julia, 1854–76

American heiress; as a teenager she was taken travelling around Europe for her health.

Nightingale, Florence, 1820–1910

Florence Nightingale's early diaries bely her iconic image as 'The Lady with the Lamp'. They record her desperate frustration before – having overcome the opposition of her wealthy family – she finally began working as a nurse. In 1854 she famously led a team to Crimea to care for soldiers wounded there – and to establish nursing as a respectable profession.

Nin, Anaïs 1903–77

Born in France to Cuban parents, spending her later life largely in America, Nin was an impassioned and lifelong diarist. An unfulfilling early marriage to a banker, Hugh Guiler, led to her *Journal of a Wife*; the diary entries on her 1930s relationships with both the writer Henry Miller and Miller's wife June would posthumously be published as *Incest*. That book also describes her adult sexual relationship with her father (and others, including her psychoanalyst René Allendy). Many of her later diaries, however, were published in an imprecisely dated form, which makes them unsuitable for this anthology.

Oates, Joyce Carol, 1938–

Prize-winning American author of more than 60 novels (under her own name and others), to say nothing of plays, poetry – and her journals, which ran to some 4,000 closely-typed pages.

Partridge, Frances, 1900–2004

In youth a member of the Bloomsbury Group, her long life saw her develop into one of the most substantial diarists of the 20th century. She and her husband Ralph were both committed pacifists.

Pepys, Emily, 1833–77

Her diary represents six months in the life of a ten-year-old rector's daughter in the mid-19th century. An unusually advanced and articulate ten-year-old, however!

Plath, Sylvia, 1932–63

Plath's suicide made her an icon to many who had never read her poetry. Both her despair and her passion for her husband, fellow poet Ted Hughes, speak through her diaries.

Pless, Princess Daisy of, 1873–1943

Born in Wales, Mary Cornwallis-West's career as an Edwardian society beauty and marriage to a wealthy German aristocrat saw her rub shoulders with the most famous names in Europe.

Potter, Beatrix, 1866–1943

Beatrix Potter's diaries were written in code, between the ages of 14 and 30; before she had found her vocation as author and, later, Lake District farmer and conservationist. But the observations of the natural world foreshadow her famous tales – *Peter Rabbit, Squirrel Nutkin, Mrs Tiggy-Winkle* and the rest.

Powell, Dawn, 1896–1965

American writer comparatively successful in her own day though since largely forgotten. Her diaries reference not only her marriage to Joseph Gousha but their son 'Jojo', who was born with what her biographer suggests was a combination of schizophrenia and cerebral palsy.

Ptashkina, Nelly, 1903–20

Nelly Ptashkina's youthful diaries describe the flight of her wealthy family from the Bolshevik revolution, from Moscow to the Ukraine and then to Paris. She died, still in her teens, in a mountain fall.

Pym, Barbara, 1913–80

The novelist famous for her wry depictions of quiet, spinsterly or clerical life could be racier in her diaries; though she never married, she had a number of romantic relationships, from her Oxford undergraduate years on.

Roberts, Rachel, 1927–80

Welsh-born actress, best known for films of the 1960s such as *This Sporting Life* and, later, *Yanks* and *Picnic at Hanging Rock*. First married to actor Alan Dobie, her tumultuous second marriage to Rex Harrison foundered on, among other things, her depression and alcoholism.

Rutherford, Edie, c.1902?–?

British Socialist, born in South Africa, married to a timber merchant in Sheffield. Her diary as a clerk and housewife during and after the Second World War was one of those contributed to the Mass Observation Project.

Sand, George, 1804–76

Pseudonym of Aurore Dupin, and known as one of the most successful writers in Europe. Born into an upper-class French family, her rebellions included separation from her husband and a number of affairs (including one with Chopin) and a habit of dressing in men's clothing.

Sarton, May, 1912–95

The pen name of Eleanore Marie Sarton, born in Belgium, but living most of her life in New England. Sarton resisted the label of 'lesbian writer', preferring to explore her relationships with the natural world around her, with the wide human range of hopes and fears.

Shelley, Mary Wollstonecraft, 1797–1851

The daughter of Mary Wollstonecraft, and the wife of Percy Bysshe Shelley, Mary was the author of *Frankenstein*. Roaming Europe in company with Shelley, her step-sister Claire Clairmont and Lord Byron, she was left a widow when Shelley died in a boating accident in Italy. She spent the bulk of her later life working as a professional novelist and biographer, protecting the reputation of her dead husband and the interests of their son.

Shore, Emily, 1819–39

A curate's daughter from Bury St Edmunds – and one of a number of diarists whose youthful observations were given poignancy (and publication!) due to their deaths at a young age.

Simcoe, Elizabeth, 1762–1850

English-born heiress Elizabeth Simcoe was wife to John Graves Simcoe, the first Lieutenant Governor of Upper Canada. Her diary describes colonial life in Ontario.

Smart, Elizabeth, 1913–86

Canadian poet and novelist, best known for *By Grand Central Station I Sat Down and Wept*, itself reflective of her affair with the married British poet George Barker (by whom she would have four children), chronicled in her diaries.

Sontag, Susan, 1933–2004

New York-born writer, philosopher and political activist, whose diaries acted as notebooks in which to chart and explore the development of her ideas.

Stark, Freya, 1893–1993

Dame Freya Stark was an explorer, and author of some two dozen books, mostly about her travels in the Middle East and Afghanistan.

Stevenson, Frances, 1888–1972

For more than 30 years Frances Stevenson was mistress and secretary to the Liberal Prime Minister David Lloyd George (who she identifies in her diaries as 'C' while he is Chancellor of the Exchequer, and then as 'D'). He was married, and reluctant to leave his first wife, Margaret. However, he and Frances were married on Margaret's death in 1943, by which time she had witnessed at first hand many of the great events of the early 20th century.

Tan, Amy, 1952–

Born in California to Chinese immigrant parents, Tan's novels – notably *The Joy Luck Club* – often explore the complications of her heritage.

Thompson, Emma, 1959–

Oscar-winning actress whose published diary records the filming of *Sense and Sensibility*, the Jane Austen adaptation which she wrote, as well as playing the role of Elinor Dashwood.

Thrale Piozzi, Hester Lynch, 1741–1821

Hester Lynch Thrale Piozzi was a Welsh-born woman of letters, known for her friendship with Dr Johnson. After the death of her first husband, the wealthy brewer Henry Thrale, she fell in love with and eventually married her children's Italian music teacher, a match which sparked considerable disapproval within her family and beyond.

Tolstoy, Sophia, 1844–1919

Countess Sophia Andreyevna Tolstaya; wife of Leo Tolstoy, author of *Anna Karenina* and *War and Peace*, and mother to their 13 children. She also acted as increasingly conflicted amanuensis to the older, difficult – sometimes almost monstrous – Leo, who however, left her ten days before his death.

Tram, Dang Thuy, 1942–70

Doctor, born in Hanoi, who became a battlefield surgeon for the People's Army of Vietnam. Her diaries were returned to her family many years after she was killed by US forces.

Truitt, Anne, 1921–2004

Though she found mid-life fame as a minimalist sculptor, Truitt also worked extensively with colour – and with words, exploring the relationship between her life as an artist, and as a wife and mother.

Vassiltchikov, Marie, 1917–78

Born into an aristocratic Russian family, Princess Marie Vassiltchikov grew up in Germany. She would later marry an American captain – and die in London – but her Berlin diaries record the Second World War from the German side, albeit that Vassiltchikov herself was connected with the anti-Nazi resistance movement.

Velmans, Edith, 1925–2023

'The Anne Frank who lived', Edith Velmans was likewise born Jewish in Holland, but survived the Second World War living under an assumed identity with a Protestant family. Most of her family were not so fortunate, but Edith would go on to have a long and successful life, working as a psychologist in America.

Victoria, Queen, 1819–1901

Starting some five years before her accession in 1837, the daily diary of Queen Victoria totals more than 140 volumes. Publication began even in her lifetime, and though inevitably – given her position – her entries have been expurgated, her voice sounds clear with considerably fewer inhibitions than one might expect!

Walker, Alice, 1944–

The diaries kept by Pulitzer Prize-winning novelist and poet Alice Walker – best known for *The Color Purple* – over four decades describe not only her experience as an African-American woman and an activist, but her emotional and artistic development.

Warner, Sylvia Townsend, 1893–1978

English novelist, poet and musicologist whose diaries describe both her work, and daily life in the country with her partner and fellow writer Valentine (Molly) Ackland.

Webb, Beatrice, 1858–1943

Sociologist, economist and a leader of the Fabian Society. Her diaries record nearly 70 years of British intellectual life, her early relationship with the Radical politician Joseph Chamberlain (which foundered on her determination to preserve her independence), and her ultimate marriage – a partnership of shared beliefs – with the socialist Sidney Webb.

Note: although any entries written before 1892 should properly be credited to her maiden name of Beatrice Potter, this author has been called Beatrice Webb throughout, to avoid confusion with Beatrix Potter.

Weeton, Ellen 1776–c.1850

The title of 'Miss' Weeton's published *Journal of a Governess* belies the sensational nature of the contents. The Lancashire schoolmistress suffered years of verbal and physical abuse at the hands of her husband Aaron Stock who – after threatening her with starvation or a Lunacy Commission hearing – threw her onto the street and attempted to deny her access to their daughter Mary, who, however, Ellen would walk for hours to visit, at her school, secretly.

Wells, Ida B., 1862–1931

African-American activist and author; a leader of the Civil Rights movement and a campaigner for women's suffrage.

Winfrey, Oprah, 1954–

Producer, actress, author, media powerhouse (at one time described as the world's only Black billionaire); and, most famously, host of *The Oprah Winfrey Show*. An impassioned believer in the utility of journal-writing, the entries quoted come from the diary she kept during the making of the film adaptation of Toni Morrison's *Beloved*, which Winfrey produced as well as starring in.

Woodforde, Nancy, 1757–1830

The diaries of the Rev. Woodforde, full of daily detail and good dinners, have long been familiar as *The Diary of a Country Parson*. The diary of his niece and housekeeper 'Nancy' (Anna Maria), however, survives intact for one year only. The family papers also include the diary of Mary Woodforde, a century before.

Woolf, Virginia, 1882–1941

Novelist, essayist, leading light of the Bloomsbury Group, Woolf's extensive diaries reflect her impact on English prose as surely as *Mrs Dalloway*, *A Room of One's Own*, or *To the Lighthouse*. Though her lifelong battles with mental health appear there, the voice that emerges is more robust and humorous than the fame of her suicide might suggest. She was married to author and publisher Leonard Woolf.

Wordsworth, Dorothy, 1771–1855

Sister and constant companion to William Wordsworth, whose observations of life in the Lake District foreshadow much of his poetry. As William said, 'she gave me eyes'.

Wyndham, Joan, 1921–2007

Would-be actress, sometime member of the Women's Auxiliary Air Force, and lifelong denizen of London's bohemian society, Joan Wyndham's youthful diaries in particular are notable for the cheerful frankness with which she explores sex.

Wynne Fremantle, Betsey, 1778–1857, Eugenia Wynne Campbell (b. 1780) and Harriet Wynne (b. 1784/6)

Elizabeth Wynne Fremantle was a lifelong diarist whose records (together, to a lesser extent, with those of her younger sisters Eugenia and Harriet) make up a formidable chronicle of life during the Napoleonic Wars. The family toured the Continent extensively, and on her marriage to the naval captain Thomas Fremantle (another diarist) Betsey often sailed with him.

Sources

Helene Hanff, *84, Charing Cross Road* (1990), Penguin Publishing Group. Copyright © Helene Hanff.

Sallie Hester, *The Diary of Sallie Hester: A Covered Wagon Girl* (2014), Capstone Publishers.

Patricia Highsmith: From *Patricia Highsmith: Her Diaries and Notebooks* edited by Anna von Planta. Copyright © 2021 Diogenes Verlag AG Zürich, Switzerland.

Etty Hillesum, *Etty: A Diary* trans. Arnold J. Pomerans, ed. K. A. D. Smelik (1985), HarperCollins UK.

Winifred Vere Hodgson, *Few Eggs and No Oranges: The Diaries of Vere Hodgson* (1976) Copyright © Persephone Books.

Loran Hurnscot, *A Prison, A Paradise* (1959), Viking Press.

Ivy Jacquier, *The Diary of Ivy Jacquier: 1907–1926* (1960), Victor Gollancz Ltd.

PD James, *Time to Be in Earnest: A Fragment of Autobiography* (2015) Copyright © Greene and Heaton.

Carolina Maria de Jesus, *Child of the Dark: The Diary of Carolina Maria de Jesus* trans. David St. Clair (2003), Penguin Publishing Group.

Lady Bird Johnson, *A White House Diary* (2007), Henry Holt and Company, LLC.

Helen Keller, *The Journal of Helen Keller* (1973), Cedric Chivers, Penguin Random House.

Oona King, *House Music* (2013) Copyright © Bloomsbury Publishing Plc.

Nella Last, *Nella Last's War* (2018), *Nella Last's Peace* (2010), *Nella Last in the 1950s* (2010) copyright © Profile Books.

Anne Morrow Lindbergh, *Bring Me A Unicorn* (1993), *Hour of Gold, Hour of Lead* (1973), *War Within and Without* (1981) Copyright © Elsevier Books.

Fanny Longfellow (Frances Appleton), *Mrs Longfellow: Selected Letters and Journals of Fanny Appleton Longfellow* (1959), ed. Edward Wagenknecht. Peter Owen Limited.

Excerpt(s) from THE CANCER JOURNALS by Audre Lorde, copyright © 1980 by Audre Lorde. Used by permission of Penguin Classics, an imprint of Penguin Publishing Group, a division of Penguin Random House LLC. All rights reserved.

Alma Mahler-Werfel, *Diaries 1898–1902* (2000), copyright © Faber and Faber.

Ma Yan, *The Diary of Ma Yan: The Struggles and Hopes of a Chinese Schoolgirl* (2009) Copyright © Little Brown Book Group Limited.

Among You Taking Notes: The Wartime Diary of Naomi Mitchison by Naomi Mitchison (Weidenfeld & Nicolson), © Lois Godfrey and the Trustees of the Mass Observation Archive, University of Sussex, 1985.

Lucy Maud Montgomery, *The Complete Journals of L. M. Montgomery*, ed. Mary Henley Rubio, Elizabeth Hillman Waterston (2017), Oxford University Press.

Helena Morley, *The Diary of 'Helena Morley'*, trans. Elizabeth Bishop (2016), Elizabeth Bishop, Virago.

Dervla Murphy, *On a Shoestring to Coorg* (1995), Hutchinson.

Anaïs Nin, *Journal of a Wife: The Early Diary of Anaïs Nin 1923–1927* (1986), *Incest: The Unexpurgated Diary of Anaïs Nin 1932–1934* (1993), *The Journals of Anaïs Nin Volume One*, ed. Gunther Stuhlmann (1973), HarperCollins.

Joyce Carol Oates, *The Journal of Joyce Carol Oates 1973–1982*, ed. Greg Johnson (2007), HarperCollins.

Frances Partridge, *Diaries 1939–1972*, ed. Rebecca Wilson (2001) Phoenix Press.

Sylvia Plath, *The Journals of Sylvia Plath* (2013), copyright © Faber and Faber.

Beatrix Potter, *The Journal of Beatrix Potter* (2012), copyright © Penguin Random House.

Dawn Powell: From *The Diaries of Dawn Powell*. Copyright © 1995 by The Estate of Dawn Powell. Reprinted with permission from Steerforth Press.

Barbara Pym, *A Very Private Eye: An Autobiography in Letters and Diaries* (1984), Macmillan.

Rachel Robert, *No Bells on Sunday: The Journals of Rachel Roberts*, ed. Alexander Walker (1985), Sphere.

May Sarton, *Journal of a Solitude* (1985), *Encore: A Journal of the Eightieth Year* (1995), Massie & McQuilkin Literary Agency, Open Road.

Elizabeth Smart, *Necessary Secrets: The Journals of Elizabeth Smart*, ed. Alice Van Wart (1991), Grafton.

Susan Sontag, *As Consciousness is Harnessed to Flesh: Diaries 1964–1980* (2013), Hamish Hamilton.

Freya Stark, *A Winter in Arabia* (1983), Century.

Frances Stevenson, *Lloyd George: A Diary by Frances Stevenson*, ed. AJP Taylor (1971), Hutchinson.

Amy Tan, *Where the Past Begins* (2018), 4th Estate.

Emma Thompson, *Sense & Sensibility: The Diaries* (2007), copyright © Emma Thompson. Reprinted with permission from The Agency on behalf of the author.

Dang Thuy Tram, *Last Night I Dreamed of Peace*, trans. Andrew X. Pham (2008), Rider.

Anne Truitt, *Daybook: The Journal of an Artist* (2023), Scribner UK.

Marie Vassiltchikov, *The Berlin Diaries of Marie 'Missie' Vassiltchikov* (1987), Methuen.

Edith Velmans: from *Edith's Story* by Edith Velmans, ed. Hester Velmans, © 2014 Van Horton Books. Used by permission of the Velmans Estate.

Alice Walker, *Gathering Blossoms Under Fire: The Journals of Alice Walker*, ed. Valerie Boyd, Weidenfeld & Nicolson (2022), Joy Harris Literary Agency.

Sylvia Townsend Warner, *The Diaries of Sylvia Townsend Warner*, ed. Claire Harman (1994), Chatto and Windus

Beatrice Webb, *The Diaries of Beatrice Webb* (2001), LSE.

Ida B. Wells: From **The Memphis Diary of Ida B. Wells** by Miriam Decosta-Willis. Copyright © 1995 by Miriam Decosta-Willis, reprinted by permission of Beacon Press, Boston.

Eve Williams, *Ladies Without Lamps* (1983), T. Harmsworth Publishing.

Oprah Winfrey, *Journey to Beloved* (1998), Hyperion.

Virginia Woolf, *Selected Diaries*, ed. Anne Olivier Bell (2008), *A Writer's Diary* (2003), Quentin Bell, Angelica Garnett, Houghton Mifflin Harcourt.

Joan Wyndham, *Love Lessons* (2001), *Love is Blue: A Wartime Diary* (1987), Flamingo, Virago.

Index

About the editor

Sarah Gristwood is a biographer, journalist and commentator on royal affairs. Her previous books include the bestselling *Arbella: England's Lost Queen*, *The Tudors in Love: The Courtly Code Behind the Last Medieval Dynasty*, and biographies of Beatrix Potter, Winston Churchill, Vita Sackville-West and Virginia Woolf, and HM Queen Elizabeth II. She is a Fellow of the Royal Historical Society and the Royal Society of Arts. She regularly contributes to TV documentary series and news channels including CNN, Sky News and the BBC.